DIANA PRINCE
WONDER WOMAN

Volume four

TRIBUNAL OF FEAR
Writer: Denny O'Neil * Artists: Don Heck / Dick Giordano

THE BEAUTY HATER
THE FIST OF FLAME
Writer: Denny O'Neil * Artist: Dick Giordano

FANGS OF FIRE
THE GRANDEE CAPER
Writer: Samuel R. Delany * Artist: Dick Giordano

PLAY NOW... DIE LATER
Writer: Bob Haney * Artist: Jim Aparo

THE SECOND LIFE OF THE ORIGINAL WONDER WOMAN
Writer: Robert Kanigher * Artists: Don Heck / Dick Giordano

Wonder Woman created by William Moulton Marston

DAN DIDIO Senior VP-Executive Editor
DENNY O'NEIL ROBERT KANIGHER MURRAY BOLTINOFF Editors-original series
BOB JOY Editor-collected edition
ROBBIN BROSTERMAN Senior Art Director
PAUL LEVITZ President & Publisher
GEORG BREWER VP-Design & DC Direct Creative
RICHARD BRUNING Senior VP-Creative Director
PATRICK CALDON Executive VP-Finance & Operations
CHRIS CARAMALIS VP-Finance
JOHN CUNNINGHAM VP-Marketing
TERRI CUNNINGHAM VP-Managing Editor
AMY GENKINS Senior VP-Business & Legal Affairs
ALISON GILL VP-Manufacturing
DAVID HYDE VP-Publicity
HANK KANALZ VP-General Manager, WildStorm
JIM LEE Editorial Director-WildStorm
GREGORY NOVECK Senior VP-Creative Affairs
SUE POHJA VP-Book Trade Sales
STEVE ROTTERDAM Senior VP-Sales & Marketing
CHERYL RUBIN Senior VP-Brand Management
ALYSSE SOLL VP-Advertising & Custom Publishing
JEFF TROJAN VP-Business Development, DC Direct
BOB WAYNE VP-Sales

Cover art by Dick Giordano

DIANA PRINCE: WONDER WOMAN Volume 4

DC Comics, 1700 Broadway, New York, NY 10019
A Warner Bros. Entertainment Company
Printed in Canada. First Printing.
ISBN: 978-1-4012-2150-8

SFI CERTIFIED SOURCING
Fiber used in this product line meets the sourcing requirements of the SFI program.
www.sfiprogram.org
PWC-SFICOC-260

DC Wonder Woman
Journey into HIGH ADVENTURE with-
DIANA PRINCE:
WONDER WOMAN
52 BIG pages DON'T TAKE LESS! ONLY 25¢
APPROVED BY THE COMICS CODE AUTHORITY
NO. 199
APR.
"TRIBUNAL of FEAR!
plus... A Wonder Girl CLASSIC

DC Wonder Woman
DIANA PRINCE:
WONDER WOMAN
52 BIG pages DON'T TAKE LESS! ONLY 25¢
APPROVED BY THE COMICS CODE AUTHORITY
NO. 200
JUNE
"THE BEAUTY HATER!"
PLUS
WONDER GIRL

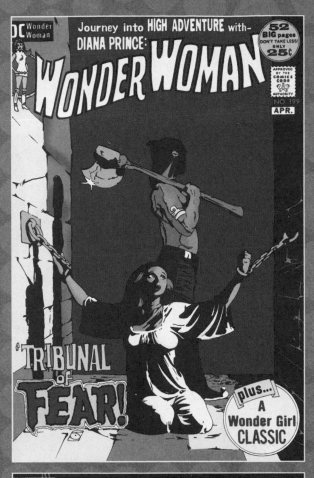

Wonder Woman 199 and 200
Covers by Jeff Jones

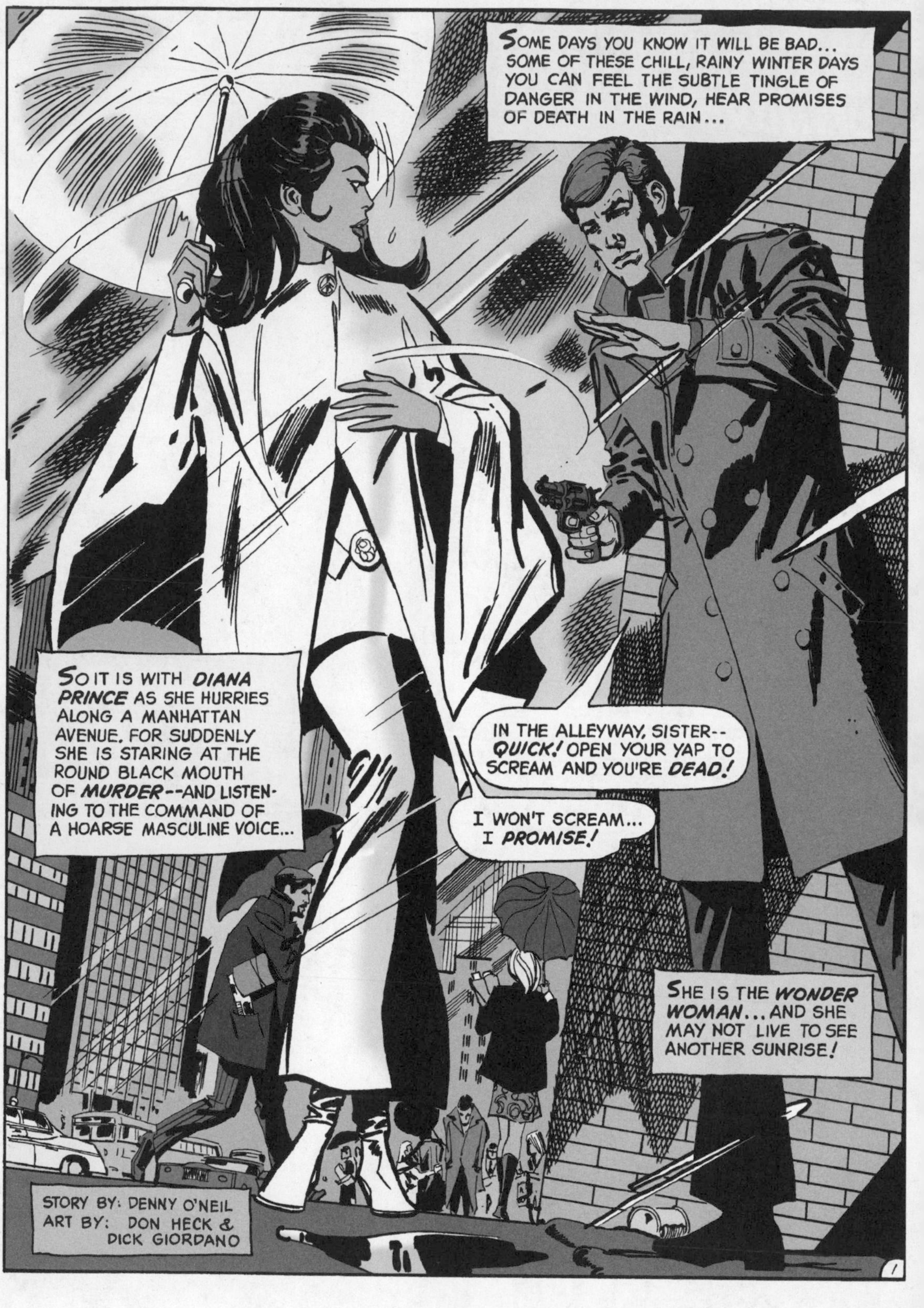
SOME DAYS YOU KNOW IT WILL BE BAD... SOME OF THESE CHILL, RAINY WINTER DAYS YOU CAN FEEL THE SUBTLE TINGLE OF DANGER IN THE WIND, HEAR PROMISES OF DEATH IN THE RAIN...
SO IT IS WITH DIANA PRINCE AS SHE HURRIES ALONG A MANHATTAN AVENUE. FOR SUDDENLY SHE IS STARING AT THE ROUND BLACK MOUTH OF MURDER--AND LISTENING TO THE COMMAND OF A HOARSE MASCULINE VOICE...
IN THE ALLEYWAY, SISTER-- QUICK! OPEN YOUR YAP TO SCREAM AND YOU'RE DEAD!
I WON'T SCREAM... I PROMISE!
SHE IS THE WONDER WOMAN... AND SHE MAY NOT LIVE TO SEE ANOTHER SUNRISE!
STORY BY: DENNY O'NEIL
ART BY: DON HECK & DICK GIORDANO
1

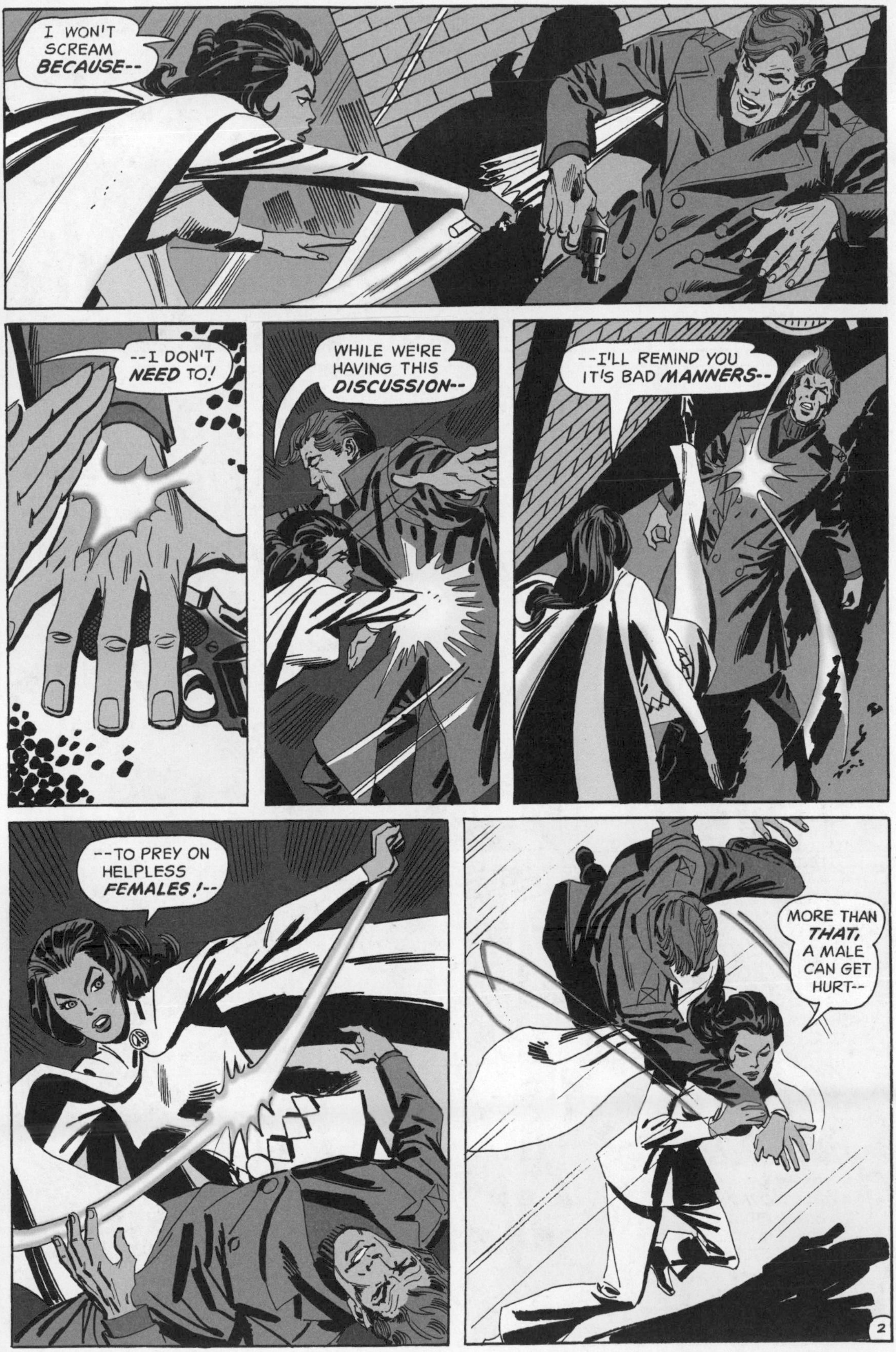
I WON'T SCREAM BECAUSE--
--I DON'T NEED TO!
WHILE WE'RE HAVING THIS DISCUSSION--
--I'LL REMIND YOU IT'S BAD MANNERS--
--TO PREY ON HELPLESS FEMALES!--
MORE THAN THAT, A MALE CAN GET HURT--
2

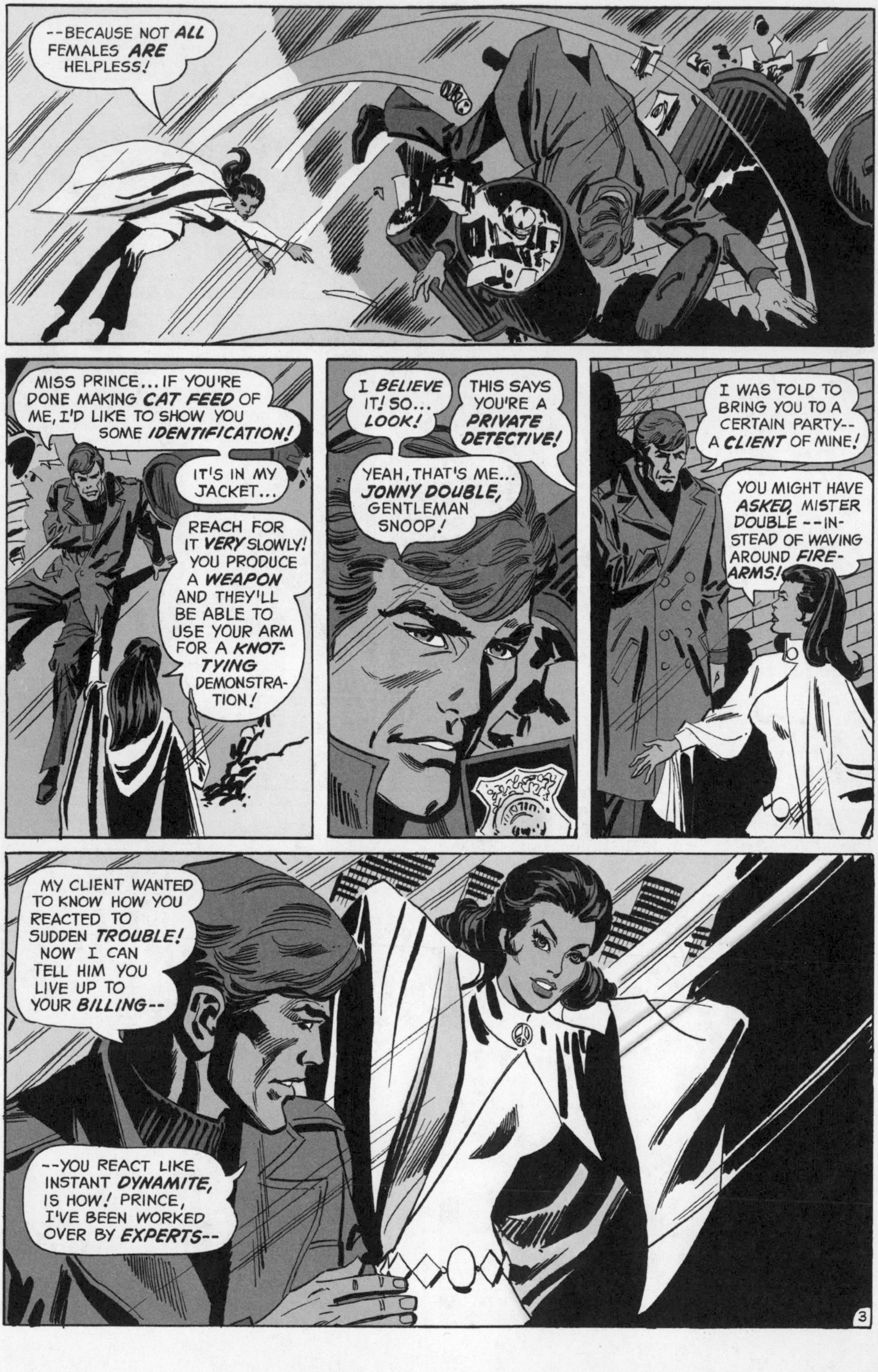
--BECAUSE NOT ALL FEMALES ARE HELPLESS!
MISS PRINCE... IF YOU'RE DONE MAKING CAT FEED OF ME, I'D LIKE TO SHOW YOU SOME IDENTIFICATION!
IT'S IN MY JACKET...
REACH FOR IT VERY SLOWLY! YOU PRODUCE A WEAPON AND THEY'LL BE ABLE TO USE YOUR ARM FOR A KNOT-TYING DEMONSTRATION!
I BELIEVE IT! SO... LOOK!
THIS SAYS YOU'RE A PRIVATE DETECTIVE!
YEAH, THAT'S ME... JONNY DOUBLE, GENTLEMAN SNOOP!
I WAS TOLD TO BRING YOU TO A CERTAIN PARTY-- A CLIENT OF MINE!
YOU MIGHT HAVE ASKED, MISTER DOUBLE --INSTEAD OF WAVING AROUND FIRE-ARMS!
MY CLIENT WANTED TO KNOW HOW YOU REACTED TO SUDDEN TROUBLE! NOW I CAN TELL HIM YOU LIVE UP TO YOUR BILLING--
--YOU REACT LIKE INSTANT DYNAMITE, IS HOW! PRINCE, I'VE BEEN WORKED OVER BY EXPERTS--
3

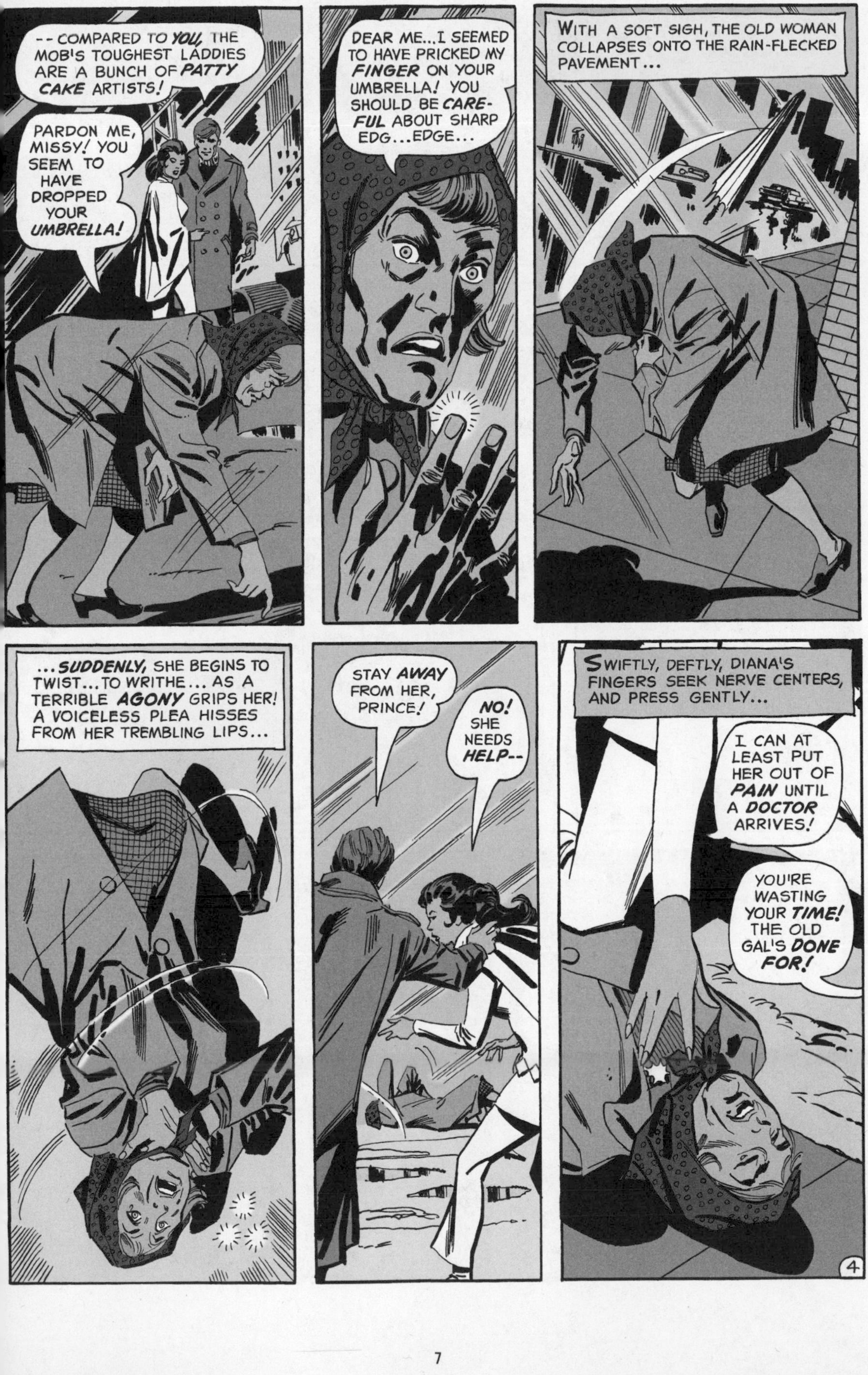

--COMPARED TO YOU, THE MOB'S TOUGHEST LADDIES ARE A BUNCH OF PATTY CAKE ARTISTS!
PARDON ME, MISSY! YOU SEEM TO HAVE DROPPED YOUR UMBRELLA!
DEAR ME...I SEEMED TO HAVE PRICKED MY FINGER ON YOUR UMBRELLA! YOU SHOULD BE CAREFUL ABOUT SHARP EDG...EDGE...
WITH A SOFT SIGH, THE OLD WOMAN COLLAPSES ONTO THE RAIN-FLECKED PAVEMENT...
...SUDDENLY, SHE BEGINS TO TWIST...TO WRITHE... AS A TERRIBLE AGONY GRIPS HER! A VOICELESS PLEA HISSES FROM HER TREMBLING LIPS...
STAY AWAY FROM HER, PRINCE!
NO! SHE NEEDS HELP--
SWIFTLY, DEFTLY, DIANA'S FINGERS SEEK NERVE CENTERS, AND PRESS GENTLY...
I CAN AT LEAST PUT HER OUT OF PAIN UNTIL A DOCTOR ARRIVES!
YOU'RE WASTING YOUR TIME! THE OLD GAL'S DONE FOR!
4

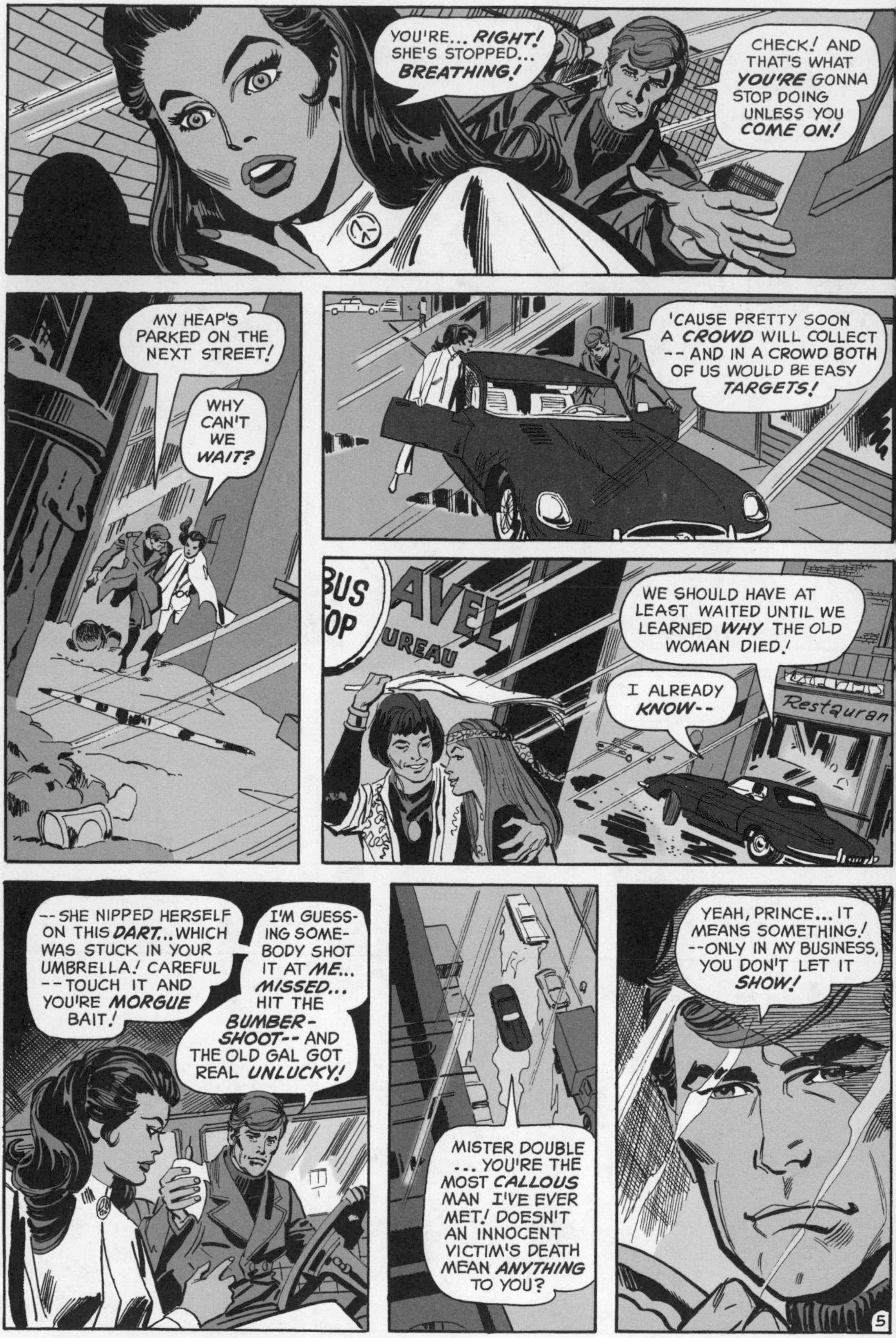
YOU'RE... RIGHT! SHE'S STOPPED... BREATHING!
CHECK! AND THAT'S WHAT YOU'RE GONNA STOP DOING UNLESS YOU COME ON!
MY HEAP'S PARKED ON THE NEXT STREET!
WHY CAN'T WE WAIT?
'CAUSE PRETTY SOON A CROWD WILL COLLECT -- AND IN A CROWD BOTH OF US WOULD BE EASY TARGETS!
BUS STOP
AVEL
UREAU
Restauran
WE SHOULD HAVE AT LEAST WAITED UNTIL WE LEARNED WHY THE OLD WOMAN DIED!
I ALREADY KNOW--
--SHE NIPPED HERSELF ON THIS DART... WHICH WAS STUCK IN YOUR UMBRELLA! CAREFUL --TOUCH IT AND YOU'RE MORGUE BAIT!
I'M GUESSING SOMEBODY SHOT IT AT ME... MISSED... HIT THE BUMBERSHOOT-- AND THE OLD GAL GOT REAL UNLUCKY!
MISTER DOUBLE ... YOU'RE THE MOST CALLOUS MAN I'VE EVER MET! DOESN'T AN INNOCENT VICTIM'S DEATH MEAN ANYTHING TO YOU?
YEAH, PRINCE... IT MEANS SOMETHING! --ONLY IN MY BUSINESS, YOU DON'T LET IT SHOW!
5

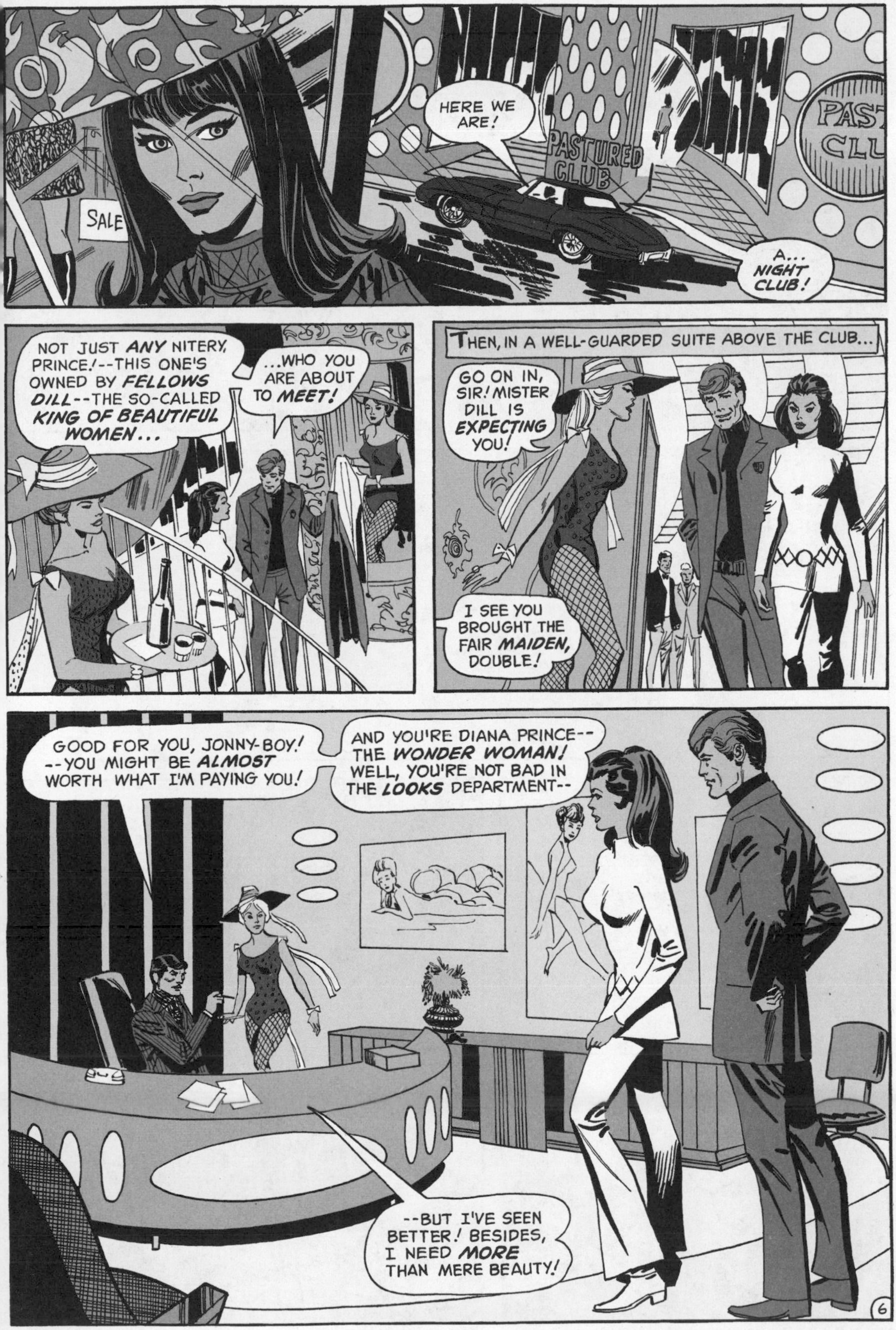
SALE
HERE WE ARE!
PASTURED CLUB
PAST CLU
A... NIGHT CLUB!
NOT JUST ANY NITERY, PRINCE!--THIS ONE'S OWNED BY FELLOWS DILL--THE SO-CALLED KING OF BEAUTIFUL WOMEN...
...WHO YOU ARE ABOUT TO MEET!
THEN, IN A WELL-GUARDED SUITE ABOVE THE CLUB...
GO ON IN, SIR! MISTER DILL IS EXPECTING YOU!
I SEE YOU BROUGHT THE FAIR MAIDEN, DOUBLE!
GOOD FOR YOU, JONNY-BOY! --YOU MIGHT BE ALMOST WORTH WHAT I'M PAYING YOU!
AND YOU'RE DIANA PRINCE--THE WONDER WOMAN! WELL, YOU'RE NOT BAD IN THE LOOKS DEPARTMENT--
--BUT I'VE SEEN BETTER! BESIDES, I NEED MORE THAN MERE BEAUTY!
6

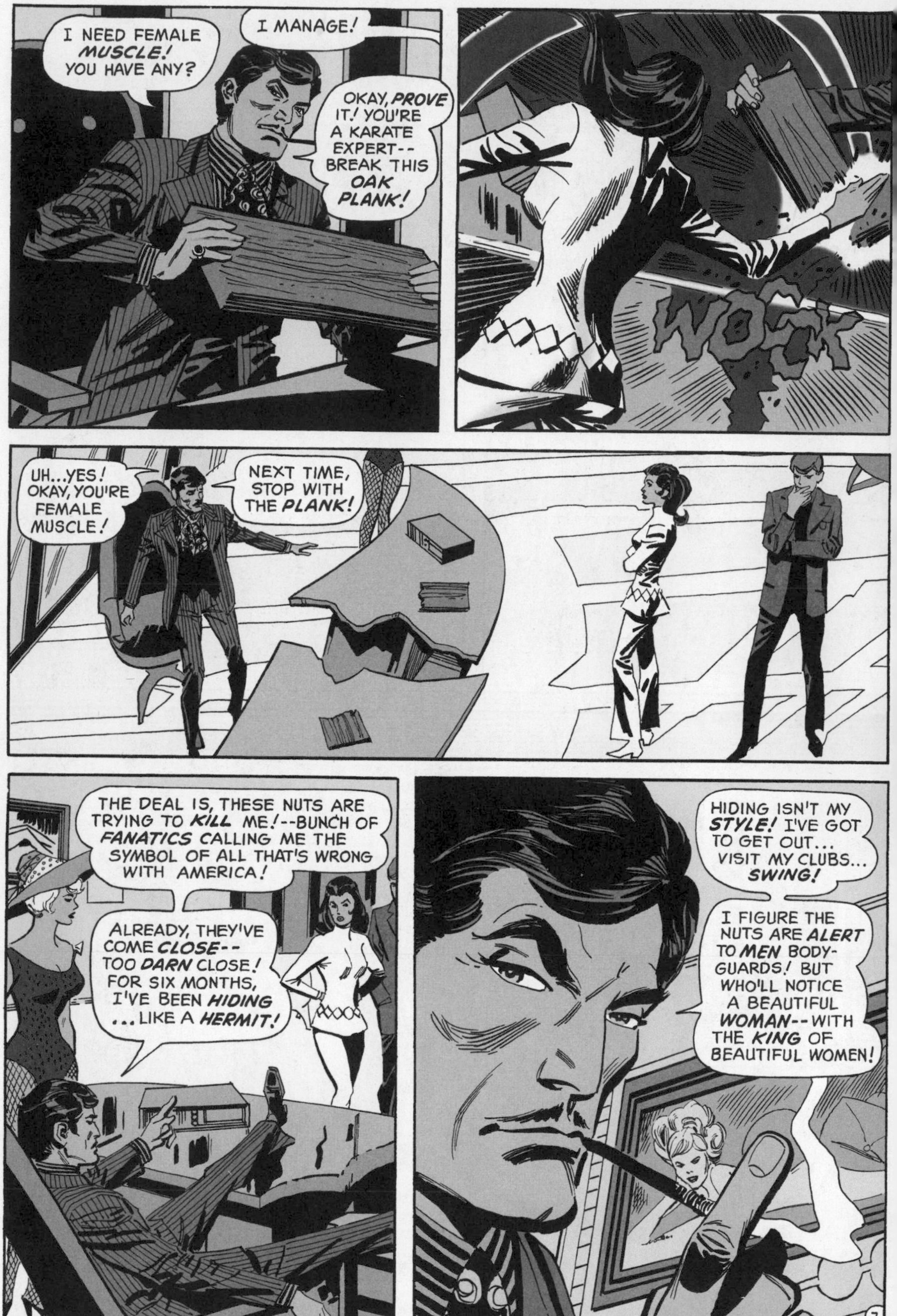
I NEED FEMALE MUSCLE! YOU HAVE ANY?
I MANAGE!
OKAY, PROVE IT! YOU'RE A KARATE EXPERT--BREAK THIS OAK PLANK!
WOCK
UH...YES! OKAY, YOU'RE FEMALE MUSCLE!
NEXT TIME, STOP WITH THE PLANK!
THE DEAL IS, THESE NUTS ARE TRYING TO KILL ME!--BUNCH OF FANATICS CALLING ME THE SYMBOL OF ALL THAT'S WRONG WITH AMERICA!
ALREADY, THEY'VE COME CLOSE--TOO DARN CLOSE! FOR SIX MONTHS, I'VE BEEN HIDING ...LIKE A HERMIT!
HIDING ISN'T MY STYLE! I'VE GOT TO GET OUT... VISIT MY CLUBS... SWING!
I FIGURE THE NUTS ARE ALERT TO MEN BODY-GUARDS! BUT WHO'LL NOTICE A BEAUTIFUL WOMAN--WITH THE KING OF BEAUTIFUL WOMEN!
7

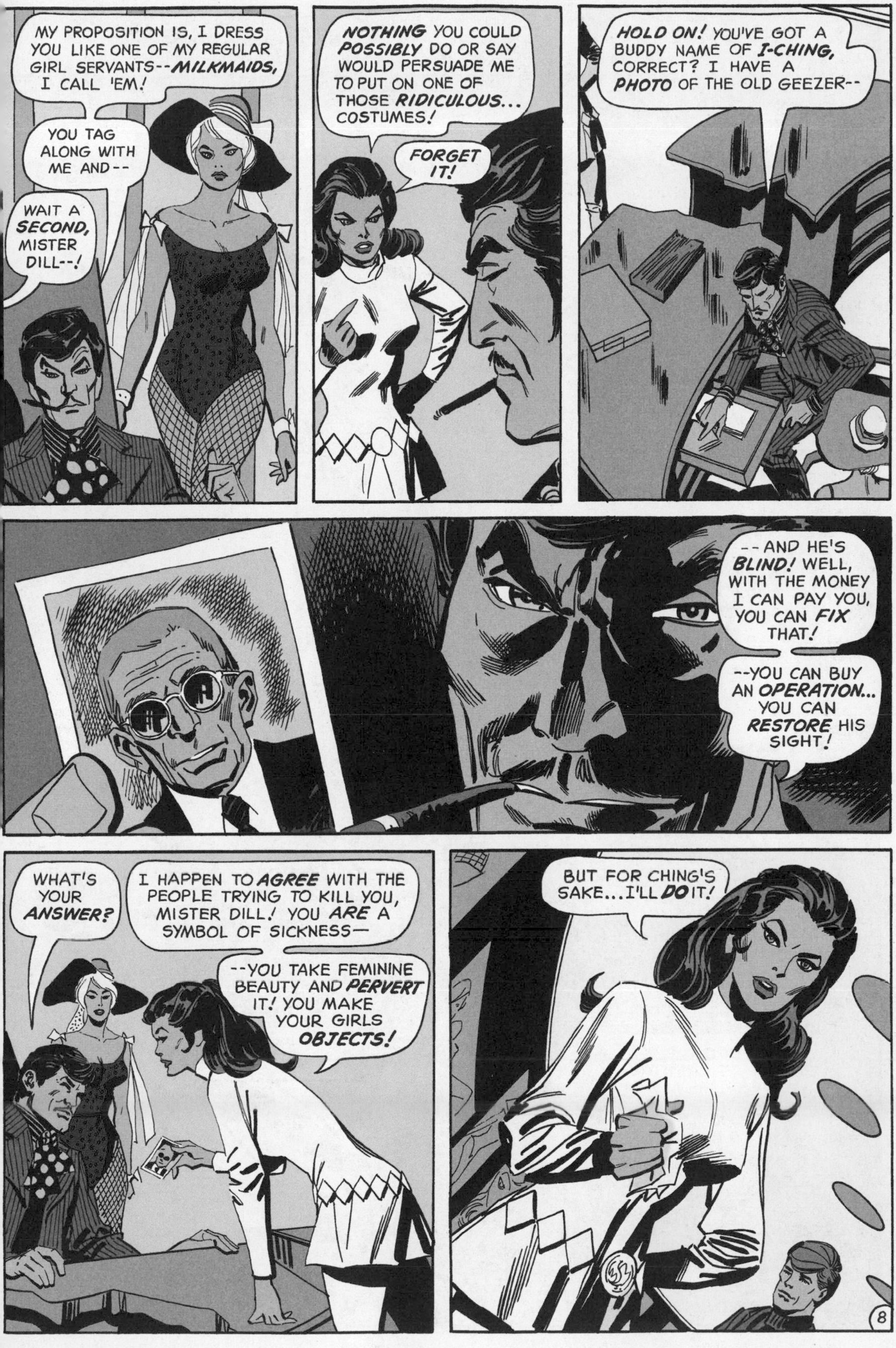
MY PROPOSITION IS, I DRESS YOU LIKE ONE OF MY REGULAR GIRL SERVANTS--MILKMAIDS, I CALL 'EM!
YOU TAG ALONG WITH ME AND--
WAIT A SECOND, MISTER DILL--!
NOTHING YOU COULD POSSIBLY DO OR SAY WOULD PERSUADE ME TO PUT ON ONE OF THOSE RIDICULOUS... COSTUMES!
FORGET IT!
HOLD ON! YOU'VE GOT A BUDDY NAME OF I-CHING, CORRECT? I HAVE A PHOTO OF THE OLD GEEZER--
--AND HE'S BLIND! WELL, WITH THE MONEY I CAN PAY YOU, YOU CAN FIX THAT!
--YOU CAN BUY AN OPERATION... YOU CAN RESTORE HIS SIGHT!
WHAT'S YOUR ANSWER?
I HAPPEN TO AGREE WITH THE PEOPLE TRYING TO KILL YOU, MISTER DILL! YOU ARE A SYMBOL OF SICKNESS—
--YOU TAKE FEMININE BEAUTY AND PERVERT IT! YOU MAKE YOUR GIRLS OBJECTS!
BUT FOR CHING'S SAKE...I'LL DO IT!
8

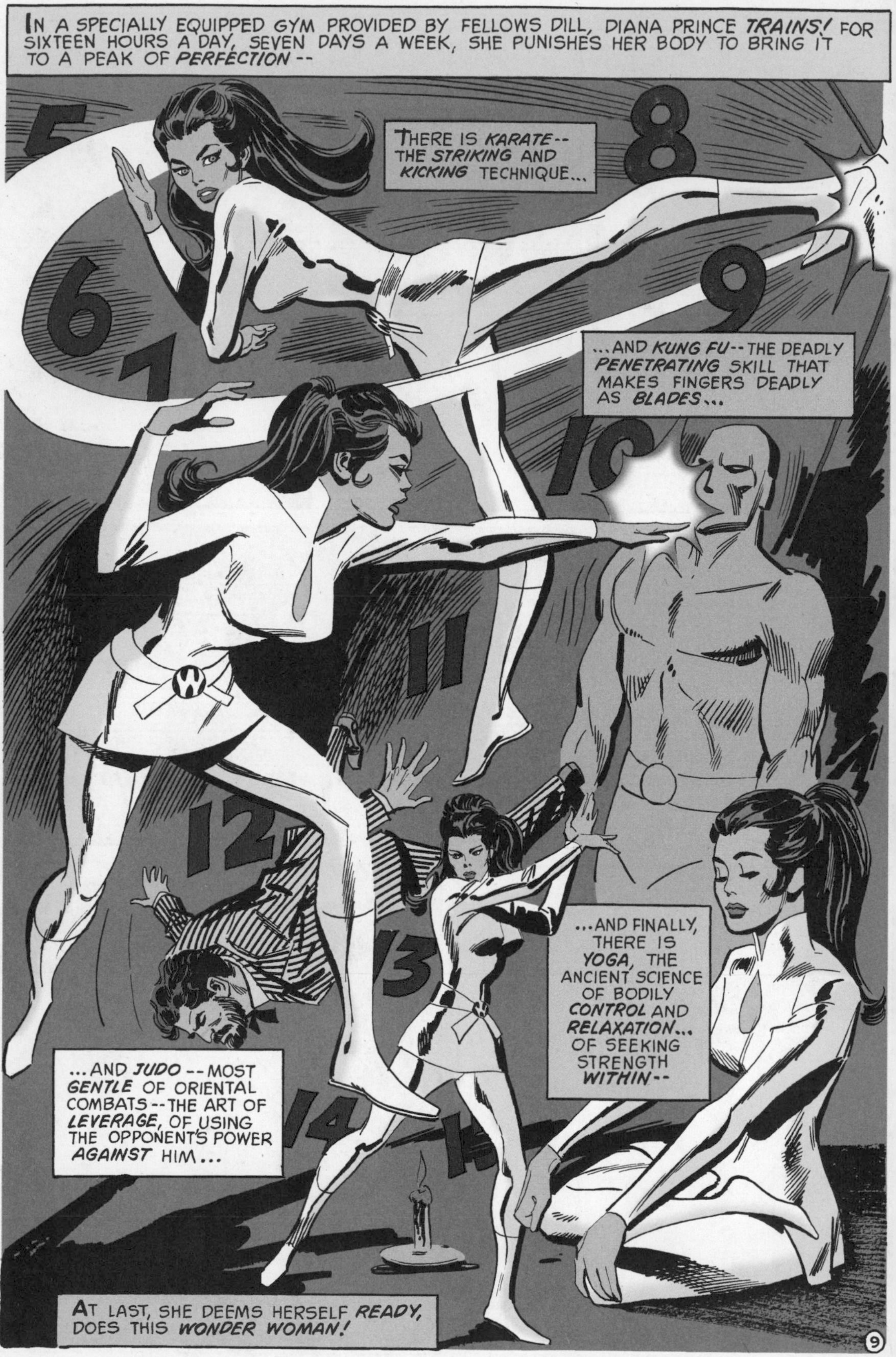
IN A SPECIALLY EQUIPPED GYM PROVIDED BY FELLOWS DILL, DIANA PRINCE TRAINS! FOR SIXTEEN HOURS A DAY, SEVEN DAYS A WEEK, SHE PUNISHES HER BODY TO BRING IT TO A PEAK OF PERFECTION --
THERE IS KARATE -- THE STRIKING AND KICKING TECHNIQUE...
...AND KUNG FU -- THE DEADLY PENETRATING SKILL THAT MAKES FINGERS DEADLY AS BLADES...
...AND JUDO -- MOST GENTLE OF ORIENTAL COMBATS -- THE ART OF LEVERAGE, OF USING THE OPPONENT'S POWER AGAINST HIM...
...AND FINALLY, THERE IS YOGA, THE ANCIENT SCIENCE OF BODILY CONTROL AND RELAXATION... OF SEEKING STRENGTH WITHIN --
AT LAST, SHE DEEMS HERSELF READY, DOES THIS WONDER WOMAN!
9

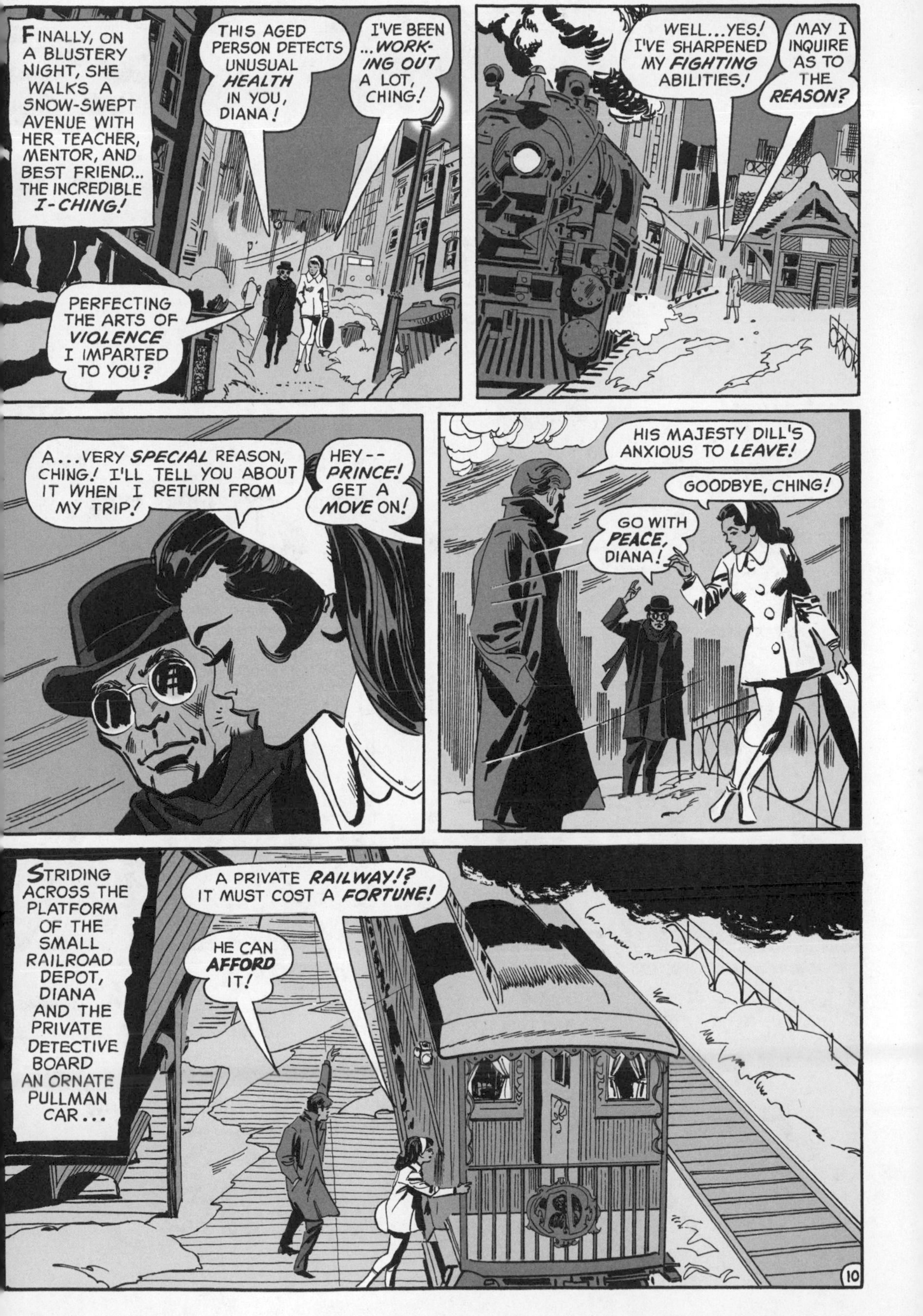
FINALLY, ON A BLUSTERY NIGHT, SHE WALKS A SNOW-SWEPT AVENUE WITH HER TEACHER, MENTOR, AND BEST FRIEND... THE INCREDIBLE I-CHING!
THIS AGED PERSON DETECTS UNUSUAL HEALTH IN YOU, DIANA!
I'VE BEEN ...WORKING OUT A LOT, CHING!
PERFECTING THE ARTS OF VIOLENCE I IMPARTED TO YOU?
WELL...YES! I'VE SHARPENED MY FIGHTING ABILITIES!
MAY I INQUIRE AS TO THE REASON?
A...VERY SPECIAL REASON, CHING! I'LL TELL YOU ABOUT IT WHEN I RETURN FROM MY TRIP!
HEY-- PRINCE! GET A MOVE ON!
HIS MAJESTY DILL'S ANXIOUS TO LEAVE!
GOODBYE, CHING!
GO WITH PEACE, DIANA!
STRIDING ACROSS THE PLATFORM OF THE SMALL RAILROAD DEPOT, DIANA AND THE PRIVATE DETECTIVE BOARD AN ORNATE PULLMAN CAR...
A PRIVATE RAILWAY!? IT MUST COST A FORTUNE!
HE CAN AFFORD IT!
10

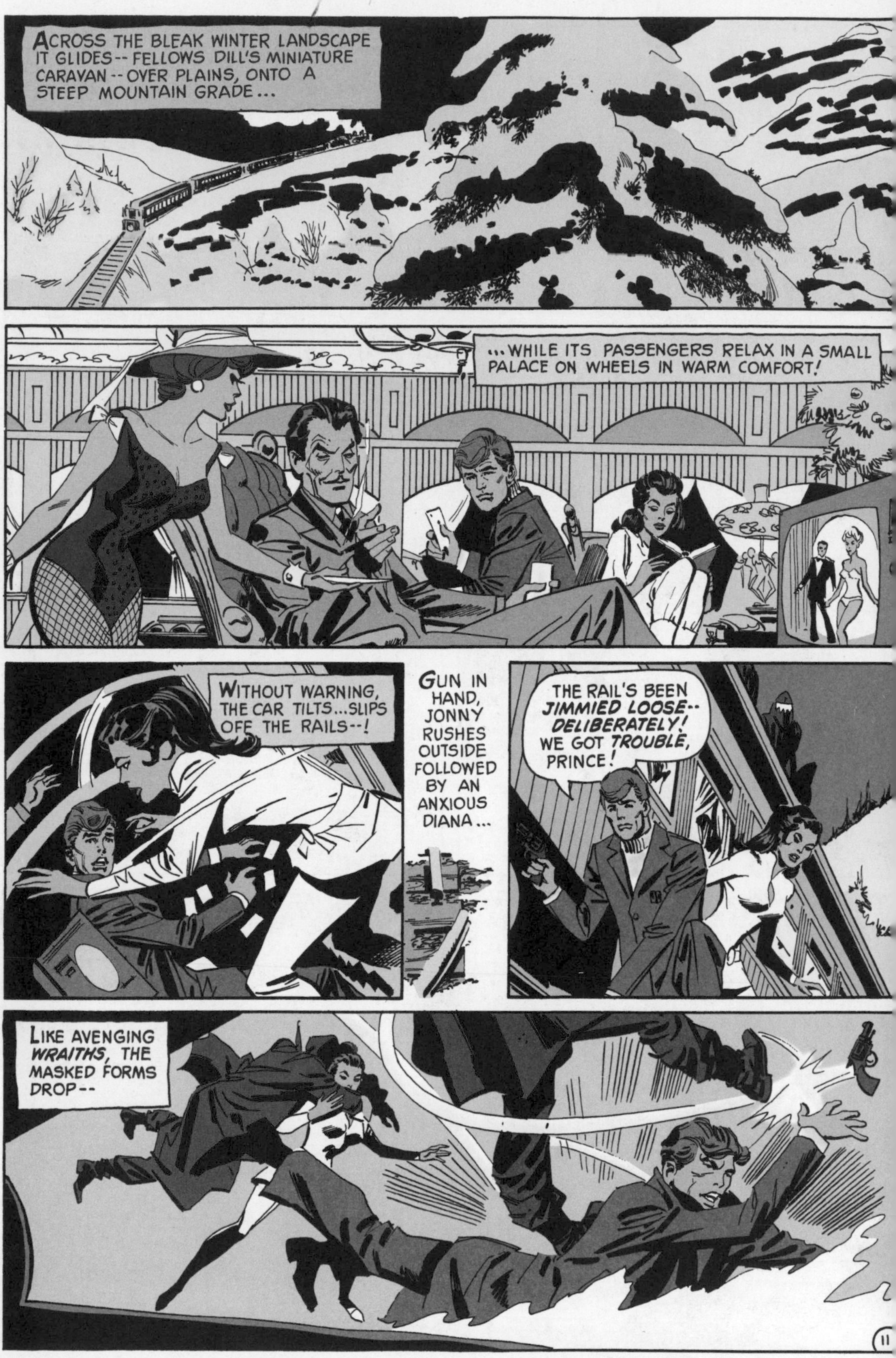

ACROSS THE BLEAK WINTER LANDSCAPE IT GLIDES -- FELLOWS DILL'S MINIATURE CARAVAN -- OVER PLAINS, ONTO A STEEP MOUNTAIN GRADE...
...WHILE ITS PASSENGERS RELAX IN A SMALL PALACE ON WHEELS IN WARM COMFORT!
WITHOUT WARNING, THE CAR TILTS...SLIPS OFF THE RAILS--!
GUN IN HAND, JONNY RUSHES OUTSIDE FOLLOWED BY AN ANXIOUS DIANA...
THE RAIL'S BEEN JIMMIED LOOSE-- DELIBERATELY! WE GOT TROUBLE, PRINCE!
LIKE AVENGING WRAITHS, THE MASKED FORMS DROP--
11

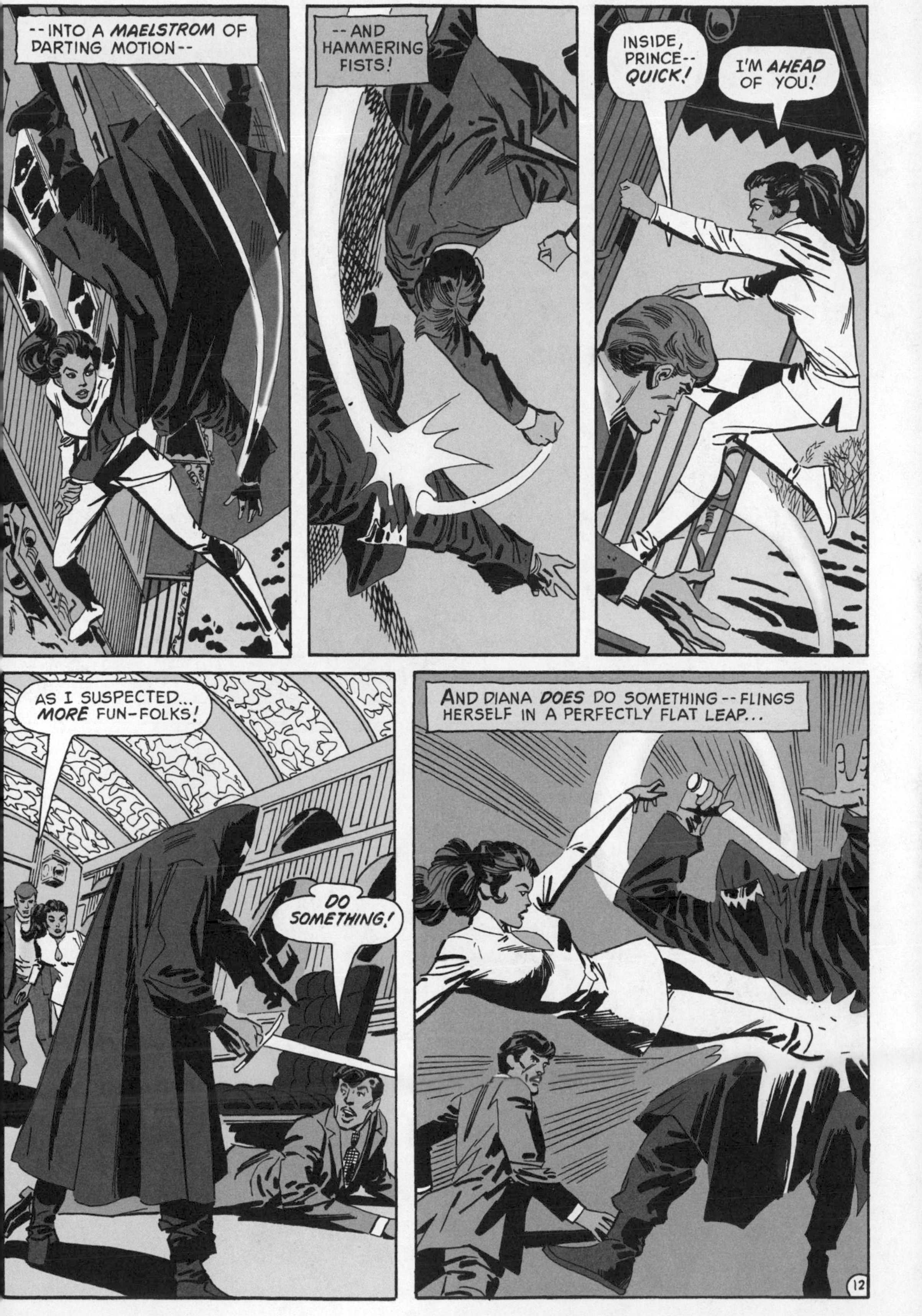
--INTO A MAELSTROM OF DARTING MOTION--
--AND HAMMERING FISTS!
INSIDE, PRINCE--QUICK!
I'M AHEAD OF YOU!
AS I SUSPECTED... MORE FUN-FOLKS!
DO SOMETHING!
AND DIANA DOES DO SOMETHING--FLINGS HERSELF IN A PERFECTLY FLAT LEAP...
12

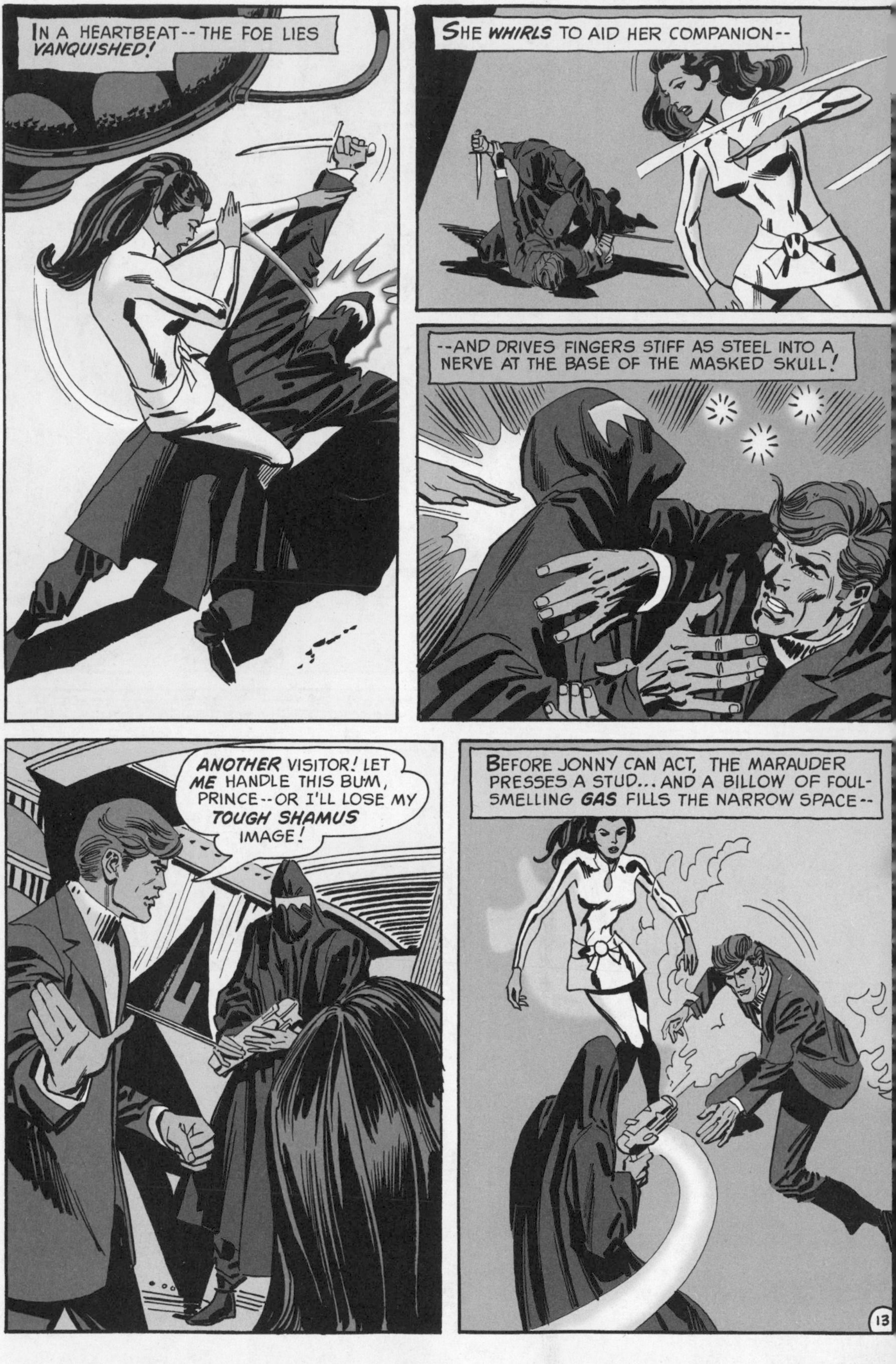
IN A HEARTBEAT--THE FOE LIES VANQUISHED!
SHE WHIRLS TO AID HER COMPANION--
--AND DRIVES FINGERS STIFF AS STEEL INTO A NERVE AT THE BASE OF THE MASKED SKULL!
ANOTHER VISITOR! LET ME HANDLE THIS BUM, PRINCE--OR I'LL LOSE MY TOUGH SHAMUS IMAGE!
BEFORE JONNY CAN ACT, THE MARAUDER PRESSES A STUD... AND A BILLOW OF FOUL-SMELLING GAS FILLS THE NARROW SPACE--
13

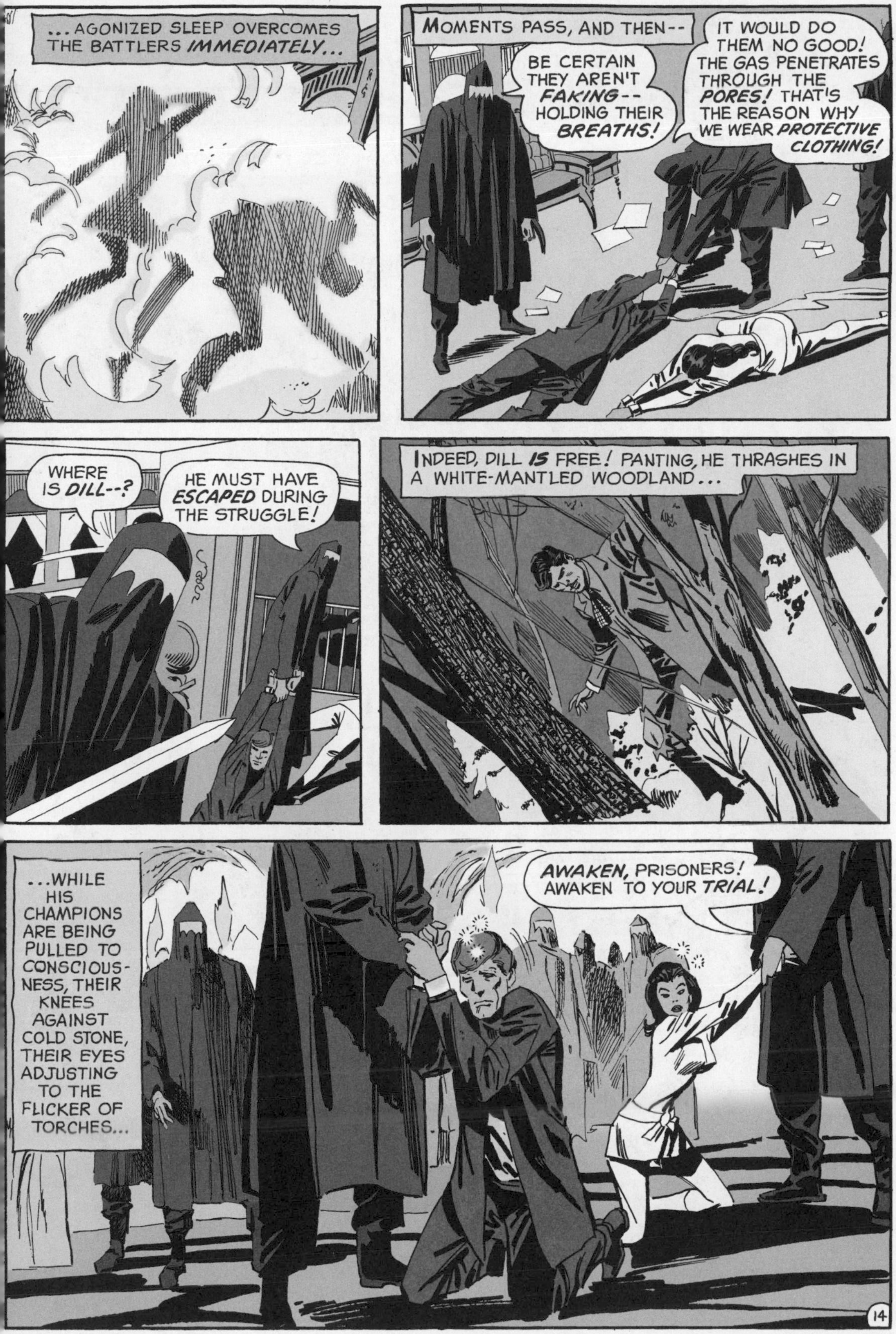
...AGONIZED SLEEP OVERCOMES THE BATTLERS IMMEDIATELY...
MOMENTS PASS, AND THEN--
BE CERTAIN THEY AREN'T FAKING-- HOLDING THEIR BREATHS!
IT WOULD DO THEM NO GOOD! THE GAS PENETRATES THROUGH THE PORES! THAT'S THE REASON WHY WE WEAR PROTECTIVE CLOTHING!
WHERE IS DILL--?
HE MUST HAVE ESCAPED DURING THE STRUGGLE!
INDEED, DILL IS FREE! PANTING, HE THRASHES IN A WHITE-MANTLED WOODLAND...
...WHILE HIS CHAMPIONS ARE BEING PULLED TO CONSCIOUSNESS, THEIR KNEES AGAINST COLD STONE, THEIR EYES ADJUSTING TO THE FLICKER OF TORCHES...
AWAKEN, PRISONERS! AWAKEN TO YOUR TRIAL!
14

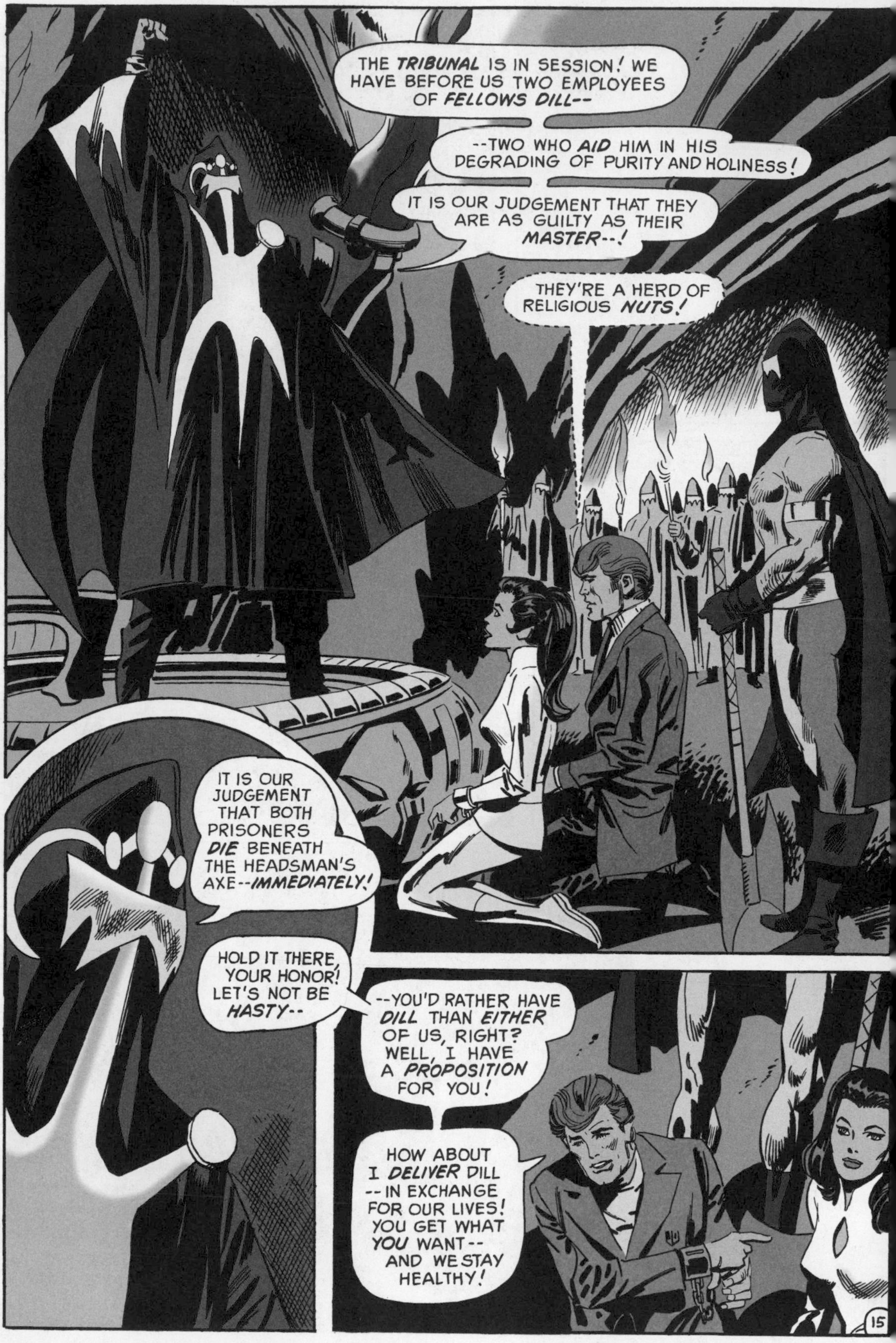
THE TRIBUNAL IS IN SESSION! WE HAVE BEFORE US TWO EMPLOYEES OF FELLOWS DILL--
--TWO WHO AID HIM IN HIS DEGRADING OF PURITY AND HOLINESS!
IT IS OUR JUDGEMENT THAT THEY ARE AS GUILTY AS THEIR MASTER--!
THEY'RE A HERD OF RELIGIOUS NUTS!
IT IS OUR JUDGEMENT THAT BOTH PRISONERS DIE BENEATH THE HEADSMAN'S AXE--IMMEDIATELY!
HOLD IT THERE, YOUR HONOR! LET'S NOT BE HASTY--
--YOU'D RATHER HAVE DILL THAN EITHER OF US, RIGHT? WELL, I HAVE A PROPOSITION FOR YOU!
HOW ABOUT I DELIVER DILL --IN EXCHANGE FOR OUR LIVES! YOU GET WHAT YOU WANT-- AND WE STAY HEALTHY!
15

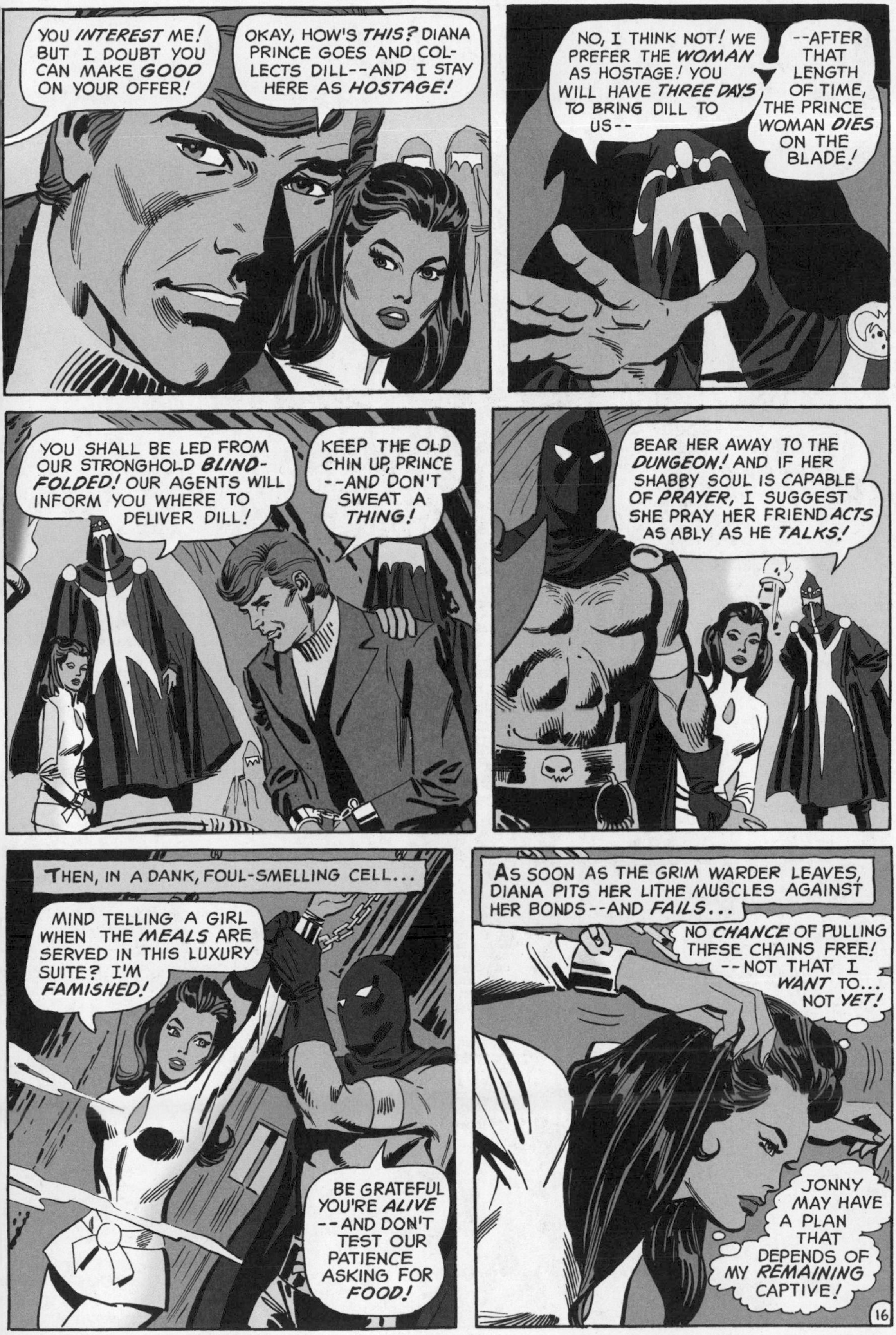
YOU INTEREST ME! BUT I DOUBT YOU CAN MAKE GOOD ON YOUR OFFER!
OKAY, HOW'S THIS? DIANA PRINCE GOES AND COL-LECTS DILL--AND I STAY HERE AS HOSTAGE!
NO, I THINK NOT! WE PREFER THE WOMAN AS HOSTAGE! YOU WILL HAVE THREE DAYS TO BRING DILL TO US--
--AFTER THAT LENGTH OF TIME, THE PRINCE WOMAN DIES ON THE BLADE!
YOU SHALL BE LED FROM OUR STRONGHOLD BLIND-FOLDED! OUR AGENTS WILL INFORM YOU WHERE TO DELIVER DILL!
KEEP THE OLD CHIN UP, PRINCE --AND DON'T SWEAT A THING!
BEAR HER AWAY TO THE DUNGEON! AND IF HER SHABBY SOUL IS CAPABLE OF PRAYER, I SUGGEST SHE PRAY HER FRIEND ACTS AS ABLY AS HE TALKS!
THEN, IN A DANK, FOUL-SMELLING CELL...
MIND TELLING A GIRL WHEN THE MEALS ARE SERVED IN THIS LUXURY SUITE? I'M FAMISHED!
BE GRATEFUL YOU'RE ALIVE --AND DON'T TEST OUR PATIENCE ASKING FOR FOOD!
AS SOON AS THE GRIM WARDER LEAVES, DIANA PITS HER LITHE MUSCLES AGAINST HER BONDS--AND FAILS...
NO CHANCE OF PULLING THESE CHAINS FREE! --NOT THAT I WANT TO... NOT YET!
JONNY MAY HAVE A PLAN THAT DEPENDS OF MY REMAINING CAPTIVE!
16

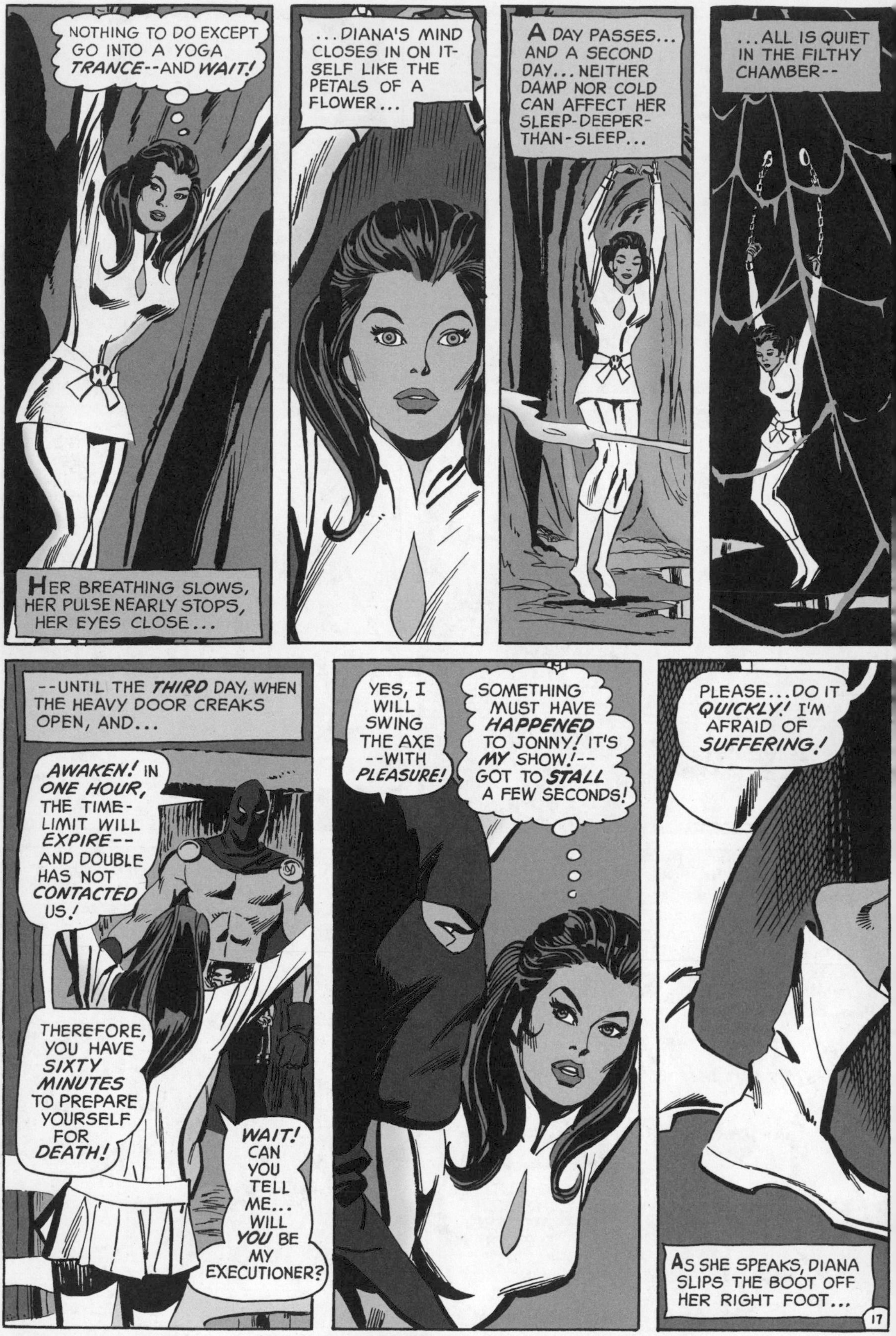
NOTHING TO DO EXCEPT GO INTO A YOGA TRANCE--AND WAIT!
HER BREATHING SLOWS, HER PULSE NEARLY STOPS, HER EYES CLOSE...
...DIANA'S MIND CLOSES IN ON IT-SELF LIKE THE PETALS OF A FLOWER...
A DAY PASSES... AND A SECOND DAY... NEITHER DAMP NOR COLD CAN AFFECT HER SLEEP-DEEPER-THAN-SLEEP...
...ALL IS QUIET IN THE FILTHY CHAMBER--
--UNTIL THE THIRD DAY, WHEN THE HEAVY DOOR CREAKS OPEN, AND...
AWAKEN! IN ONE HOUR, THE TIME-LIMIT WILL EXPIRE--AND DOUBLE HAS NOT CONTACTED US!
THEREFORE, YOU HAVE SIXTY MINUTES TO PREPARE YOURSELF FOR DEATH!
WAIT! CAN YOU TELL ME... WILL YOU BE MY EXECUTIONER?
YES, I WILL SWING THE AXE --WITH PLEASURE!
SOMETHING MUST HAVE HAPPENED TO JONNY! IT'S MY SHOW!--GOT TO STALL A FEW SECONDS!
PLEASE...DO IT QUICKLY! I'M AFRAID OF SUFFERING!
AS SHE SPEAKS, DIANA SLIPS THE BOOT OFF HER RIGHT FOOT...
17

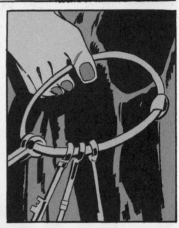

No QUESTION OF IT... SHE REALLY *IS* A *WONDER WOMAN!*

18

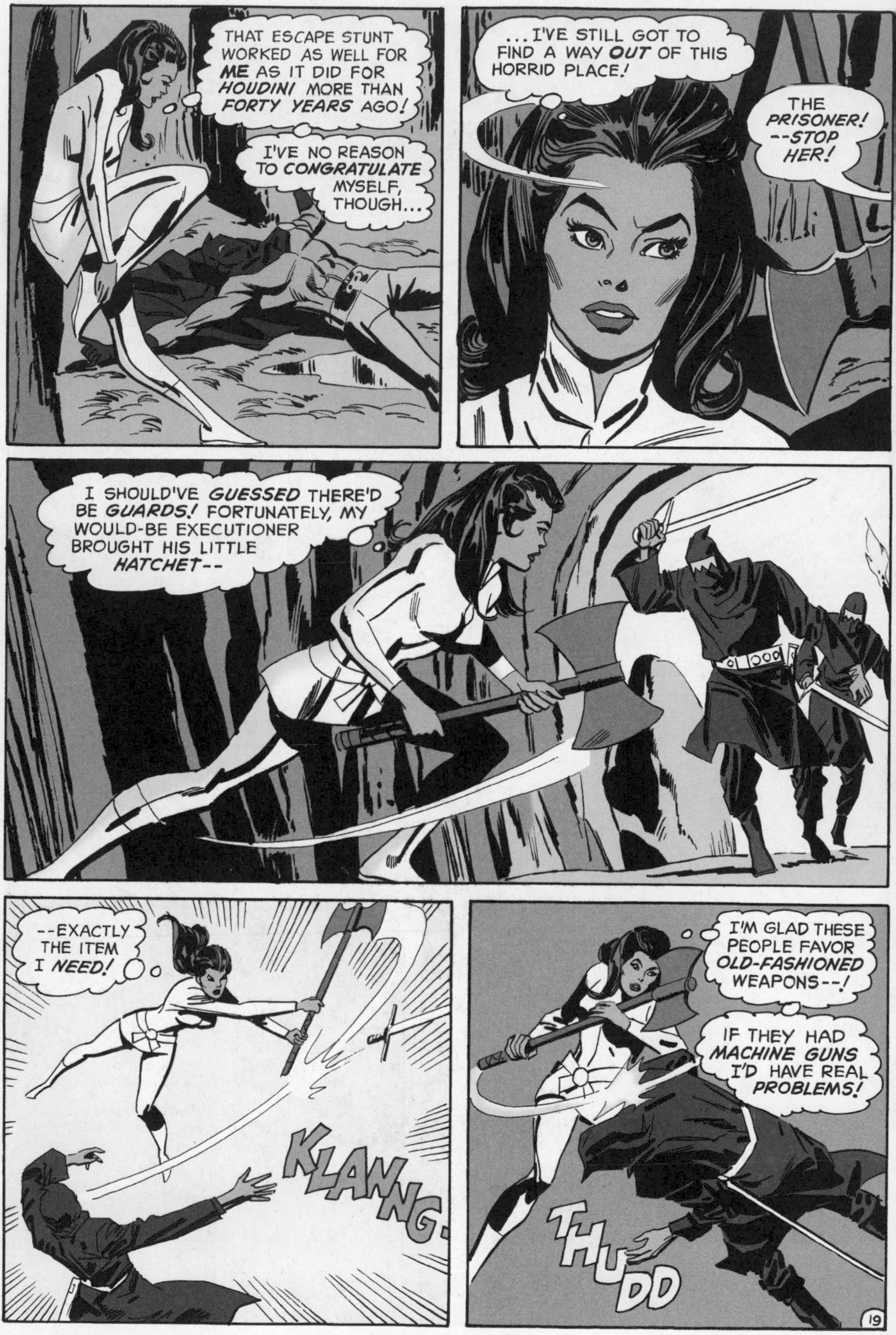
THAT ESCAPE STUNT WORKED AS WELL FOR ME AS IT DID FOR HOUDINI MORE THAN FORTY YEARS AGO!
I'VE NO REASON TO CONGRATULATE MYSELF, THOUGH...
...I'VE STILL GOT TO FIND A WAY OUT OF THIS HORRID PLACE!
THE PRISONER! --STOP HER!
I SHOULD'VE GUESSED THERE'D BE GUARDS! FORTUNATELY, MY WOULD-BE EXECUTIONER BROUGHT HIS LITTLE HATCHET--
--EXACTLY THE ITEM I NEED!
KLANNG!
I'M GLAD THESE PEOPLE FAVOR OLD-FASHIONED WEAPONS--!
IF THEY HAD MACHINE GUNS I'D HAVE REAL PROBLEMS!
THUDD
19

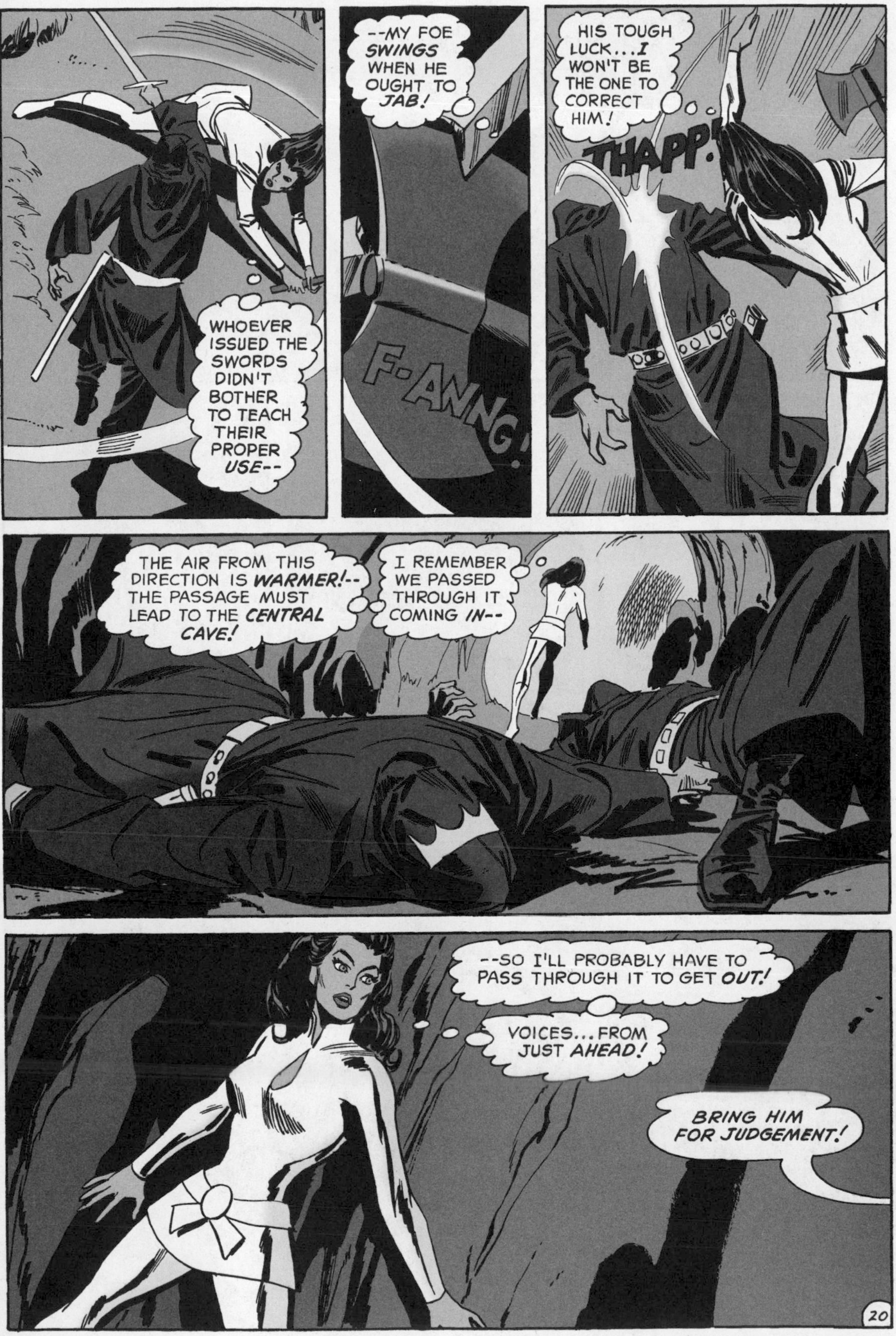
WHOEVER ISSUED THE SWORDS DIDN'T BOTHER TO TEACH THEIR PROPER USE--
--MY FOE SWINGS WHEN HE OUGHT TO JAB!
F-ANNG!
HIS TOUGH LUCK...I WON'T BE THE ONE TO CORRECT HIM!
THAPP!
THE AIR FROM THIS DIRECTION IS WARMER!-- THE PASSAGE MUST LEAD TO THE CENTRAL CAVE!
I REMEMBER WE PASSED THROUGH IT COMING IN--
--SO I'LL PROBABLY HAVE TO PASS THROUGH IT TO GET OUT!
VOICES...FROM JUST AHEAD!
BRING HIM FOR JUDGEMENT!
20

CREEPING FORWARD, DIANA PEERS THROUGH THE SMOKY GLOOM AND SEES...

JONNY DOUBLE! HE *DID* RETURN...BUT *ALONE!* I DON'T SEE *DILL!*

I'VE GOT TO GET IN THE CENTRAL CAVERN...AND I THINK I KNOW *HOW!*

MY PASSPORT IS *STANDING* THERE--IF I CAN MOVE *QUIETLY* ENOUGH!

MEANWHILE...

YOU *FAILED* IN YOUR MISSION--?

I MISSED NABBING FELLOWS DILL FOR YOU, YEAH! SORRY...CAN'T WIN 'EM ALL!

I SEARCHED EVERY SQUARE *INCH* OF NEW YORK! DILL HAS *VANISHED...GONE!*

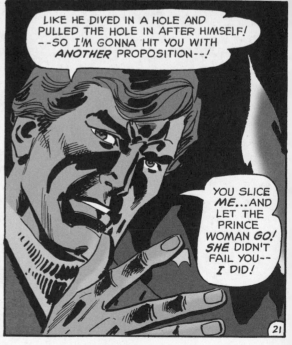

LIKE HE DIVED IN A HOLE AND PULLED THE HOLE IN AFTER HIMSELF! --SO I'M GONNA HIT YOU WITH *ANOTHER* PROPOSITION--!

YOU SLICE *ME*...AND LET THE PRINCE WOMAN *GO! SHE* DIDN'T FAIL YOU-- *I* DID!

21

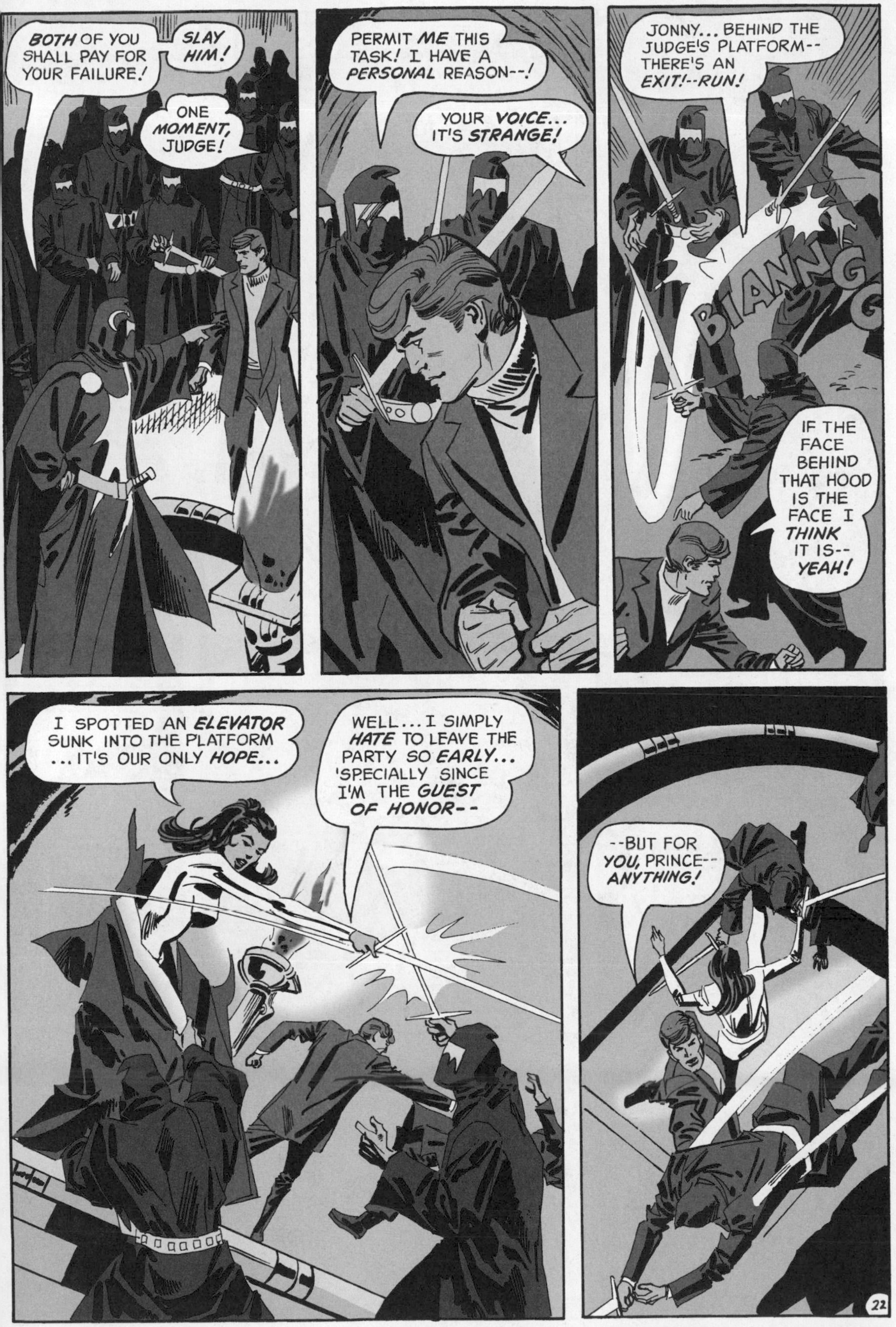
BOTH OF YOU SHALL PAY FOR YOUR FAILURE!
SLAY HIM!
ONE MOMENT, JUDGE!
PERMIT ME THIS TASK! I HAVE A PERSONAL REASON--!
YOUR VOICE... IT'S STRANGE!
JONNY... BEHIND THE JUDGE'S PLATFORM--THERE'S AN EXIT!--RUN!
BIANNGG
IF THE FACE BEHIND THAT HOOD IS THE FACE I THINK IT IS--YEAH!
I SPOTTED AN ELEVATOR SUNK INTO THE PLATFORM ...IT'S OUR ONLY HOPE...
WELL... I SIMPLY HATE TO LEAVE THE PARTY SO EARLY... 'SPECIALLY SINCE I'M THE GUEST OF HONOR--
--BUT FOR YOU, PRINCE--ANYTHING!
22

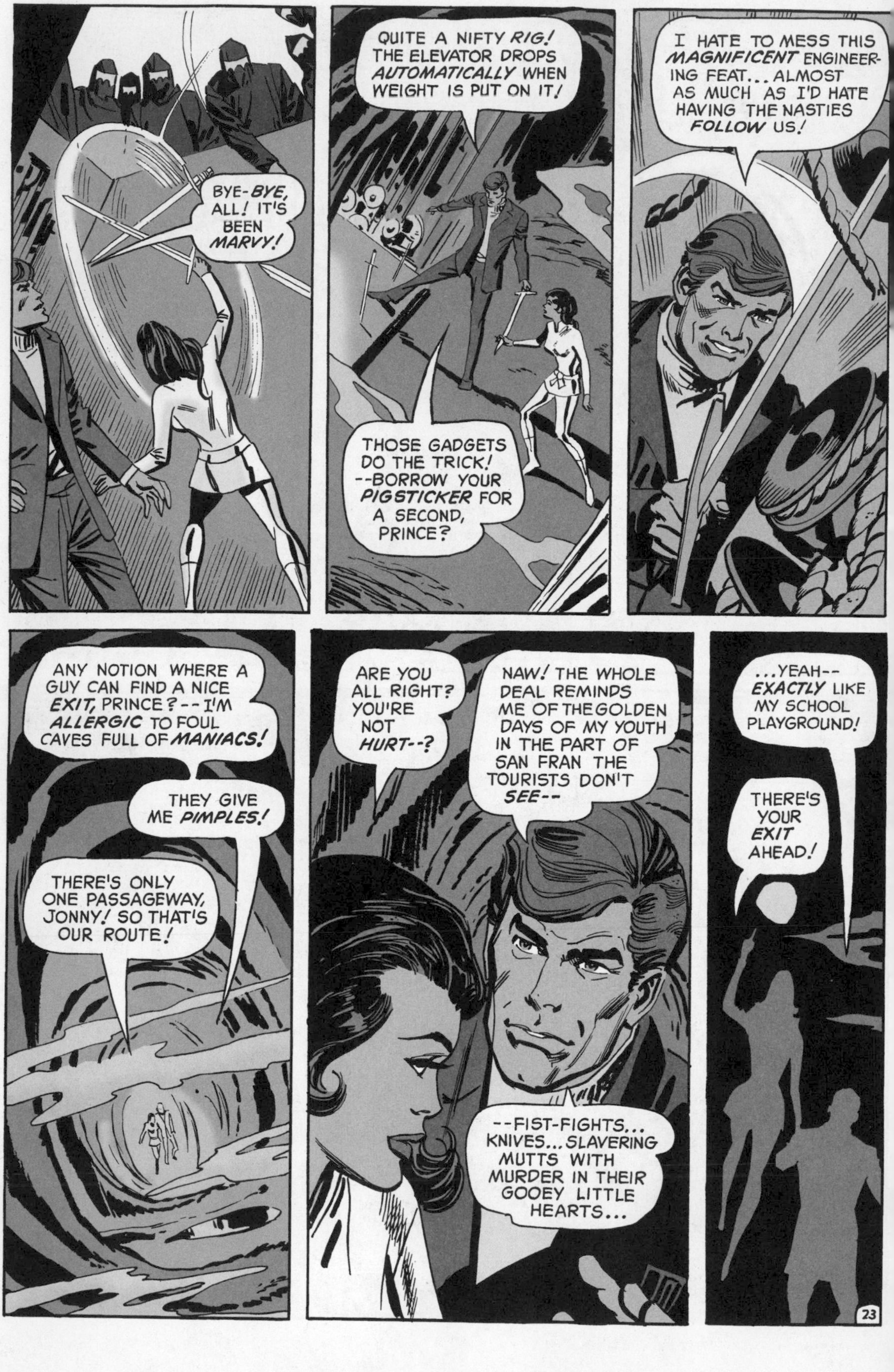
BYE-BYE, ALL! IT'S BEEN MARVY!
QUITE A NIFTY RIG! THE ELEVATOR DROPS AUTOMATICALLY WHEN WEIGHT IS PUT ON IT!
THOSE GADGETS DO THE TRICK! --BORROW YOUR PIGSTICKER FOR A SECOND, PRINCE?
I HATE TO MESS THIS MAGNIFICENT ENGINEERING FEAT... ALMOST AS MUCH AS I'D HATE HAVING THE NASTIES FOLLOW US!
ANY NOTION WHERE A GUY CAN FIND A NICE EXIT, PRINCE? -- I'M ALLERGIC TO FOUL CAVES FULL OF MANIACS!
THEY GIVE ME PIMPLES!
THERE'S ONLY ONE PASSAGEWAY, JONNY! SO THAT'S OUR ROUTE!
ARE YOU ALL RIGHT? YOU'RE NOT HURT--?
NAW! THE WHOLE DEAL REMINDS ME OF THE GOLDEN DAYS OF MY YOUTH IN THE PART OF SAN FRAN THE TOURISTS DON'T SEE--
--FIST-FIGHTS... KNIVES... SLAVERING MUTTS WITH MURDER IN THEIR GOOEY LITTLE HEARTS...
...YEAH-- EXACTLY LIKE MY SCHOOL PLAYGROUND!
THERE'S YOUR EXIT AHEAD!
23

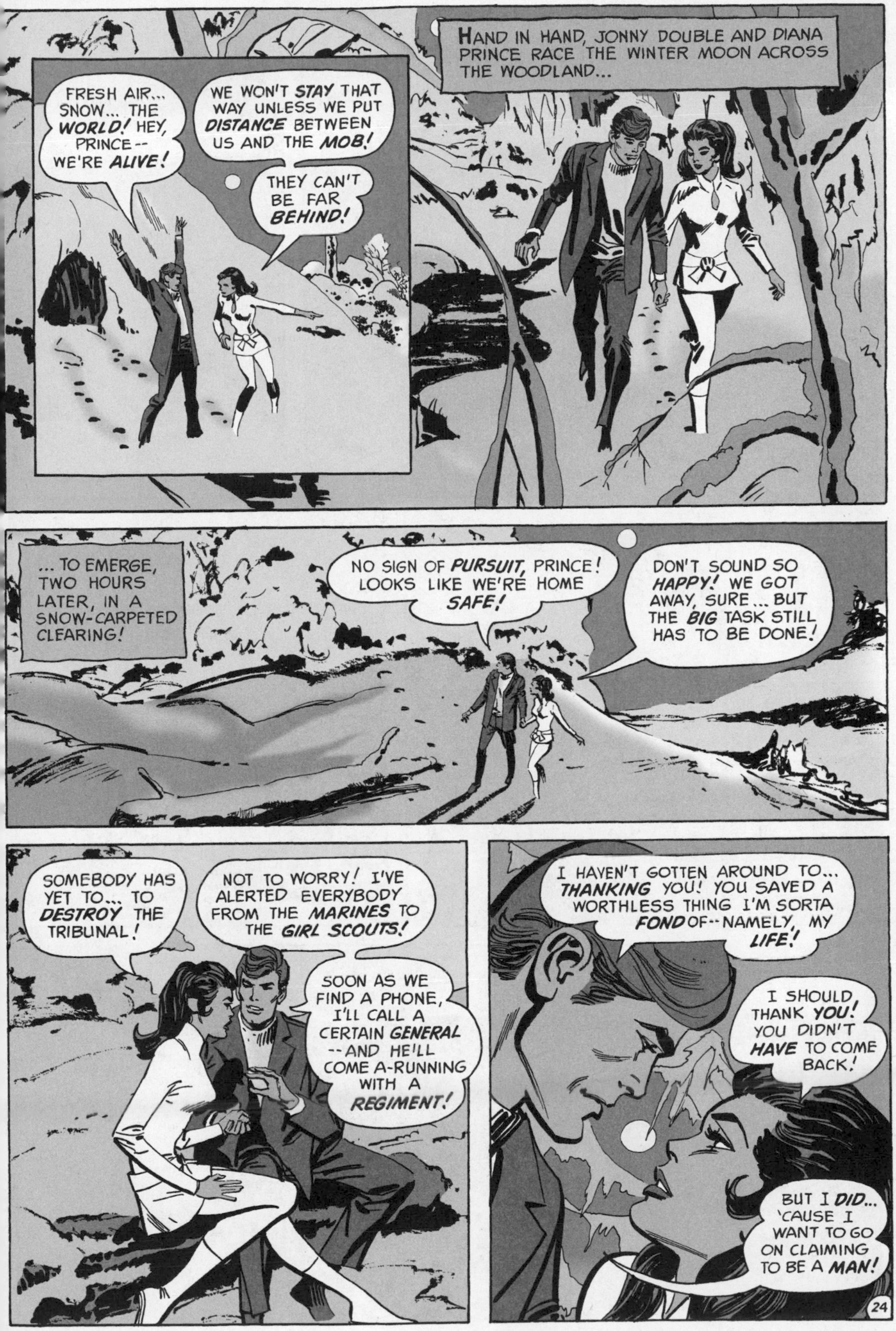
HAND IN HAND, JONNY DOUBLE AND DIANA PRINCE RACE THE WINTER MOON ACROSS THE WOODLAND...
FRESH AIR... SNOW... THE WORLD! HEY, PRINCE-- WE'RE ALIVE!
WE WON'T STAY THAT WAY UNLESS WE PUT DISTANCE BETWEEN US AND THE MOB!
THEY CAN'T BE FAR BEHIND!
... TO EMERGE, TWO HOURS LATER, IN A SNOW-CARPETED CLEARING!
NO SIGN OF PURSUIT, PRINCE! LOOKS LIKE WE'RE HOME SAFE!
DON'T SOUND SO HAPPY! WE GOT AWAY, SURE... BUT THE BIG TASK STILL HAS TO BE DONE!
SOMEBODY HAS YET TO... TO DESTROY THE TRIBUNAL!
NOT TO WORRY! I'VE ALERTED EVERYBODY FROM THE MARINES TO THE GIRL SCOUTS!
SOON AS WE FIND A PHONE, I'LL CALL A CERTAIN GENERAL --AND HE'LL COME A-RUNNING WITH A REGIMENT!
I HAVEN'T GOTTEN AROUND TO... THANKING YOU! YOU SAVED A WORTHLESS THING I'M SORTA FOND OF--NAMELY, MY LIFE!
I SHOULD THANK YOU! YOU DIDN'T HAVE TO COME BACK!
BUT I DID... 'CAUSE I WANT TO GO ON CLAIMING TO BE A MAN!
24

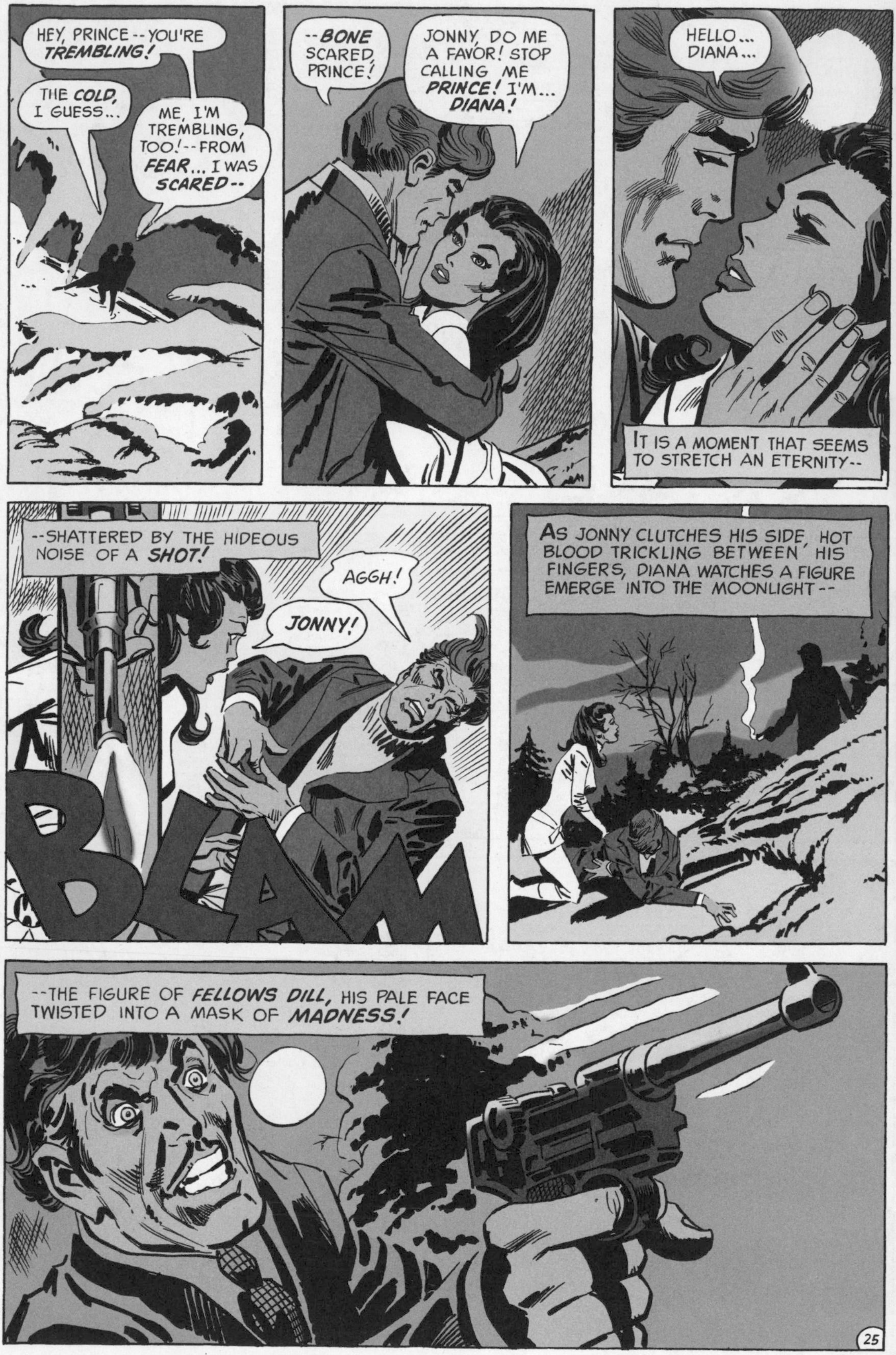
HEY, PRINCE -- YOU'RE TREMBLING!
THE COLD, I GUESS...
ME, I'M TREMBLING, TOO!-- FROM FEAR... I WAS SCARED--
--BONE SCARED, PRINCE!
JONNY, DO ME A FAVOR! STOP CALLING ME PRINCE! I'M... DIANA!
HELLO... DIANA...
IT IS A MOMENT THAT SEEMS TO STRETCH AN ETERNITY--
--SHATTERED BY THE HIDEOUS NOISE OF A SHOT!
AGGH!
JONNY!
BLAM
AS JONNY CLUTCHES HIS SIDE, HOT BLOOD TRICKLING BETWEEN HIS FINGERS, DIANA WATCHES A FIGURE EMERGE INTO THE MOONLIGHT--
--THE FIGURE OF FELLOWS DILL, HIS PALE FACE TWISTED INTO A MASK OF MADNESS!
25

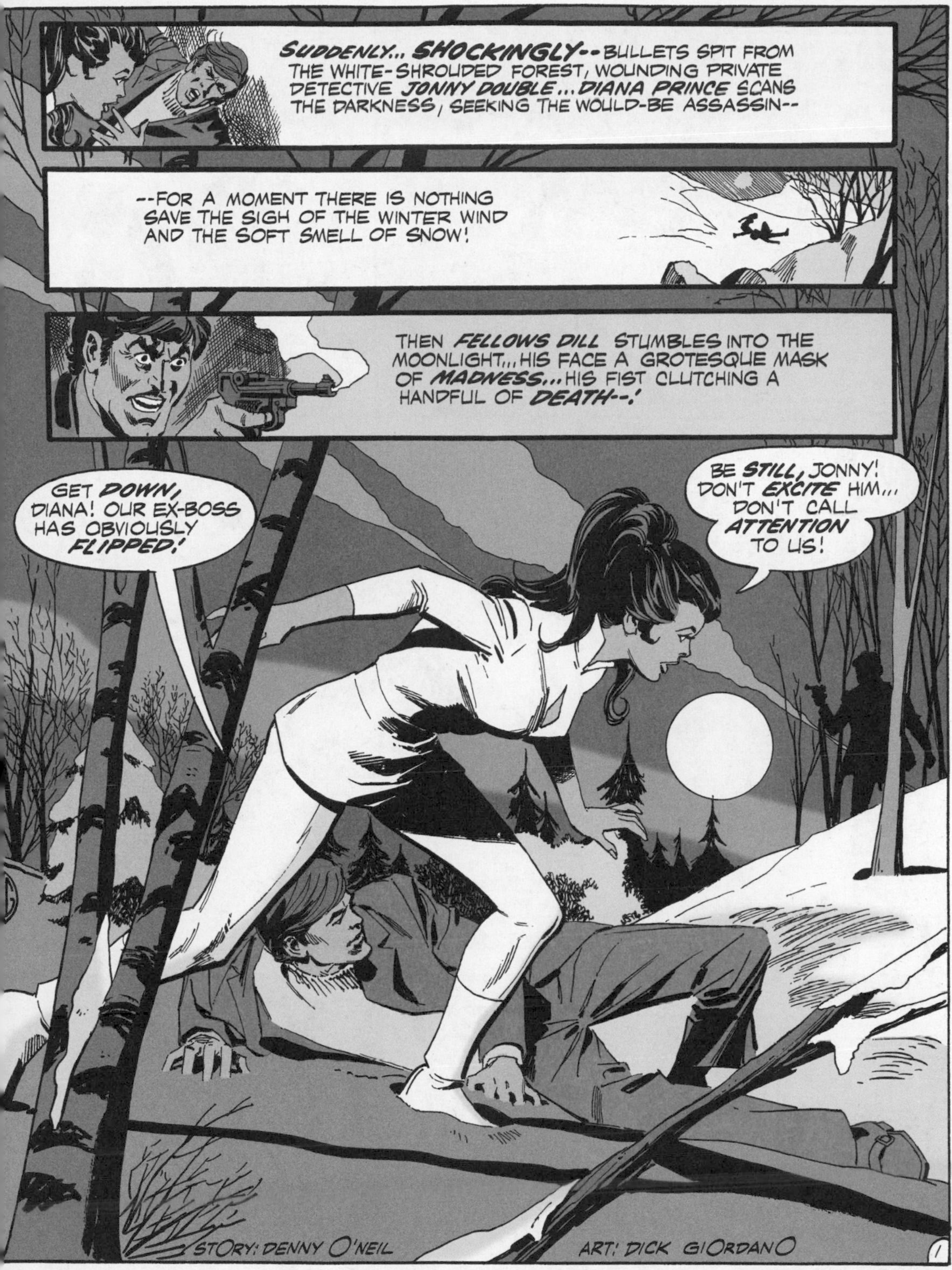
SUDDENLY... SHOCKINGLY--BULLETS SPIT FROM THE WHITE-SHROUDED FOREST, WOUNDING PRIVATE DETECTIVE JONNY DOUBLE...DIANA PRINCE SCANS THE DARKNESS, SEEKING THE WOULD-BE ASSASSIN--
--FOR A MOMENT THERE IS NOTHING SAVE THE SIGH OF THE WINTER WIND AND THE SOFT SMELL OF SNOW!
THEN FELLOWS DILL STUMBLES INTO THE MOONLIGHT... HIS FACE A GROTESQUE MASK OF MADNESS... HIS FIST CLUTCHING A HANDFUL OF DEATH--!
GET DOWN, DIANA! OUR EX-BOSS HAS OBVIOUSLY FLIPPED!
BE STILL, JONNY! DON'T EXCITE HIM... DON'T CALL ATTENTION TO US!
STORY: DENNY O'NEIL
ART: DICK GIORDANO
1

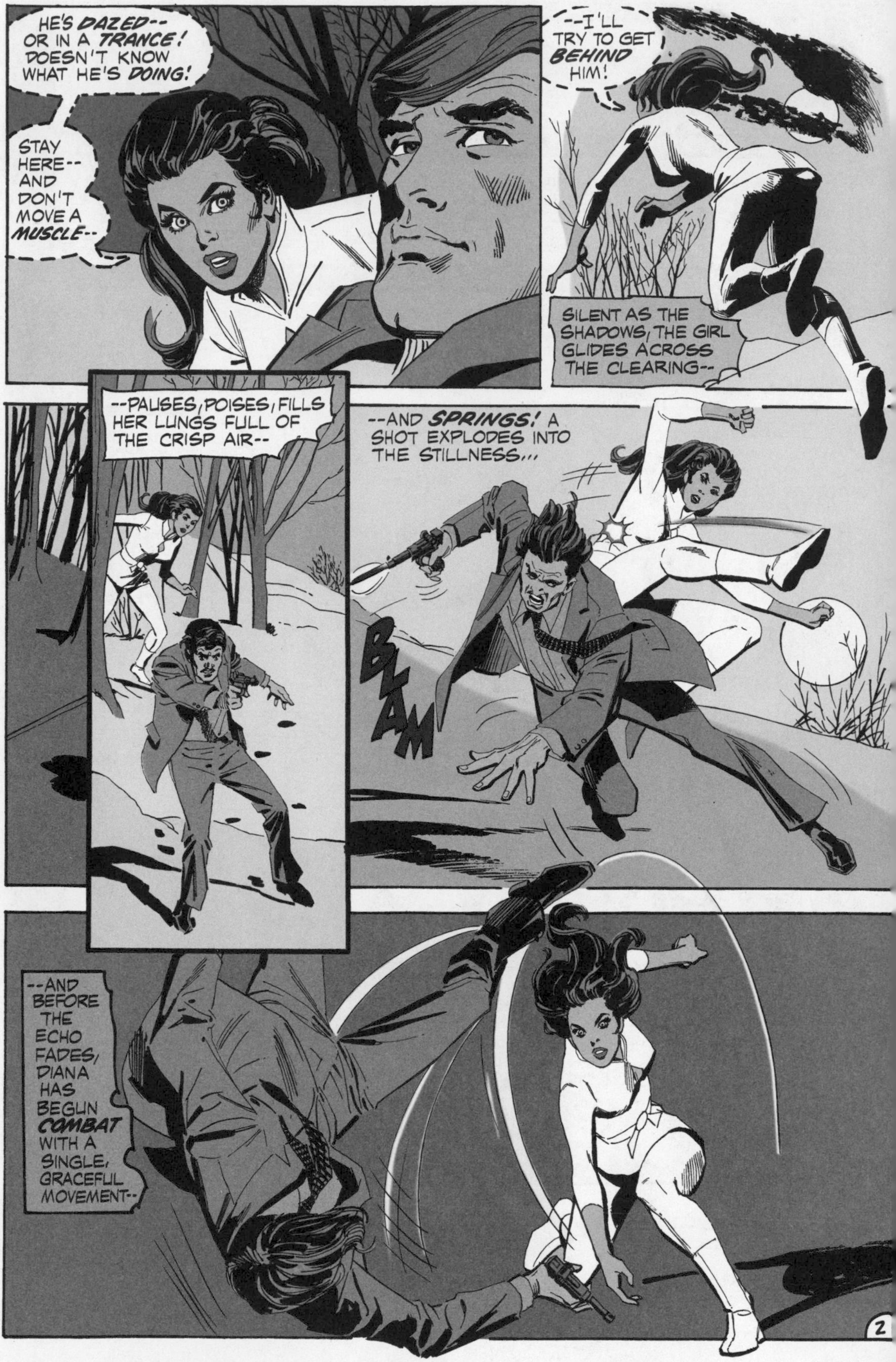
HE'S DAZED-- OR IN A TRANCE! DOESN'T KNOW WHAT HE'S DOING!
STAY HERE-- AND DON'T MOVE A MUSCLE--
--I'LL TRY TO GET BEHIND HIM!
SILENT AS THE SHADOWS, THE GIRL GLIDES ACROSS THE CLEARING--
--PAUSES, POISES, FILLS HER LUNGS FULL OF THE CRISP AIR--
--AND SPRINGS! A SHOT EXPLODES INTO THE STILLNESS...
BLAM
--AND BEFORE THE ECHO FADES, DIANA HAS BEGUN COMBAT WITH A SINGLE, GRACEFUL MOVEMENT--
2

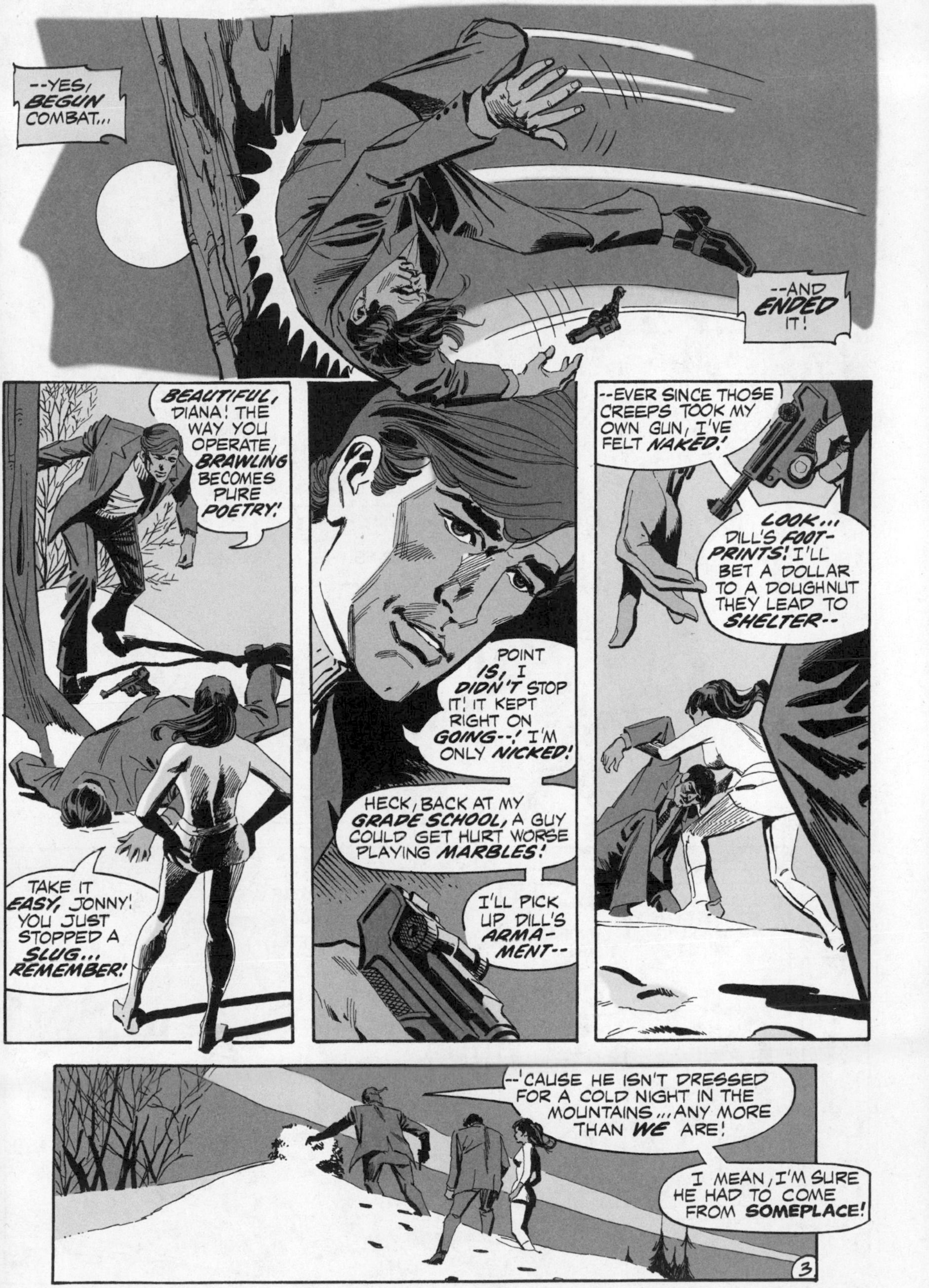
--YES, BEGUN COMBAT...
--AND ENDED IT!
BEAUTIFUL, DIANA! THE WAY YOU OPERATE, BRAWLING BECOMES PURE POETRY!
TAKE IT EASY, JONNY! YOU JUST STOPPED A SLUG... REMEMBER!
POINT IS, I DIDN'T STOP IT! IT KEPT RIGHT ON GOING--! I'M ONLY NICKED!
HECK, BACK AT MY GRADE SCHOOL, A GUY COULD GET HURT WORSE PLAYING MARBLES!
I'LL PICK UP DILL'S ARMA-MENT--
--EVER SINCE THOSE CREEPS TOOK MY OWN GUN, I'VE FELT NAKED!
LOOK... DILL'S FOOT-PRINTS! I'LL BET A DOLLAR TO A DOUGHNUT THEY LEAD TO SHELTER--
--'CAUSE HE ISN'T DRESSED FOR A COLD NIGHT IN THE MOUNTAINS... ANY MORE THAN WE ARE!
I MEAN, I'M SURE HE HAD TO COME FROM SOMEPLACE!
3

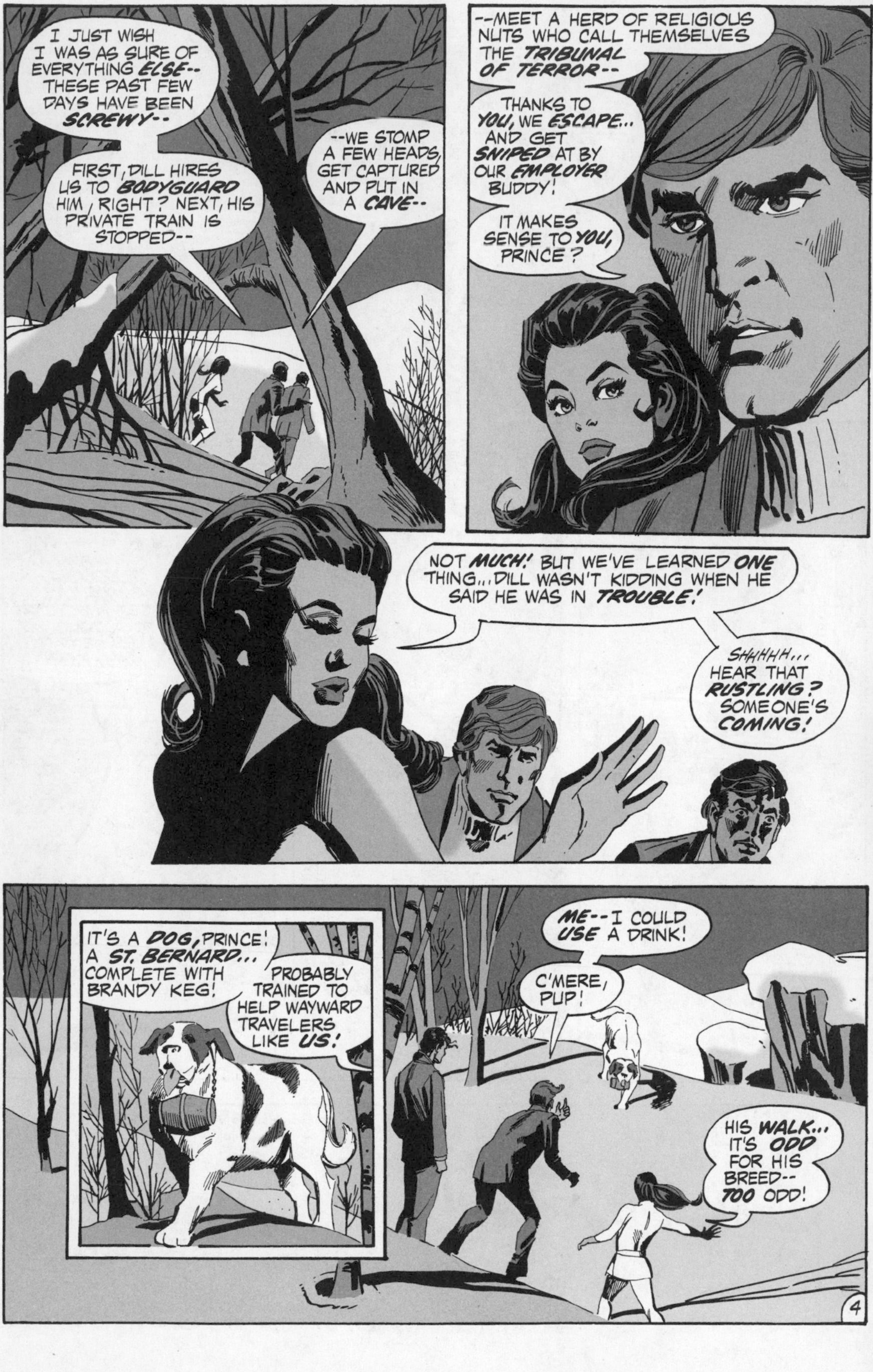
I JUST WISH I WAS AS SURE OF EVERYTHING *ELSE*-- THESE PAST FEW DAYS HAVE BEEN *SCREWY*--
FIRST, DILL HIRES US TO *BODYGUARD* HIM, RIGHT? NEXT, HIS PRIVATE TRAIN IS STOPPED--
--WE STOMP A FEW HEADS, GET CAPTURED AND PUT IN A *CAVE*--
--MEET A HERD OF RELIGIOUS NUTS WHO CALL THEMSELVES THE *TRIBUNAL OF TERROR*--
THANKS TO *YOU*, WE *ESCAPE*... AND GET *SNIPED* AT BY OUR *EMPLOYER* BUDDY!
IT MAKES SENSE TO *YOU*, PRINCE?
NOT *MUCH!* BUT WE'VE LEARNED *ONE* THING... DILL WASN'T KIDDING WHEN HE SAID HE WAS IN *TROUBLE!*
SHHHHH... HEAR THAT *RUSTLING?* SOMEONE'S *COMING!*
IT'S A *DOG*, PRINCE! A *ST. BERNARD*... COMPLETE WITH BRANDY KEG!
PROBABLY TRAINED TO HELP WAYWARD TRAVELERS LIKE *US!*
ME-- I COULD *USE* A DRINK!
C'MERE, PUP!
HIS *WALK*... IT'S *ODD* FOR HIS BREED-- *TOO* ODD!
4

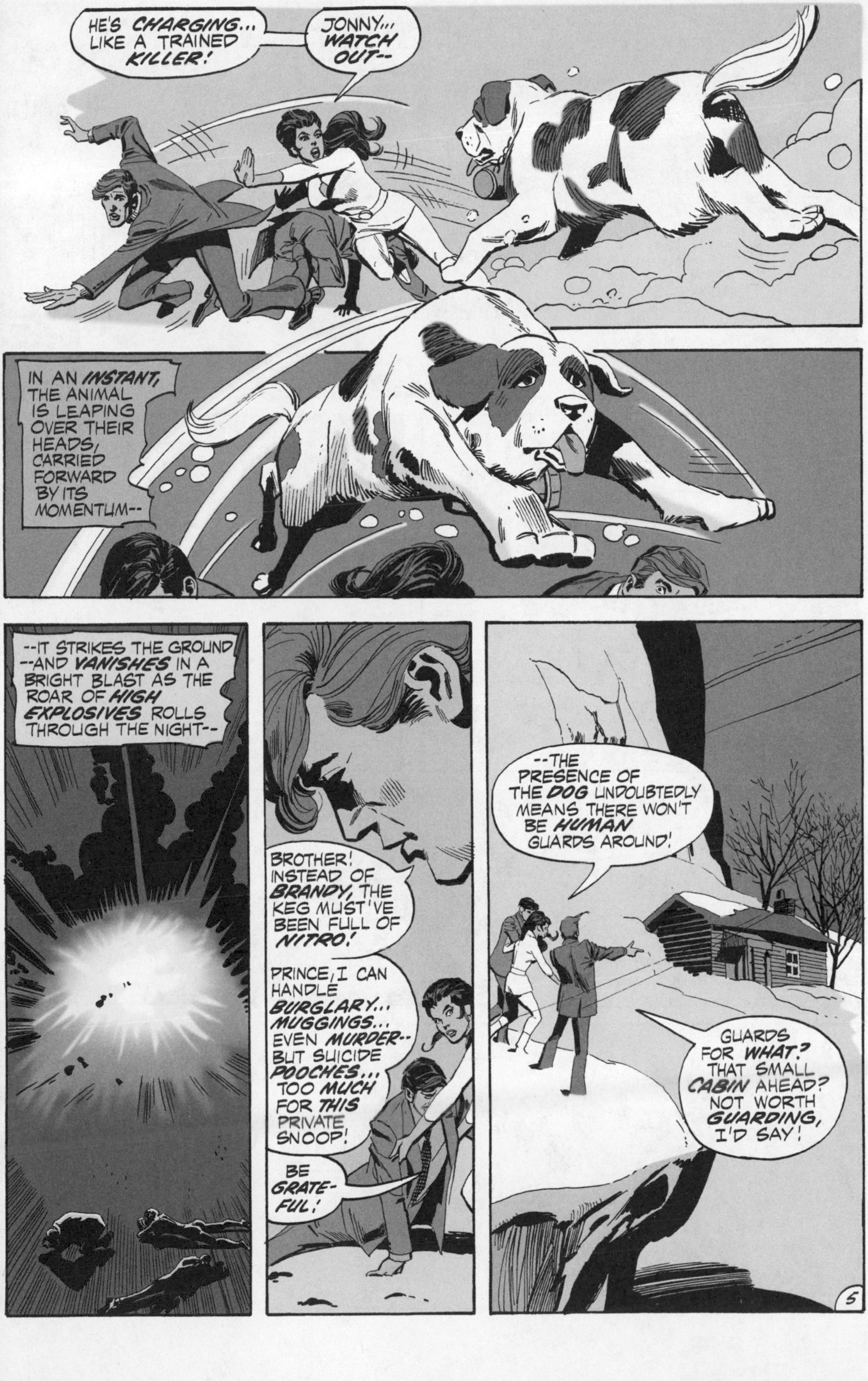
HE'S CHARGING... LIKE A TRAINED KILLER!
JONNY... WATCH OUT--
IN AN INSTANT, THE ANIMAL IS LEAPING OVER THEIR HEADS, CARRIED FORWARD BY ITS MOMENTUM--
--IT STRIKES THE GROUND --AND VANISHES IN A BRIGHT BLAST AS THE ROAR OF HIGH EXPLOSIVES ROLLS THROUGH THE NIGHT--
BROTHER! INSTEAD OF BRANDY, THE KEG MUST'VE BEEN FULL OF NITRO!
PRINCE, I CAN HANDLE BURGLARY... MUGGINGS... EVEN MURDER-- BUT SUICIDE POOCHES... TOO MUCH FOR THIS PRIVATE SNOOP!
BE GRATEFUL!
--THE PRESENCE OF THE DOG UNDOUBTEDLY MEANS THERE WON'T BE HUMAN GUARDS AROUND!
GUARDS FOR WHAT? THAT SMALL CABIN AHEAD? NOT WORTH GUARDING, I'D SAY!
5

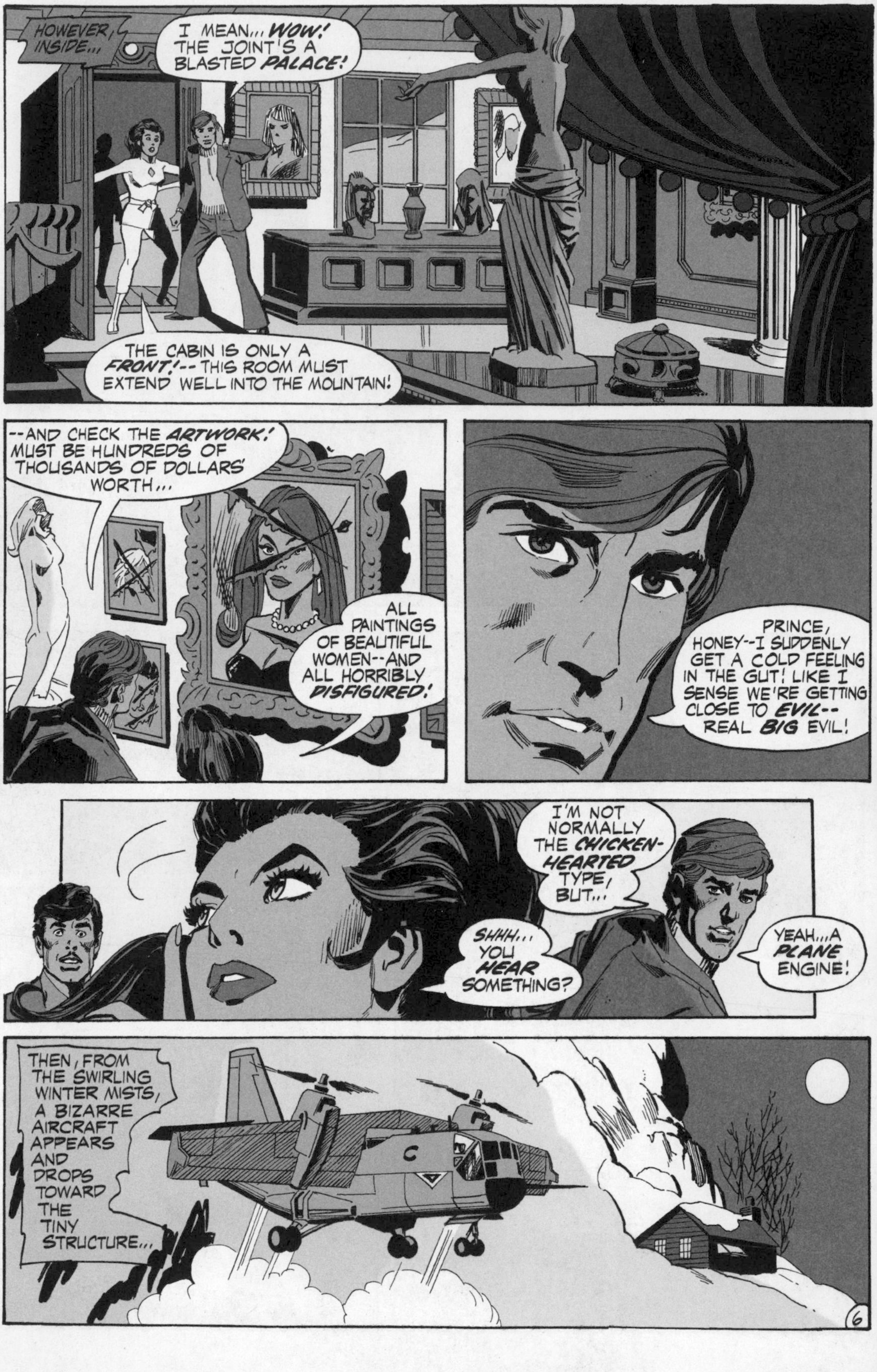

HOWEVER, INSIDE...
I MEAN... WOW! THE JOINT'S A BLASTED PALACE!
THE CABIN IS ONLY A FRONT!-- THIS ROOM MUST EXTEND WELL INTO THE MOUNTAIN!
--AND CHECK THE ARTWORK! MUST BE HUNDREDS OF THOUSANDS OF DOLLARS' WORTH...
ALL PAINTINGS OF BEAUTIFUL WOMEN--AND ALL HORRIBLY DISFIGURED!
PRINCE, HONEY--I SUDDENLY GET A COLD FEELING IN THE GUT! LIKE I SENSE WE'RE GETTING CLOSE TO EVIL-- REAL BIG EVIL!
I'M NOT NORMALLY THE CHICKEN-HEARTED TYPE, BUT...
SHHH... YOU HEAR SOMETHING?
YEAH... A PLANE ENGINE!
THEN, FROM THE SWIRLING WINTER MISTS, A BIZARRE AIRCRAFT APPEARS AND DROPS TOWARD THE TINY STRUCTURE...
C
6

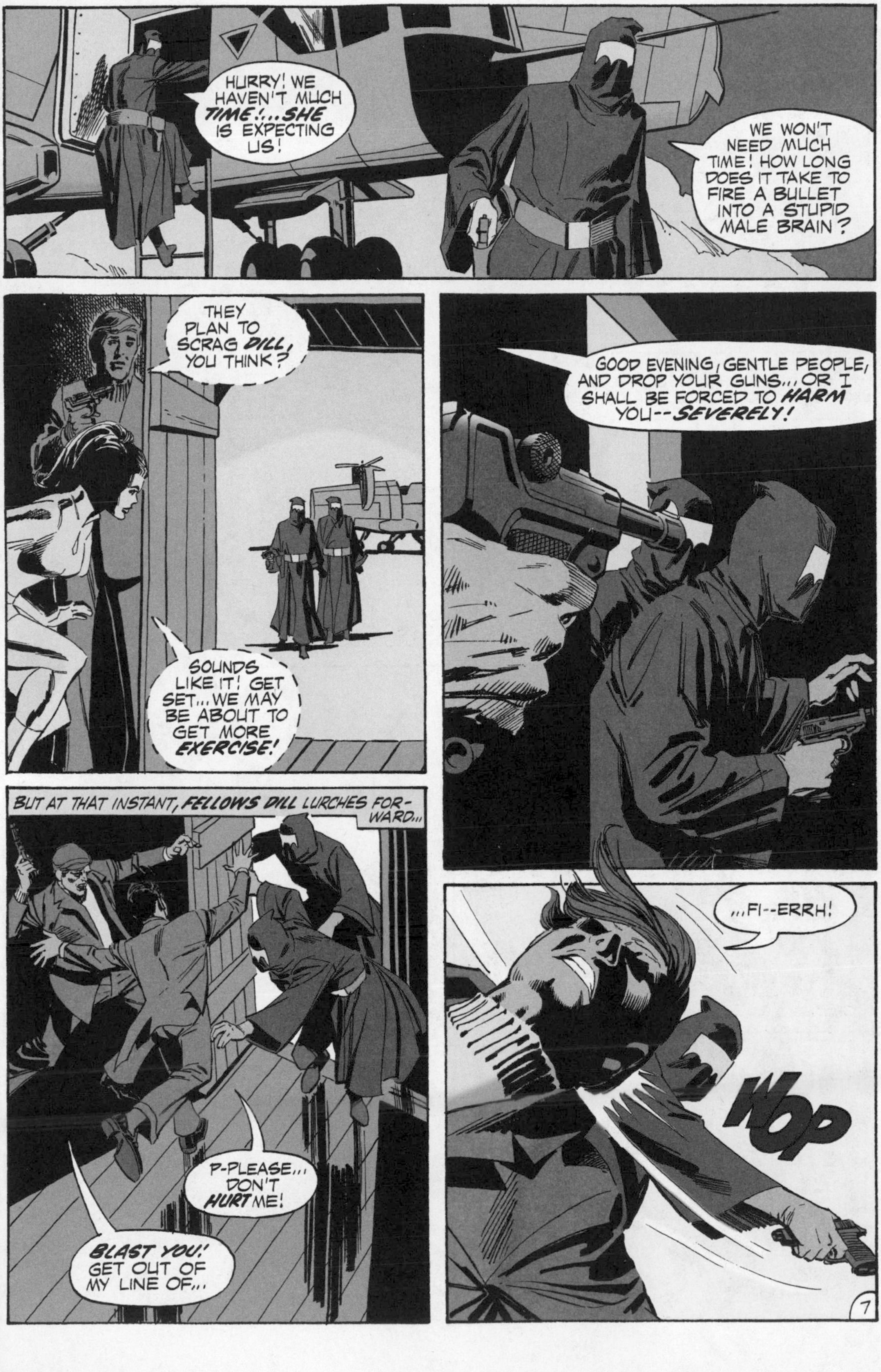
HURRY! WE HAVEN'T MUCH TIME!...SHE IS EXPECTING US!
WE WON'T NEED MUCH TIME! HOW LONG DOES IT TAKE TO FIRE A BULLET INTO A STUPID MALE BRAIN?
THEY PLAN TO SCRAG DILL, YOU THINK?
SOUNDS LIKE IT! GET SET...WE MAY BE ABOUT TO GET MORE EXERCISE!
GOOD EVENING, GENTLE PEOPLE, AND DROP YOUR GUNS...OR I SHALL BE FORCED TO HARM YOU--SEVERELY!
BUT AT THAT INSTANT, FELLOWS DILL LURCHES FOR-WARD...
P-PLEASE... DON'T HURT ME!
BLAST YOU! GET OUT OF MY LINE OF...
...FI--ERRH!
WOP
7

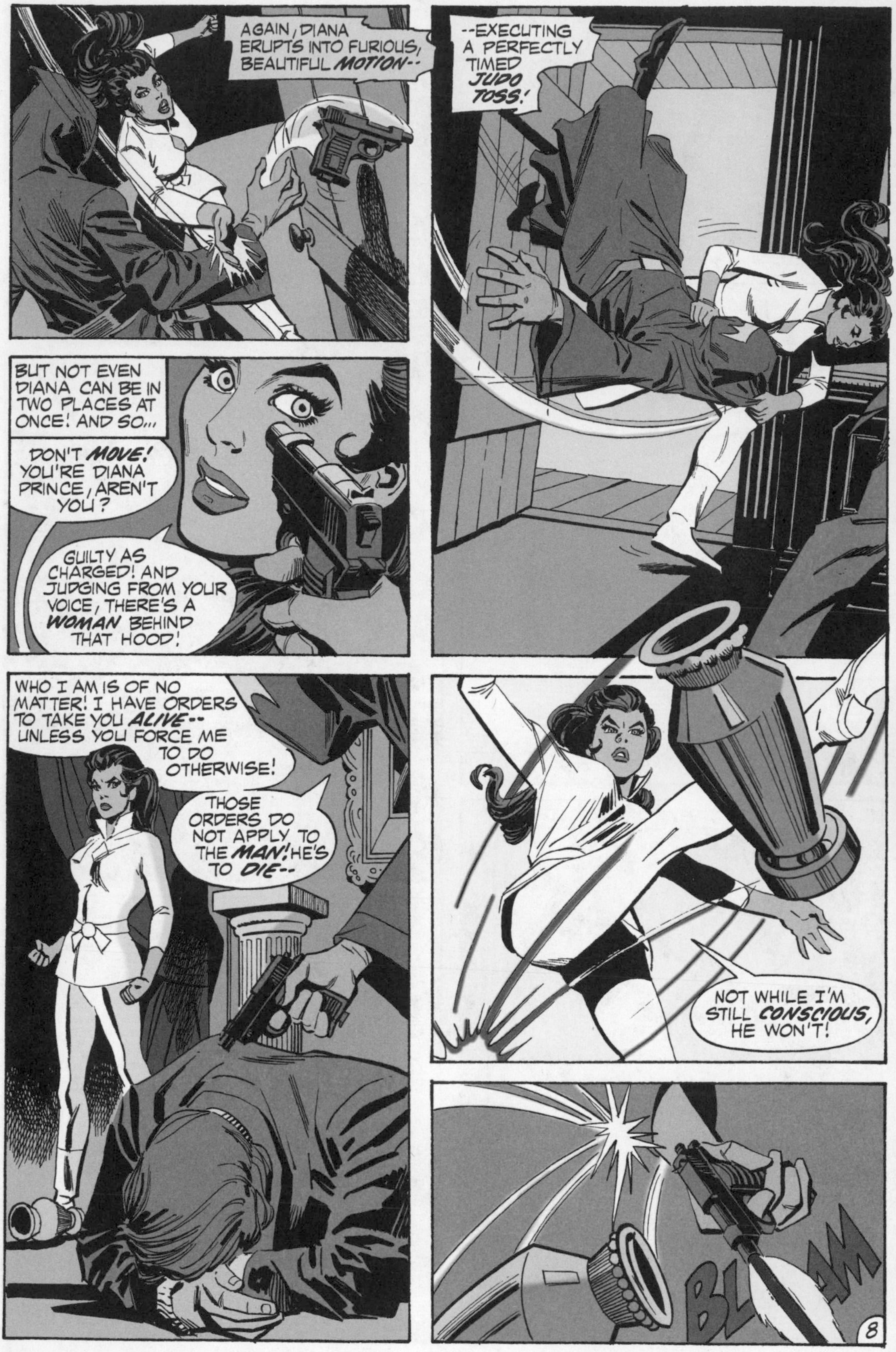
AGAIN, DIANA ERUPTS INTO FURIOUS, BEAUTIFUL MOTION--
--EXECUTING A PERFECTLY TIMED JUDO TOSS!
BUT NOT EVEN DIANA CAN BE IN TWO PLACES AT ONCE! AND SO...
DON'T MOVE! YOU'RE DIANA PRINCE, AREN'T YOU?
GUILTY AS CHARGED! AND JUDGING FROM YOUR VOICE, THERE'S A WOMAN BEHIND THAT HOOD!
WHO I AM IS OF NO MATTER! I HAVE ORDERS TO TAKE YOU ALIVE-- UNLESS YOU FORCE ME TO DO OTHERWISE!
THOSE ORDERS DO NOT APPLY TO THE MAN! HE'S TO DIE--
NOT WHILE I'M STILL CONSCIOUS, HE WON'T!
BLAM
8

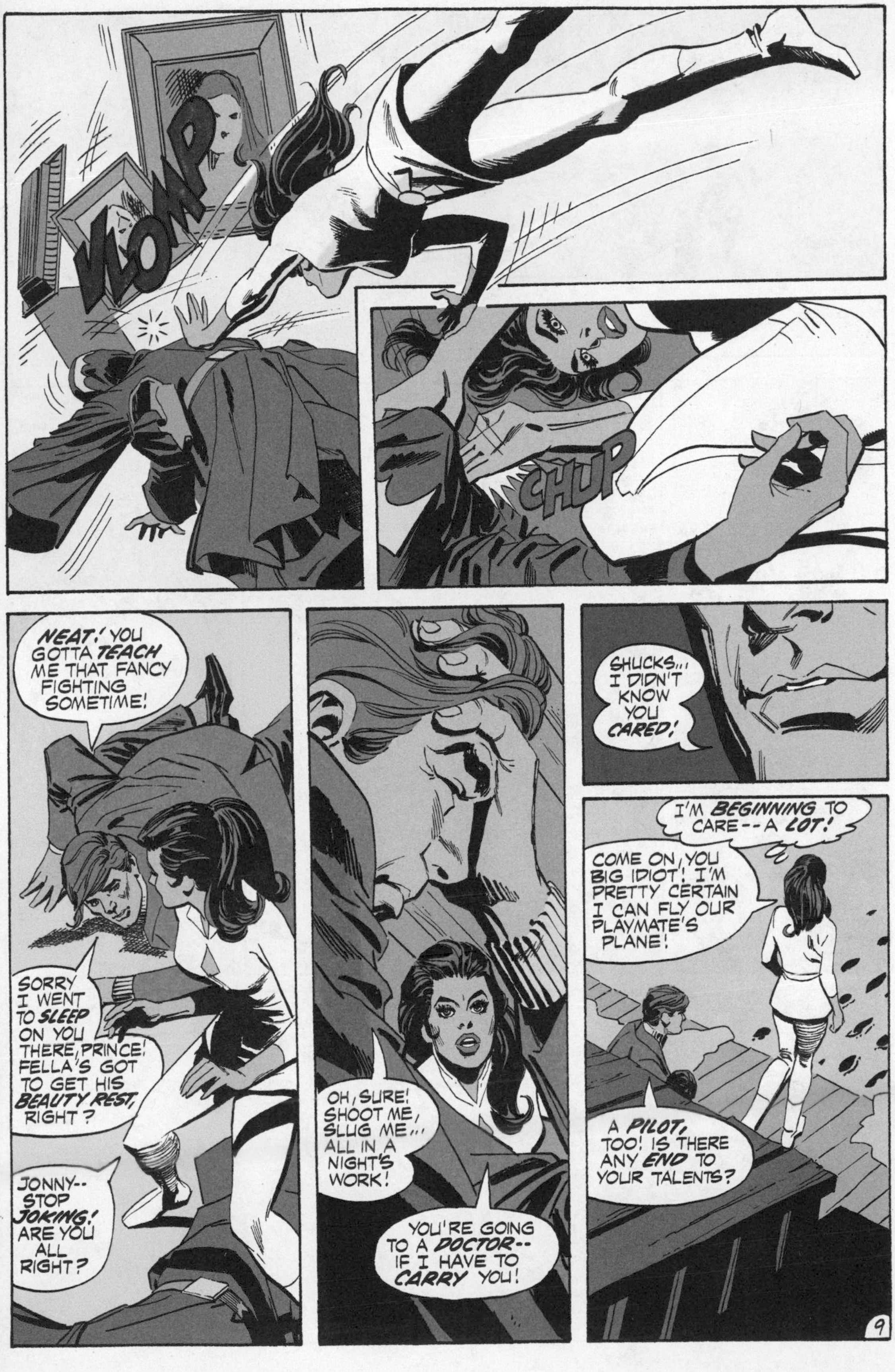
VLOMP
CHUP
NEAT! YOU GOTTA TEACH ME THAT FANCY FIGHTING SOMETIME!
SORRY I WENT TO SLEEP ON YOU THERE, PRINCE! FELLA'S GOT TO GET HIS BEAUTY REST, RIGHT?
JONNY-- STOP JOKING! ARE YOU ALL RIGHT?
OH, SURE! SHOOT ME, SLUG ME... ALL IN A NIGHT'S WORK!
YOU'RE GOING TO A DOCTOR-- IF I HAVE TO CARRY YOU!
SHUCKS... I DIDN'T KNOW YOU CARED!
I'M BEGINNING TO CARE-- A LOT!
COME ON, YOU BIG IDIOT! I'M PRETTY CERTAIN I CAN FLY OUR PLAYMATE'S PLANE!
A PILOT, TOO! IS THERE ANY END TO YOUR TALENTS?
9

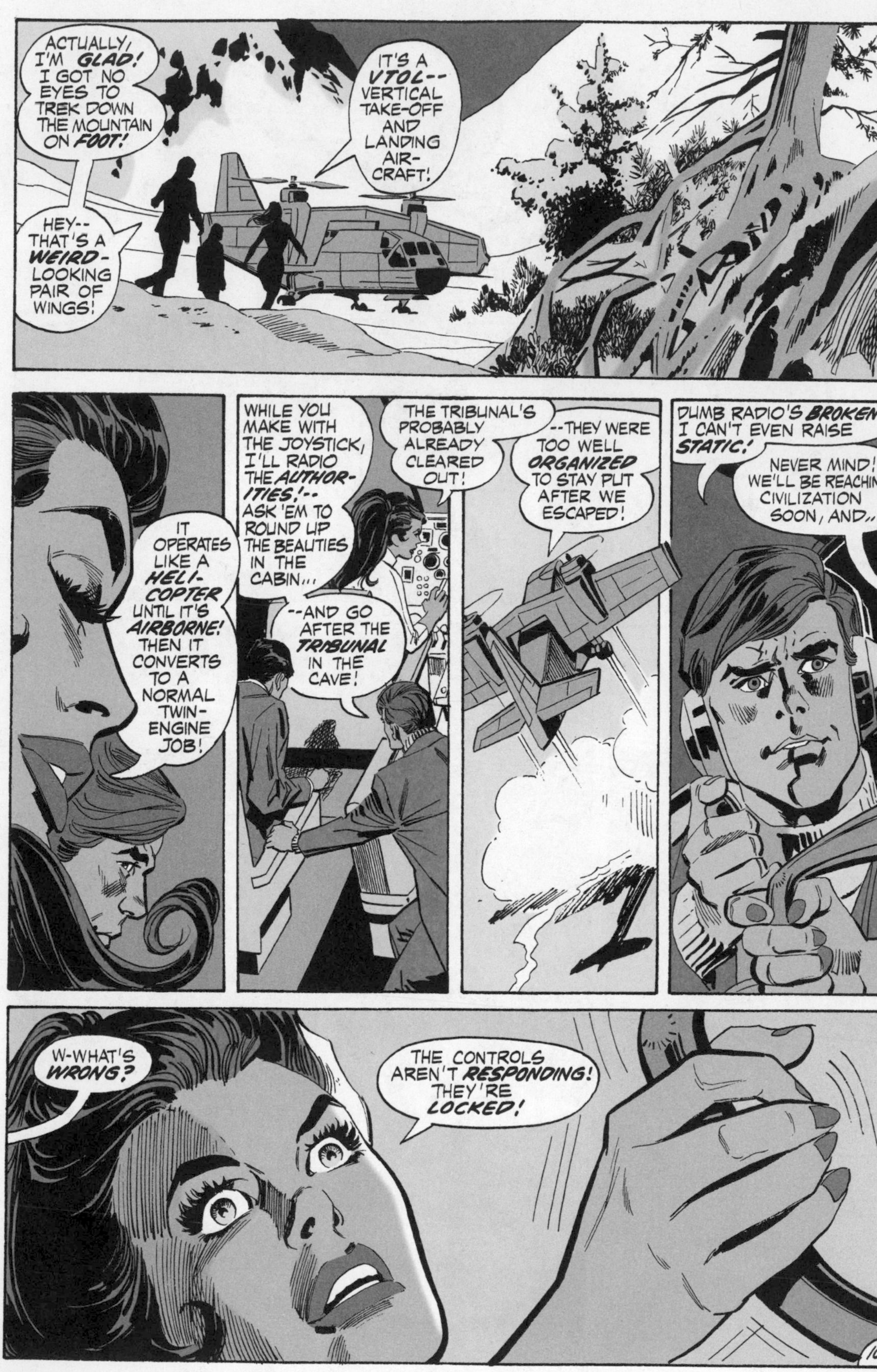
ACTUALLY, I'M GLAD! I GOT NO EYES TO TREK DOWN THE MOUNTAIN ON FOOT!
IT'S A VTOL-- VERTICAL TAKE-OFF AND LANDING AIR-CRAFT!
HEY-- THAT'S A WEIRD-LOOKING PAIR OF WINGS!
IT OPERATES LIKE A HELI-COPTER UNTIL IT'S AIRBORNE! THEN IT CONVERTS TO A NORMAL TWIN-ENGINE JOB!
WHILE YOU MAKE WITH THE JOYSTICK, I'LL RADIO THE AUTHOR-ITIES!-- ASK 'EM TO ROUND UP THE BEAUTIES IN THE CABIN...
--AND GO AFTER THE TRIBUNAL IN THE CAVE!
THE TRIBUNAL'S PROBABLY ALREADY CLEARED OUT!
--THEY WERE TOO WELL ORGANIZED TO STAY PUT AFTER WE ESCAPED!
DUMB RADIO'S BROKEN! I CAN'T EVEN RAISE STATIC!
NEVER MIND! WE'LL BE REACHING CIVILIZATION SOON, AND...
W-WHAT'S WRONG?
THE CONTROLS AREN'T RESPONDING! THEY'RE LOCKED!
10

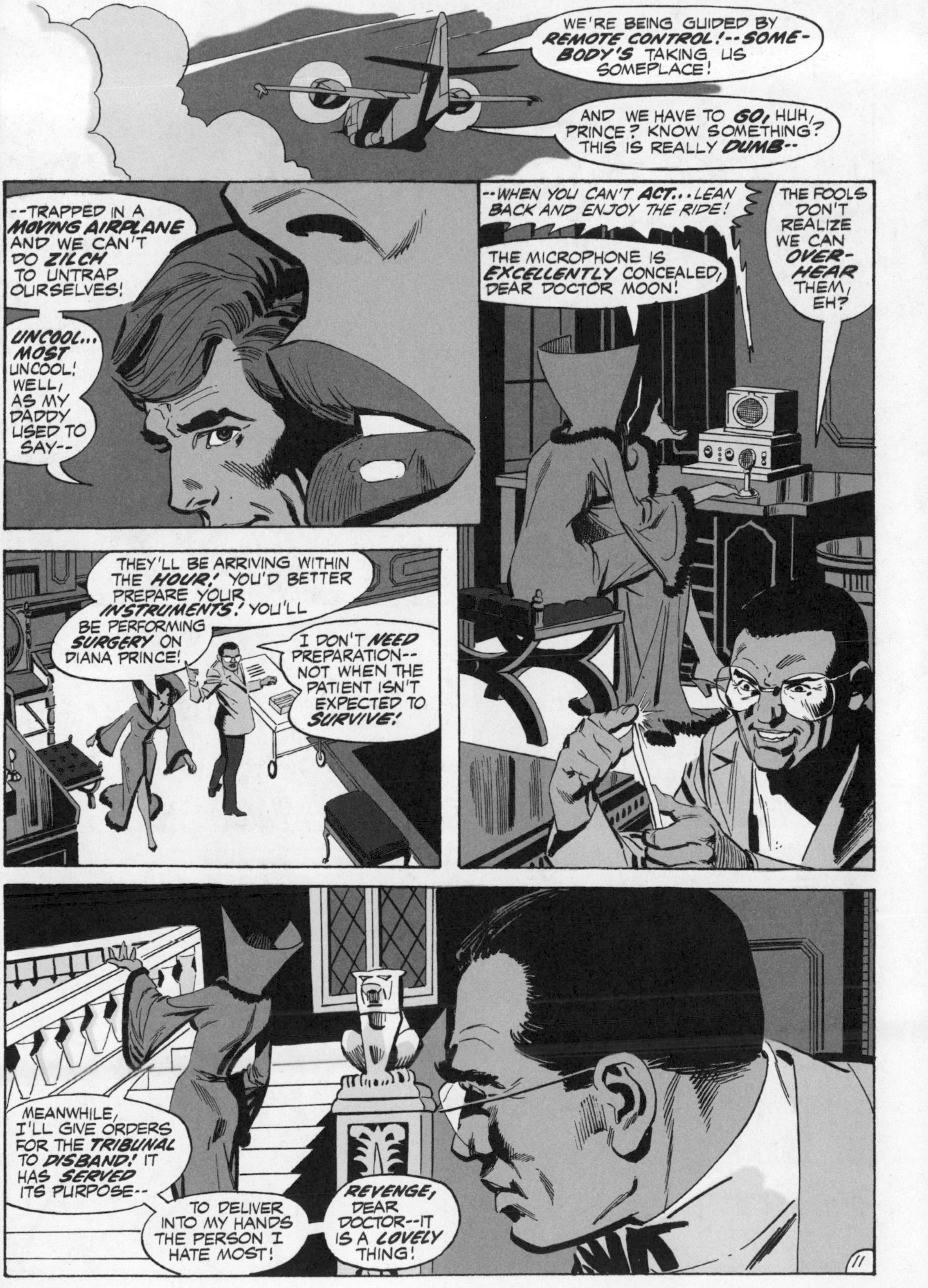
WE'RE BEING GUIDED BY REMOTE CONTROL!--SOME-BODY'S TAKING US SOMEPLACE!
AND WE HAVE TO GO, HUH, PRINCE? KNOW SOMETHING? THIS IS REALLY DUMB--
--TRAPPED IN A MOVING AIRPLANE AND WE CAN'T DO ZILCH TO UNTRAP OURSELVES!
UNCOOL... MOST UNCOOL! WELL, AS MY DADDY USED TO SAY--
--WHEN YOU CAN'T ACT...LEAN BACK AND ENJOY THE RIDE!
THE MICROPHONE IS EXCELLENTLY CONCEALED, DEAR DOCTOR MOON!
THE FOOLS DON'T REALIZE WE CAN OVER-HEAR THEM, EH?
THEY'LL BE ARRIVING WITHIN THE HOUR! YOU'D BETTER PREPARE YOUR INSTRUMENTS! YOU'LL BE PERFORMING SURGERY ON DIANA PRINCE!
I DON'T NEED PREPARATION--NOT WHEN THE PATIENT ISN'T EXPECTED TO SURVIVE!
MEANWHILE, I'LL GIVE ORDERS FOR THE TRIBUNAL TO DISBAND! IT HAS SERVED ITS PURPOSE--
TO DELIVER INTO MY HANDS THE PERSON I HATE MOST!
REVENGE, DEAR DOCTOR--IT IS A LOVELY THING!
11

AND AS THE SUN'S FIRST GLOW SPREADS OVER THE CLOUDS....

WE'RE *LANDING*, JONNY!

YEAH.... AND I *RECOGNIZE* THE PLACE!

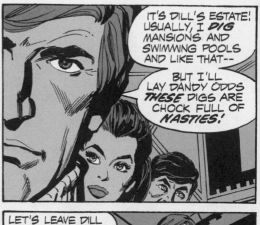

IT'S DILL'S ESTATE! USUALLY, I *DIG* MANSIONS AND SWIMMING POOLS AND LIKE THAT--

BUT I'LL LAY DANDY ODDS *THESE* DIGS ARE CHOCK FULL OF *NASTIES*!

LET'S LEAVE DILL HERE! I'M TIRED OF *NURSE-MAIDING* THE ZOMBIE MILLIONAIRE!

GOOD IDEA! HE'LL *SLOW* US.... ....AND WE MAY HAVE TO MOVE *FAST*!

I'LL SAY *THIS* FOR YOU, PRINCE-- SINCE I MET YOU LIFE HASN'T BEEN *DULL*!

IN FACT, I SORTA MISS THE GOOD OLD DAYS WHEN I WAS *BORED*!

SURELY YOU DON'T BLAME *ME* FOR WHAT'S HAPPENED!

MISTER DOUBLE, YOU HAVE A *NERVE*! YOU RECRUITED *ME* FOR THIS DUMB BODY-GUARDING CHORE!

IF IT HADN'T BEEN FOR *YOU*, I'D NEVER HAVE *HEARD* OF DILL....OR THE TRIBUNAL....

EASY, PRINCE--!

I'VE GOT NO INTEREST IN *SCALDING YOU OFF*, LADY! IN MY OWN BUMBLING FASHION, I WAS TRYING TO MAKE *FUNNY*!

--'CAUSE THE *CHUCKLE ROUTINE* MAY CAUSE ME TO FORGET I'M *SCARED*!

12

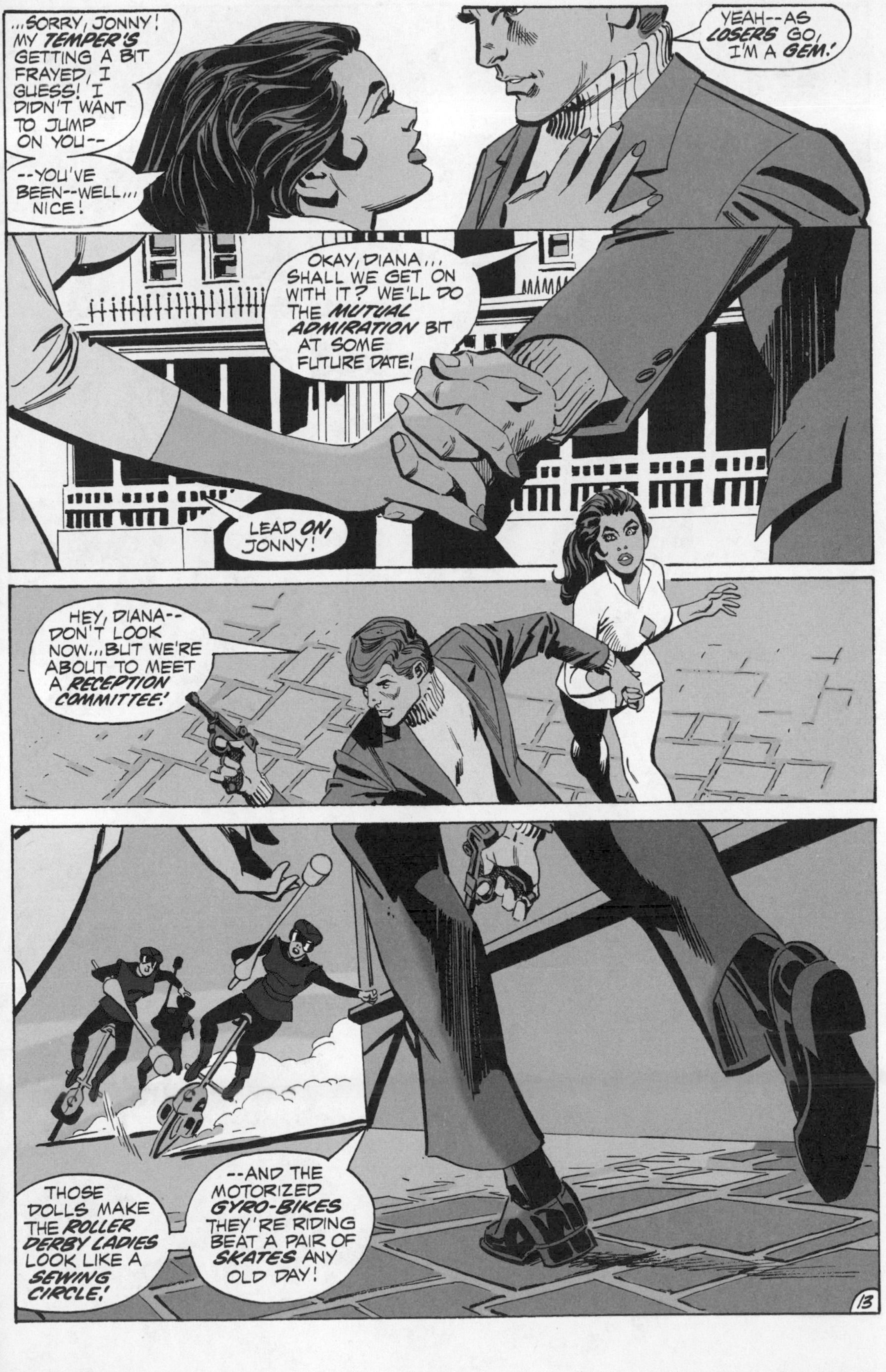
...SORRY, JONNY! MY TEMPER'S GETTING A BIT FRAYED, I GUESS! I DIDN'T WANT TO JUMP ON YOU--
--YOU'VE BEEN--WELL... NICE!
YEAH--AS LOSERS GO, I'M A GEM!
OKAY, DIANA... SHALL WE GET ON WITH IT? WE'LL DO THE MUTUAL ADMIRATION BIT AT SOME FUTURE DATE!
LEAD ON, JONNY!
HEY, DIANA-- DON'T LOOK NOW...BUT WE'RE ABOUT TO MEET A RECEPTION COMMITTEE!
THOSE DOLLS MAKE THE ROLLER DERBY LADIES LOOK LIKE A SEWING CIRCLE!
--AND THE MOTORIZED GYRO-BIKES THEY'RE RIDING BEAT A PAIR OF SKATES ANY OLD DAY!
13

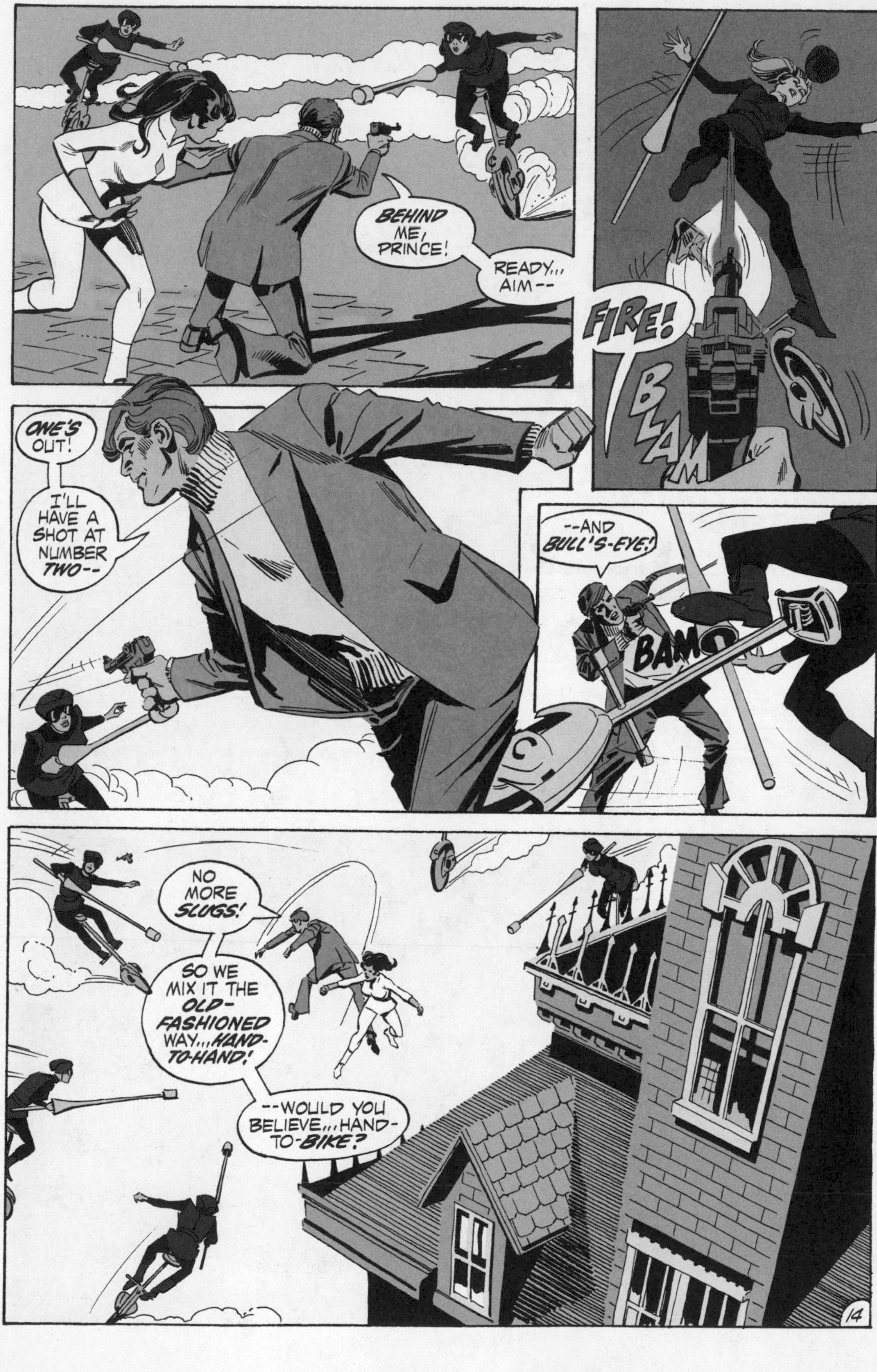
BEHIND ME, PRINCE!
READY... AIM--
FIRE!
BLAM
ONE'S OUT!
I'LL HAVE A SHOT AT NUMBER TWO--
--AND BULL'S-EYE!
BAMO
NO MORE SLUGS!
SO WE MIX IT THE OLD-FASHIONED WAY... HAND-TO-HAND!
--WOULD YOU BELIEVE... HAND-TO-BIKE?
14

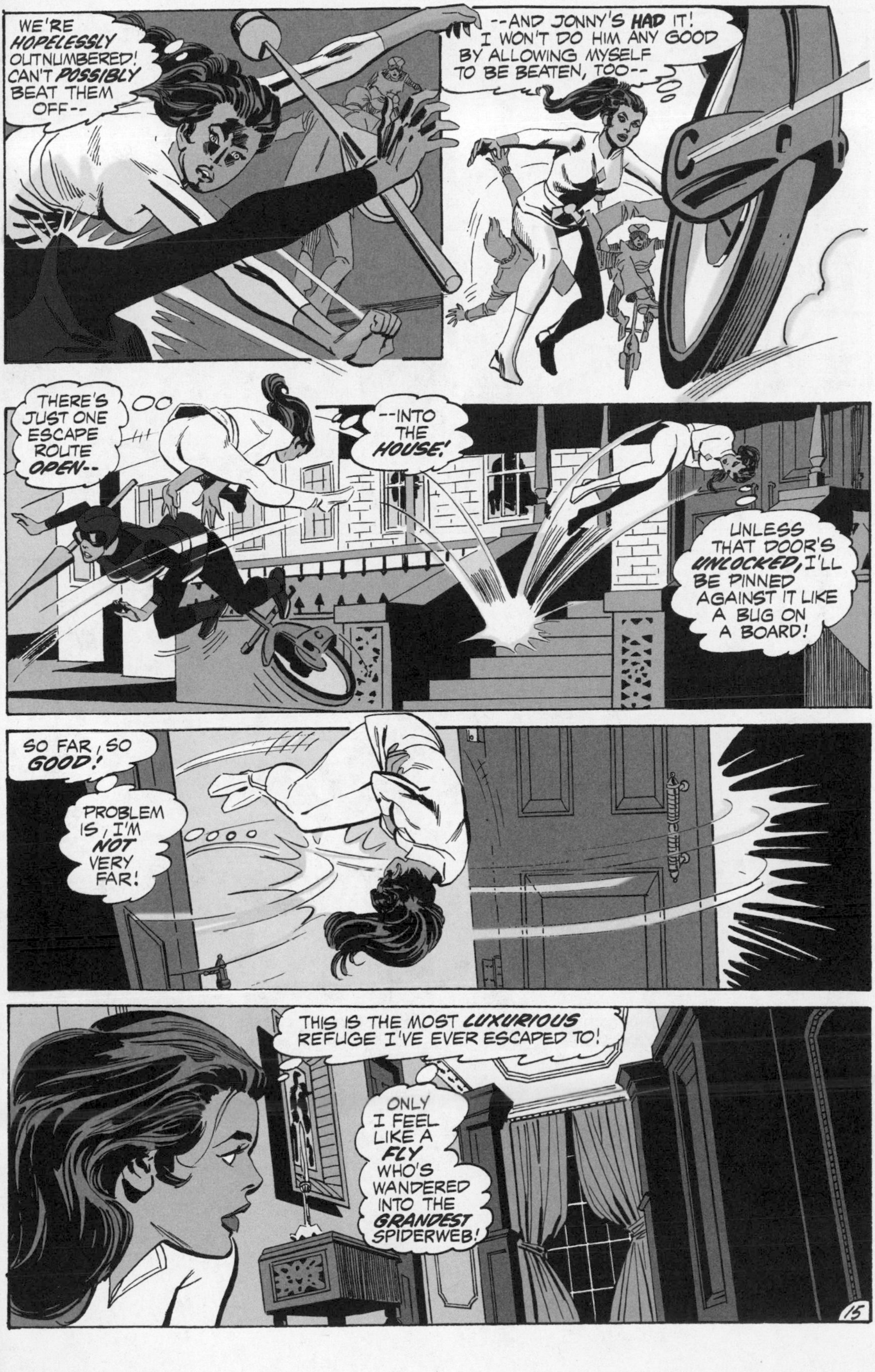
WE'RE HOPELESSLY OUTNUMBERED! CAN'T POSSIBLY BEAT THEM OFF--
--AND JONNY'S HAD IT! I WON'T DO HIM ANY GOOD BY ALLOWING MYSELF TO BE BEATEN, TOO--
THERE'S JUST ONE ESCAPE ROUTE OPEN--
--INTO THE HOUSE!
UNLESS THAT DOOR'S UNLOCKED, I'LL BE PINNED AGAINST IT LIKE A BUG ON A BOARD!
SO FAR, SO GOOD!
PROBLEM IS, I'M NOT VERY FAR!
THIS IS THE MOST LUXURIOUS REFUGE I'VE EVER ESCAPED TO!
ONLY I FEEL LIKE A FLY WHO'S WANDERED INTO THE GRANDEST SPIDERWEB!
15

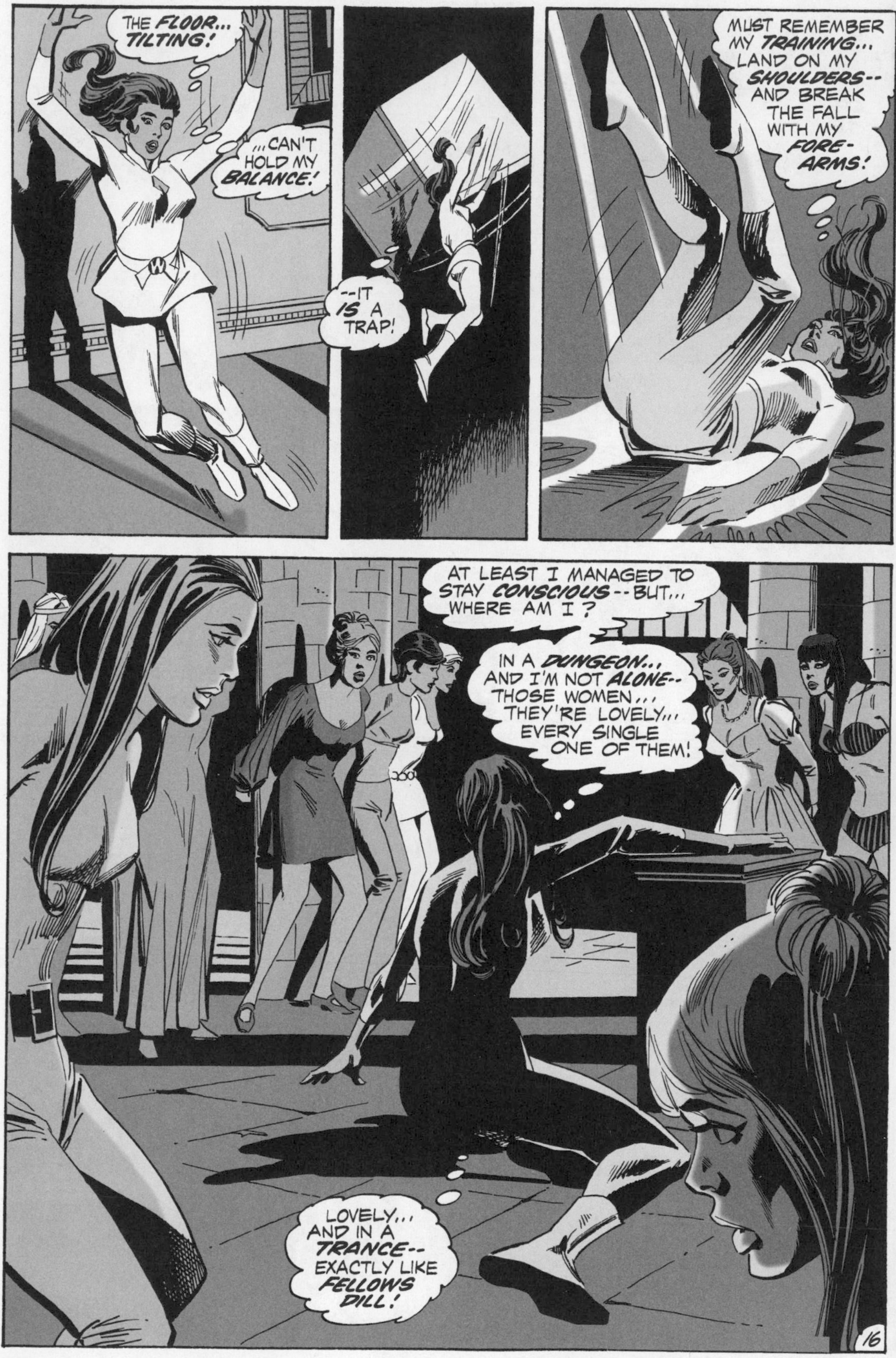
THE FLOOR... TILTING!
...CAN'T HOLD MY BALANCE!
--IT IS A TRAP!
MUST REMEMBER MY TRAINING... LAND ON MY SHOULDERS-- AND BREAK THE FALL WITH MY FORE-ARMS!
AT LEAST I MANAGED TO STAY CONSCIOUS--BUT... WHERE AM I?
IN A DUNGEON... AND I'M NOT ALONE-- THOSE WOMEN... THEY'RE LOVELY... EVERY SINGLE ONE OF THEM!
LOVELY... AND IN A TRANCE-- EXACTLY LIKE FELLOWS DILL!
16

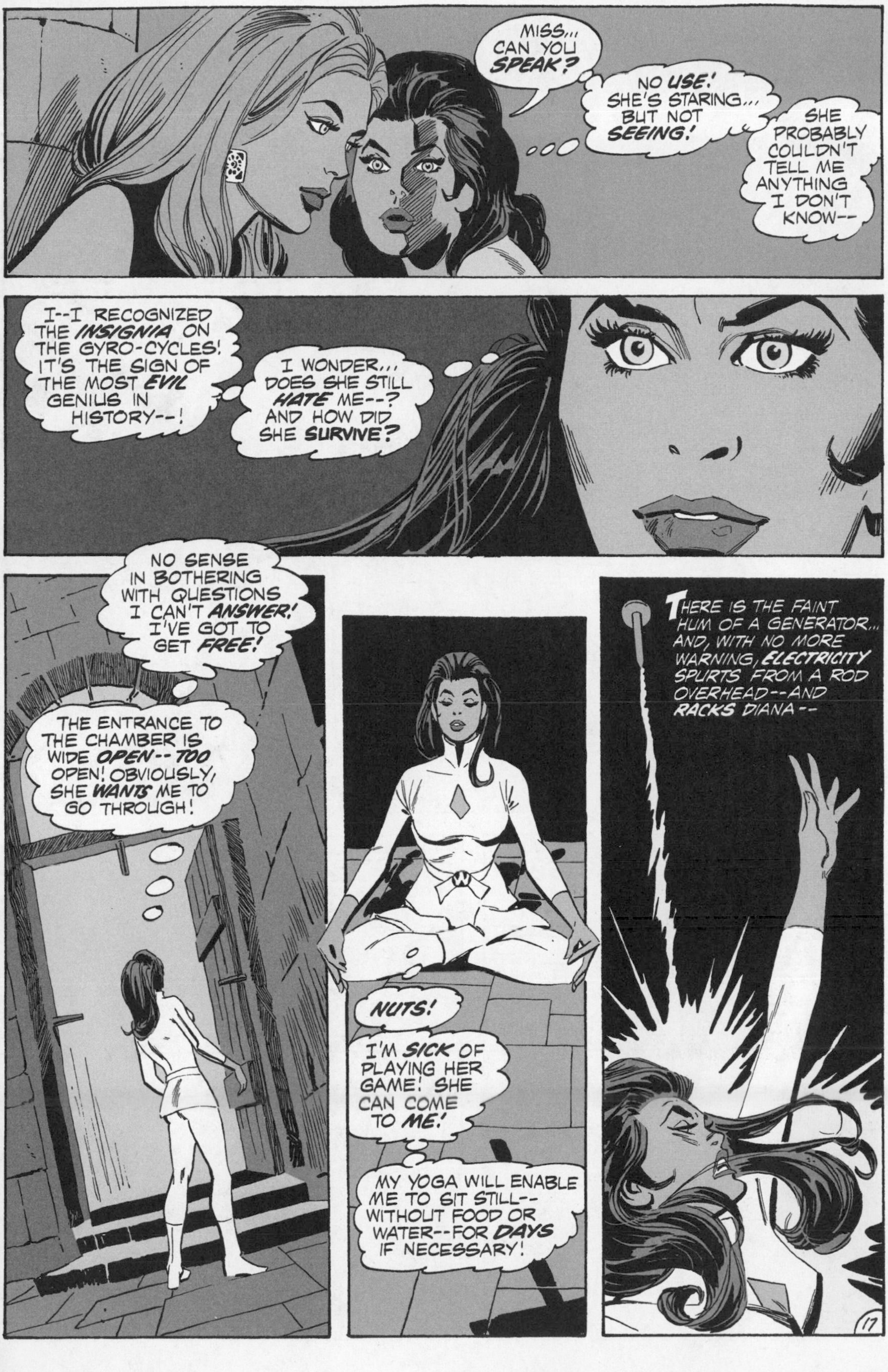
MISS... CAN YOU SPEAK?
NO USE! SHE'S STARING... BUT NOT SEEING!
SHE PROBABLY COULDN'T TELL ME ANYTHING I DON'T KNOW--
I--I RECOGNIZED THE INSIGNIA ON THE GYRO-CYCLES! IT'S THE SIGN OF THE MOST EVIL GENIUS IN HISTORY--!
I WONDER... DOES SHE STILL HATE ME--? AND HOW DID SHE SURVIVE?
NO SENSE IN BOTHERING WITH QUESTIONS I CAN'T ANSWER! I'VE GOT TO GET FREE!
THE ENTRANCE TO THE CHAMBER IS WIDE OPEN--TOO OPEN! OBVIOUSLY, SHE WANTS ME TO GO THROUGH!
NUTS!
I'M SICK OF PLAYING HER GAME! SHE CAN COME TO ME!
MY YOGA WILL ENABLE ME TO SIT STILL--WITHOUT FOOD OR WATER--FOR DAYS IF NECESSARY!
THERE IS THE FAINT HUM OF A GENERATOR... AND, WITH NO MORE WARNING, ELECTRICITY SPURTS FROM A ROD OVERHEAD--AND RACKS DIANA--
17

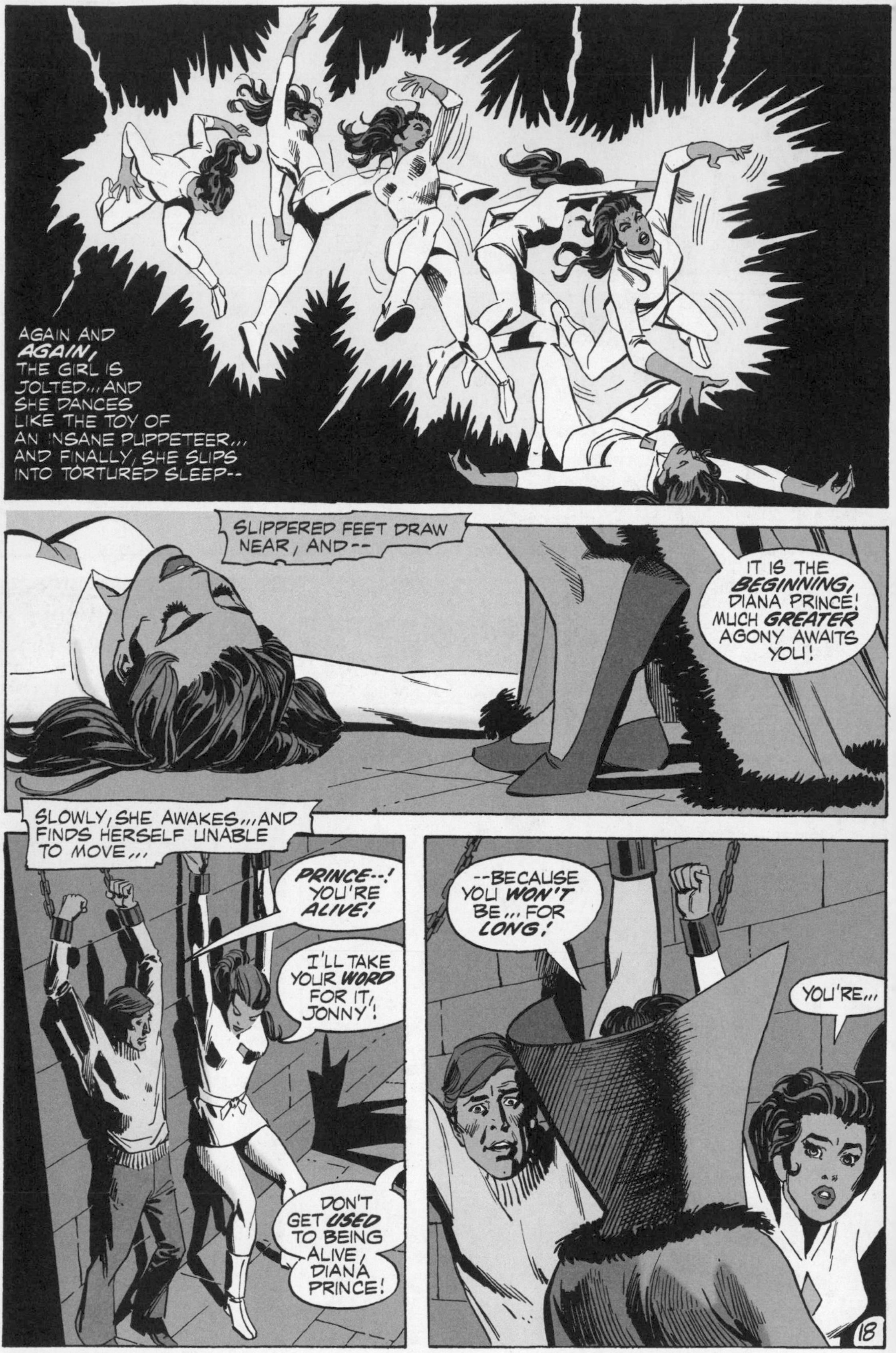
AGAIN AND *AGAIN*, THE GIRL IS JOLTED... AND SHE DANCES LIKE THE TOY OF AN INSANE PUPPETEER... AND FINALLY, SHE SLIPS INTO TORTURED SLEEP--
SLIPPERED FEET DRAW NEAR, AND--
IT IS THE *BEGINNING*, DIANA PRINCE! MUCH *GREATER* AGONY AWAITS YOU!
SLOWLY, SHE AWAKES... AND FINDS HERSELF UNABLE TO MOVE...
PRINCE--! YOU'RE *ALIVE*!
I'LL TAKE YOUR *WORD* FOR IT, JONNY!
DON'T GET *USED* TO BEING ALIVE, DIANA PRINCE!
--BECAUSE YOU *WON'T* BE... FOR *LONG*!
YOU'RE...
18

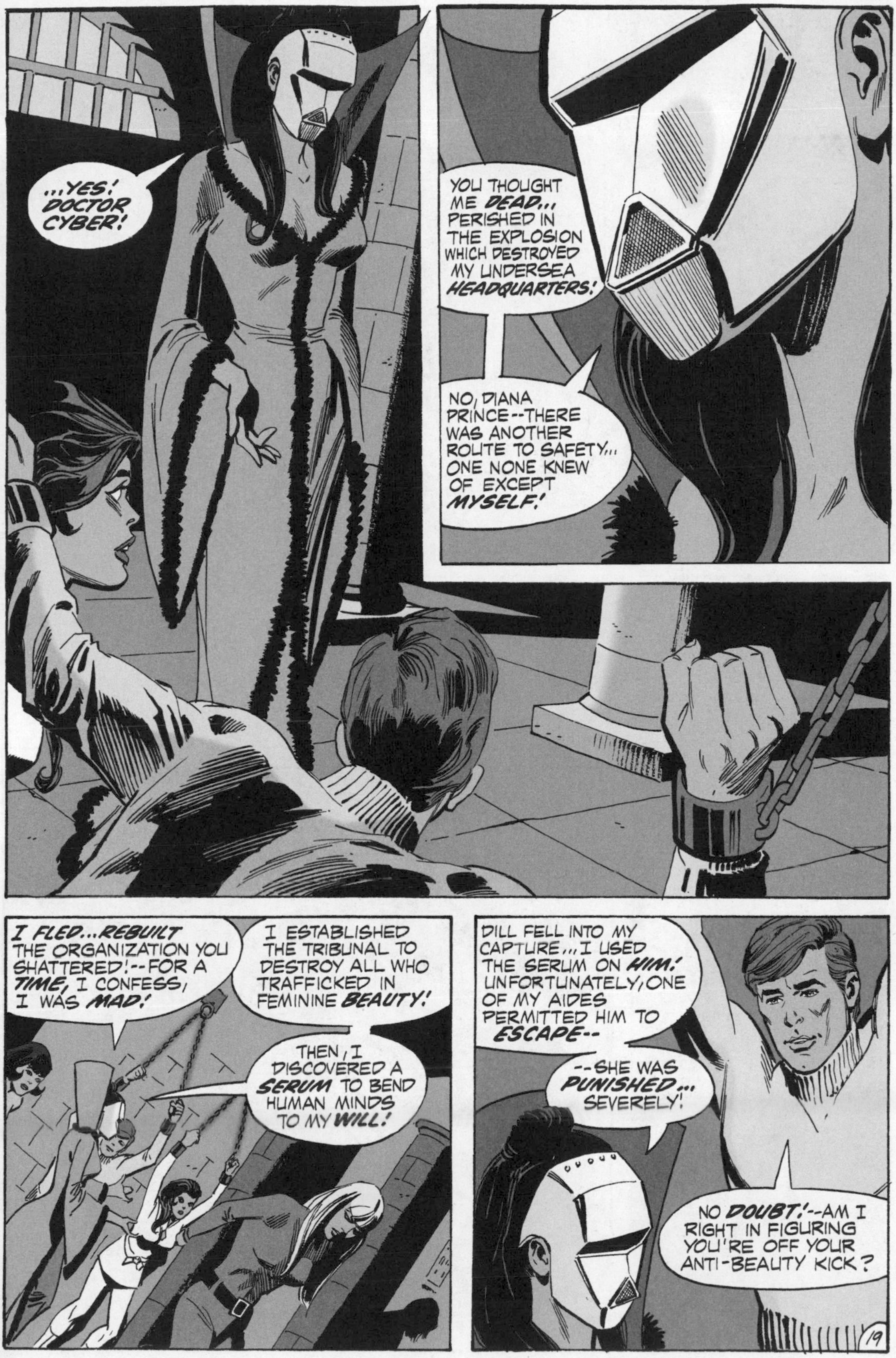

...YES! DOCTOR CYBER!
YOU THOUGHT ME DEAD... PERISHED IN THE EXPLOSION WHICH DESTROYED MY UNDERSEA HEADQUARTERS!
NO, DIANA PRINCE--THERE WAS ANOTHER ROUTE TO SAFETY... ONE NONE KNEW OF EXCEPT MYSELF!
I FLED...REBUILT THE ORGANIZATION YOU SHATTERED!--FOR A TIME, I CONFESS, I WAS MAD!
I ESTABLISHED THE TRIBUNAL TO DESTROY ALL WHO TRAFFICKED IN FEMININE BEAUTY!
THEN, I DISCOVERED A SERUM TO BEND HUMAN MINDS TO MY WILL!
DILL FELL INTO MY CAPTURE... I USED THE SERUM ON HIM! UNFORTUNATELY, ONE OF MY AIDES PERMITTED HIM TO ESCAPE--
--SHE WAS PUNISHED... SEVERELY!
NO DOUBT!--AM I RIGHT IN FIGURING YOU'RE OFF YOUR ANTI-BEAUTY KICK?
19

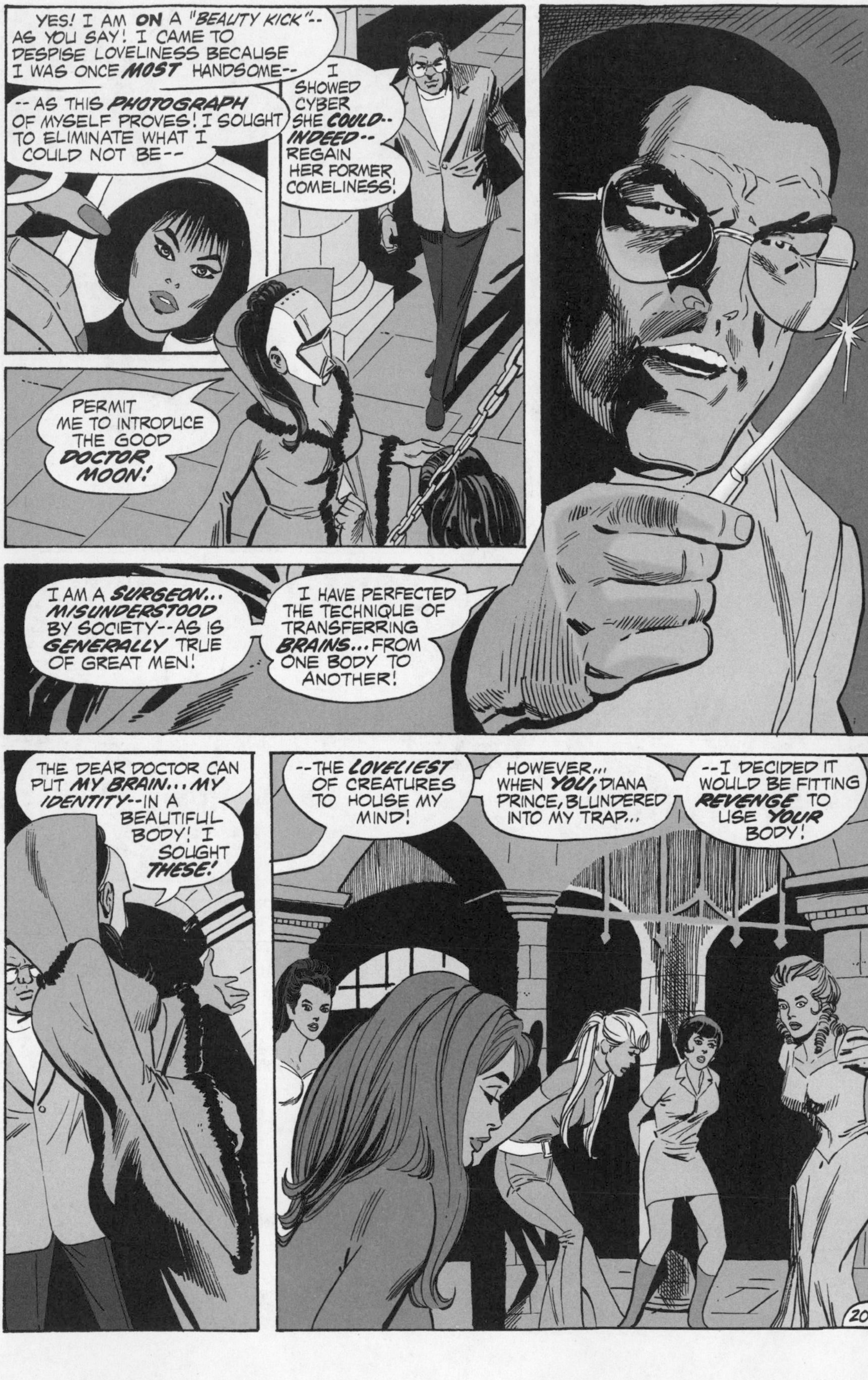
YES! I AM ON A "BEAUTY KICK"-- AS YOU SAY! I CAME TO DESPISE LOVELINESS BECAUSE I WAS ONCE MOST HANDSOME--
-- AS THIS PHOTOGRAPH OF MYSELF PROVES! I SOUGHT TO ELIMINATE WHAT I COULD NOT BE--
I SHOWED CYBER SHE COULD-- INDEED-- REGAIN HER FORMER COMELINESS!
PERMIT ME TO INTRODUCE THE GOOD DOCTOR MOON!
I AM A SURGEON... MISUNDERSTOOD BY SOCIETY--AS IS GENERALLY TRUE OF GREAT MEN!
I HAVE PERFECTED THE TECHNIQUE OF TRANSFERRING BRAINS... FROM ONE BODY TO ANOTHER!
THE DEAR DOCTOR CAN PUT MY BRAIN... MY IDENTITY--IN A BEAUTIFUL BODY! I SOUGHT THESE!
--THE LOVELIEST OF CREATURES TO HOUSE MY MIND!
HOWEVER... WHEN YOU, DIANA PRINCE, BLUNDERED INTO MY TRAP...
--I DECIDED IT WOULD BE FITTING REVENGE TO USE YOUR BODY!
20

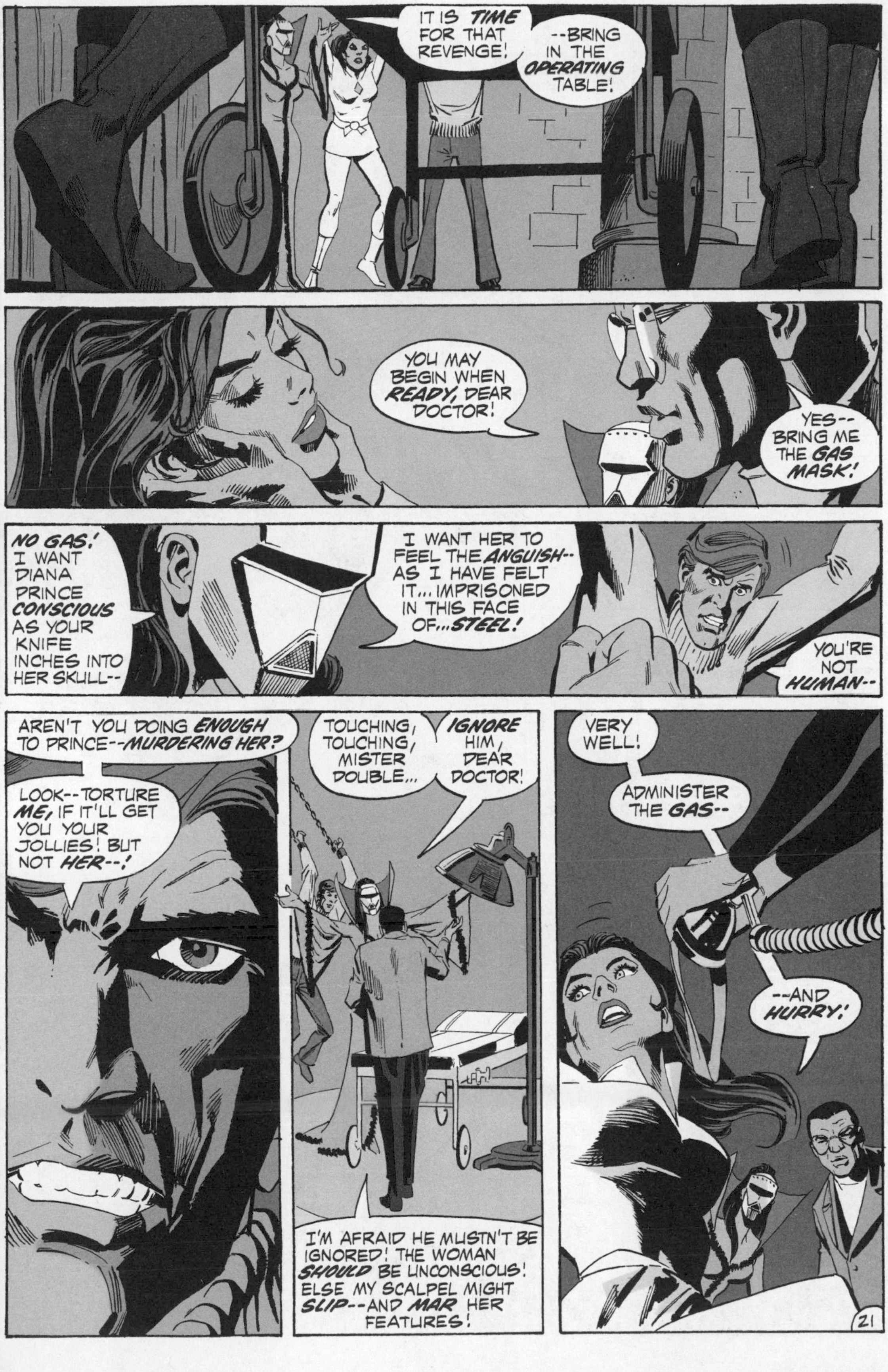
IT IS TIME FOR THAT REVENGE!
--BRING IN THE OPERATING TABLE!
YOU MAY BEGIN WHEN READY, DEAR DOCTOR!
YES-- BRING ME THE GAS MASK!
NO GAS! I WANT DIANA PRINCE CONSCIOUS AS YOUR KNIFE INCHES INTO HER SKULL--
I WANT HER TO FEEL THE ANGUISH-- AS I HAVE FELT IT... IMPRISONED IN THIS FACE OF... STEEL!
YOU'RE NOT HUMAN--
AREN'T YOU DOING ENOUGH TO PRINCE--MURDERING HER?
LOOK--TORTURE ME, IF IT'LL GET YOU YOUR JOLLIES! BUT NOT HER--!
TOUCHING, TOUCHING, MISTER DOUBLE...
IGNORE HIM, DEAR DOCTOR!
I'M AFRAID HE MUSTN'T BE IGNORED! THE WOMAN SHOULD BE UNCONSCIOUS! ELSE MY SCALPEL MIGHT SLIP--AND MAR HER FEATURES!
VERY WELL!
ADMINISTER THE GAS--
--AND HURRY!
21

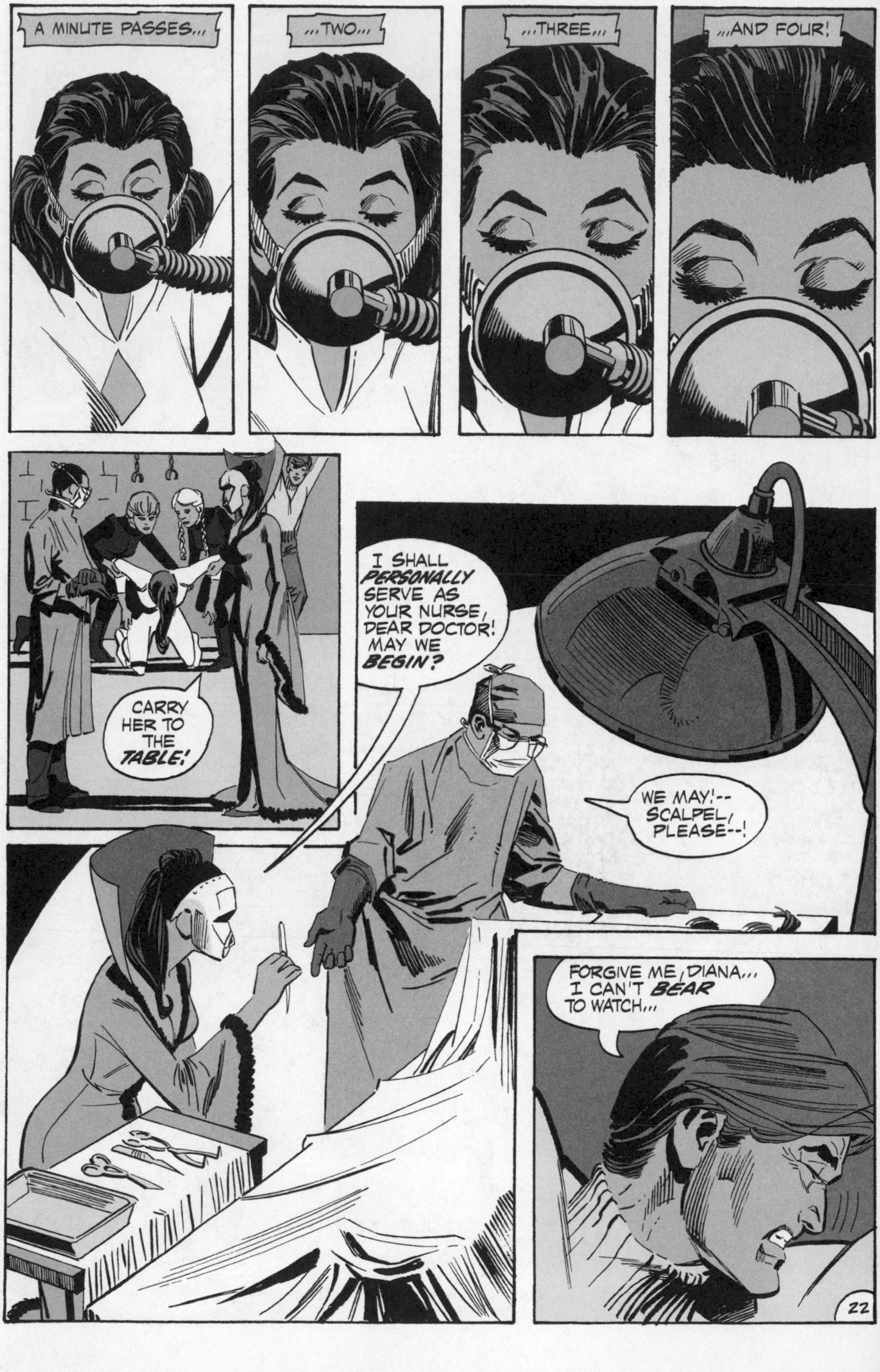
A MINUTE PASSES...
...TWO...
...THREE...
...AND FOUR!
CARRY HER TO THE TABLE!
I SHALL PERSONALLY SERVE AS YOUR NURSE, DEAR DOCTOR! MAY WE BEGIN?
WE MAY!-- SCALPEL, PLEASE--!
FORGIVE ME, DIANA... I CAN'T BEAR TO WATCH...
22

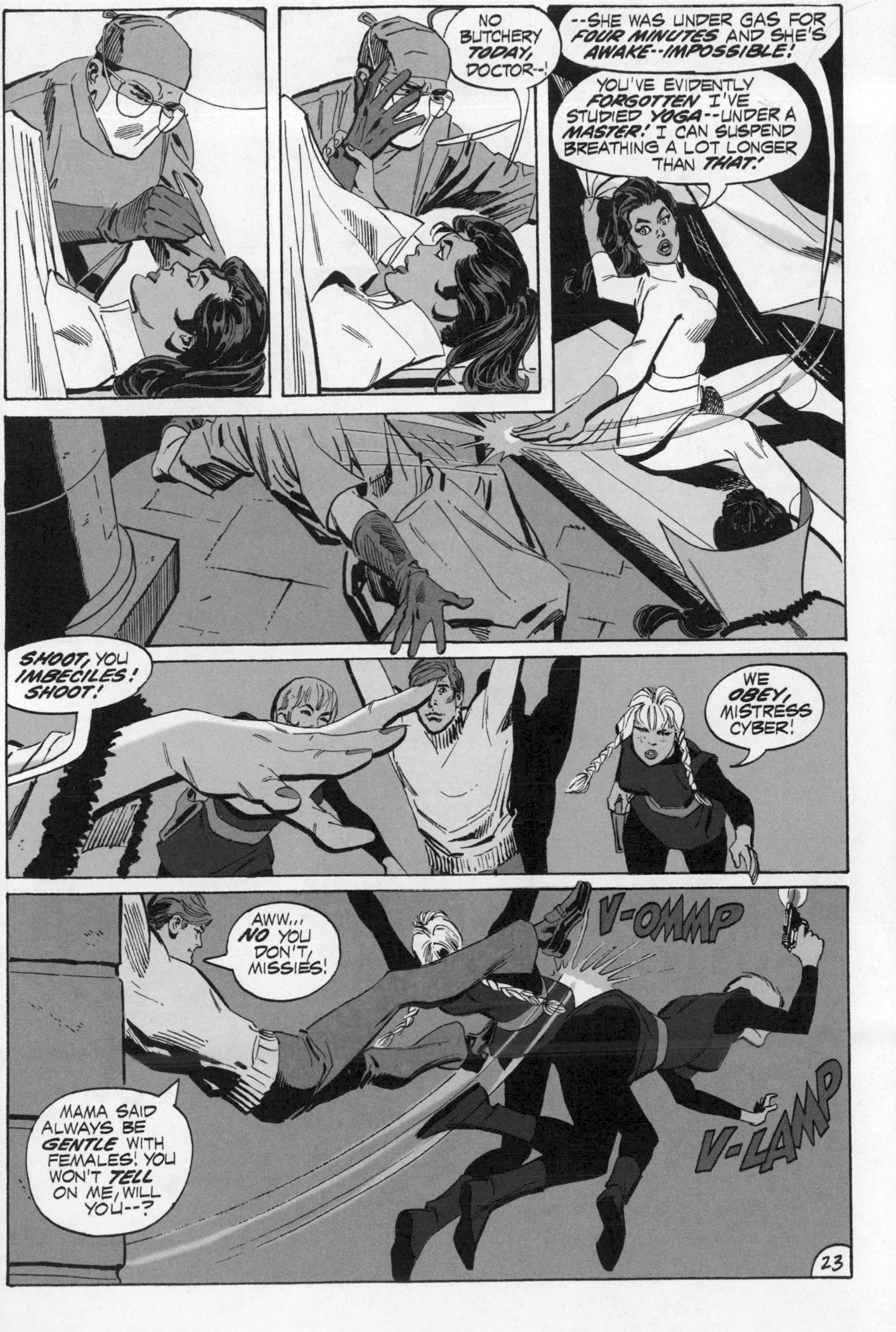
NO BUTCHERY TODAY, DOCTOR--!
--SHE WAS UNDER GAS FOR FOUR MINUTES AND SHE'S AWAKE--IMPOSSIBLE!
YOU'VE EVIDENTLY FORGOTTEN I'VE STUDIED YOGA--UNDER A MASTER! I CAN SUSPEND BREATHING A LOT LONGER THAN THAT!
SHOOT, YOU IMBECILES! SHOOT!
WE OBEY, MISTRESS CYBER!
AWW... NO YOU DON'T, MISSIES!
V-OMMP
MAMA SAID ALWAYS BE GENTLE WITH FEMALES! YOU WON'T TELL ON ME, WILL YOU--?
V-LAMP
23

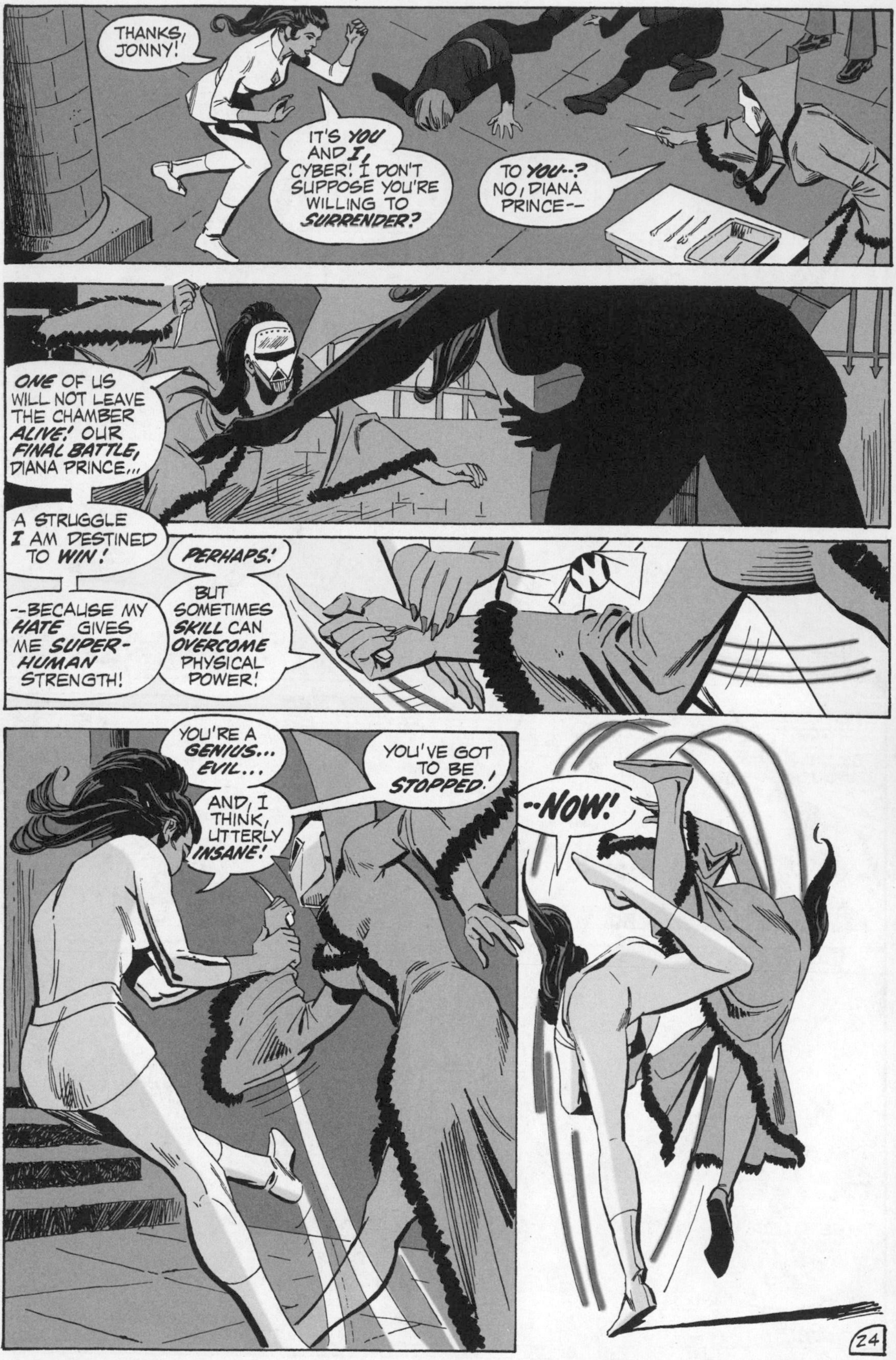
THANKS, JONNY!
IT'S YOU AND I, CYBER! I DON'T SUPPOSE YOU'RE WILLING TO SURRENDER?
TO YOU--? NO, DIANA PRINCE--
ONE OF US WILL NOT LEAVE THE CHAMBER ALIVE! OUR FINAL BATTLE, DIANA PRINCE...
A STRUGGLE I AM DESTINED TO WIN!
--BECAUSE MY HATE GIVES ME SUPER-HUMAN STRENGTH!
PERHAPS!
BUT SOMETIMES SKILL CAN OVERCOME PHYSICAL POWER!
YOU'RE A GENIUS... EVIL...
AND, I THINK, UTTERLY INSANE!
YOU'VE GOT TO BE STOPPED!
--NOW!
24

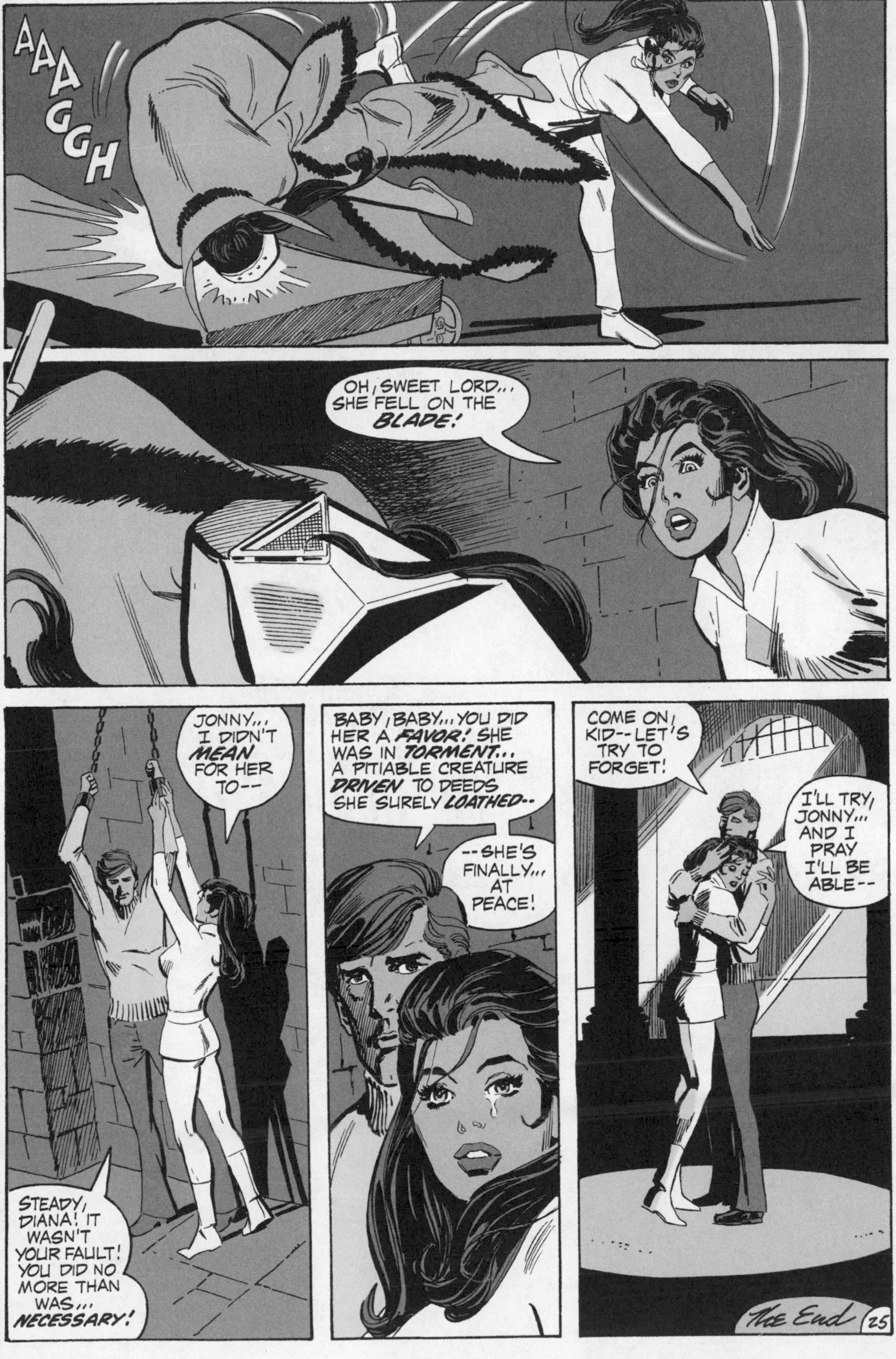
AAAGGH
OH, SWEET LORD... SHE FELL ON THE BLADE!
JONNY... I DIDN'T MEAN FOR HER TO--
STEADY, DIANA! IT WASN'T YOUR FAULT! YOU DID NO MORE THAN WAS... NECESSARY!
BABY, BABY... YOU DID HER A FAVOR! SHE WAS IN TORMENT... A PITIABLE CREATURE DRIVEN TO DEEDS SHE SURELY LOATHED..
--SHE'S FINALLY... AT PEACE!
COME ON, KID--LET'S TRY TO FORGET!
I'LL TRY, JONNY... AND I PRAY I'LL BE ABLE--
The End
25

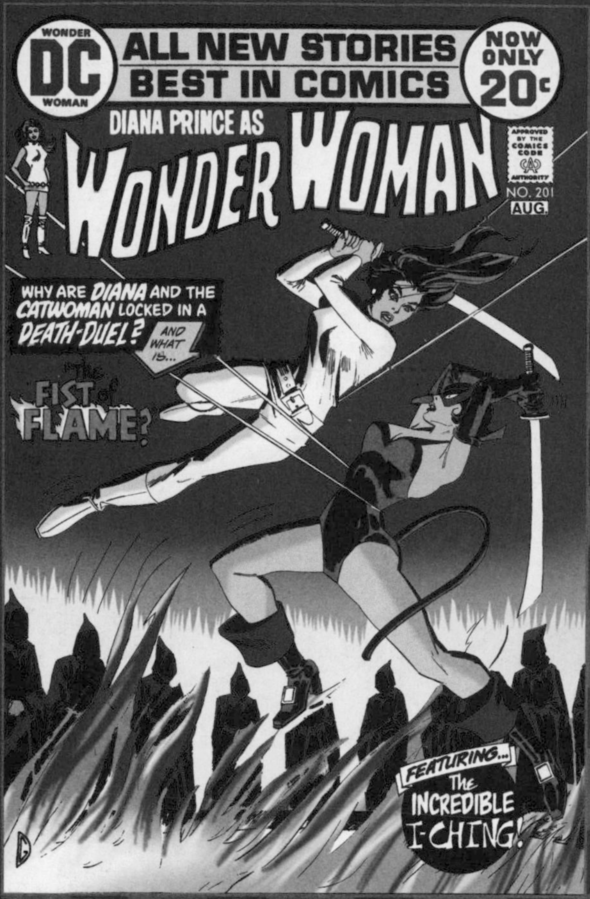
WONDER WOMAN DC WOMAN
ALL NEW STORIES
BEST IN COMICS
NOW ONLY 20c
DIANA PRINCE AS
WONDER WOMAN
NO. 201
AUG.
WHY ARE DIANA AND THE CATWOMAN LOCKED IN A DEATH-DUEL?
AND WHAT IS...
"The FIST of FLAME?"
FEATURING... The INCREDIBLE I-CHING!

Wonder Woman 201 and 202
Covers by Dick Giordano

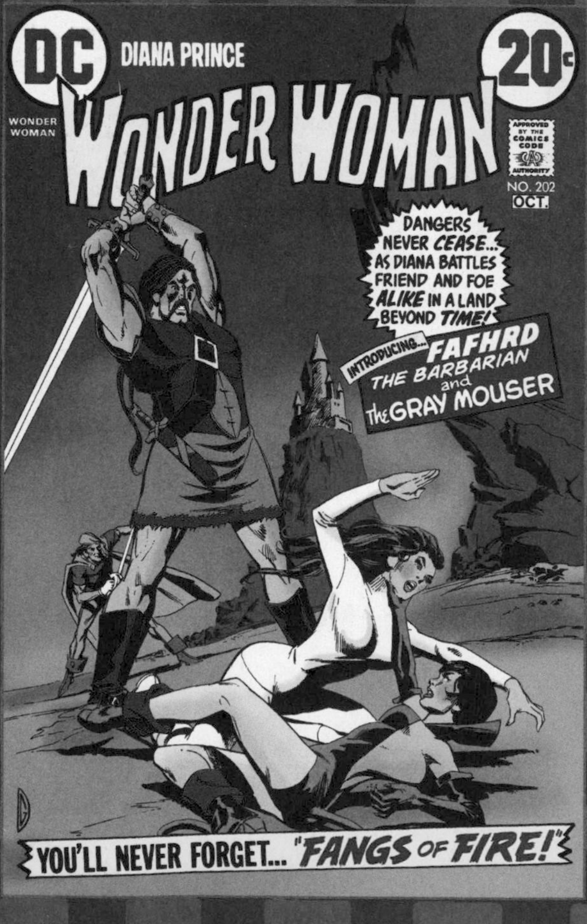
DC
DIANA PRINCE
20c
WONDER WOMAN
WONDER WOMAN
NO. 202
OCT.
DANGERS NEVER CEASE... AS DIANA BATTLES FRIEND AND FOE ALIKE IN A LAND BEYOND TIME!
INTRODUCING... FAFHRD THE BARBARIAN and The GRAY MOUSER
YOU'LL NEVER FORGET... "FANGS OF FIRE!"

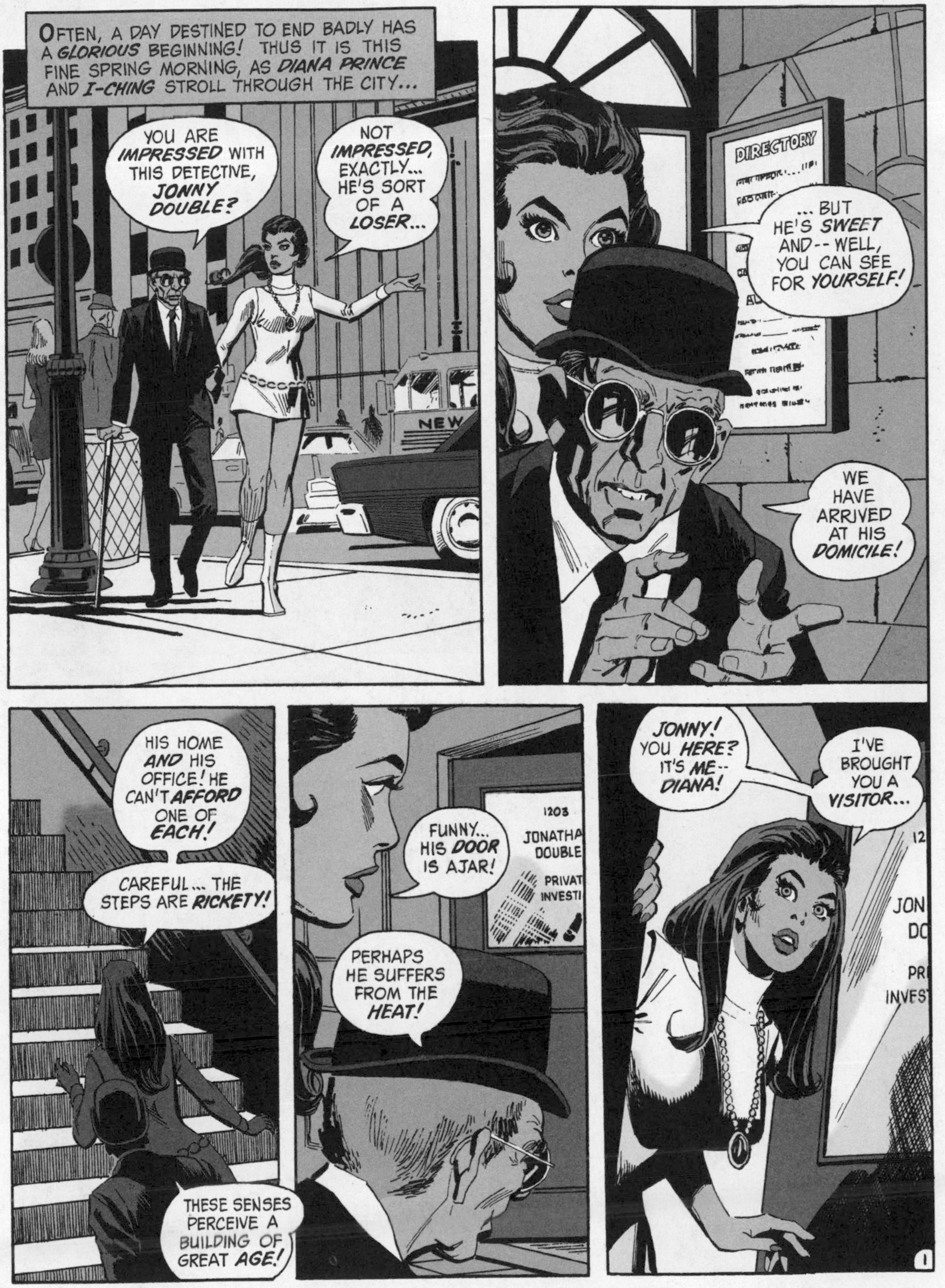

OFTEN, A DAY DESTINED TO END BADLY HAS A GLORIOUS BEGINNING! THUS IT IS THIS FINE SPRING MORNING, AS DIANA PRINCE AND I-CHING STROLL THROUGH THE CITY...
YOU ARE IMPRESSED WITH THIS DETECTIVE, JONNY DOUBLE?
NOT IMPRESSED, EXACTLY... HE'S SORT OF A LOSER...
DIRECTORY
... BUT HE'S SWEET AND-- WELL, YOU CAN SEE FOR YOURSELF!
WE HAVE ARRIVED AT HIS DOMICILE!
HIS HOME AND HIS OFFICE! HE CAN'T AFFORD ONE OF EACH!
CAREFUL... THE STEPS ARE RICKETY!
THESE SENSES PERCEIVE A BUILDING OF GREAT AGE!
1203
JONATHA
DOUBLE
PRIVAT
INVESTI
FUNNY... HIS DOOR IS AJAR!
PERHAPS HE SUFFERS FROM THE HEAT!
JONNY! YOU HERE? IT'S ME-- DIANA!
I'VE BROUGHT YOU A VISITOR...
1

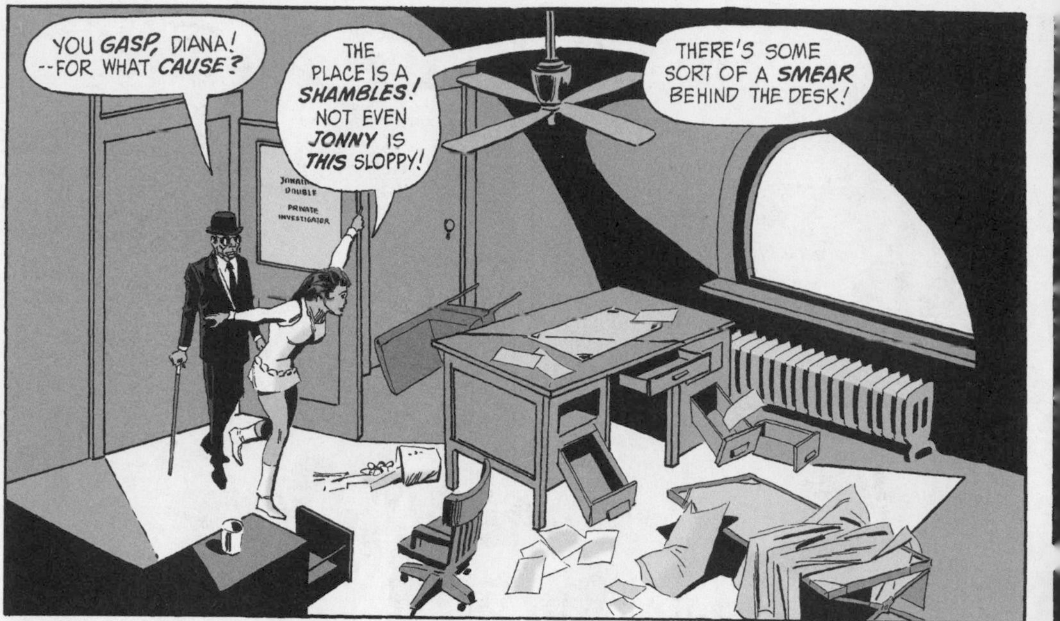
YOU GASP, DIANA! --FOR WHAT CAUSE?
THE PLACE IS A SHAMBLES! NOT EVEN JONNY IS THIS SLOPPY!
THERE'S SOME SORT OF A SMEAR BEHIND THE DESK!
PRIVATE INVESTIGATOR

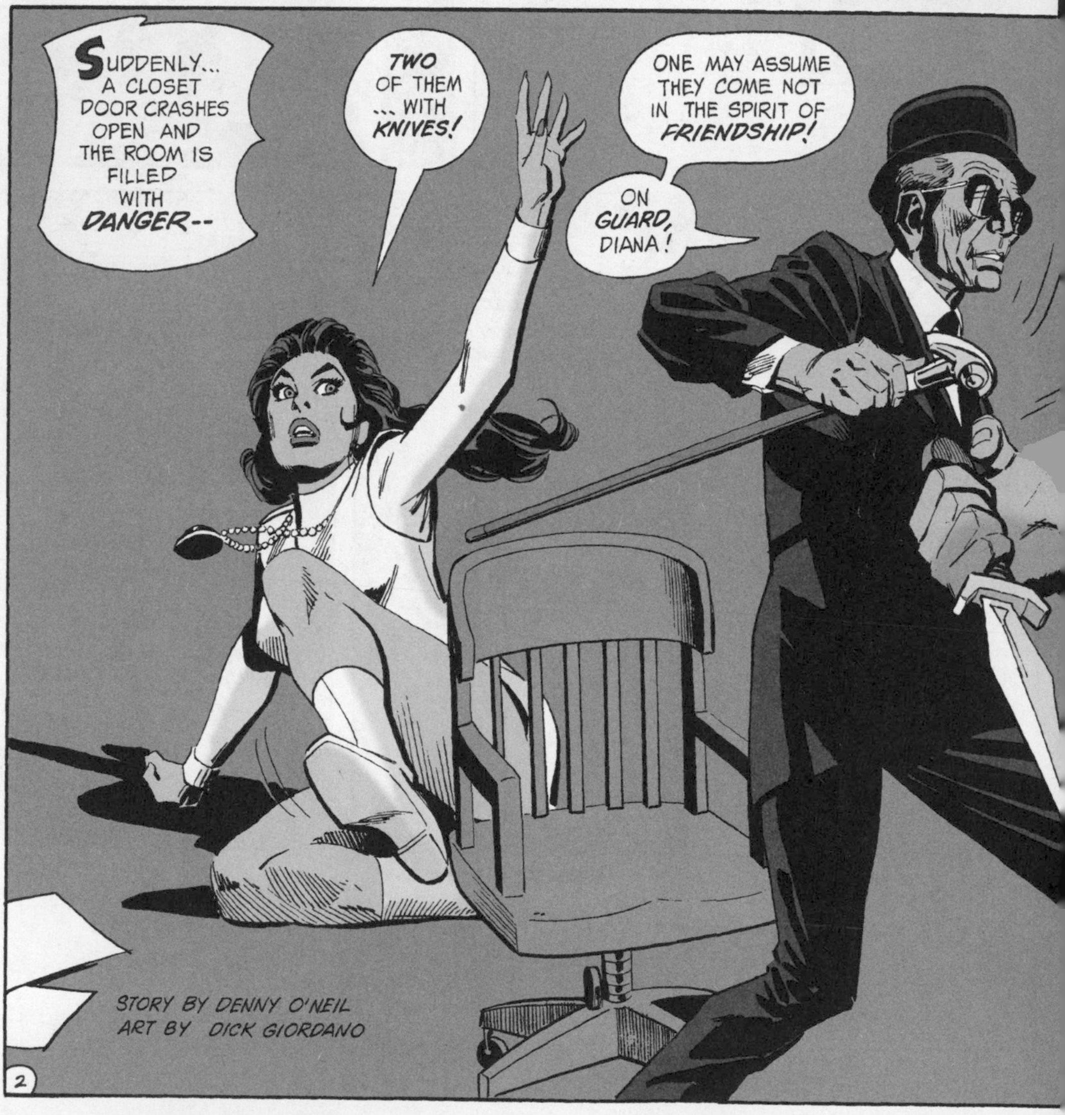
SUDDENLY... A CLOSET DOOR CRASHES OPEN AND THE ROOM IS FILLED WITH DANGER--
TWO OF THEM ... WITH KNIVES!
ONE MAY ASSUME THEY COME NOT IN THE SPIRIT OF FRIENDSHIP!
ON GUARD, DIANA!
STORY BY DENNY O'NEIL
ART BY DICK GIORDANO
2

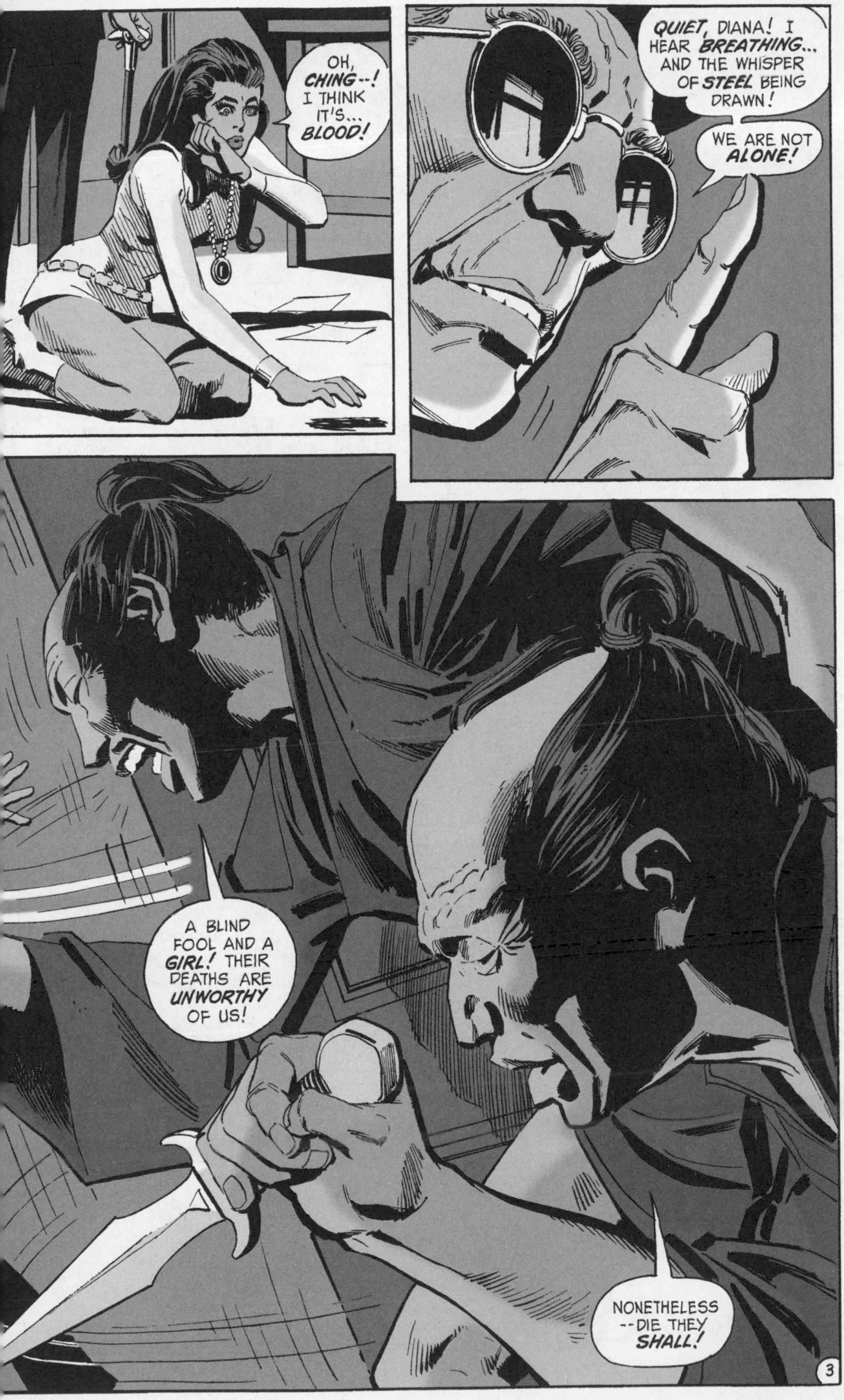
OH, CHING--! I THINK IT'S... BLOOD!
QUIET, DIANA! I HEAR BREATHING... AND THE WHISPER OF STEEL BEING DRAWN!
WE ARE NOT ALONE!
A BLIND FOOL AND A GIRL! THEIR DEATHS ARE UNWORTHY OF US!
NONETHELESS --DIE THEY SHALL!
3

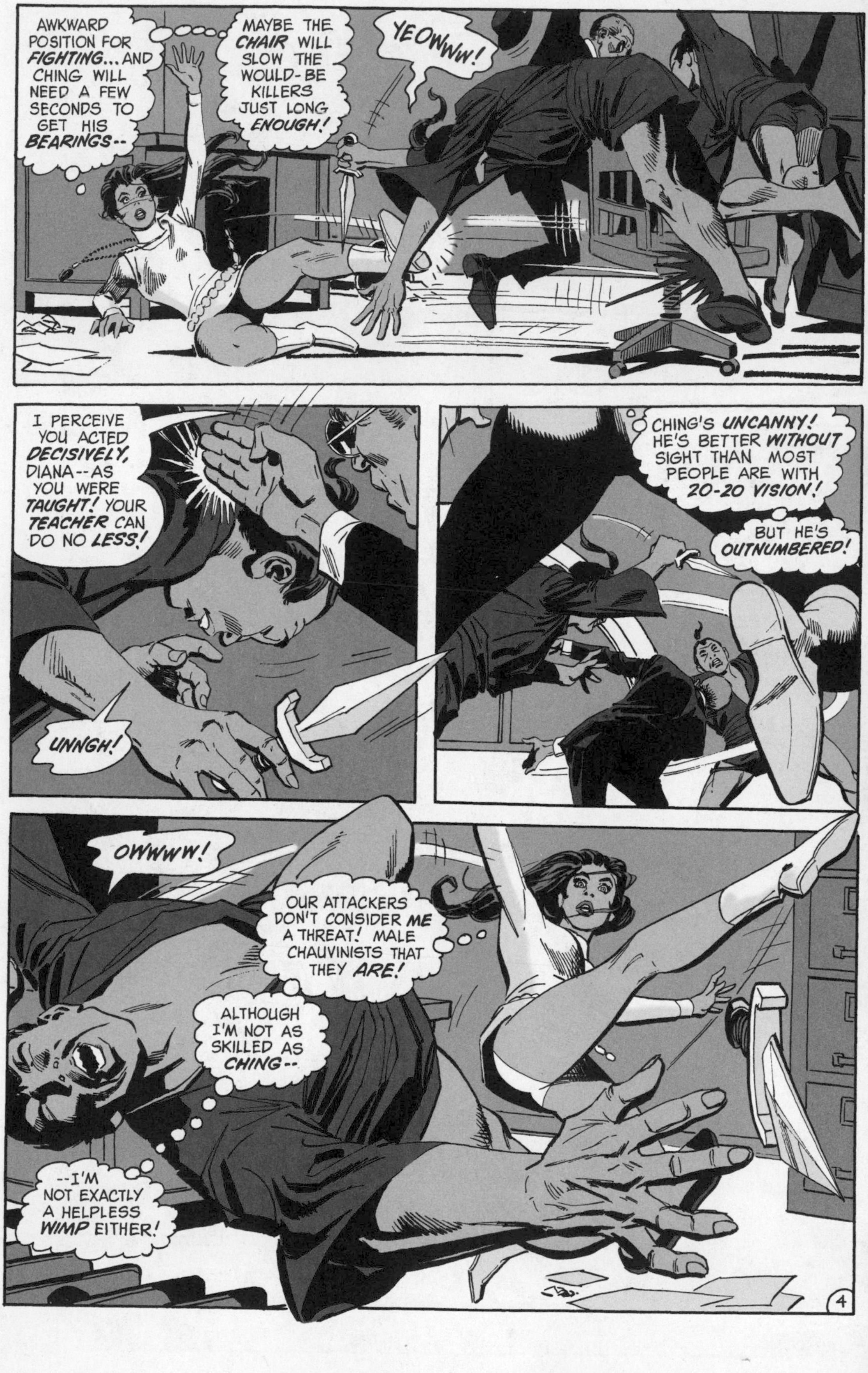
AWKWARD POSITION FOR FIGHTING... AND CHING WILL NEED A FEW SECONDS TO GET HIS BEARINGS--
MAYBE THE CHAIR WILL SLOW THE WOULD-BE KILLERS JUST LONG ENOUGH!
YEOWWW!
I PERCEIVE YOU ACTED DECISIVELY, DIANA--AS YOU WERE TAUGHT! YOUR TEACHER CAN DO NO LESS!
UNNGH!
CHING'S UNCANNY! HE'S BETTER WITHOUT SIGHT THAN MOST PEOPLE ARE WITH 20-20 VISION!
BUT HE'S OUTNUMBERED!
OWWWW!
OUR ATTACKERS DON'T CONSIDER ME A THREAT! MALE CHAUVINISTS THAT THEY ARE!
ALTHOUGH I'M NOT AS SKILLED AS CHING--
--I'M NOT EXACTLY A HELPLESS WIMP EITHER!
4

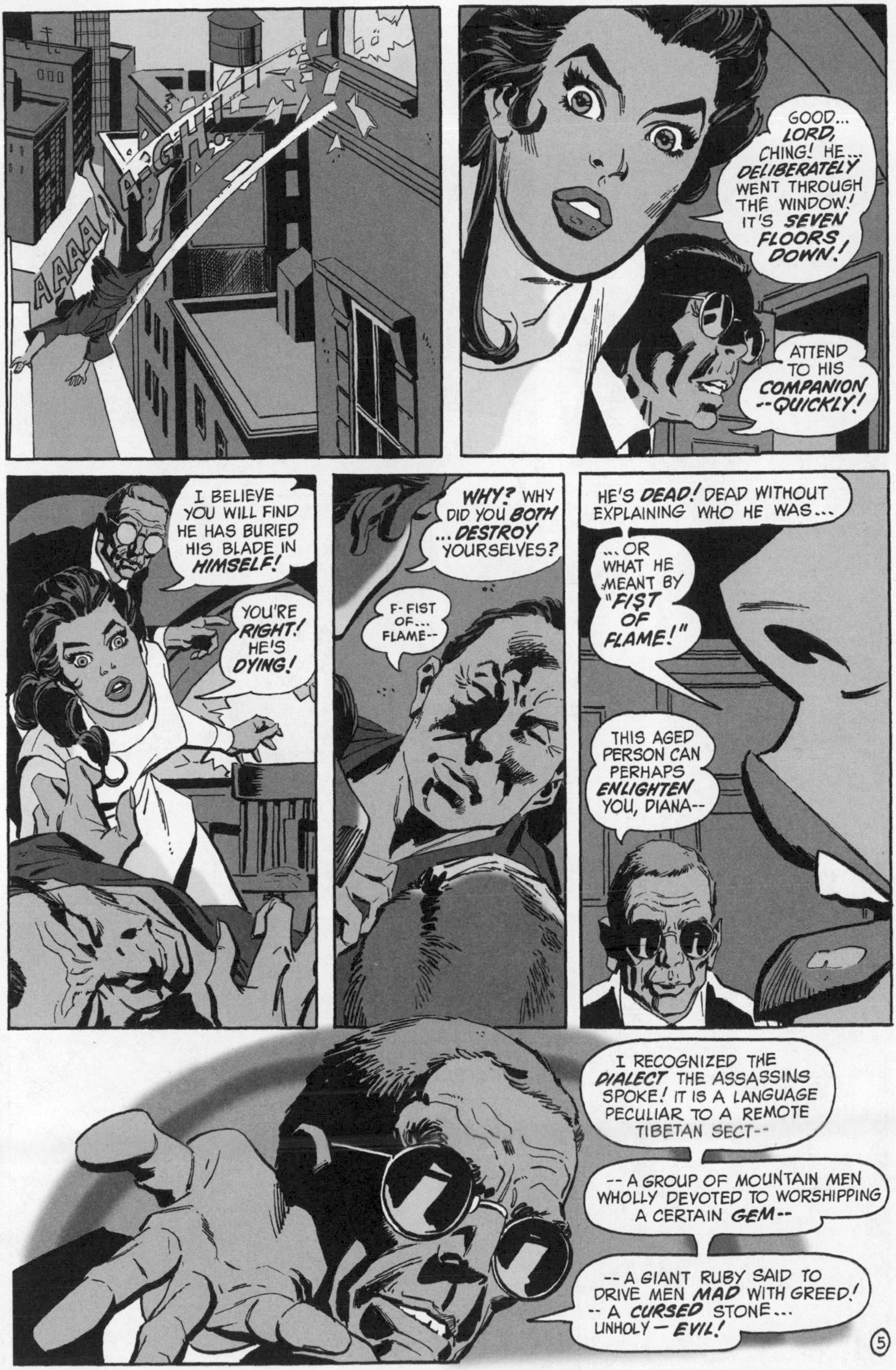
AAAAA-A-GH!
GOOD... LORD, CHING! HE... DELIBERATELY WENT THROUGH THE WINDOW! IT'S SEVEN FLOORS DOWN!
ATTEND TO HIS COMPANION --QUICKLY!
I BELIEVE YOU WILL FIND HE HAS BURIED HIS BLADE IN HIMSELF!
YOU'RE RIGHT! HE'S DYING!
WHY? WHY DID YOU BOTH ...DESTROY YOURSELVES?
F-FIST OF... FLAME--
HE'S DEAD! DEAD WITHOUT EXPLAINING WHO HE WAS...
...OR WHAT HE MEANT BY "FIST OF FLAME!"
THIS AGED PERSON CAN PERHAPS ENLIGHTEN YOU, DIANA--
I RECOGNIZED THE DIALECT THE ASSASSINS SPOKE! IT IS A LANGUAGE PECULIAR TO A REMOTE TIBETAN SECT--
-- A GROUP OF MOUNTAIN MEN WHOLLY DEVOTED TO WORSHIPPING A CERTAIN GEM--
-- A GIANT RUBY SAID TO DRIVE MEN MAD WITH GREED! -- A CURSED STONE... UNHOLY -- EVIL!
5

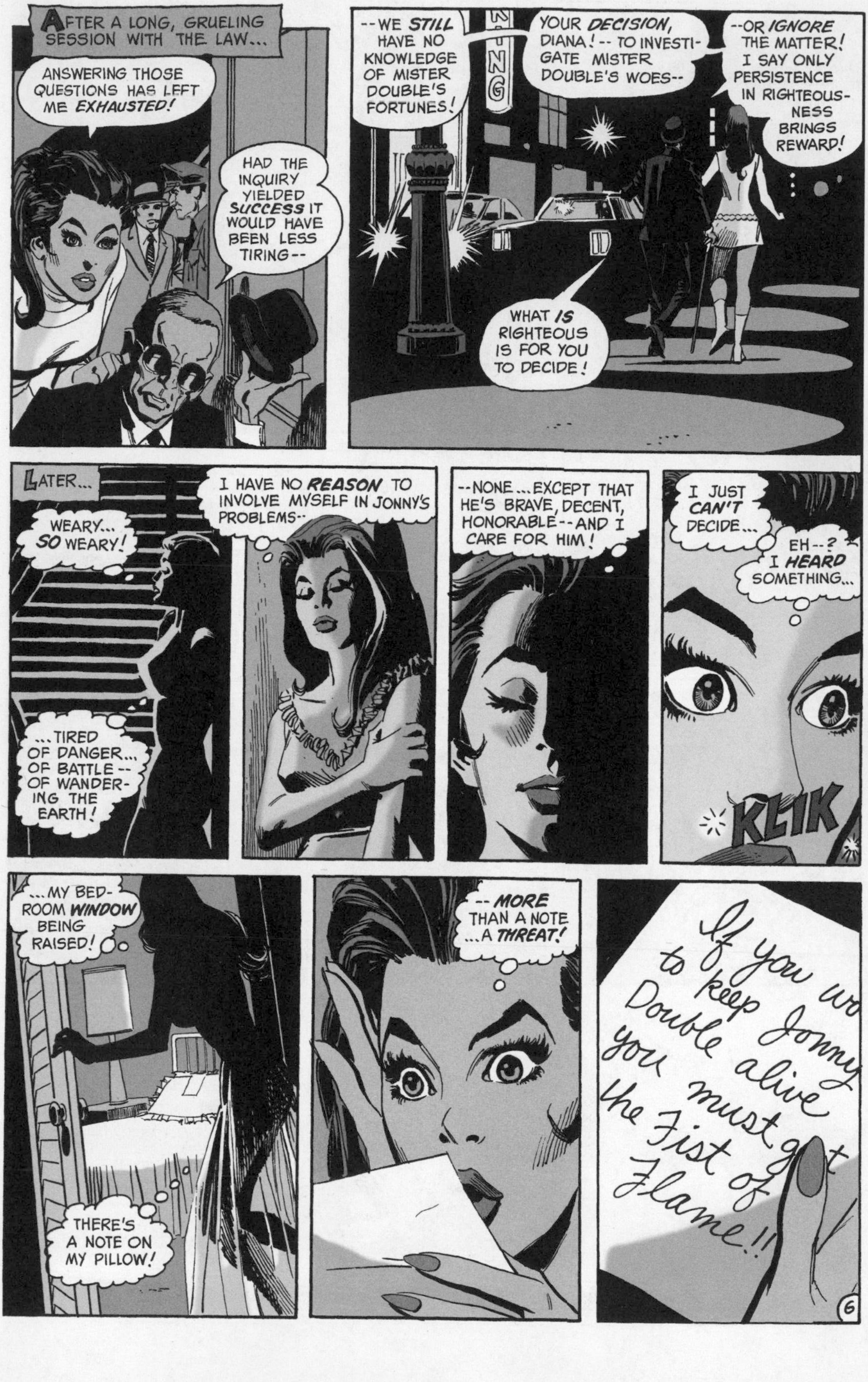

AFTER A LONG, GRUELING SESSION WITH THE LAW...
ANSWERING THOSE QUESTIONS HAS LEFT ME EXHAUSTED!
HAD THE INQUIRY YIELDED SUCCESS IT WOULD HAVE BEEN LESS TIRING--
--WE STILL HAVE NO KNOWLEDGE OF MISTER DOUBLE'S FORTUNES!
YOUR DECISION, DIANA! -- TO INVESTIGATE MISTER DOUBLE'S WOES--
--OR IGNORE THE MATTER! I SAY ONLY PERSISTENCE IN RIGHTEOUSNESS BRINGS REWARD!
WHAT IS RIGHTEOUS IS FOR YOU TO DECIDE!
LATER...
WEARY... SO WEARY!
...TIRED OF DANGER... OF BATTLE -- OF WANDERING THE EARTH!
I HAVE NO REASON TO INVOLVE MYSELF IN JONNY'S PROBLEMS--
--NONE... EXCEPT THAT HE'S BRAVE, DECENT, HONORABLE -- AND I CARE FOR HIM!
I JUST CAN'T DECIDE...
EH--? I HEARD SOMETHING...
KLIK
...MY BEDROOM WINDOW BEING RAISED!
THERE'S A NOTE ON MY PILLOW!
-- MORE THAN A NOTE ...A THREAT!
If you w
to keep Jonny
Double alive
you must get
the Fist of
Flame!!
6

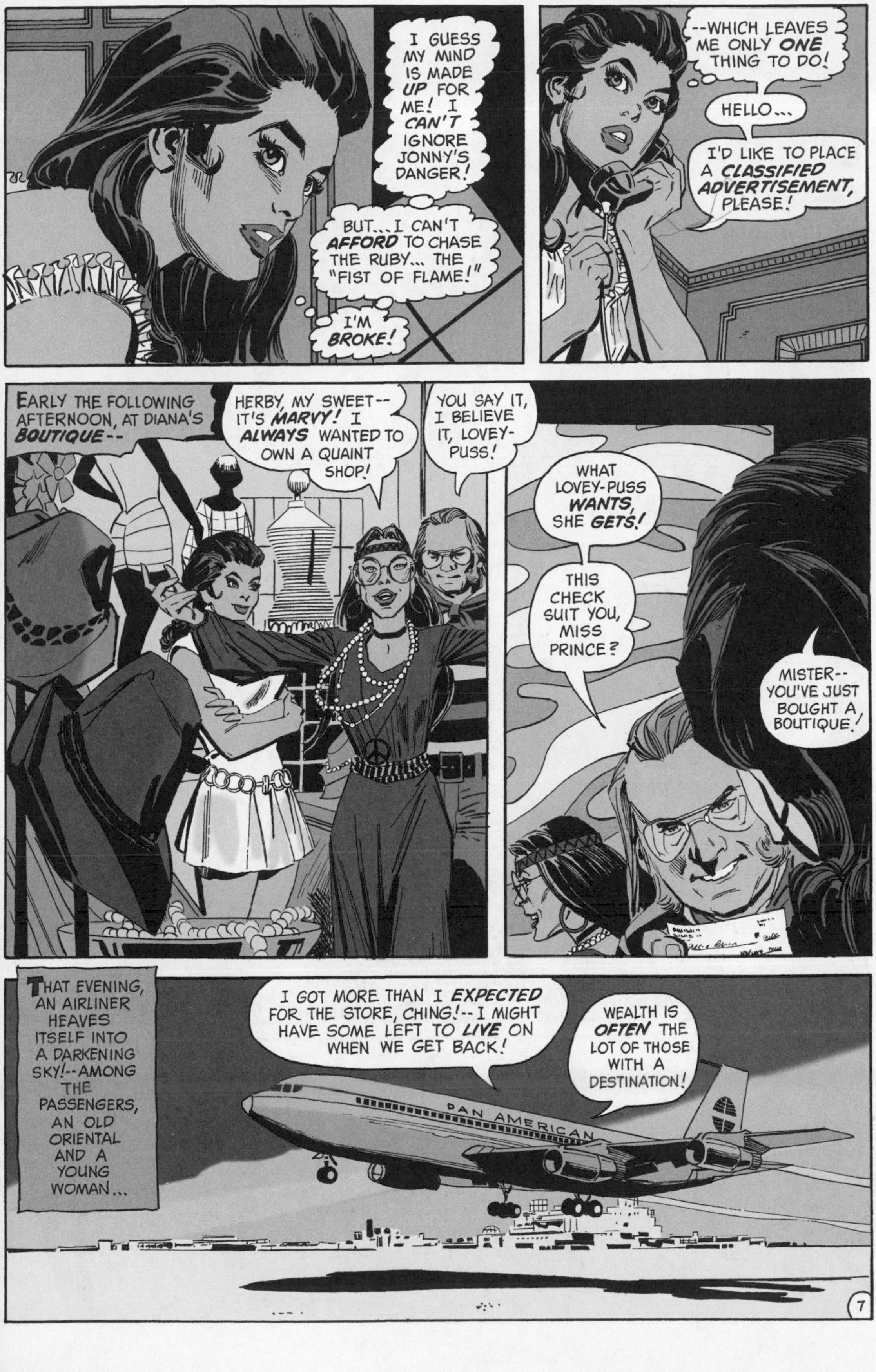
I GUESS MY MIND IS MADE UP FOR ME! I CAN'T IGNORE JONNY'S DANGER!
BUT... I CAN'T AFFORD TO CHASE THE RUBY... THE "FIST OF FLAME!"
I'M BROKE!
--WHICH LEAVES ME ONLY ONE THING TO DO!
HELLO...
I'D LIKE TO PLACE A CLASSIFIED ADVERTISEMENT, PLEASE!
EARLY THE FOLLOWING AFTERNOON, AT DIANA'S BOUTIQUE--
HERBY, MY SWEET--IT'S MARVY! I ALWAYS WANTED TO OWN A QUAINT SHOP!
YOU SAY IT, I BELIEVE IT, LOVEY-PUSS!
WHAT LOVEY-PUSS WANTS, SHE GETS!
THIS CHECK SUIT YOU, MISS PRINCE?
MISTER--YOU'VE JUST BOUGHT A BOUTIQUE!
THAT EVENING, AN AIRLINER HEAVES ITSELF INTO A DARKENING SKY!--AMONG THE PASSENGERS, AN OLD ORIENTAL AND A YOUNG WOMAN...
I GOT MORE THAN I EXPECTED FOR THE STORE, CHING!--I MIGHT HAVE SOME LEFT TO LIVE ON WHEN WE GET BACK!
WEALTH IS OFTEN THE LOT OF THOSE WITH A DESTINATION!
PAN AMERICAN
7

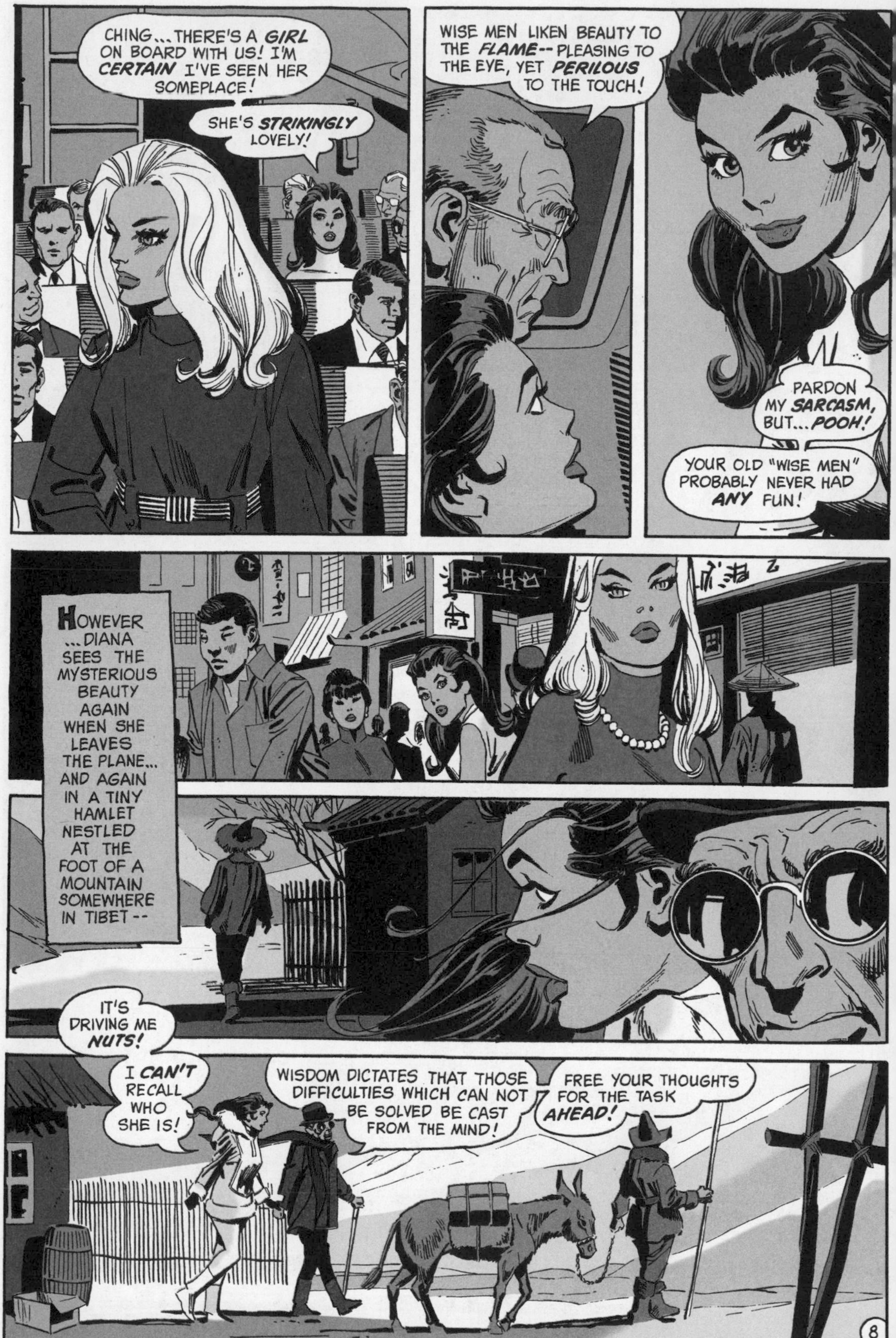
CHING... THERE'S A GIRL ON BOARD WITH US! I'M CERTAIN I'VE SEEN HER SOMEPLACE!
SHE'S STRIKINGLY LOVELY!
WISE MEN LIKEN BEAUTY TO THE FLAME-- PLEASING TO THE EYE, YET PERILOUS TO THE TOUCH!
PARDON MY SARCASM, BUT... POOH!
YOUR OLD "WISE MEN" PROBABLY NEVER HAD ANY FUN!
HOWEVER ...DIANA SEES THE MYSTERIOUS BEAUTY AGAIN WHEN SHE LEAVES THE PLANE... AND AGAIN IN A TINY HAMLET NESTLED AT THE FOOT OF A MOUNTAIN SOMEWHERE IN TIBET --
IT'S DRIVING ME NUTS!
I CAN'T RECALL WHO SHE IS!
WISDOM DICTATES THAT THOSE DIFFICULTIES WHICH CAN NOT BE SOLVED BE CAST FROM THE MIND!
FREE YOUR THOUGHTS FOR THE TASK AHEAD!
8

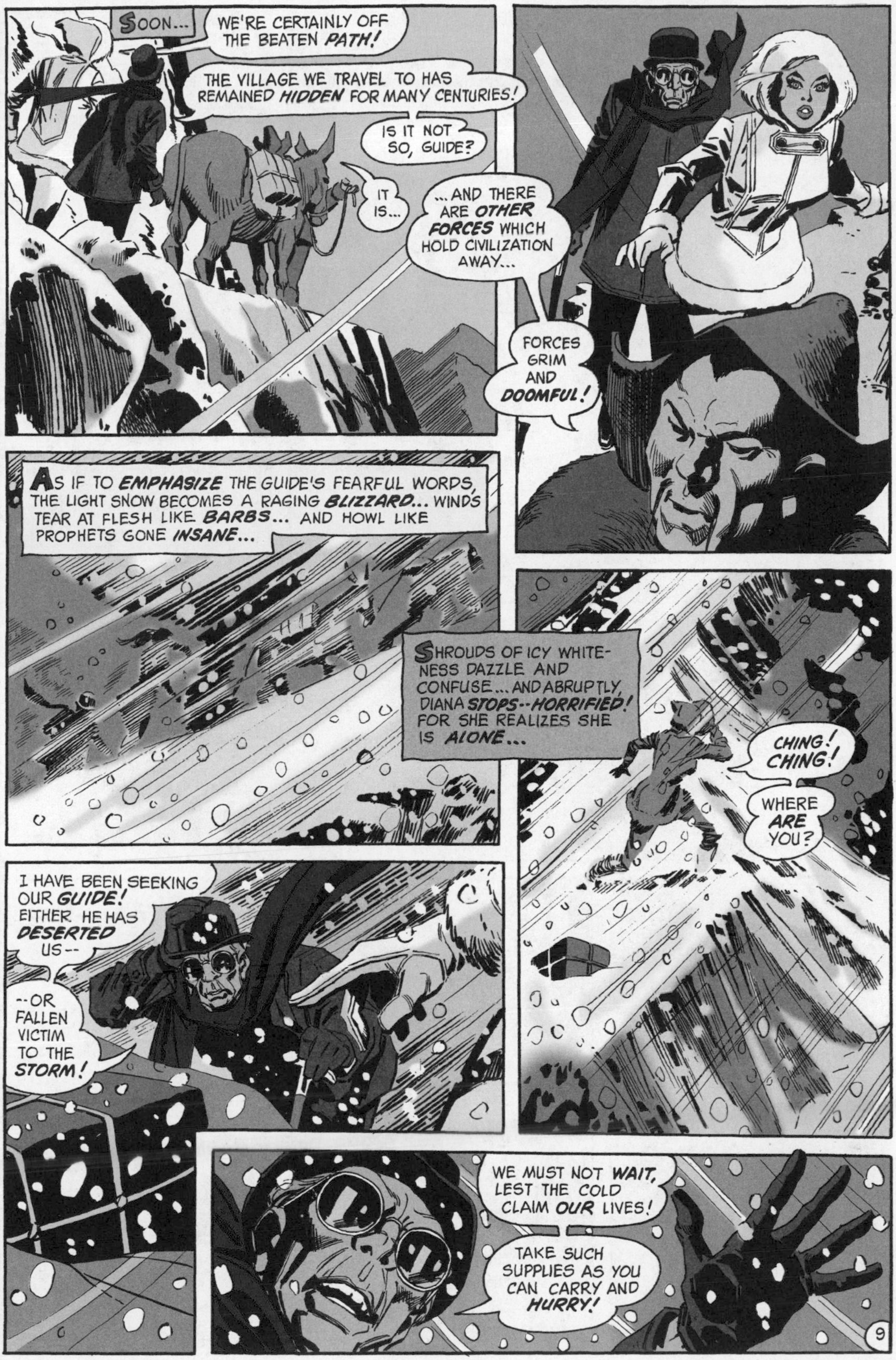
SOON...
WE'RE CERTAINLY OFF THE BEATEN PATH!
THE VILLAGE WE TRAVEL TO HAS REMAINED HIDDEN FOR MANY CENTURIES!
IS IT NOT SO, GUIDE?
IT IS...
...AND THERE ARE OTHER FORCES WHICH HOLD CIVILIZATION AWAY...
FORCES GRIM AND DOOMFUL!
AS IF TO EMPHASIZE THE GUIDE'S FEARFUL WORDS, THE LIGHT SNOW BECOMES A RAGING BLIZZARD... WIND'S TEAR AT FLESH LIKE BARBS... AND HOWL LIKE PROPHETS GONE INSANE...
SHROUDS OF ICY WHITENESS DAZZLE AND CONFUSE... AND ABRUPTLY, DIANA STOPS--HORRIFIED! FOR SHE REALIZES SHE IS ALONE...
CHING! CHING!
WHERE ARE YOU?
I HAVE BEEN SEEKING OUR GUIDE! EITHER HE HAS DESERTED US--
--OR FALLEN VICTIM TO THE STORM!
WE MUST NOT WAIT, LEST THE COLD CLAIM OUR LIVES!
TAKE SUCH SUPPLIES AS YOU CAN CARRY AND HURRY!
9

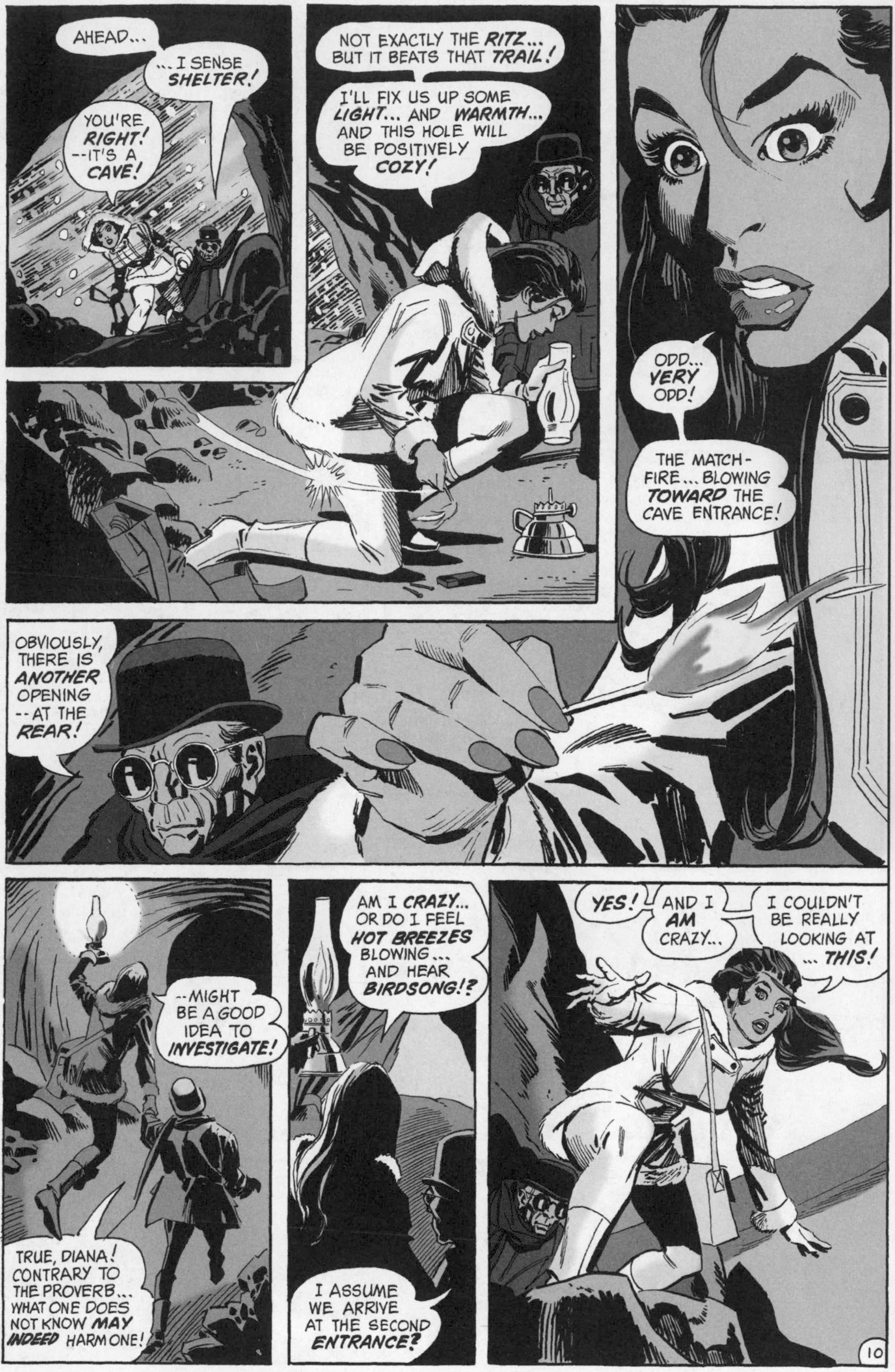
AHEAD...
...I SENSE SHELTER!
YOU'RE RIGHT! --IT'S A CAVE!
NOT EXACTLY THE RITZ... BUT IT BEATS THAT TRAIL!
I'LL FIX US UP SOME LIGHT... AND WARMTH... AND THIS HOLE WILL BE POSITIVELY COZY!
ODD... VERY ODD!
THE MATCH-FIRE... BLOWING TOWARD THE CAVE ENTRANCE!
OBVIOUSLY, THERE IS ANOTHER OPENING --AT THE REAR!
--MIGHT BE A GOOD IDEA TO INVESTIGATE!
TRUE, DIANA! CONTRARY TO THE PROVERB... WHAT ONE DOES NOT KNOW MAY INDEED HARM ONE!
AM I CRAZY... OR DO I FEEL HOT BREEZES BLOWING... AND HEAR BIRDSONG!?
I ASSUME WE ARRIVE AT THE SECOND ENTRANCE?
YES!
AND I AM CRAZY...
I COULDN'T BE REALLY LOOKING AT ...THIS!
10

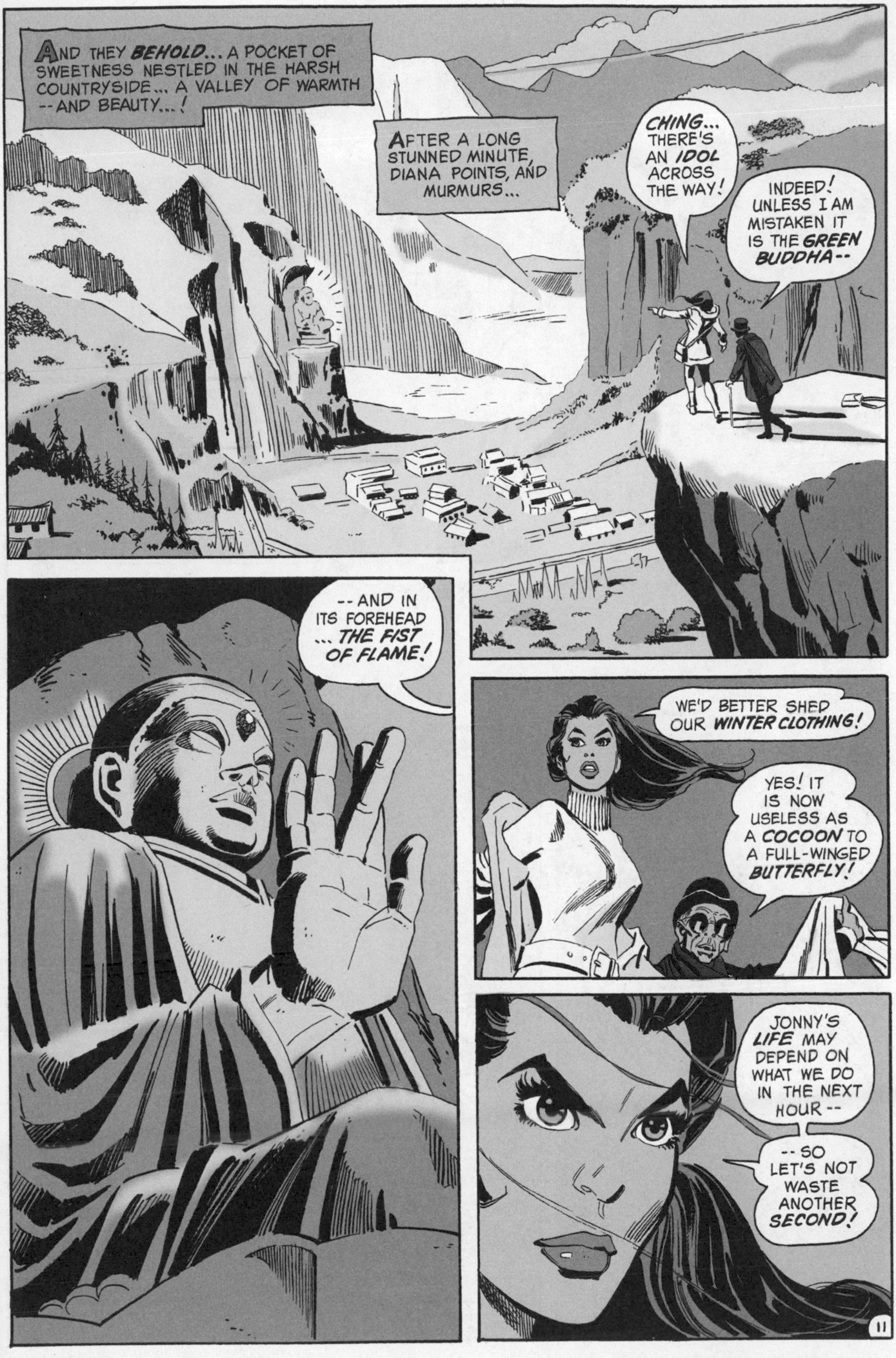
AND THEY BEHOLD... A POCKET OF SWEETNESS NESTLED IN THE HARSH COUNTRYSIDE... A VALLEY OF WARMTH --AND BEAUTY...!
AFTER A LONG STUNNED MINUTE, DIANA POINTS, AND MURMURS...
CHING... THERE'S AN IDOL ACROSS THE WAY!
INDEED! UNLESS I AM MISTAKEN IT IS THE GREEN BUDDHA--
--AND IN ITS FOREHEAD ...THE FIST OF FLAME!
WE'D BETTER SHED OUR WINTER CLOTHING!
YES! IT IS NOW USELESS AS A COCOON TO A FULL-WINGED BUTTERFLY!
JONNY'S LIFE MAY DEPEND ON WHAT WE DO IN THE NEXT HOUR--
--SO LET'S NOT WASTE ANOTHER SECOND!
11

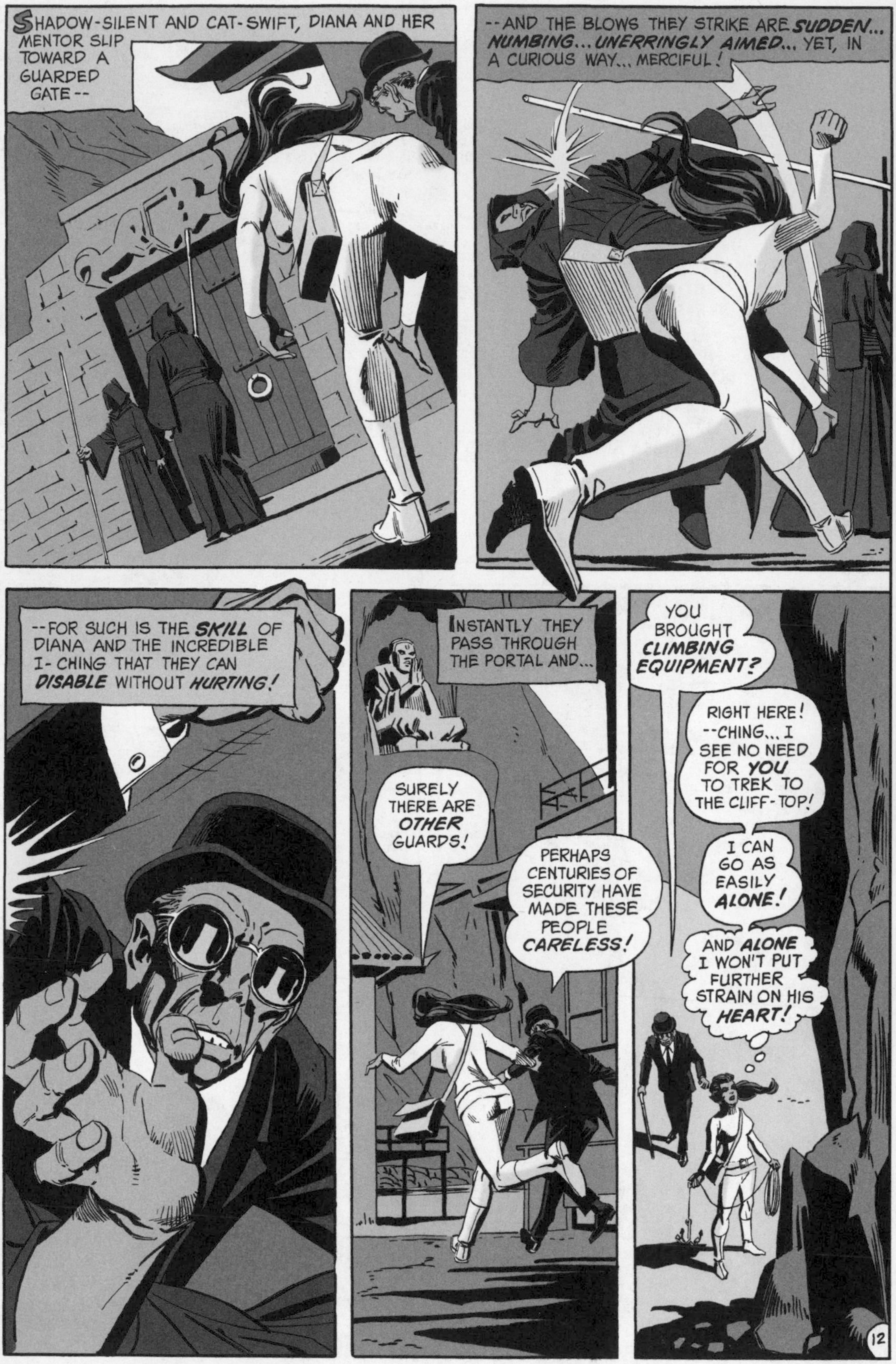
SHADOW-SILENT AND CAT-SWIFT, DIANA AND HER MENTOR SLIP TOWARD A GUARDED GATE--
--AND THE BLOWS THEY STRIKE ARE SUDDEN... NUMBING... UNERRINGLY AIMED... YET, IN A CURIOUS WAY... MERCIFUL!
--FOR SUCH IS THE SKILL OF DIANA AND THE INCREDIBLE I-CHING THAT THEY CAN DISABLE WITHOUT HURTING!
INSTANTLY THEY PASS THROUGH THE PORTAL AND...
SURELY THERE ARE OTHER GUARDS!
PERHAPS CENTURIES OF SECURITY HAVE MADE THESE PEOPLE CARELESS!
YOU BROUGHT CLIMBING EQUIPMENT?
RIGHT HERE! --CHING... I SEE NO NEED FOR YOU TO TREK TO THE CLIFF-TOP!
I CAN GO AS EASILY ALONE!
AND ALONE I WON'T PUT FURTHER STRAIN ON HIS HEART!
12

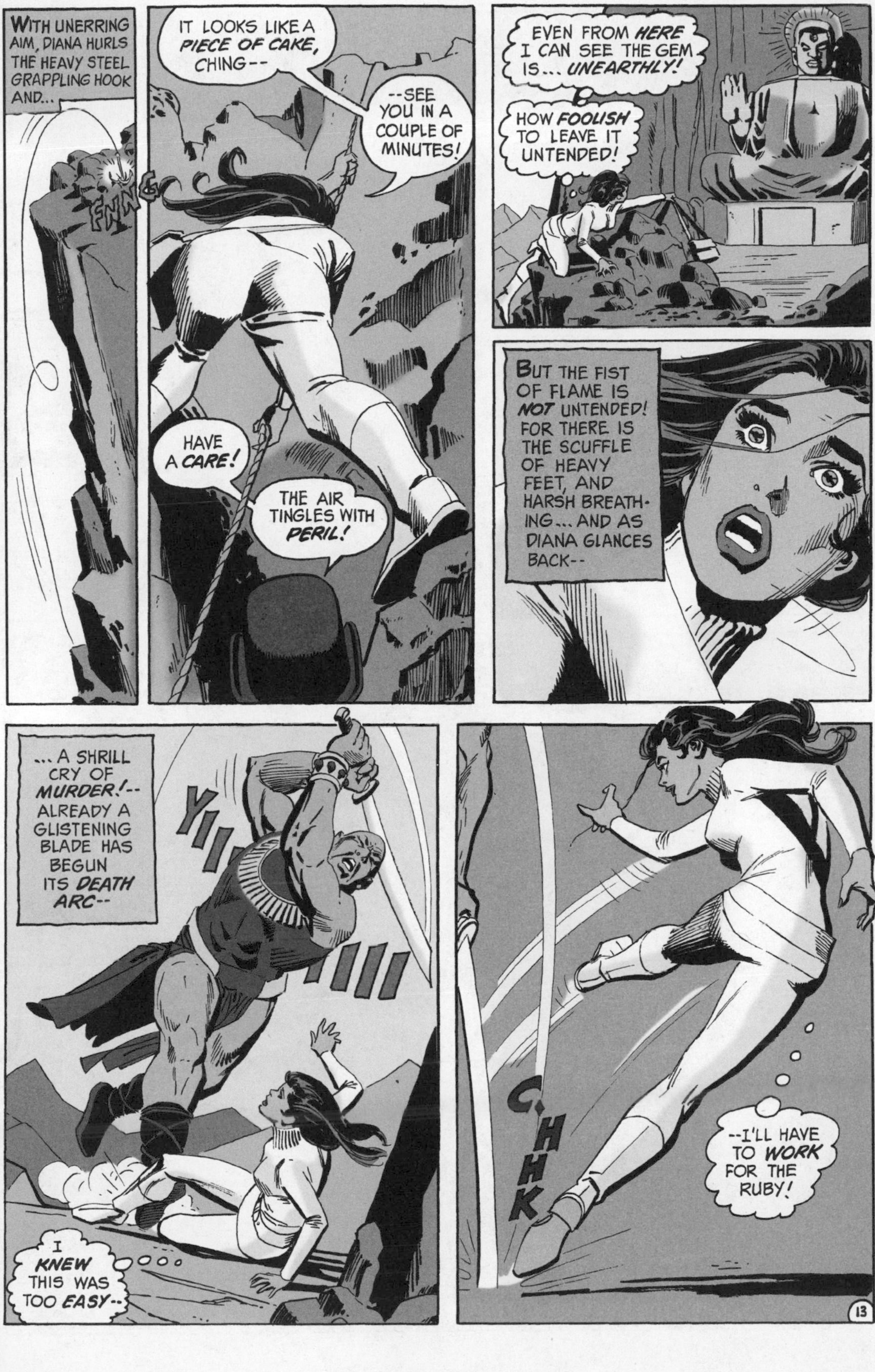
WITH UNERRING AIM, DIANA HURLS THE HEAVY STEEL GRAPPLING HOOK AND...
FNNG
IT LOOKS LIKE A PIECE OF CAKE, CHING--
--SEE YOU IN A COUPLE OF MINUTES!
HAVE A CARE!
THE AIR TINGLES WITH PERIL!
EVEN FROM HERE I CAN SEE THE GEM IS... UNEARTHLY!
HOW FOOLISH TO LEAVE IT UNTENDED!
BUT THE FIST OF FLAME IS NOT UNTENDED! FOR THERE IS THE SCUFFLE OF HEAVY FEET, AND HARSH BREATHING... AND AS DIANA GLANCES BACK--
... A SHRILL CRY OF MURDER!-- ALREADY A GLISTENING BLADE HAS BEGUN ITS DEATH ARC--
YIIIIIII
I KNEW THIS WAS TOO EASY--
CHHK
--I'LL HAVE TO WORK FOR THE RUBY!
13

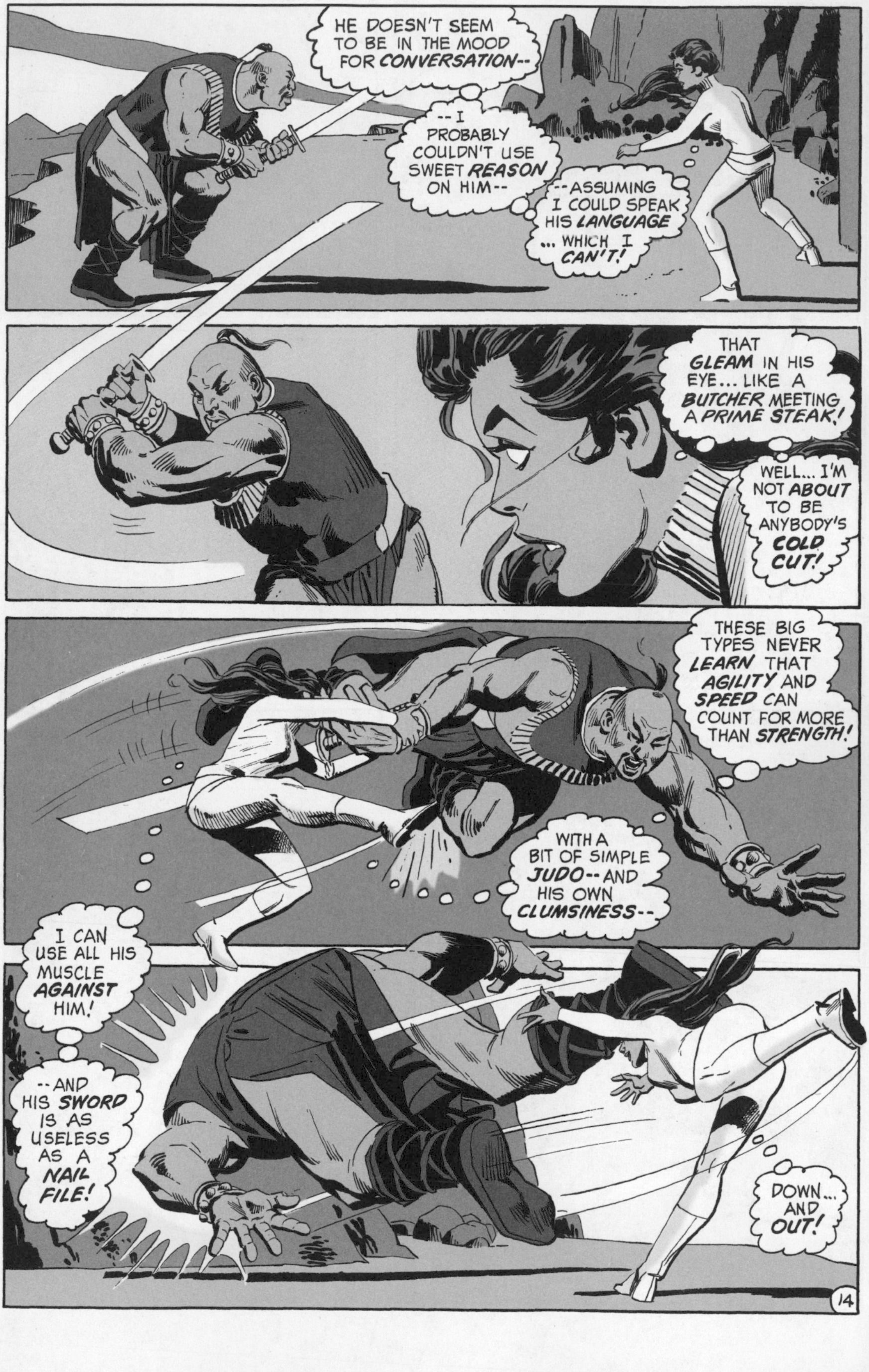
HE DOESN'T SEEM TO BE IN THE MOOD FOR CONVERSATION--
--I PROBABLY COULDN'T USE SWEET REASON ON HIM--
--ASSUMING I COULD SPEAK HIS LANGUAGE ... WHICH I CAN'T!
THAT GLEAM IN HIS EYE... LIKE A BUTCHER MEETING A PRIME STEAK!
WELL... I'M NOT ABOUT TO BE ANYBODY'S COLD CUT!
THESE BIG TYPES NEVER LEARN THAT AGILITY AND SPEED CAN COUNT FOR MORE THAN STRENGTH!
WITH A BIT OF SIMPLE JUDO--AND HIS OWN CLUMSINESS--
I CAN USE ALL HIS MUSCLE AGAINST HIM!
--AND HIS SWORD IS AS USELESS AS A NAIL FILE!
DOWN... AND OUT!
14

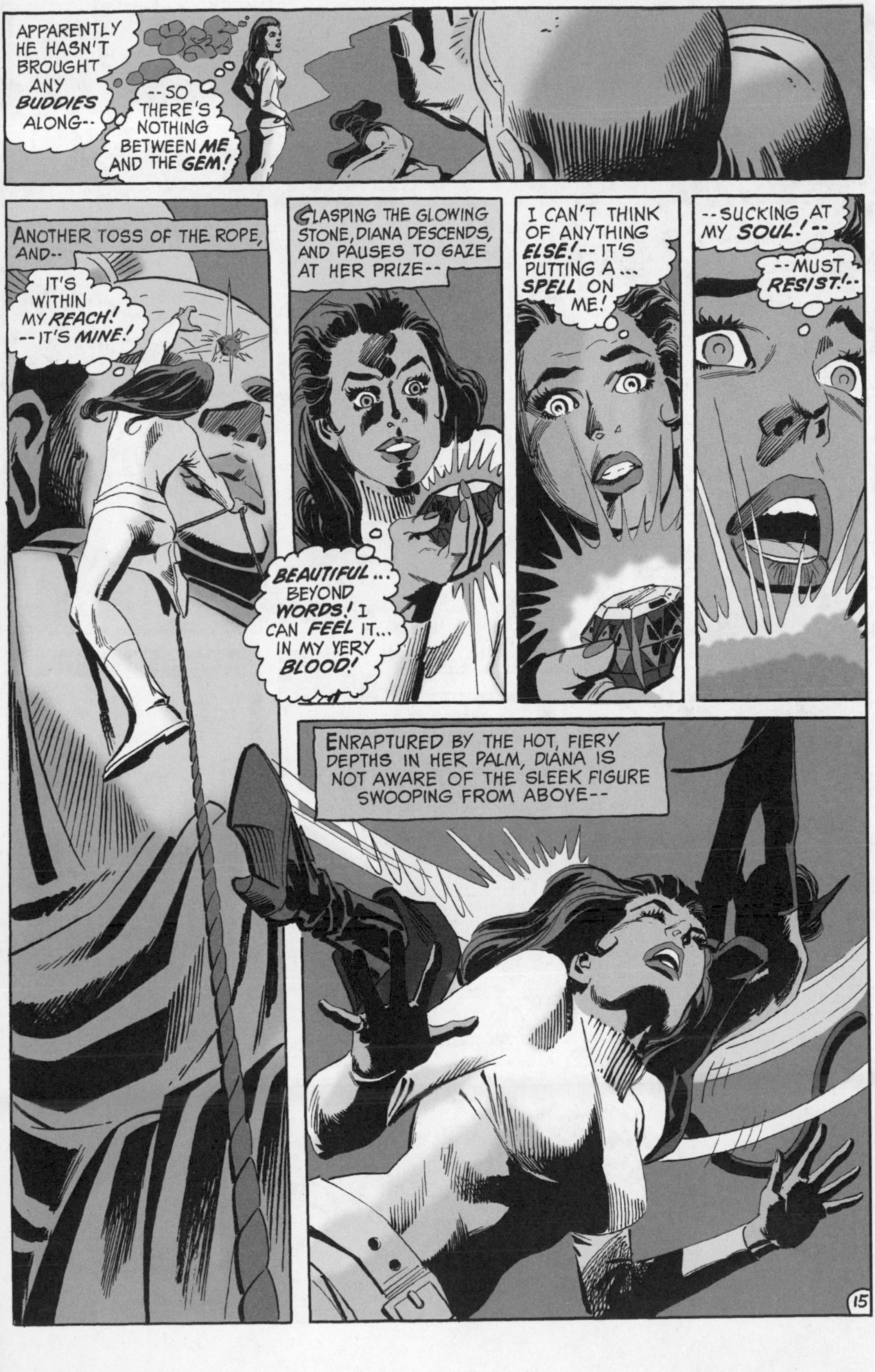
APPARENTLY HE HASN'T BROUGHT ANY BUDDIES ALONG--
--SO THERE'S NOTHING BETWEEN ME AND THE GEM!
ANOTHER TOSS OF THE ROPE, AND--
IT'S WITHIN MY REACH! --IT'S MINE!
GLASPING THE GLOWING STONE, DIANA DESCENDS, AND PAUSES TO GAZE AT HER PRIZE--
BEAUTIFUL... BEYOND WORDS! I CAN FEEL IT... IN MY VERY BLOOD!
I CAN'T THINK OF ANYTHING ELSE!-- IT'S PUTTING A... SPELL ON ME!
--SUCKING AT MY SOUL!--
--MUST RESIST!--
ENRAPTURED BY THE HOT, FIERY DEPTHS IN HER PALM, DIANA IS NOT AWARE OF THE SLEEK FIGURE SWOOPING FROM ABOVE--
15

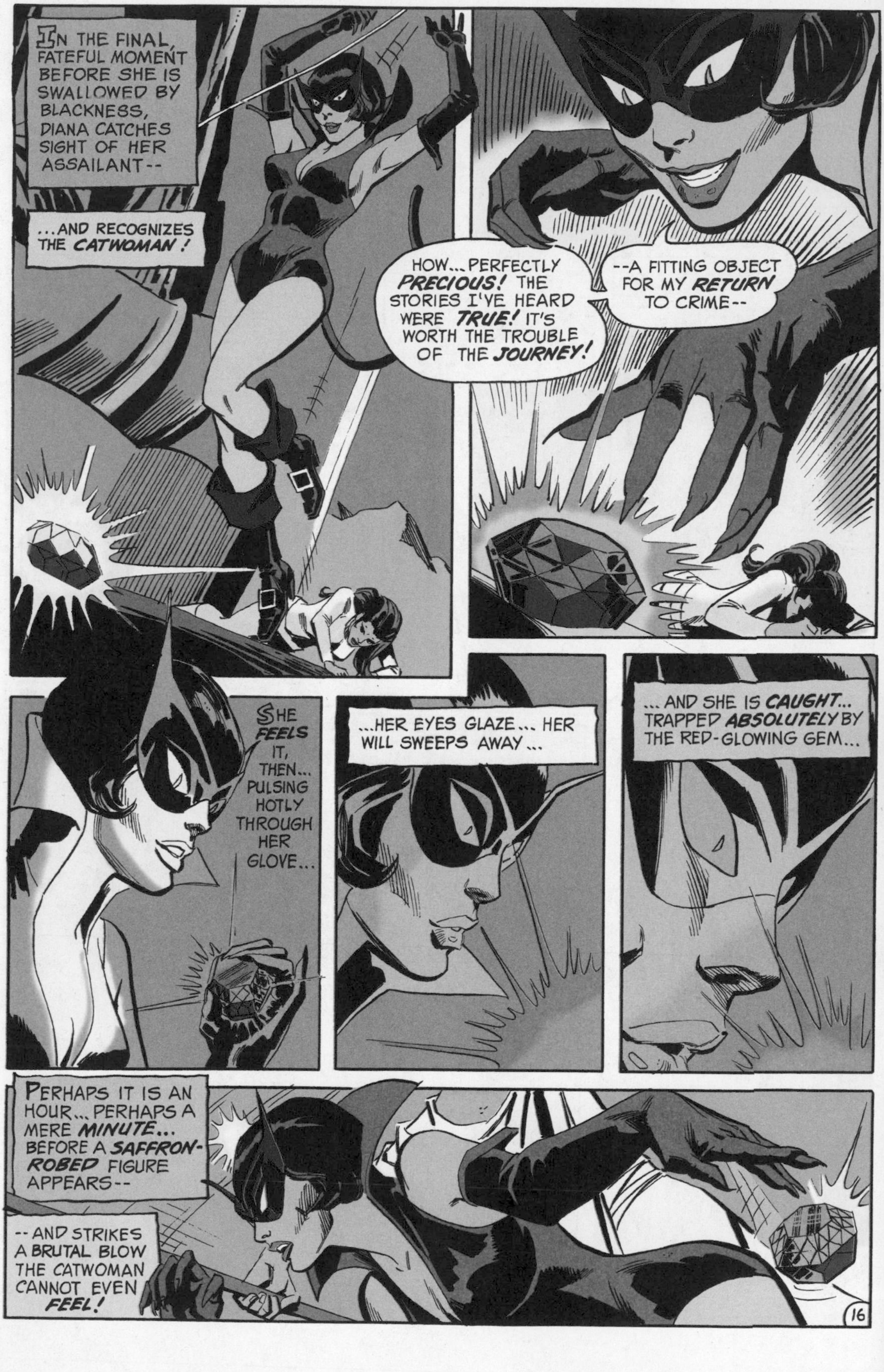
IN THE FINAL, FATEFUL MOMENT BEFORE SHE IS SWALLOWED BY BLACKNESS, DIANA CATCHES SIGHT OF HER ASSAILANT--
...AND RECOGNIZES THE CATWOMAN!
HOW... PERFECTLY PRECIOUS! THE STORIES I'VE HEARD WERE TRUE! IT'S WORTH THE TROUBLE OF THE JOURNEY!
--A FITTING OBJECT FOR MY RETURN TO CRIME--
SHE FEELS IT, THEN... PULSING HOTLY THROUGH HER GLOVE...
...HER EYES GLAZE... HER WILL SWEEPS AWAY...
...AND SHE IS CAUGHT... TRAPPED ABSOLUTELY BY THE RED-GLOWING GEM...
PERHAPS IT IS AN HOUR... PERHAPS A MERE MINUTE... BEFORE A SAFFRON-ROBED FIGURE APPEARS--
--AND STRIKES A BRUTAL BLOW THE CATWOMAN CANNOT EVEN FEEL!
16

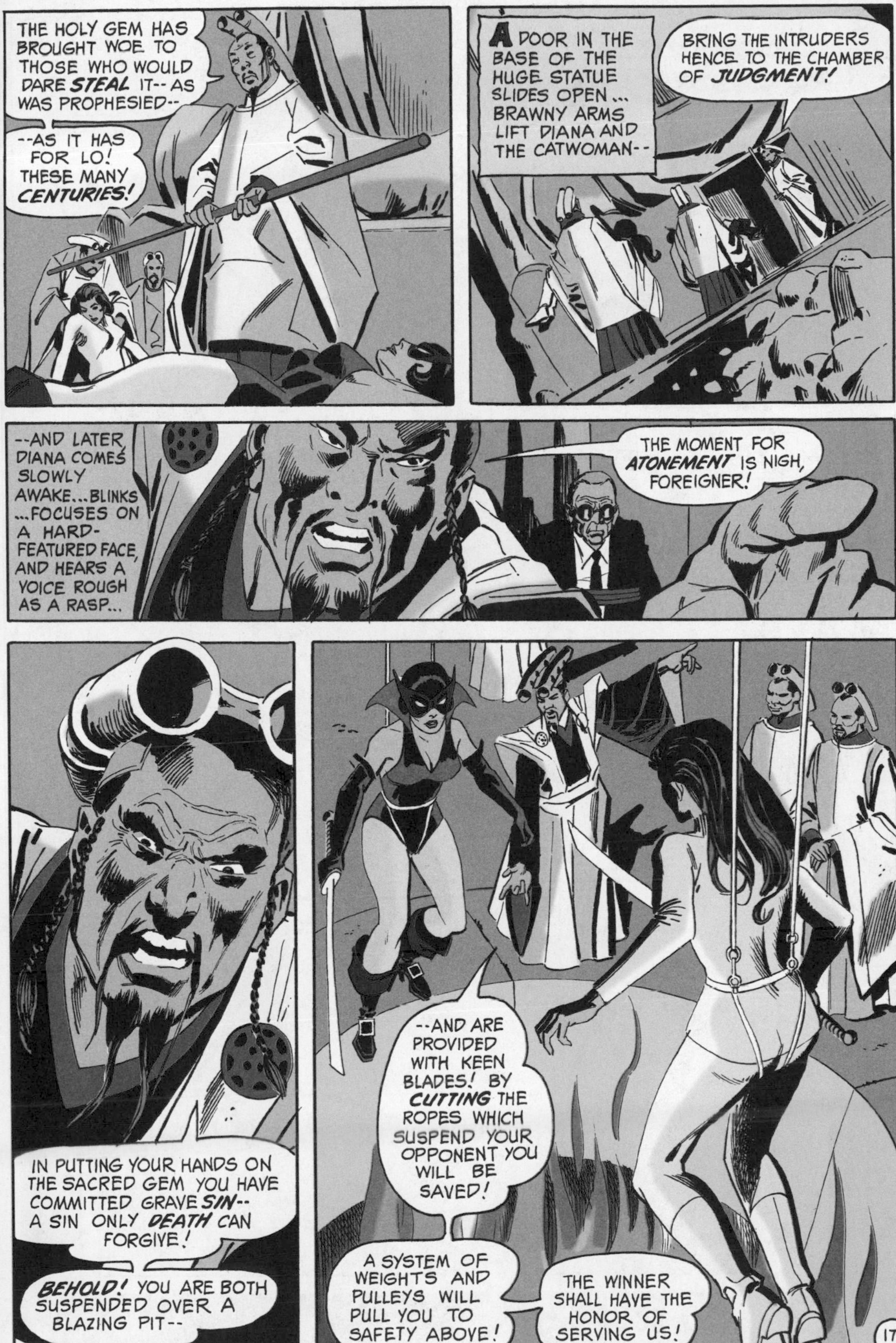
THE HOLY GEM HAS BROUGHT WOE TO THOSE WHO WOULD DARE STEAL IT-- AS WAS PROPHESIED--
--AS IT HAS FOR LO! THESE MANY CENTURIES!
A DOOR IN THE BASE OF THE HUGE STATUE SLIDES OPEN... BRAWNY ARMS LIFT DIANA AND THE CATWOMAN--
BRING THE INTRUDERS HENCE TO THE CHAMBER OF JUDGMENT!
--AND LATER, DIANA COMES SLOWLY AWAKE...BLINKS ...FOCUSES ON A HARD-FEATURED FACE, AND HEARS A VOICE ROUGH AS A RASP...
THE MOMENT FOR ATONEMENT IS NIGH, FOREIGNER!
IN PUTTING YOUR HANDS ON THE SACRED GEM YOU HAVE COMMITTED GRAVE SIN-- A SIN ONLY DEATH CAN FORGIVE!
BEHOLD! YOU ARE BOTH SUSPENDED OVER A BLAZING PIT--
--AND ARE PROVIDED WITH KEEN BLADES! BY CUTTING THE ROPES WHICH SUSPEND YOUR OPPONENT YOU WILL BE SAVED!
A SYSTEM OF WEIGHTS AND PULLEYS WILL PULL YOU TO SAFETY ABOVE!
THE WINNER SHALL HAVE THE HONOR OF SERVING US!
17

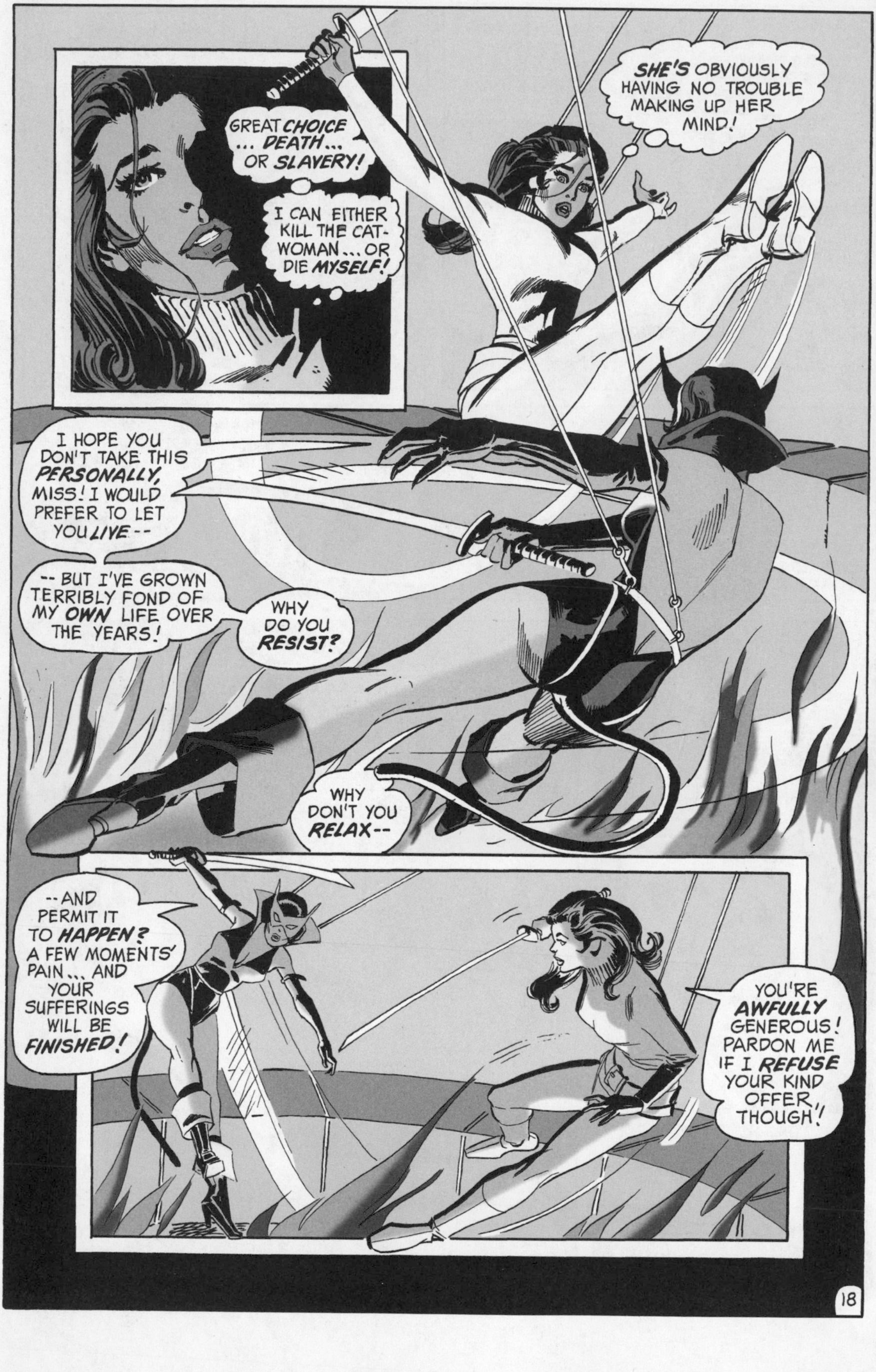
GREAT CHOICE ... DEATH ... OR SLAVERY!
I CAN EITHER KILL THE CAT-WOMAN ... OR DIE MYSELF!
SHE'S OBVIOUSLY HAVING NO TROUBLE MAKING UP HER MIND!
I HOPE YOU DON'T TAKE THIS PERSONALLY, MISS! I WOULD PREFER TO LET YOU LIVE --
-- BUT I'VE GROWN TERRIBLY FOND OF MY OWN LIFE OVER THE YEARS!
WHY DO YOU RESIST?
WHY DON'T YOU RELAX--
--AND PERMIT IT TO HAPPEN? A FEW MOMENTS' PAIN ... AND YOUR SUFFERINGS WILL BE FINISHED!
YOU'RE AWFULLY GENEROUS! PARDON ME IF I REFUSE YOUR KIND OFFER, THOUGH!
18

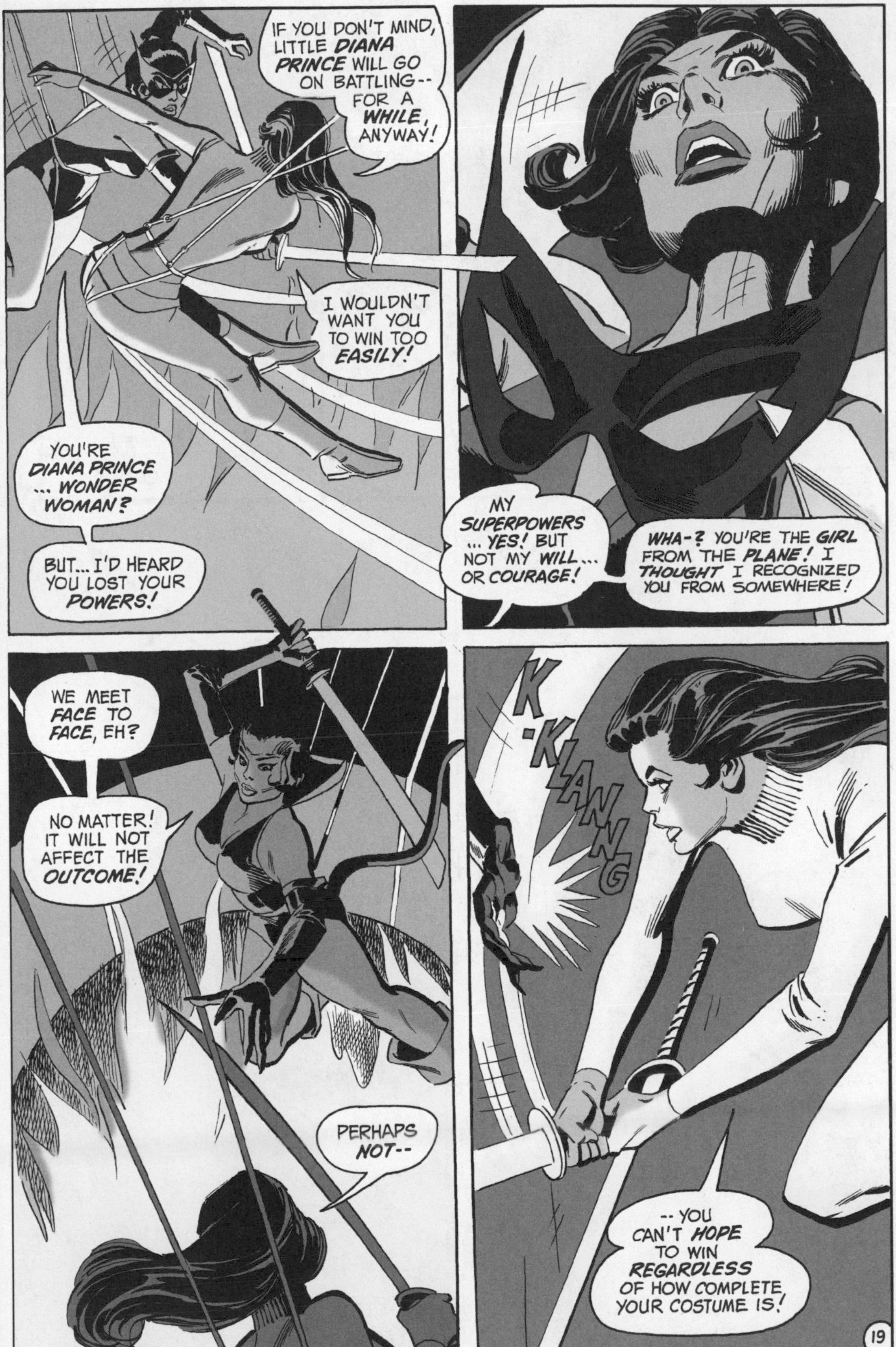
IF YOU DON'T MIND, LITTLE DIANA PRINCE WILL GO ON BATTLING-- FOR A WHILE, ANYWAY!
I WOULDN'T WANT YOU TO WIN TOO EASILY!
YOU'RE DIANA PRINCE ... WONDER WOMAN?
BUT... I'D HEARD YOU LOST YOUR POWERS!
MY SUPERPOWERS ... YES! BUT NOT MY WILL... OR COURAGE!
WHA-? YOU'RE THE GIRL FROM THE PLANE! I THOUGHT I RECOGNIZED YOU FROM SOMEWHERE!
WE MEET FACE TO FACE, EH?
NO MATTER! IT WILL NOT AFFECT THE OUTCOME!
PERHAPS NOT--
K-KLANNG
--YOU CAN'T HOPE TO WIN REGARDLESS OF HOW COMPLETE YOUR COSTUME IS!
19

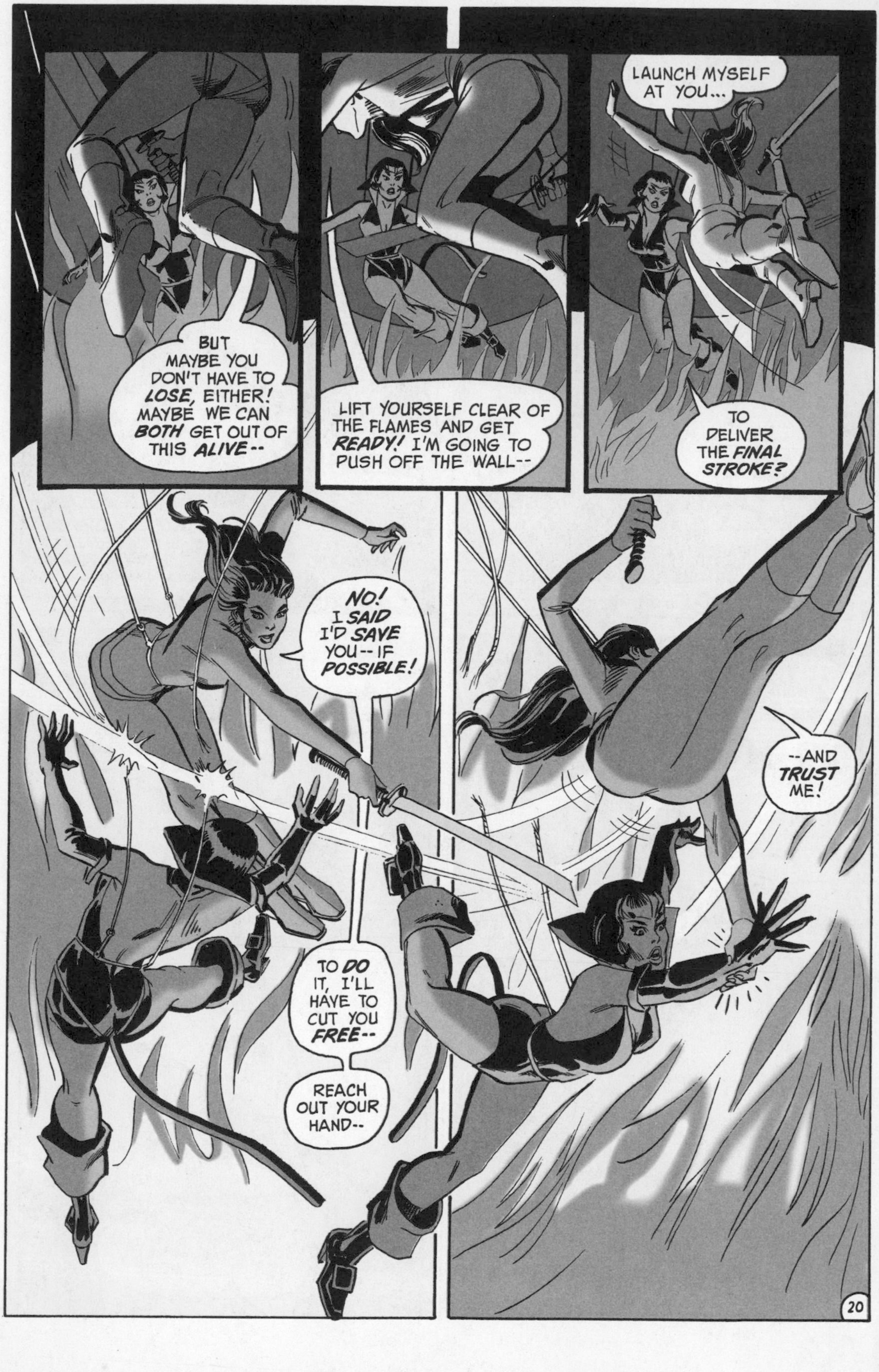
BUT MAYBE YOU DON'T HAVE TO LOSE, EITHER! MAYBE WE CAN BOTH GET OUT OF THIS ALIVE--
LIFT YOURSELF CLEAR OF THE FLAMES AND GET READY! I'M GOING TO PUSH OFF THE WALL--
LAUNCH MYSELF AT YOU...
TO DELIVER THE FINAL STROKE?
NO! I SAID I'D SAVE YOU-- IF POSSIBLE!
TO DO IT, I'LL HAVE TO CUT YOU FREE--
REACH OUT YOUR HAND--
--AND TRUST ME!
20

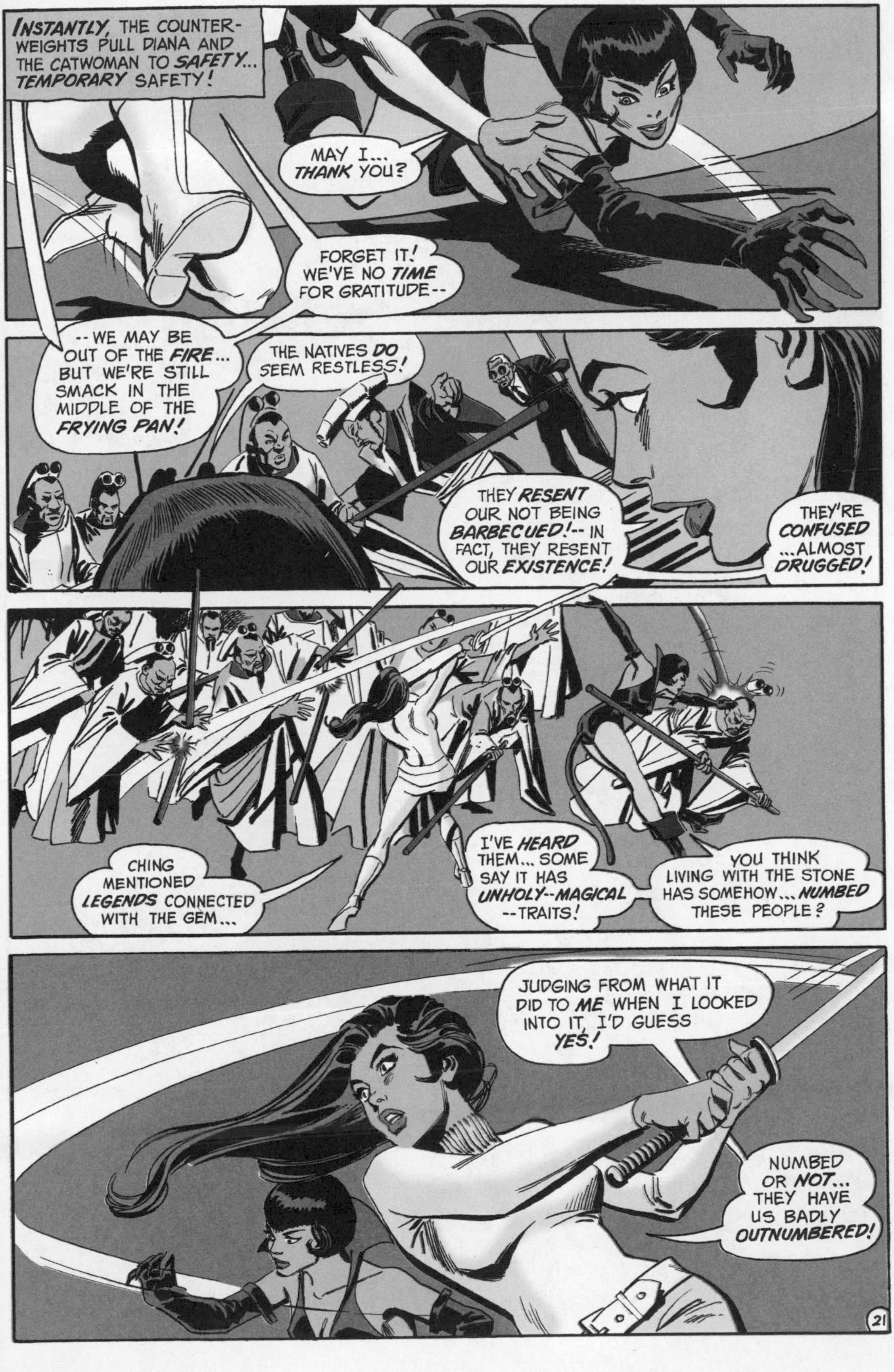
INSTANTLY, THE COUNTER-WEIGHTS PULL DIANA AND THE CATWOMAN TO SAFETY... TEMPORARY SAFETY!
MAY I... THANK YOU?
FORGET IT! WE'VE NO TIME FOR GRATITUDE--
--WE MAY BE OUT OF THE FIRE... BUT WE'RE STILL SMACK IN THE MIDDLE OF THE FRYING PAN!
THE NATIVES DO SEEM RESTLESS!
THEY RESENT OUR NOT BEING BARBECUED!-- IN FACT, THEY RESENT OUR EXISTENCE!
THEY'RE CONFUSED ...ALMOST DRUGGED!
CHING MENTIONED LEGENDS CONNECTED WITH THE GEM...
I'VE HEARD THEM... SOME SAY IT HAS UNHOLY--MAGICAL --TRAITS!
YOU THINK LIVING WITH THE STONE HAS SOMEHOW... NUMBED THESE PEOPLE?
JUDGING FROM WHAT IT DID TO ME WHEN I LOOKED INTO IT, I'D GUESS YES!
NUMBED OR NOT... THEY HAVE US BADLY OUTNUMBERED!
21

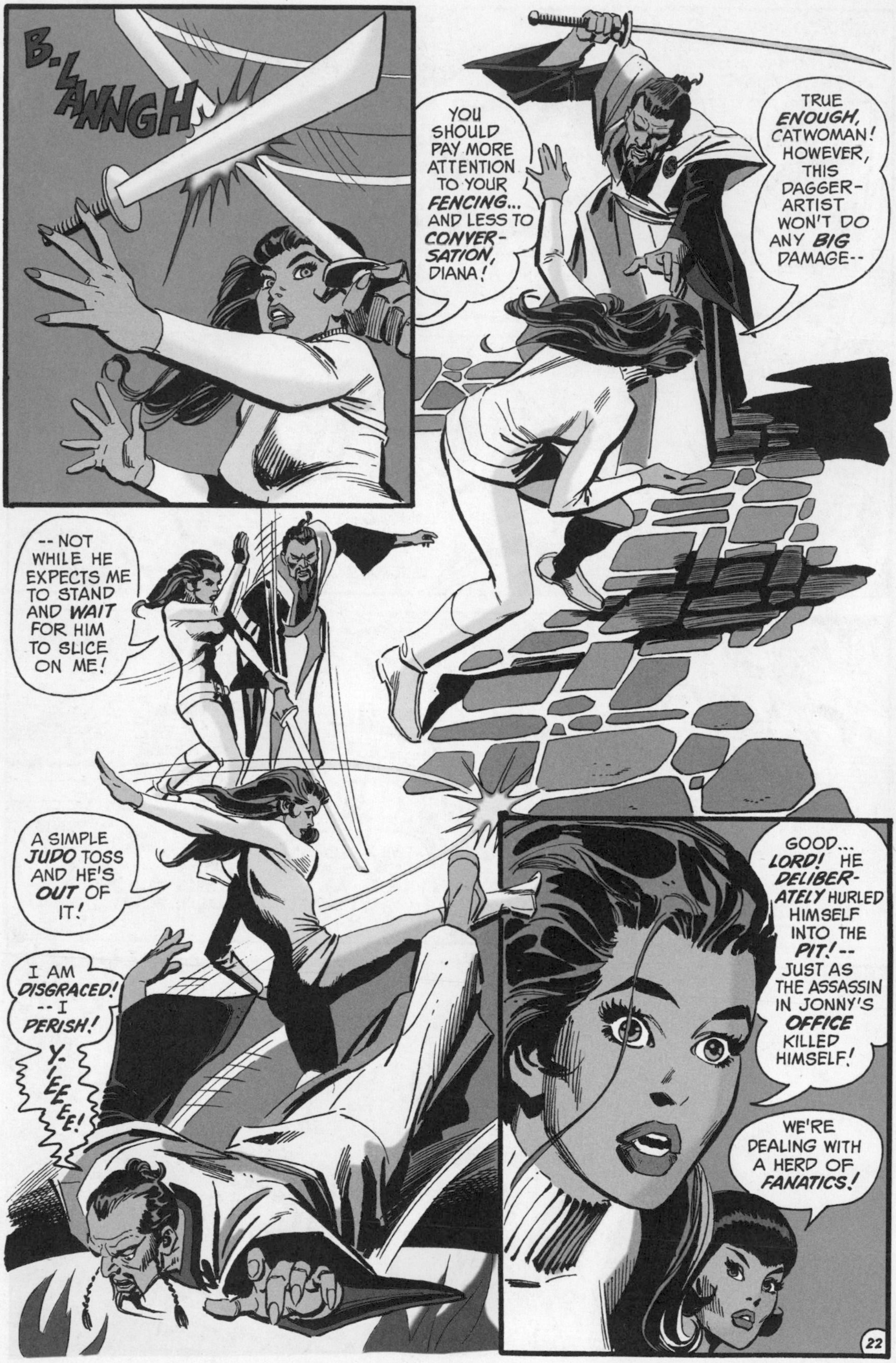
B-LANNGH
YOU SHOULD PAY MORE ATTENTION TO YOUR FENCING... AND LESS TO CONVER-SATION, DIANA!
TRUE ENOUGH, CATWOMAN! HOWEVER, THIS DAGGER-ARTIST WON'T DO ANY BIG DAMAGE--
--NOT WHILE HE EXPECTS ME TO STAND AND WAIT FOR HIM TO SLICE ON ME!
A SIMPLE JUDO TOSS AND HE'S OUT OF IT!
I AM DISGRACED! --I PERISH!
Y-IEEEE!
GOOD... LORD! HE DELIBER-ATELY HURLED HIMSELF INTO THE PIT! --JUST AS THE ASSASSIN IN JONNY'S OFFICE KILLED HIMSELF!
WE'RE DEALING WITH A HERD OF FANATICS!
22

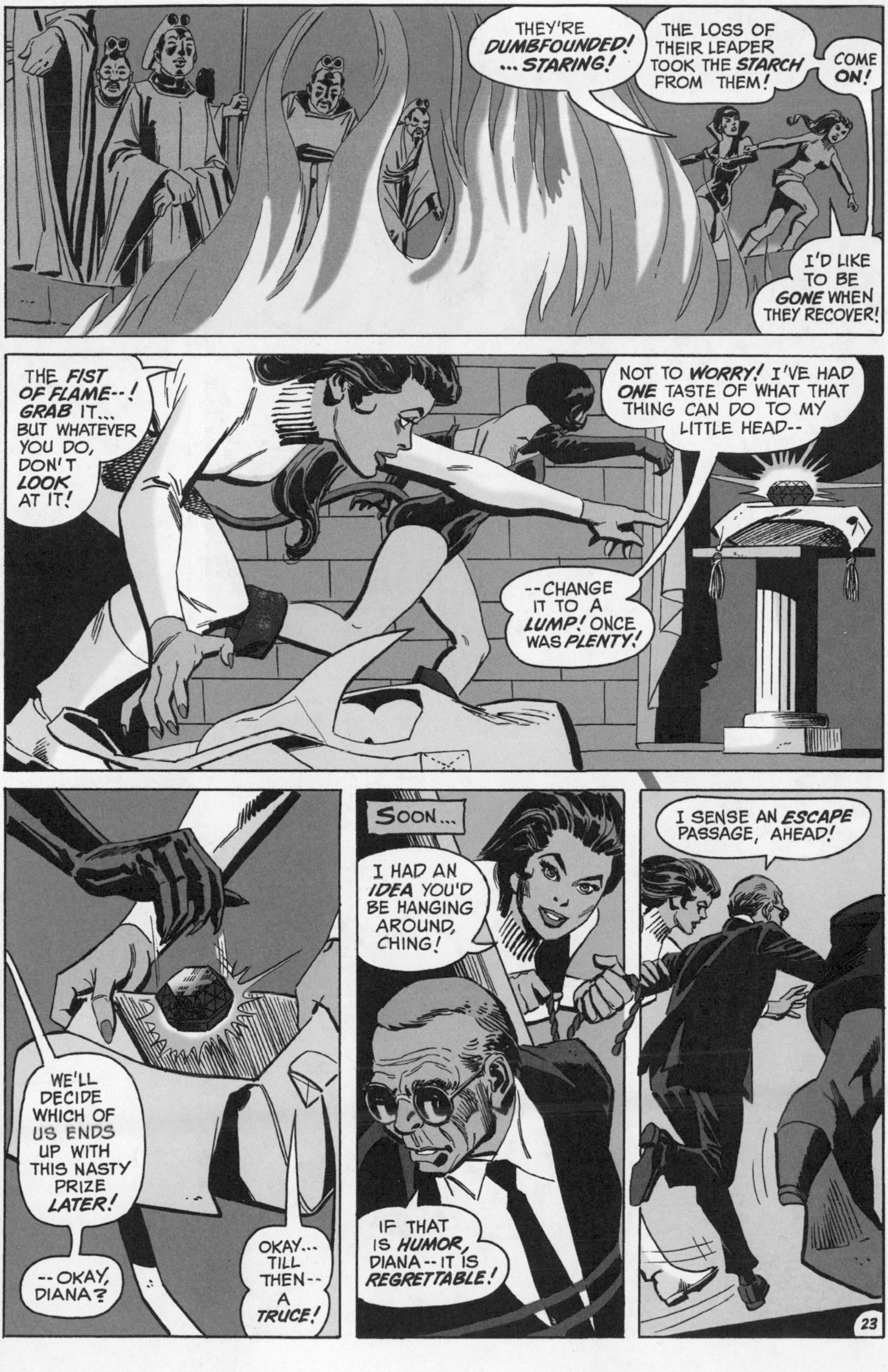
THEY'RE DUMBFOUNDED! ... STARING!
THE LOSS OF THEIR LEADER TOOK THE STARCH FROM THEM!
COME ON!
I'D LIKE TO BE GONE WHEN THEY RECOVER!
THE FIST OF FLAME--! GRAB IT... BUT WHATEVER YOU DO, DON'T LOOK AT IT!
NOT TO WORRY! I'VE HAD ONE TASTE OF WHAT THAT THING CAN DO TO MY LITTLE HEAD--
--CHANGE IT TO A LUMP! ONCE WAS PLENTY!
WE'LL DECIDE WHICH OF US ENDS UP WITH THIS NASTY PRIZE LATER!
--OKAY, DIANA?
OKAY... TILL THEN-- A TRUCE!
SOON...
I HAD AN IDEA YOU'D BE HANGING AROUND, CHING!
IF THAT IS HUMOR, DIANA--IT IS REGRETTABLE!
I SENSE AN ESCAPE PASSAGE, AHEAD!
23

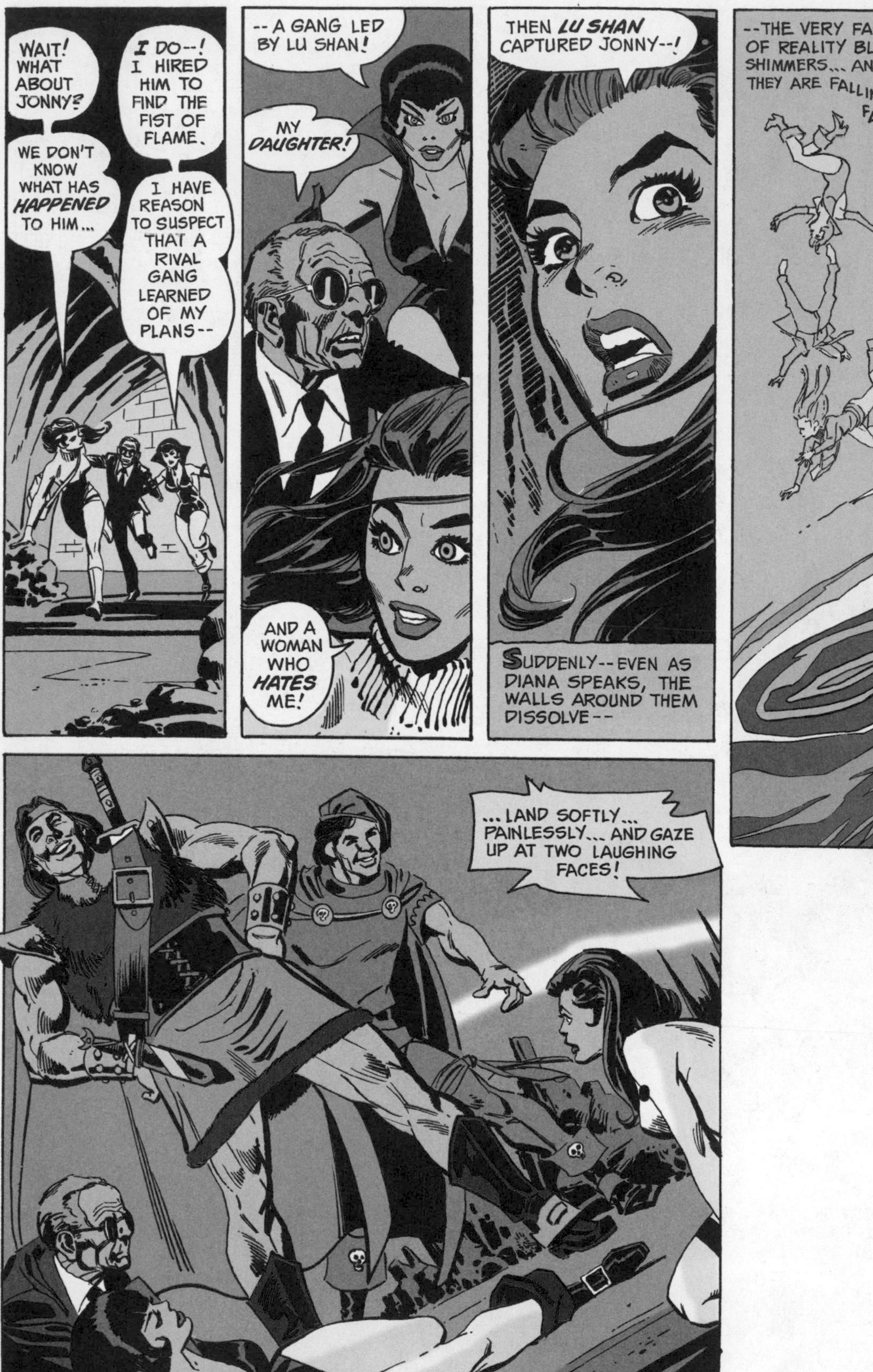

WAIT! WHAT ABOUT JONNY?
I DO--! I HIRED HIM TO FIND THE FIST OF FLAME.
WE DON'T KNOW WHAT HAS HAPPENED TO HIM...
I HAVE REASON TO SUSPECT THAT A RIVAL GANG LEARNED OF MY PLANS--
-- A GANG LED BY LU SHAN!
MY DAUGHTER!
AND A WOMAN WHO HATES ME!
THEN LU SHAN CAPTURED JONNY--!
SUDDENLY-- EVEN AS DIANA SPEAKS, THE WALLS AROUND THEM DISSOLVE--
--THE VERY FABRIC OF REALITY BLURS... SHIMMERS... AND THEY ARE FALLING,
FALLING...
... LAND SOFTLY... PAINLESSLY... AND GAZE UP AT TWO LAUGHING FACES!

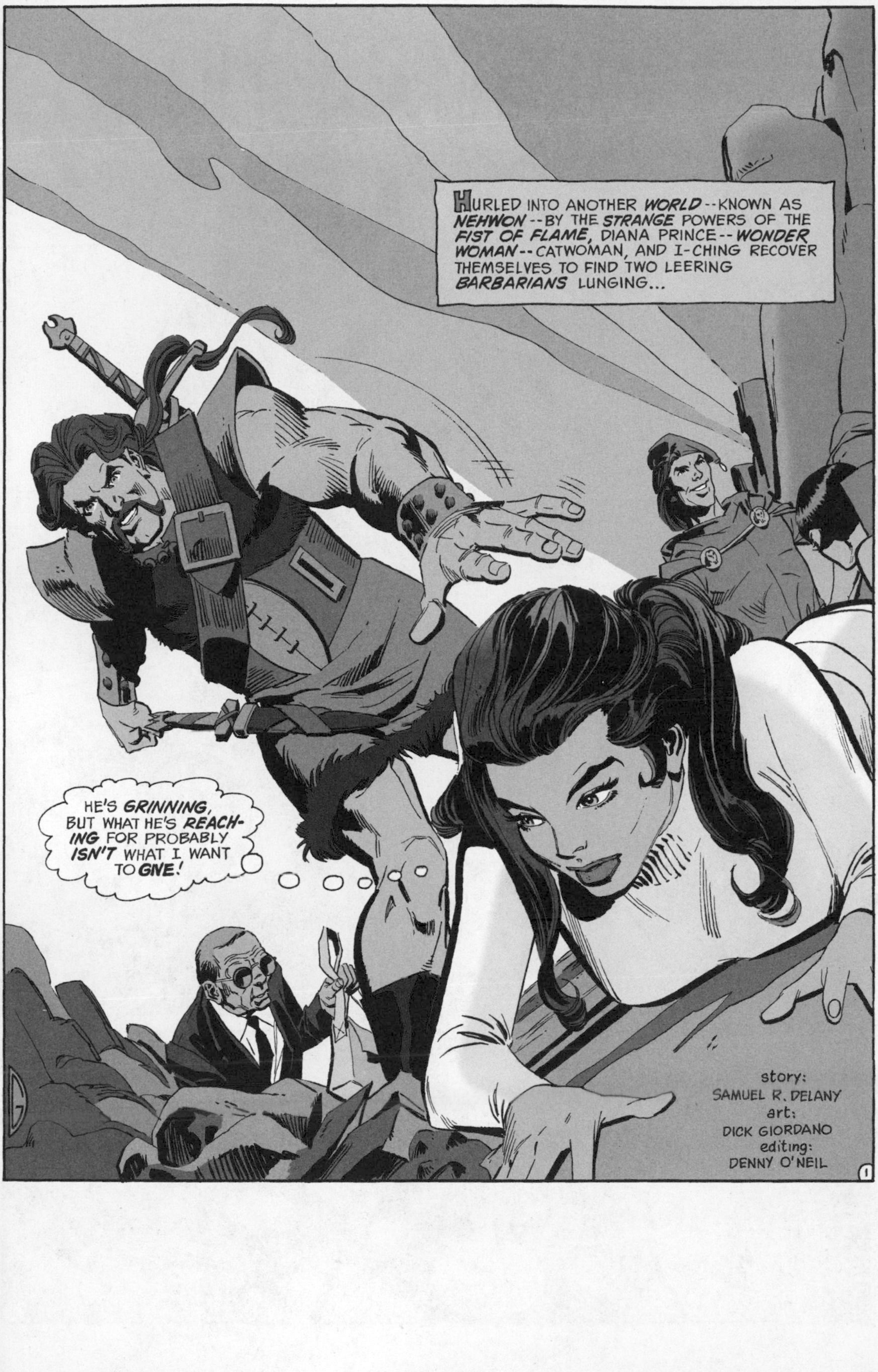
HURLED INTO ANOTHER WORLD--KNOWN AS NEHWON--BY THE STRANGE POWERS OF THE FIST OF FLAME, DIANA PRINCE--WONDER WOMAN--CATWOMAN, AND I-CHING RECOVER THEMSELVES TO FIND TWO LEERING BARBARIANS LUNGING...
HE'S GRINNING, BUT WHAT HE'S REACH-ING FOR PROBABLY ISN'T WHAT I WANT TO GIVE!
story: SAMUEL R. DELANY art: DICK GIORDANO editing: DENNY O'NEIL
1

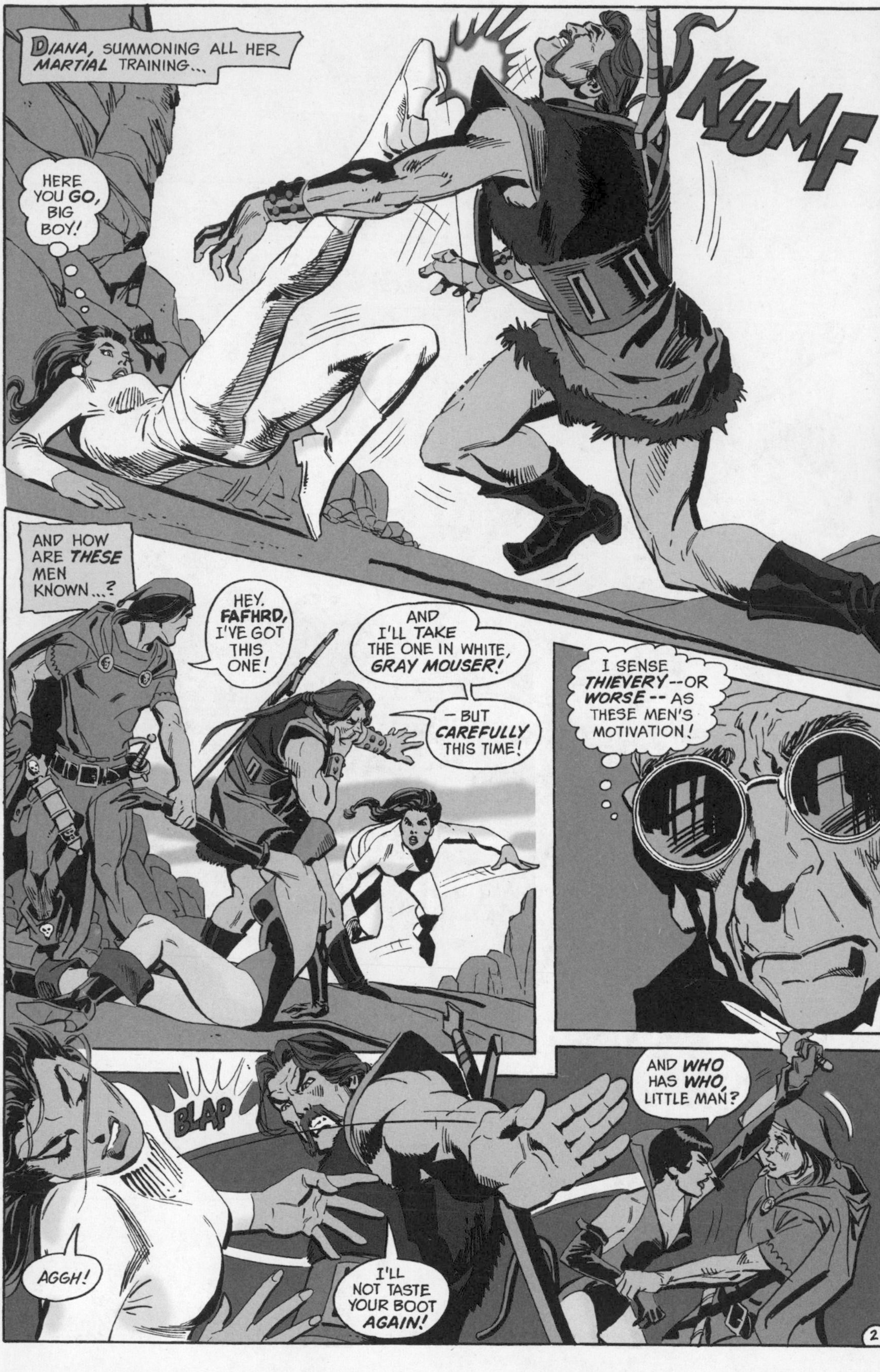
DIANA, SUMMONING ALL HER MARTIAL TRAINING...
HERE YOU GO, BIG BOY!
KLUMF
AND HOW ARE THESE MEN KNOWN...?
HEY. FAFHRD, I'VE GOT THIS ONE!
AND I'LL TAKE THE ONE IN WHITE, GRAY MOUSER!
— BUT CAREFULLY THIS TIME!
I SENSE THIEVERY -- OR WORSE -- AS THESE MEN'S MOTIVATION!
BLAP
AGGH!
I'LL NOT TASTE YOUR BOOT AGAIN!
AND WHO HAS WHO, LITTLE MAN?
2

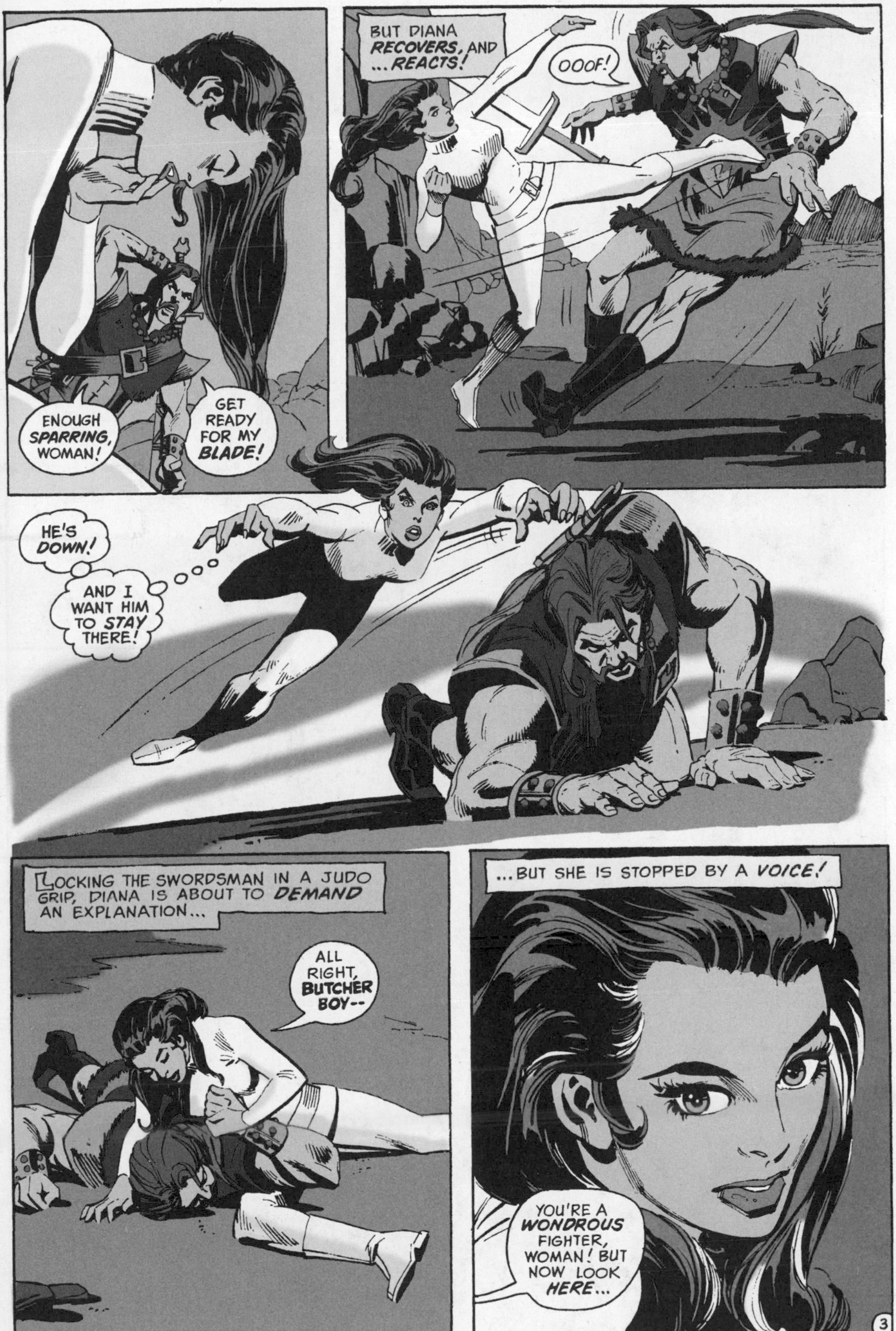
ENOUGH SPARRING, WOMAN!
GET READY FOR MY BLADE!
BUT DIANA RECOVERS, AND ...REACTS!
OOOF!
HE'S DOWN!
AND I WANT HIM TO STAY THERE!
LOCKING THE SWORDSMAN IN A JUDO GRIP, DIANA IS ABOUT TO DEMAND AN EXPLANATION...
ALL RIGHT, BUTCHER BOY--
...BUT SHE IS STOPPED BY A VOICE!
YOU'RE A WONDROUS FIGHTER, WOMAN! BUT NOW LOOK HERE...
3

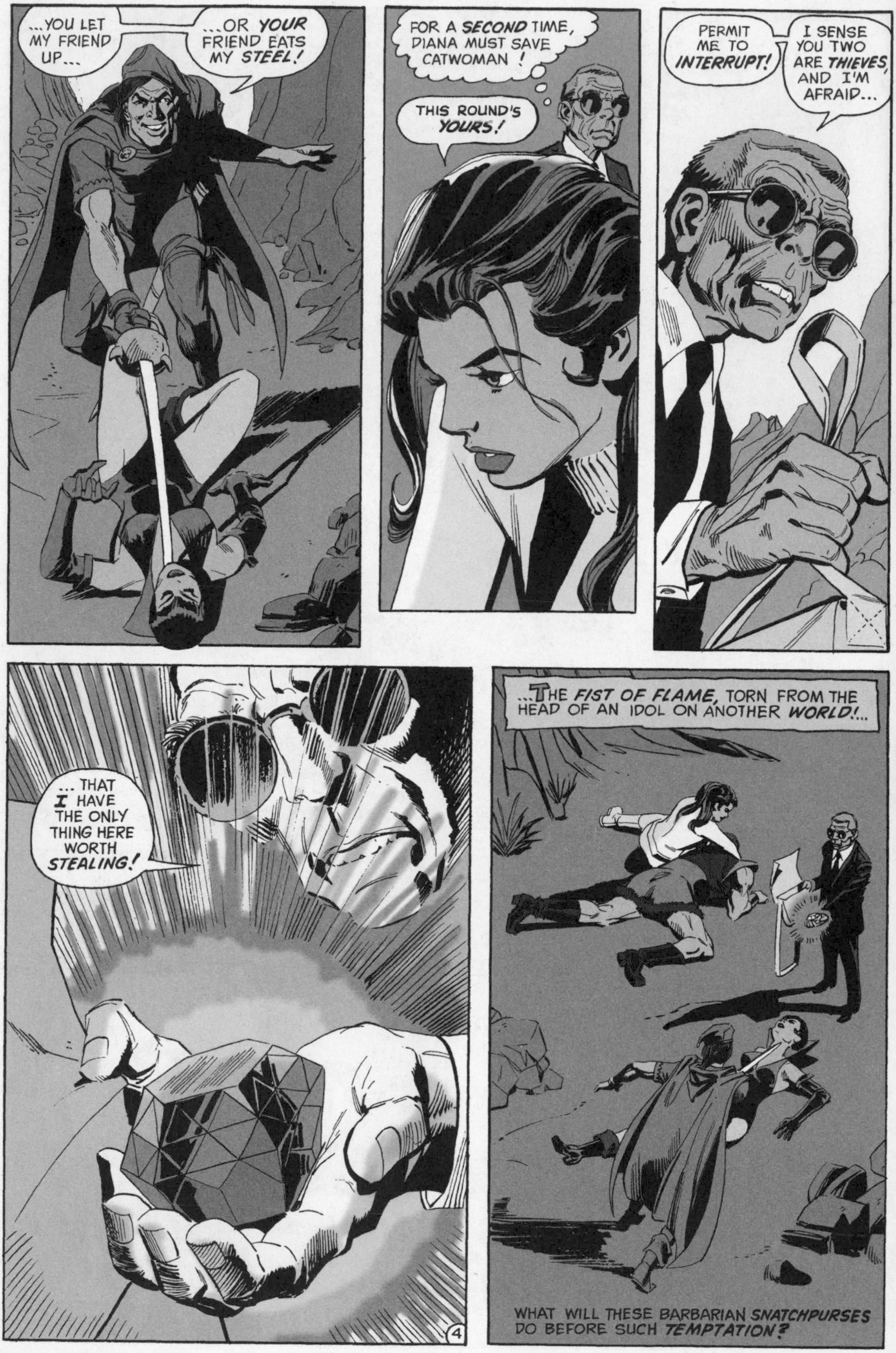
...YOU LET MY FRIEND UP...
...OR YOUR FRIEND EATS MY STEEL!
FOR A SECOND TIME, DIANA MUST SAVE CATWOMAN!
THIS ROUND'S YOURS!
PERMIT ME TO INTERRUPT!
I SENSE YOU TWO ARE THIEVES, AND I'M AFRAID...
... THAT I HAVE THE ONLY THING HERE WORTH STEALING!
4
...THE FIST OF FLAME, TORN FROM THE HEAD OF AN IDOL ON ANOTHER WORLD!...
WHAT WILL THESE BARBARIAN SNATCHPURSES DO BEFORE SUCH TEMPTATION?

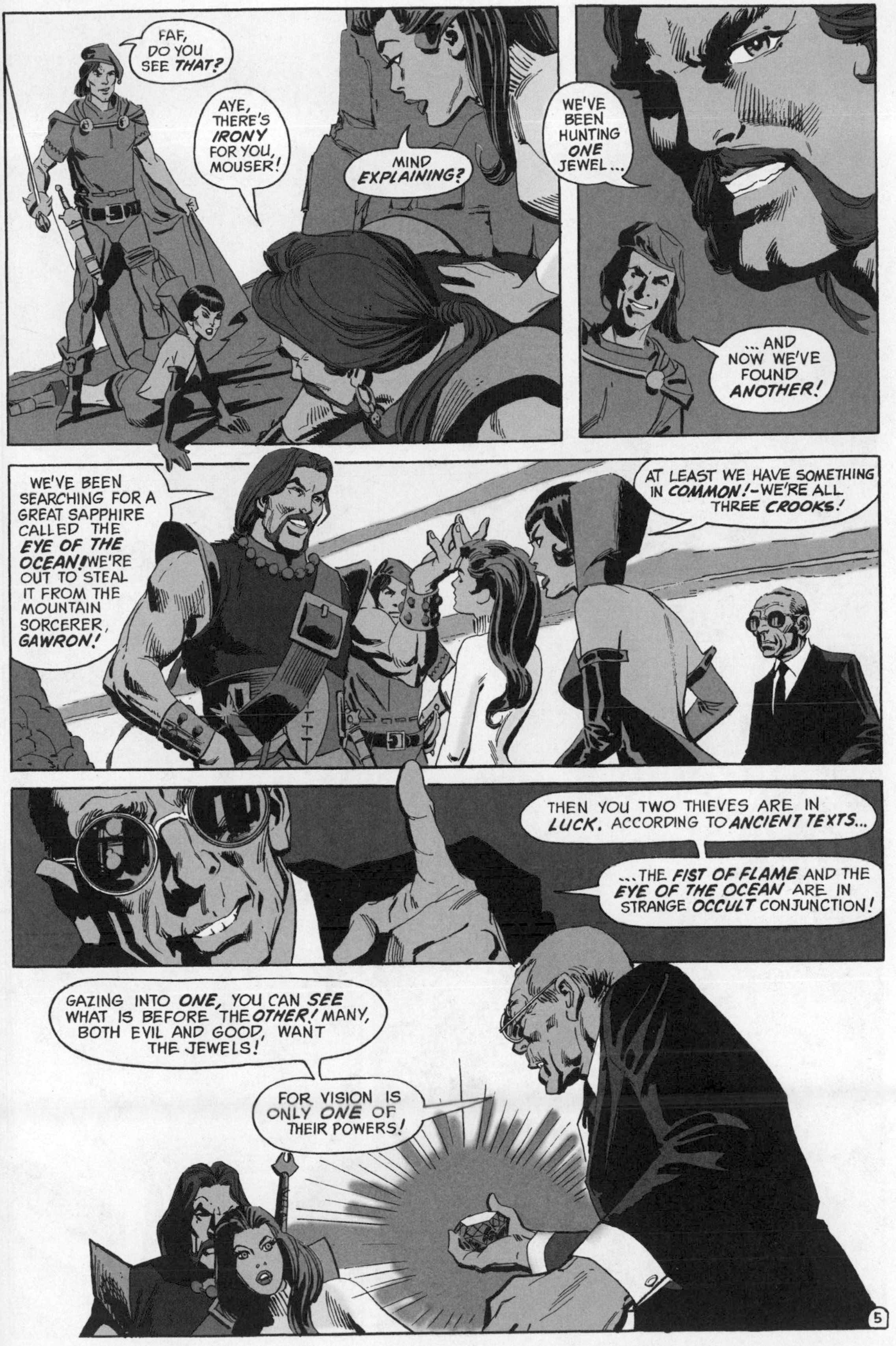

FAF, DO YOU SEE THAT?
AYE, THERE'S IRONY FOR YOU, MOUSER!
MIND EXPLAINING?
WE'VE BEEN HUNTING ONE JEWEL...
...AND NOW WE'VE FOUND ANOTHER!
WE'VE BEEN SEARCHING FOR A GREAT SAPPHIRE CALLED THE EYE OF THE OCEAN! WE'RE OUT TO STEAL IT FROM THE MOUNTAIN SORCERER, GAWRON!
AT LEAST WE HAVE SOMETHING IN COMMON! -WE'RE ALL THREE CROOKS!
THEN YOU TWO THIEVES ARE IN LUCK. ACCORDING TO ANCIENT TEXTS...
...THE FIST OF FLAME AND THE EYE OF THE OCEAN ARE IN STRANGE OCCULT CONJUNCTION!
GAZING INTO ONE, YOU CAN SEE WHAT IS BEFORE THE OTHER! MANY, BOTH EVIL AND GOOD, WANT THE JEWELS!
FOR VISION IS ONLY ONE OF THEIR POWERS!
5

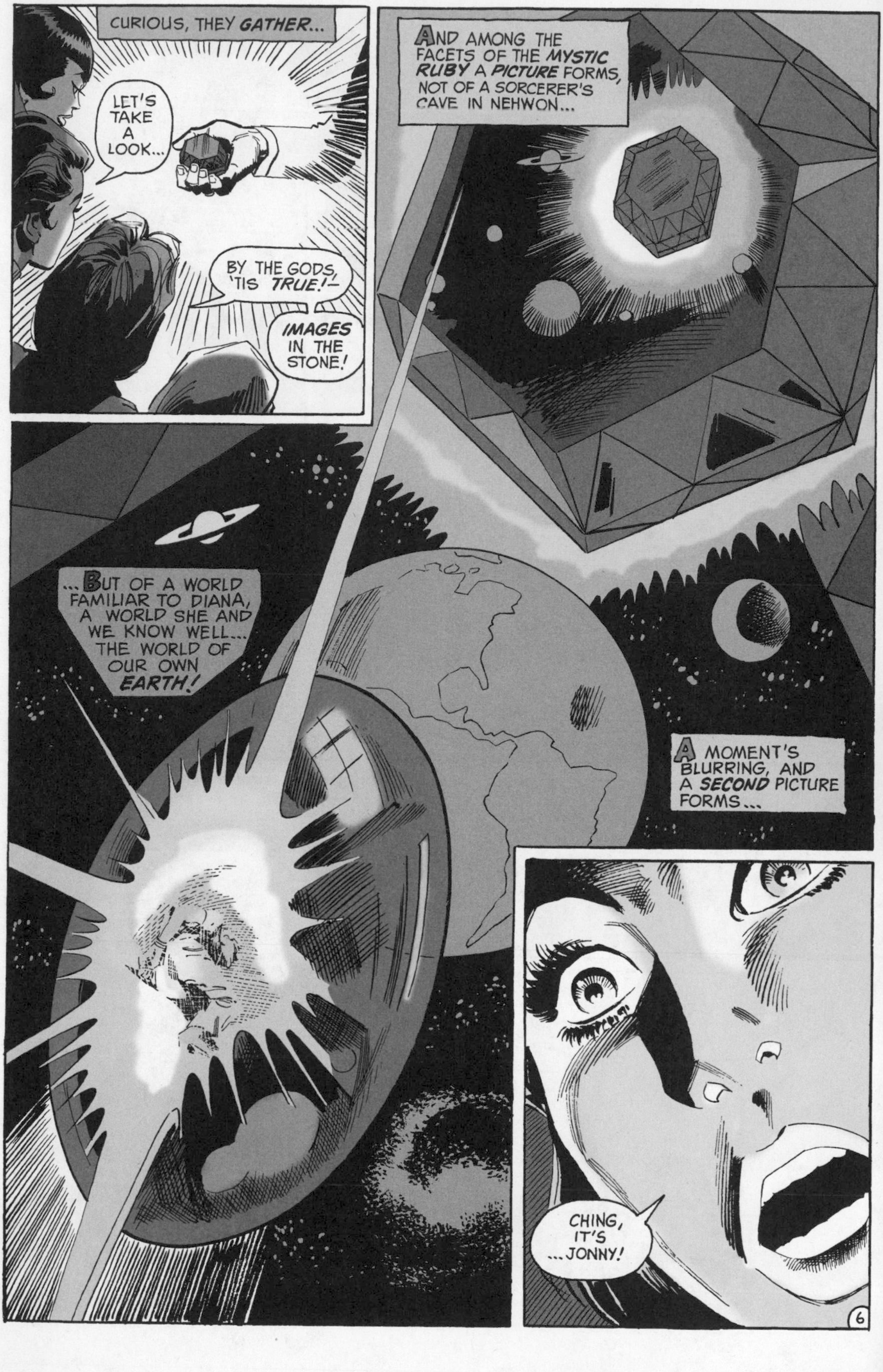
CURIOUS, THEY GATHER...
LET'S TAKE A LOOK...
BY THE GODS, 'TIS TRUE!--
IMAGES IN THE STONE!
AND AMONG THE FACETS OF THE MYSTIC RUBY A PICTURE FORMS, NOT OF A SORCERER'S CAVE IN NEHWON...
...BUT OF A WORLD FAMILIAR TO DIANA, A WORLD SHE AND WE KNOW WELL... THE WORLD OF OUR OWN EARTH!
A MOMENT'S BLURRING, AND A SECOND PICTURE FORMS...
CHING, IT'S ...JONNY!
6

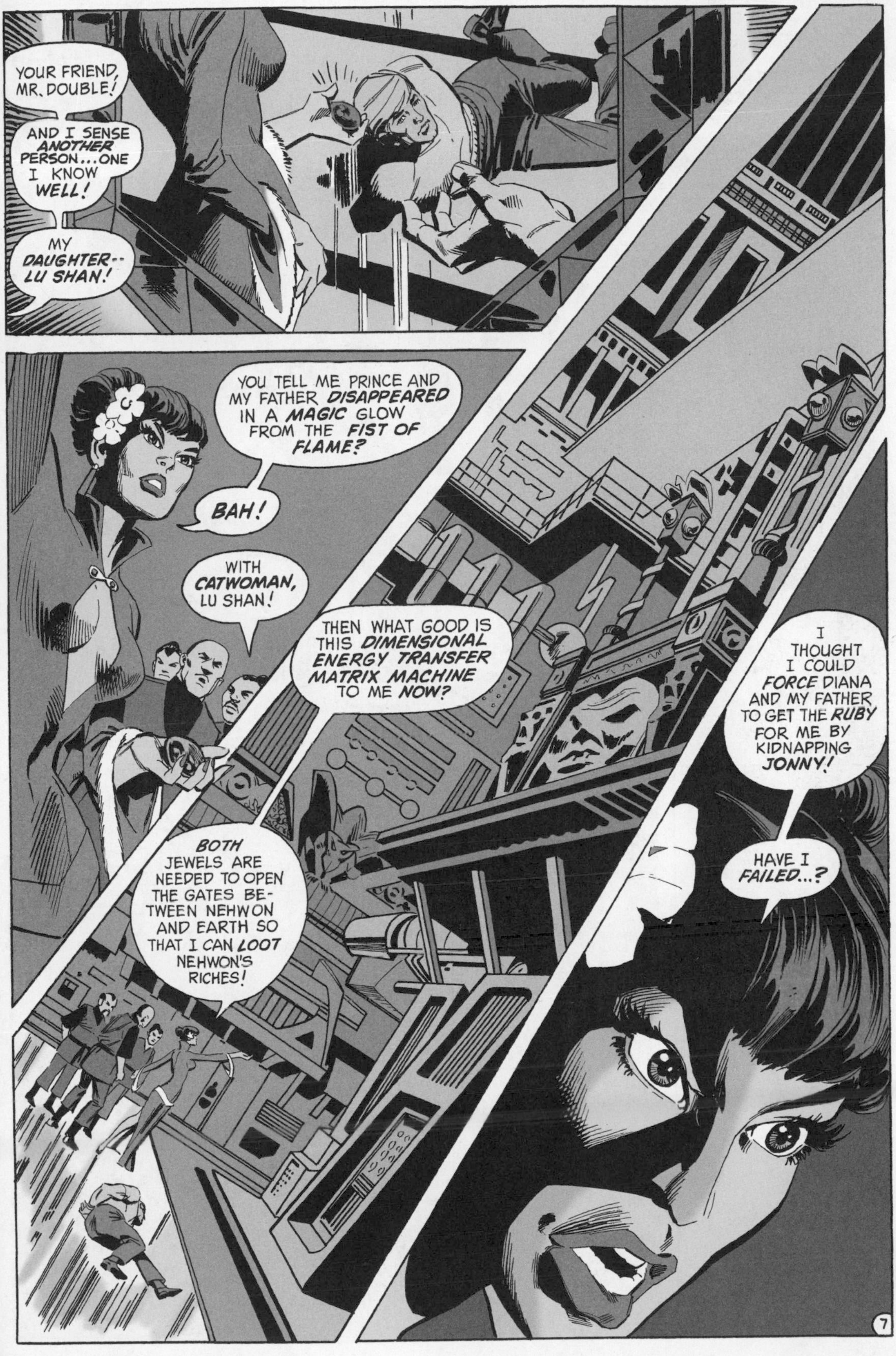
YOUR FRIEND, MR. DOUBLE!
AND I SENSE ANOTHER PERSON...ONE I KNOW WELL!
MY DAUGHTER-- LU SHAN!
YOU TELL ME PRINCE AND MY FATHER DISAPPEARED IN A MAGIC GLOW FROM THE FIST OF FLAME?
BAH!
WITH CATWOMAN, LU SHAN!
THEN WHAT GOOD IS THIS DIMENSIONAL ENERGY TRANSFER MATRIX MACHINE TO ME NOW?
BOTH JEWELS ARE NEEDED TO OPEN THE GATES BE- TWEEN NEHWON AND EARTH SO THAT I CAN LOOT NEHWON'S RICHES!
I THOUGHT I COULD FORCE DIANA AND MY FATHER TO GET THE RUBY FOR ME BY KIDNAPPING JONNY!
HAVE I FAILED...?
7

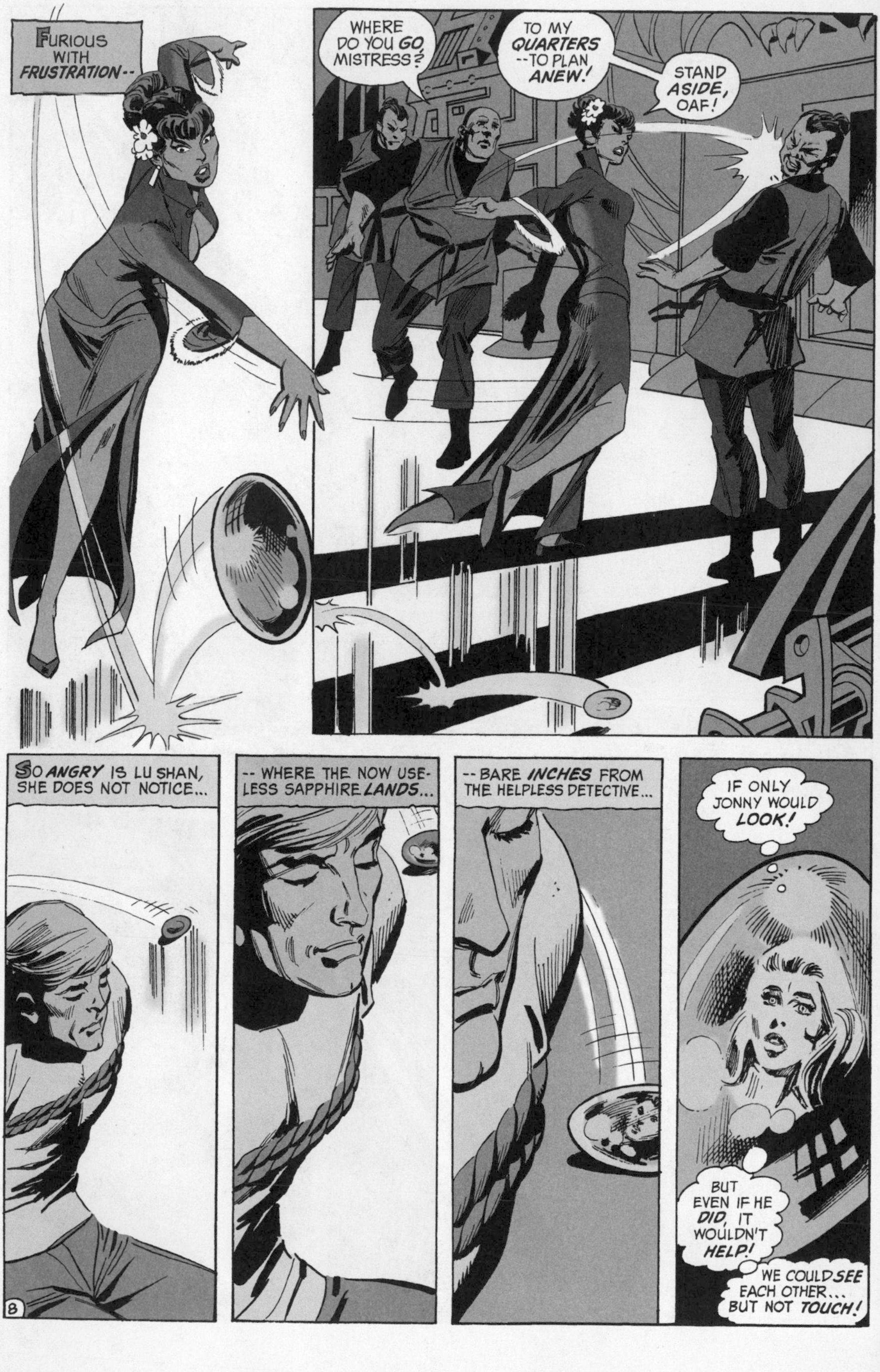
FURIOUS WITH FRUSTRATION--
WHERE DO YOU GO, MISTRESS?
TO MY QUARTERS --TO PLAN ANEW!
STAND ASIDE, OAF!
SO ANGRY IS LU SHAN, SHE DOES NOT NOTICE...
8
-- WHERE THE NOW USELESS SAPPHIRE LANDS...
-- BARE INCHES FROM THE HELPLESS DETECTIVE...
IF ONLY JONNY WOULD LOOK!
BUT EVEN IF HE DID, IT WOULDN'T HELP!
WE COULD SEE EACH OTHER... BUT NOT TOUCH!

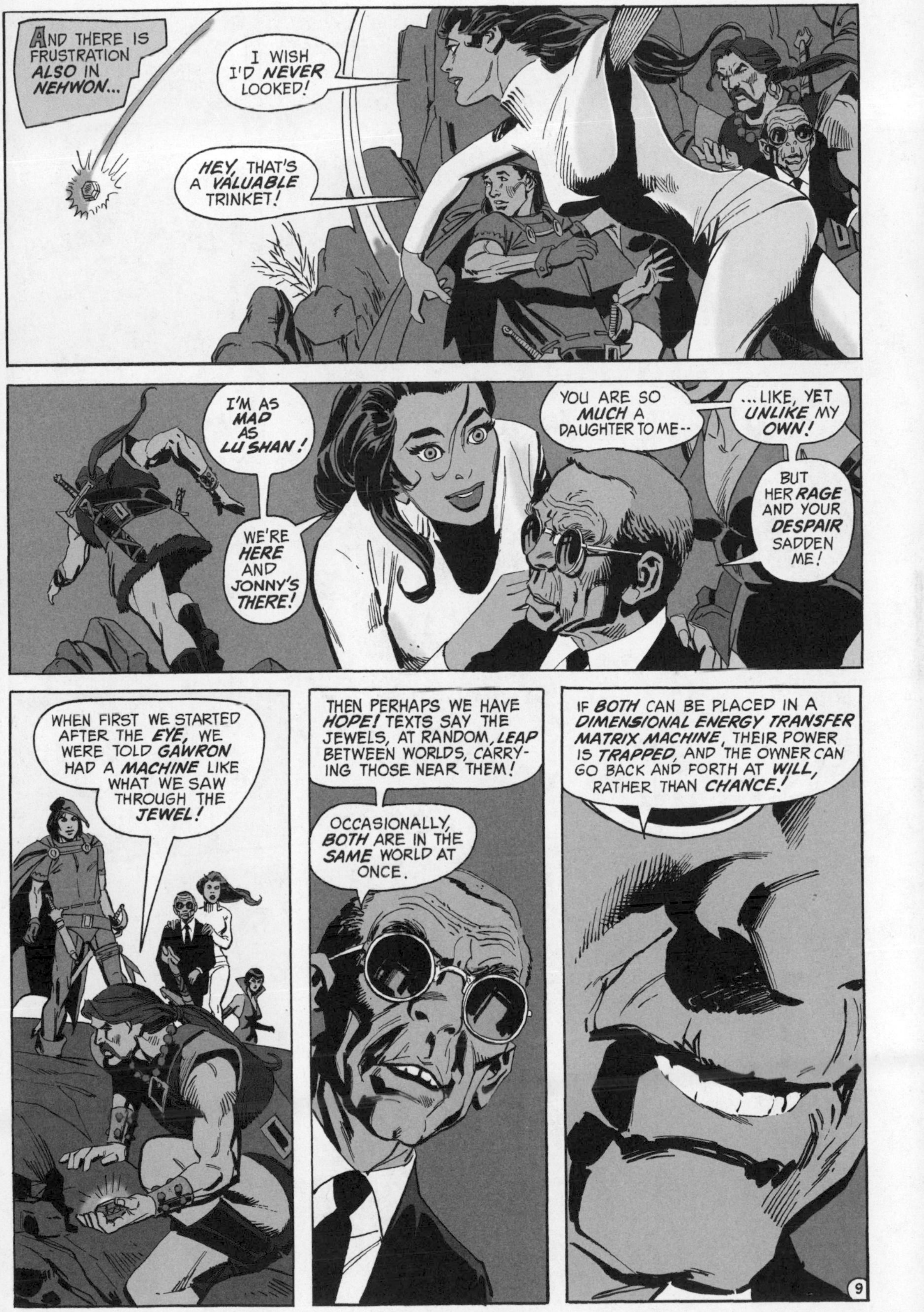
AND THERE IS FRUSTRATION ALSO IN NEHWON...
I WISH I'D NEVER LOOKED!
HEY, THAT'S A VALUABLE TRINKET!
I'M AS MAD AS LU SHAN!
WE'RE HERE AND JONNY'S THERE!
YOU ARE SO MUCH A DAUGHTER TO ME--
...LIKE, YET UNLIKE MY OWN!
BUT HER RAGE AND YOUR DESPAIR SADDEN ME!
WHEN FIRST WE STARTED AFTER THE EYE, WE WERE TOLD GAWRON HAD A MACHINE LIKE WHAT WE SAW THROUGH THE JEWEL!
THEN PERHAPS WE HAVE HOPE! TEXTS SAY THE JEWELS, AT RANDOM, LEAP BETWEEN WORLDS, CARRYING THOSE NEAR THEM!
OCCASIONALLY, BOTH ARE IN THE SAME WORLD AT ONCE.
IF BOTH CAN BE PLACED IN A DIMENSIONAL ENERGY TRANSFER MATRIX MACHINE, THEIR POWER IS TRAPPED, AND THE OWNER CAN GO BACK AND FORTH AT WILL, RATHER THAN CHANCE!
9

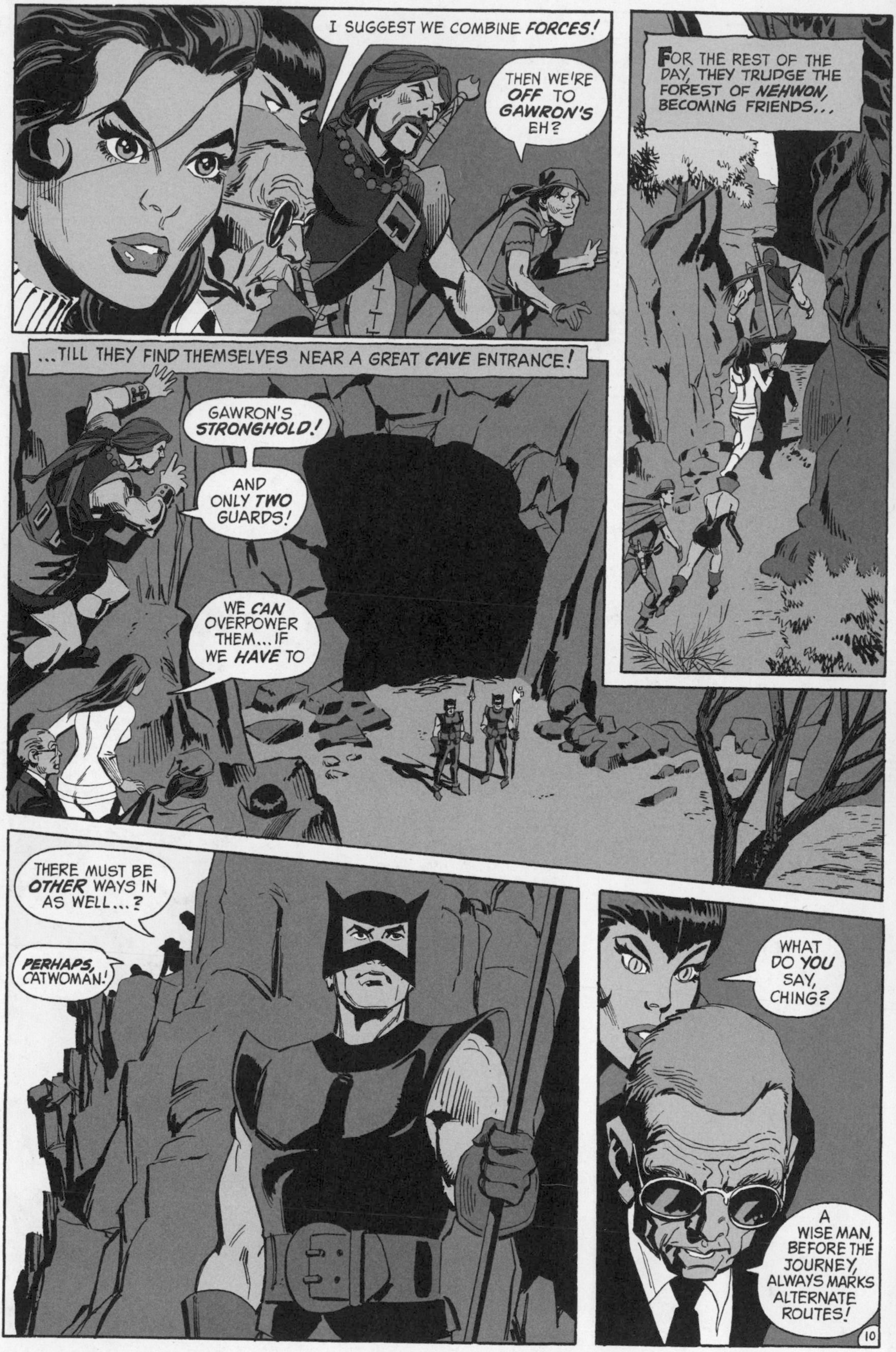

I SUGGEST WE COMBINE FORCES!
THEN WE'RE OFF TO GAWRON'S EH?
FOR THE REST OF THE DAY, THEY TRUDGE THE FOREST OF NEHWON, BECOMING FRIENDS...
...TILL THEY FIND THEMSELVES NEAR A GREAT CAVE ENTRANCE!
GAWRON'S STRONGHOLD!
AND ONLY TWO GUARDS!
WE CAN OVERPOWER THEM...IF WE HAVE TO
THERE MUST BE OTHER WAYS IN AS WELL...?
PERHAPS, CATWOMAN!
WHAT DO YOU SAY, CHING?
A WISE MAN, BEFORE THE JOURNEY, ALWAYS MARKS ALTERNATE ROUTES!
10

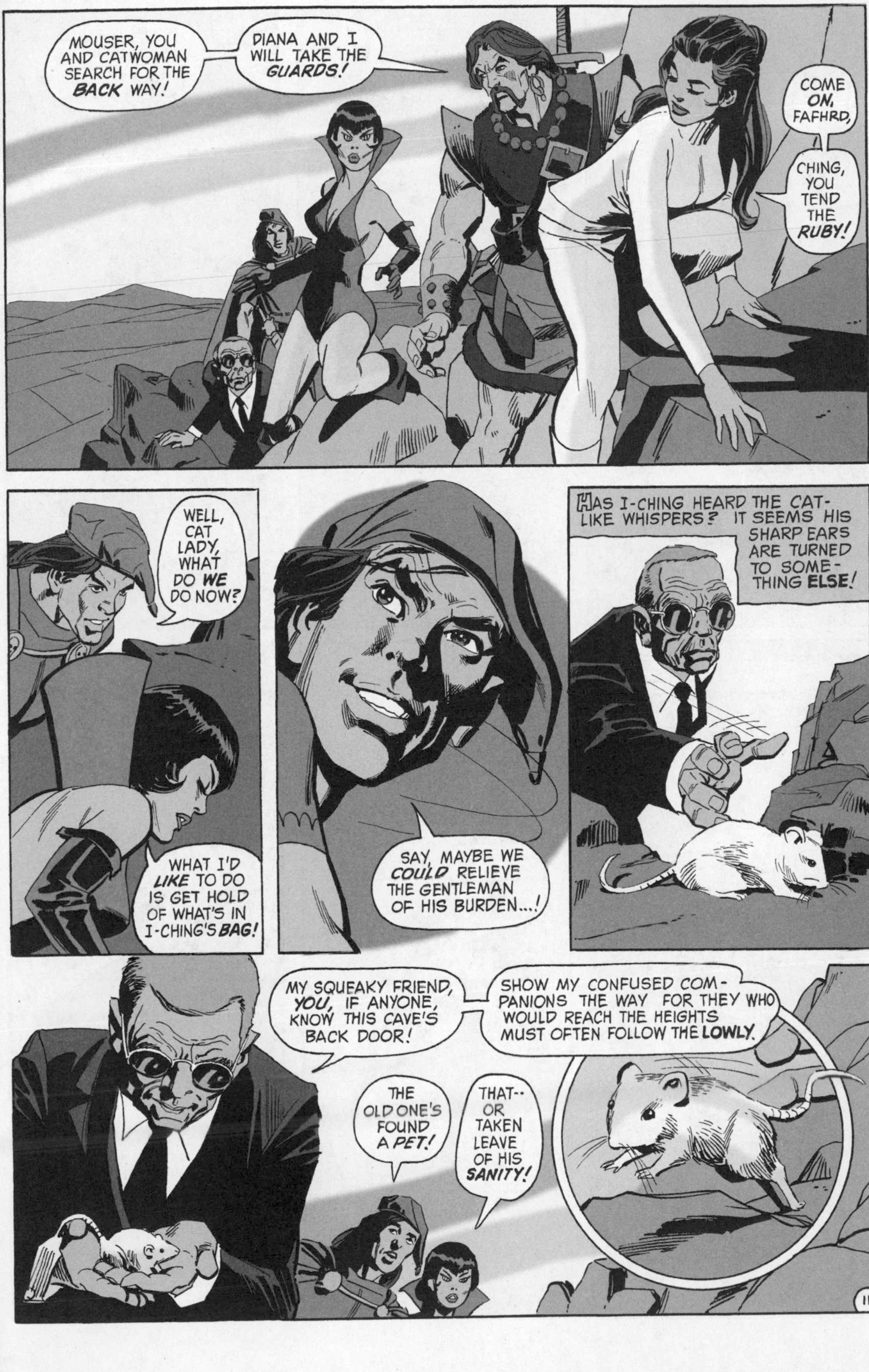
MOUSER, YOU AND CATWOMAN SEARCH FOR THE BACK WAY!
DIANA AND I WILL TAKE THE GUARDS!
COME ON, FAFHRD,
CHING, YOU TEND THE RUBY!
WELL, CAT LADY, WHAT DO WE DO NOW?
WHAT I'D LIKE TO DO IS GET HOLD OF WHAT'S IN I-CHING'S BAG!
SAY, MAYBE WE COULD RELIEVE THE GENTLEMAN OF HIS BURDEN...!
HAS I-CHING HEARD THE CAT-LIKE WHISPERS? IT SEEMS HIS SHARP EARS ARE TURNED TO SOME-THING ELSE!
MY SQUEAKY FRIEND, YOU, IF ANYONE, KNOW THIS CAVE'S BACK DOOR!
SHOW MY CONFUSED COM-PANIONS THE WAY FOR THEY WHO WOULD REACH THE HEIGHTS MUST OFTEN FOLLOW THE LOWLY.
THE OLD ONE'S FOUND A PET!
THAT-- OR TAKEN LEAVE OF HIS SANITY!
11

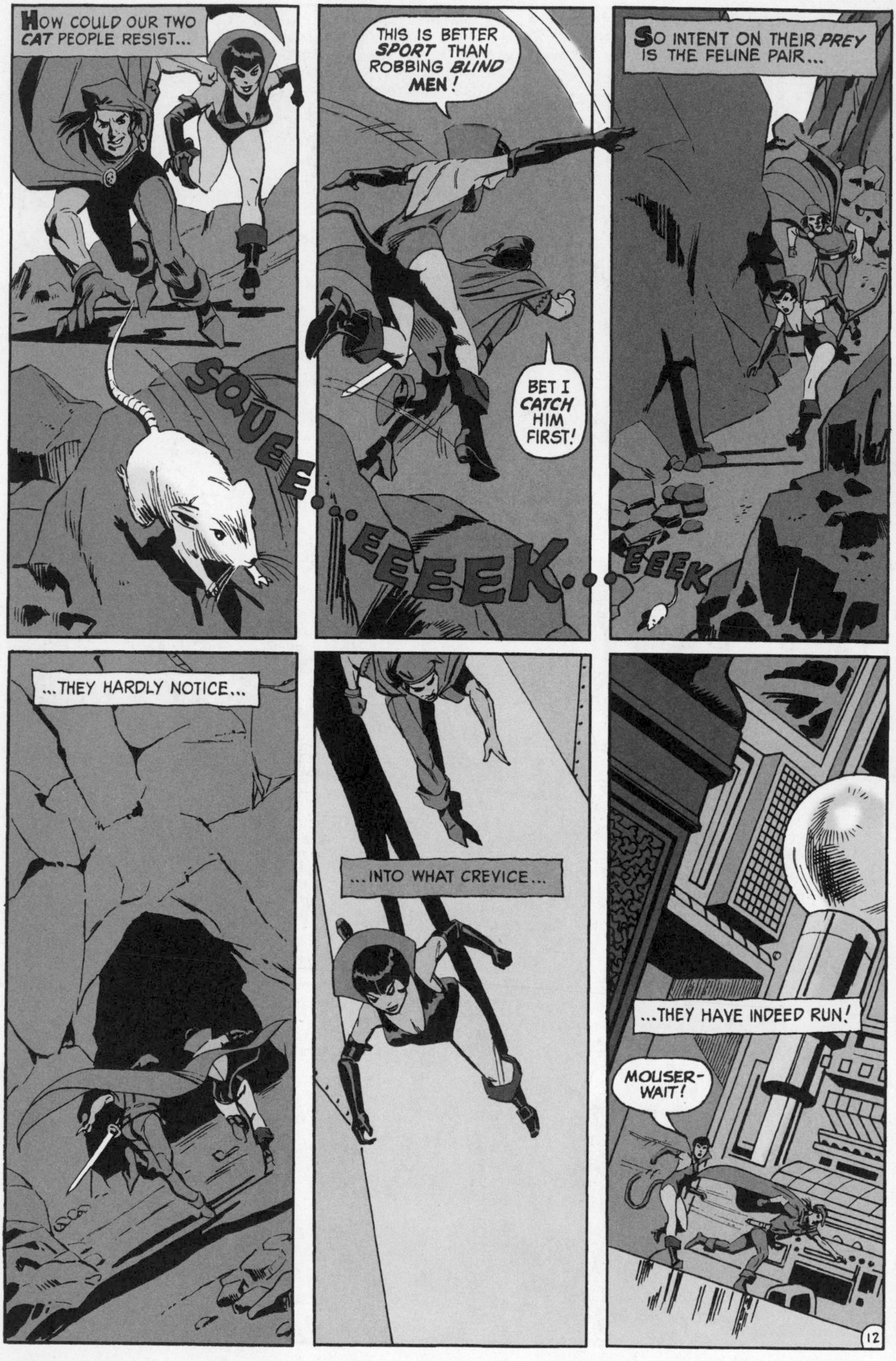
HOW COULD OUR TWO CAT PEOPLE RESIST...
SQUEEE...EEEEK...EEEK
THIS IS BETTER SPORT THAN ROBBING BLIND MEN!
BET I CATCH HIM FIRST!
SO INTENT ON THEIR PREY IS THE FELINE PAIR...
...THEY HARDLY NOTICE...
...INTO WHAT CREVICE...
...THEY HAVE INDEED RUN!
MOUSER-WAIT!
12

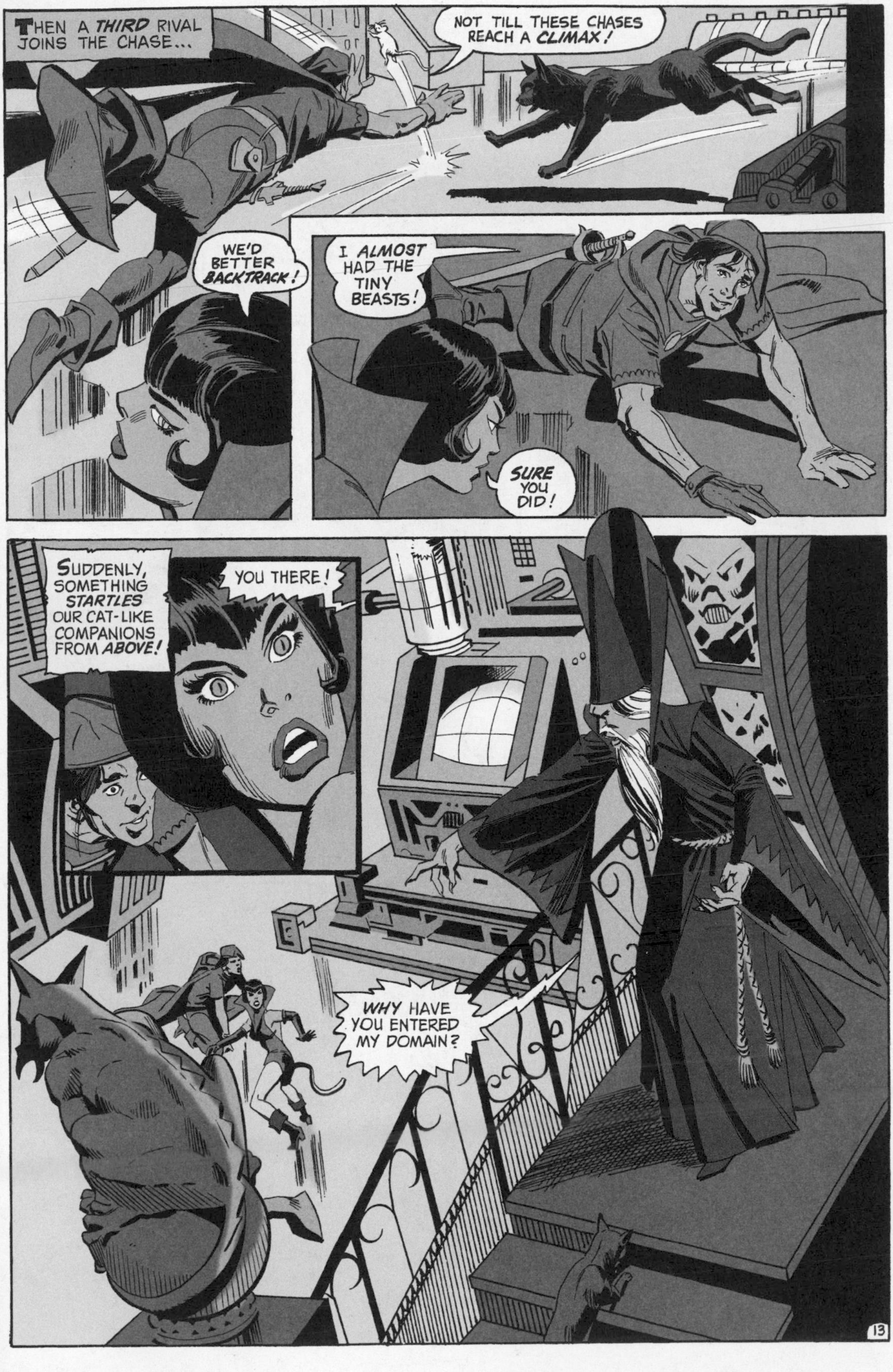
THEN A THIRD RIVAL JOINS THE CHASE...
NOT TILL THESE CHASES REACH A CLIMAX!
WE'D BETTER BACKTRACK!
I ALMOST HAD THE TINY BEASTS!
SURE YOU DID!
SUDDENLY, SOMETHING STARTLES OUR CAT-LIKE COMPANIONS FROM ABOVE!
YOU THERE!
WHY HAVE YOU ENTERED MY DOMAIN?
13

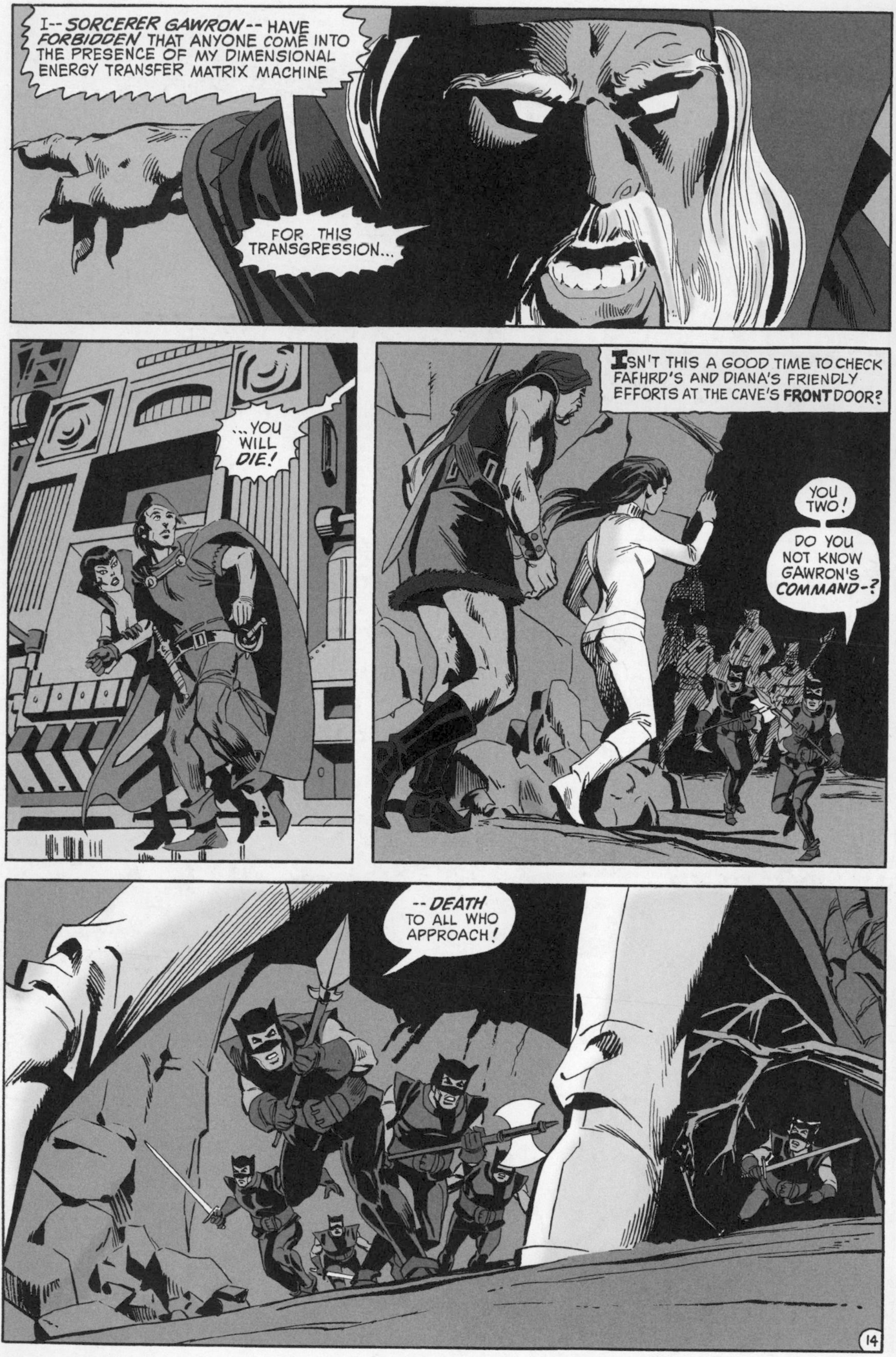
I-- SORCERER GAWRON -- HAVE FORBIDDEN THAT ANYONE COME INTO THE PRESENCE OF MY DIMENSIONAL ENERGY TRANSFER MATRIX MACHINE
FOR THIS TRANSGRESSION...
...YOU WILL DIE!
ISN'T THIS A GOOD TIME TO CHECK FAFHRD'S AND DIANA'S FRIENDLY EFFORTS AT THE CAVE'S FRONT DOOR?
YOU TWO!
DO YOU NOT KNOW GAWRON'S COMMAND-?
-- DEATH TO ALL WHO APPROACH!
14

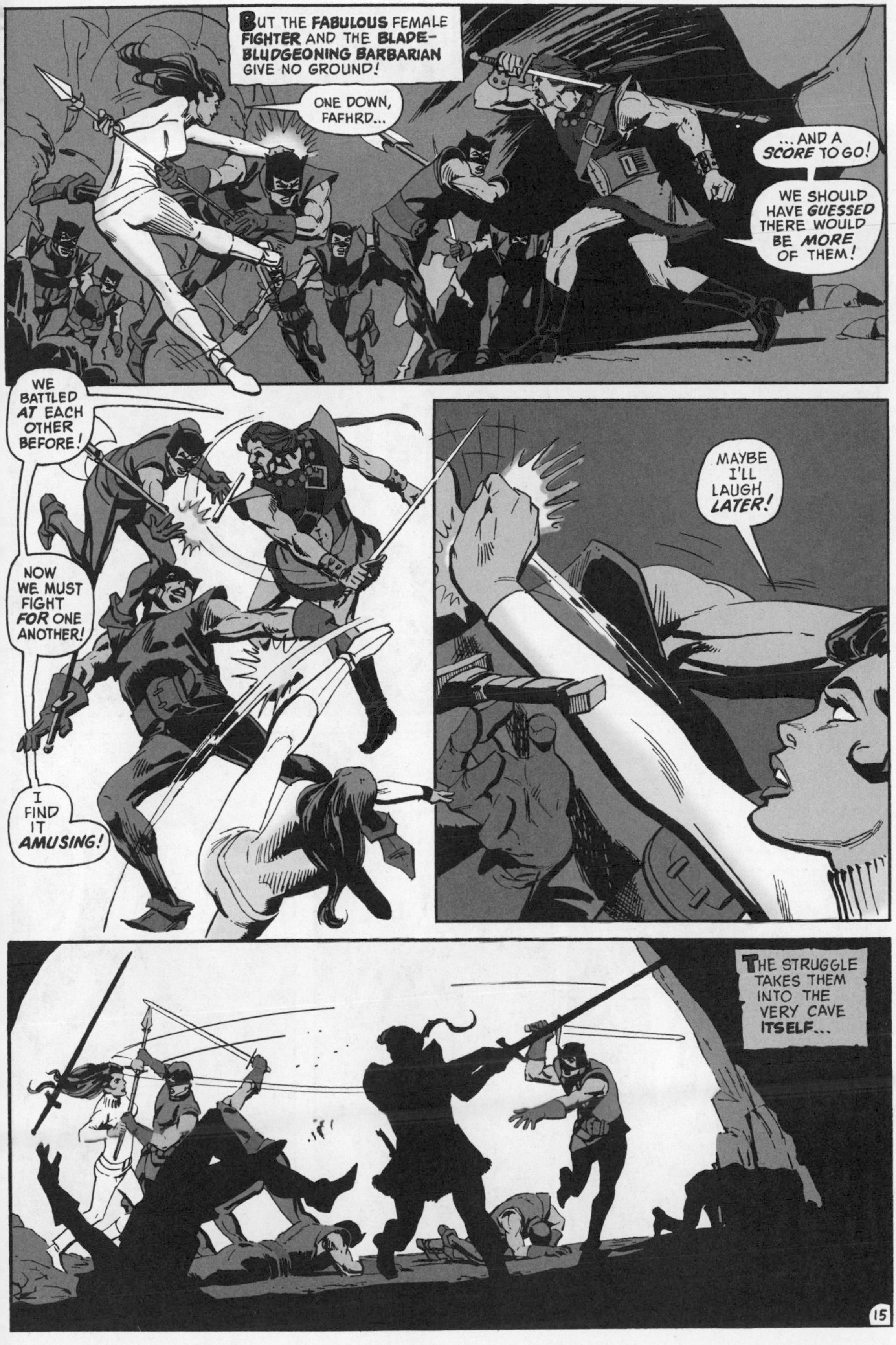
BUT THE FABULOUS FEMALE FIGHTER AND THE BLADE-BLUDGEONING BARBARIAN GIVE NO GROUND!
ONE DOWN, FAFHRD...
...AND A SCORE TO GO!
WE SHOULD HAVE GUESSED THERE WOULD BE MORE OF THEM!
WE BATTLED AT EACH OTHER BEFORE!
NOW WE MUST FIGHT FOR ONE ANOTHER!
I FIND IT AMUSING!
MAYBE I'LL LAUGH LATER!
THE STRUGGLE TAKES THEM INTO THE VERY CAVE ITSELF...
15

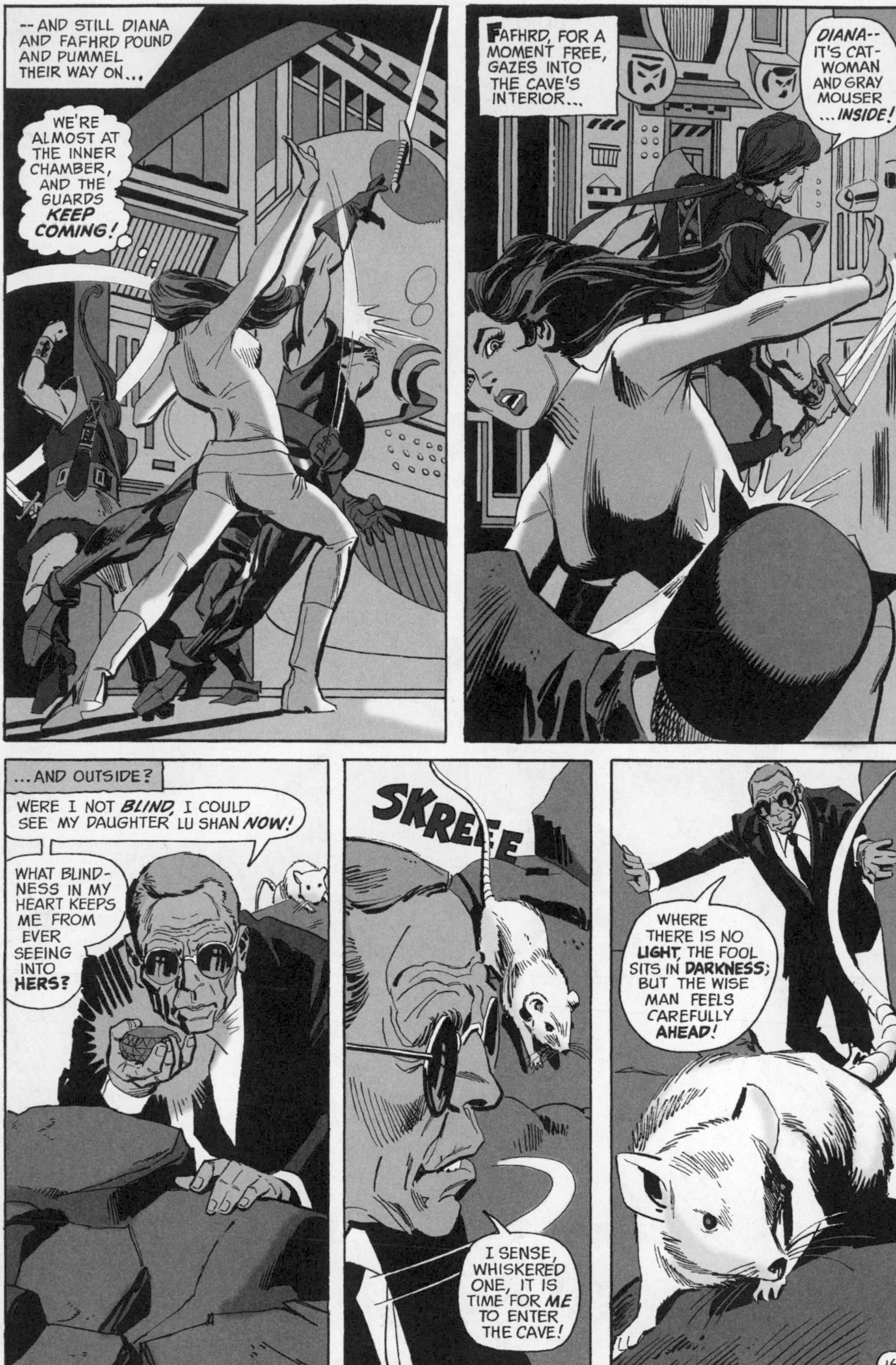
--AND STILL DIANA AND FAFHRD POUND AND PUMMEL THEIR WAY ON...
WE'RE ALMOST AT THE INNER CHAMBER, AND THE GUARDS KEEP COMING!
FAFHRD, FOR A MOMENT FREE, GAZES INTO THE CAVE'S INTERIOR...
DIANA-- IT'S CAT-WOMAN AND GRAY MOUSER ...INSIDE!
...AND OUTSIDE?
WERE I NOT BLIND, I COULD SEE MY DAUGHTER LU SHAN NOW!
WHAT BLINDNESS IN MY HEART KEEPS ME FROM EVER SEEING INTO HERS?
SKREEE
I SENSE, WHISKERED ONE, IT IS TIME FOR ME TO ENTER THE CAVE!
WHERE THERE IS NO LIGHT, THE FOOL SITS IN DARKNESS; BUT THE WISE MAN FEELS CAREFULLY AHEAD!
16

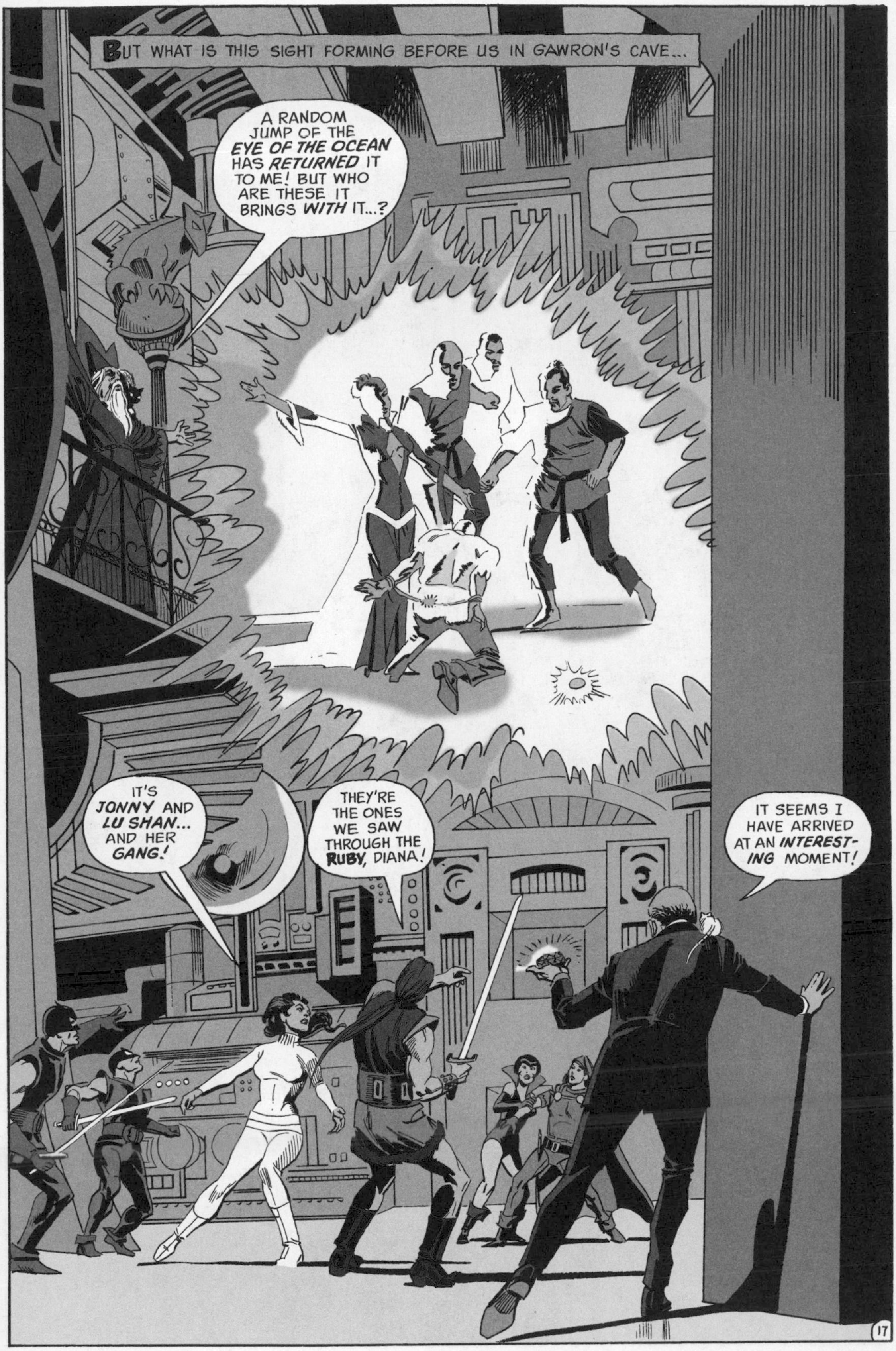
BUT WHAT IS THIS SIGHT FORMING BEFORE US IN GAWRON'S CAVE...
A RANDOM JUMP OF THE EYE OF THE OCEAN HAS RETURNED IT TO ME! BUT WHO ARE THESE IT BRINGS WITH IT...?
IT'S JONNY AND LU SHAN... AND HER GANG!
THEY'RE THE ONES WE SAW THROUGH THE RUBY, DIANA!
IT SEEMS I HAVE ARRIVED AT AN INTERESTING MOMENT!
17

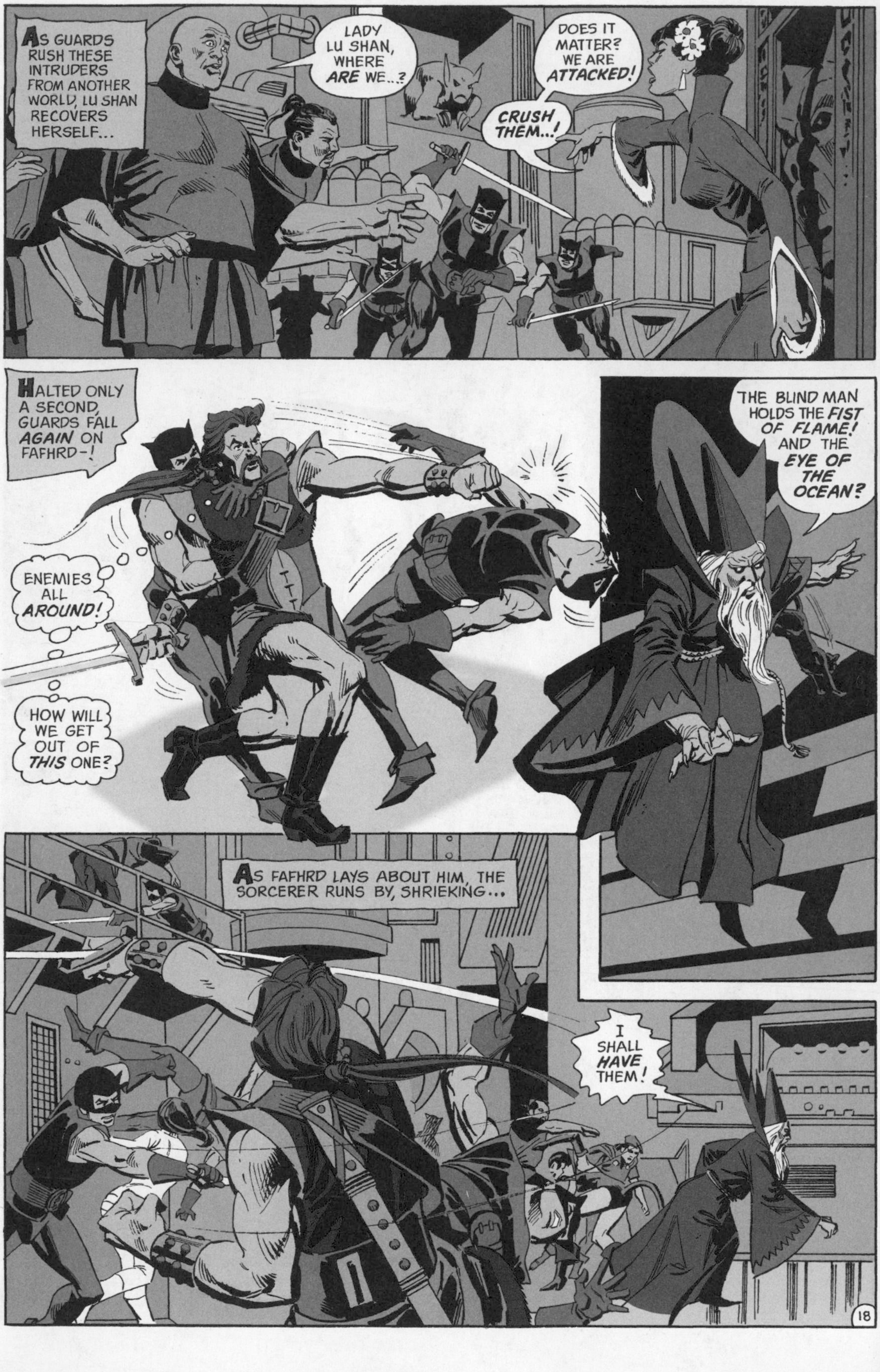
AS GUARDS RUSH THESE INTRUDERS FROM ANOTHER WORLD, LU SHAN RECOVERS HERSELF...
LADY LU SHAN, WHERE ARE WE...?
DOES IT MATTER? WE ARE ATTACKED!
CRUSH THEM...!
HALTED ONLY A SECOND, GUARDS FALL AGAIN ON FAFHRD-!
ENEMIES ALL AROUND!
HOW WILL WE GET OUT OF THIS ONE?
THE BLIND MAN HOLDS THE FIST OF FLAME! AND THE EYE OF THE OCEAN?
AS FAFHRD LAYS ABOUT HIM, THE SORCERER RUNS BY, SHRIEKING...
I SHALL HAVE THEM!
18

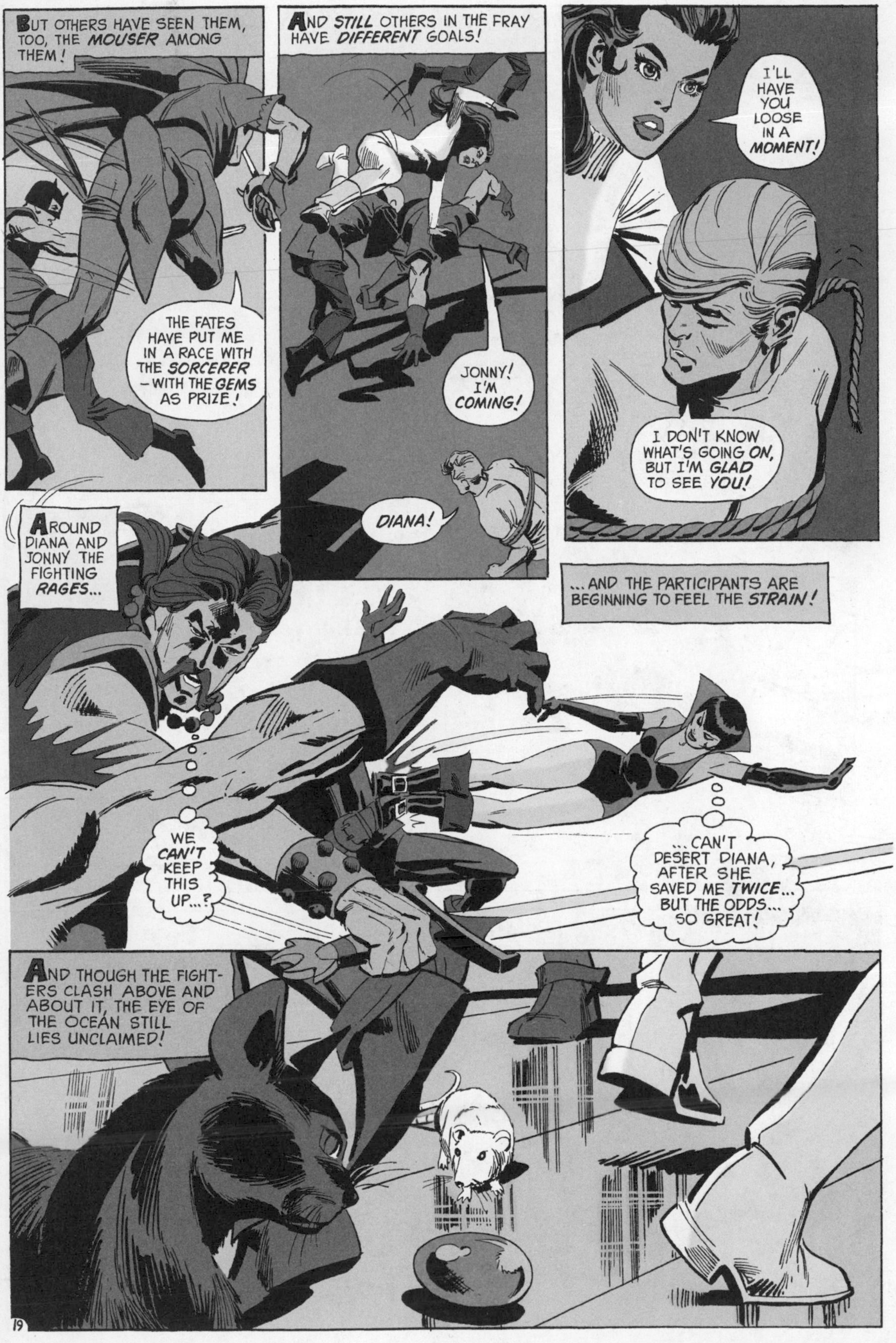
BUT OTHERS HAVE SEEN THEM, TOO, THE MOUSER AMONG THEM!
THE FATES HAVE PUT ME IN A RACE WITH THE SORCERER —WITH THE GEMS AS PRIZE!
AND STILL OTHERS IN THE FRAY HAVE DIFFERENT GOALS!
JONNY! I'M COMING!
DIANA!
I'LL HAVE YOU LOOSE IN A MOMENT!
I DON'T KNOW WHAT'S GOING ON, BUT I'M GLAD TO SEE YOU!
AROUND DIANA AND JONNY THE FIGHTING RAGES...
...AND THE PARTICIPANTS ARE BEGINNING TO FEEL THE STRAIN!
WE CAN'T KEEP THIS UP...?
...CAN'T DESERT DIANA, AFTER SHE SAVED ME TWICE... BUT THE ODDS... SO GREAT!
AND THOUGH THE FIGHTERS CLASH ABOVE AND ABOUT IT, THE EYE OF THE OCEAN STILL LIES UNCLAIMED!
19

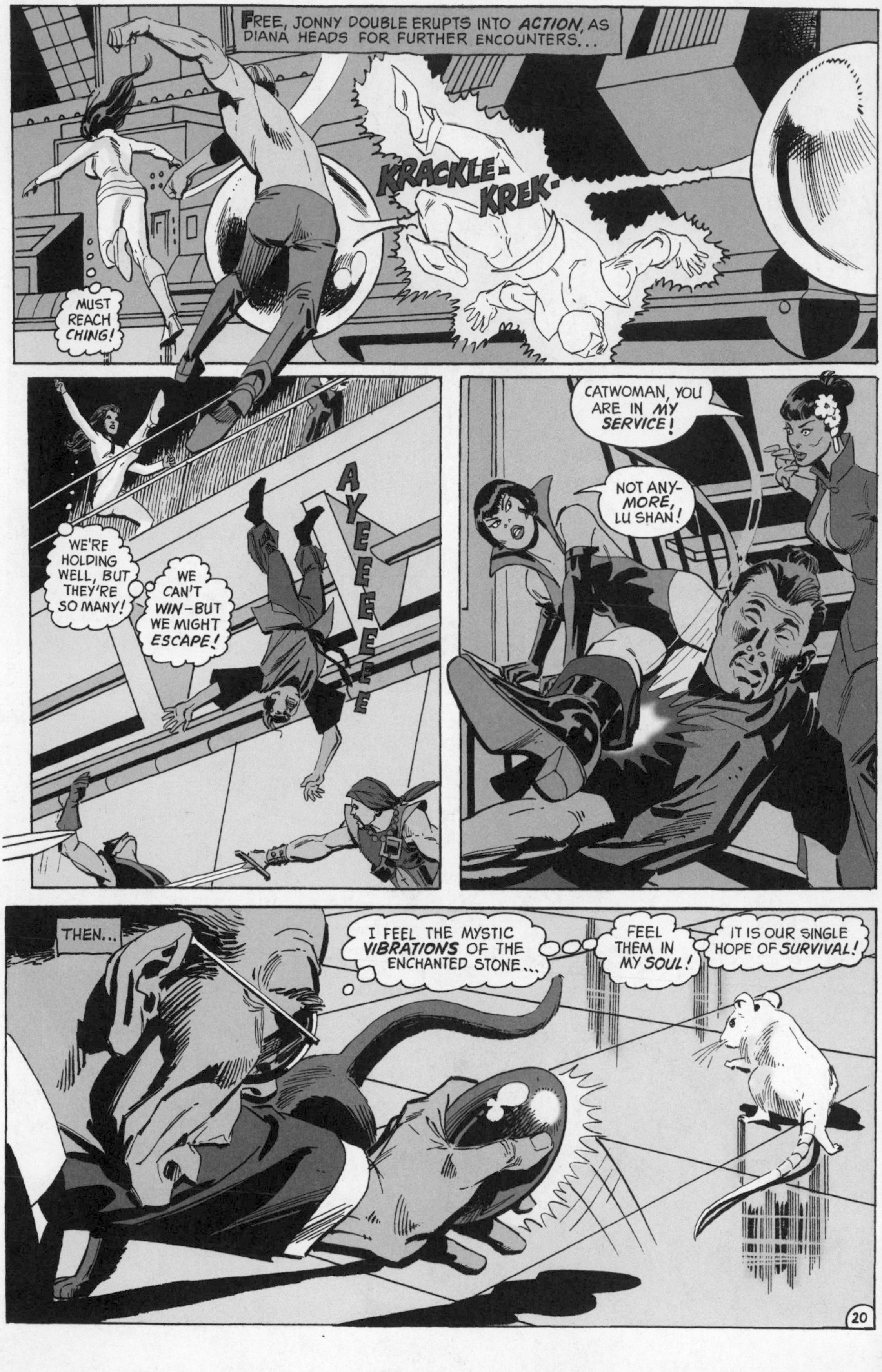
FREE, JONNY DOUBLE ERUPTS INTO ACTION, AS DIANA HEADS FOR FURTHER ENCOUNTERS...
KRACKLE-KREK-
MUST REACH CHING!
WE'RE HOLDING WELL, BUT THEY'RE SO MANY!
WE CAN'T WIN-BUT WE MIGHT ESCAPE!
AYEEEEEE
CATWOMAN, YOU ARE IN MY SERVICE!
NOT ANY-MORE, LU SHAN!
THEN...
I FEEL THE MYSTIC VIBRATIONS OF THE ENCHANTED STONE...
FEEL THEM IN MY SOUL!
IT IS OUR SINGLE HOPE OF SURVIVAL!
20

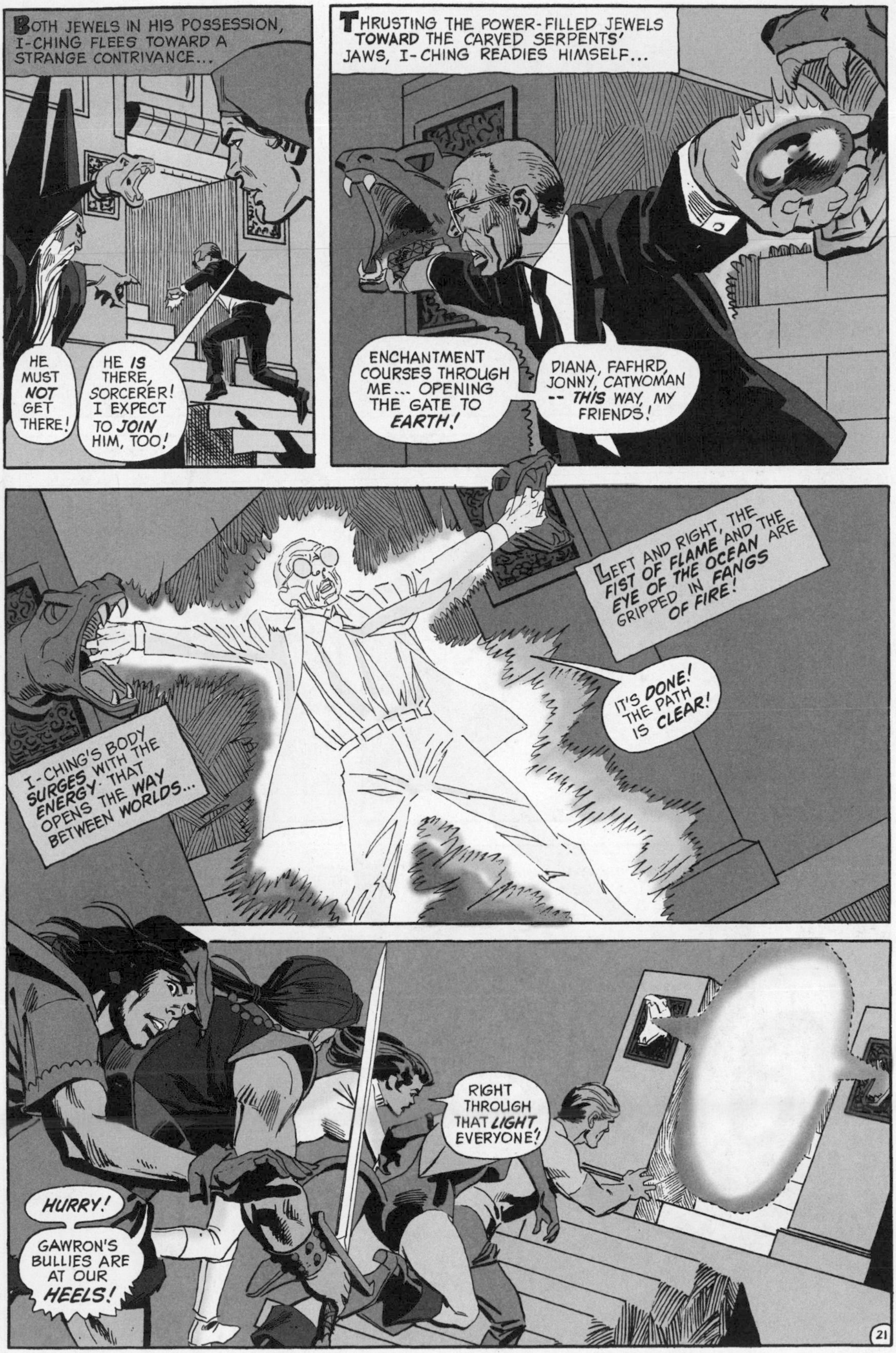
BOTH JEWELS IN HIS POSSESSION, I-CHING FLEES TOWARD A STRANGE CONTRIVANCE...
HE MUST NOT GET THERE!
HE IS THERE, SORCERER! I EXPECT TO JOIN HIM, TOO!
THRUSTING THE POWER-FILLED JEWELS TOWARD THE CARVED SERPENTS' JAWS, I-CHING READIES HIMSELF...
ENCHANTMENT COURSES THROUGH ME... OPENING THE GATE TO EARTH!
DIANA, FAFHRD, JONNY, CATWOMAN -- THIS WAY, MY FRIENDS!
LEFT AND RIGHT, THE FIST OF FLAME AND THE EYE OF THE OCEAN ARE GRIPPED IN FANGS OF FIRE!
IT'S DONE! THE PATH IS CLEAR!
I-CHING'S BODY SURGES WITH THE ENERGY THAT OPENS THE WAY BETWEEN WORLDS...
RIGHT THROUGH THAT LIGHT, EVERYONE!
HURRY!
GAWRON'S BULLIES ARE AT OUR HEELS!
21

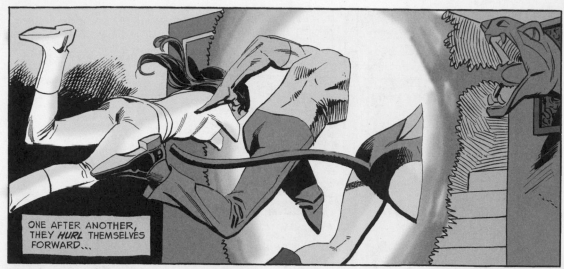

ONE AFTER ANOTHER, THEY *HURL* THEMSELVES FORWARD...

I'M *LAST* --AS *USUAL!* 'TIS THE PRICE I PAY FOR BEING *POLITE!*

...ALMOST AS AN **AFTERTHOUGHT**...

I THINK I'LL JUST TAKE *THIS* ALONG WITH ME!

ONE JEWEL GONE, THE CURRENT IS CUT AND THE GATE IS GONE, PERHAPS *FOREVER!*

THEY'VE STOLEN MY *GEM* AND ESCAPED MY *TRAP!*

...WHILE *I* AM *TRAPPED* HERE!

22

100

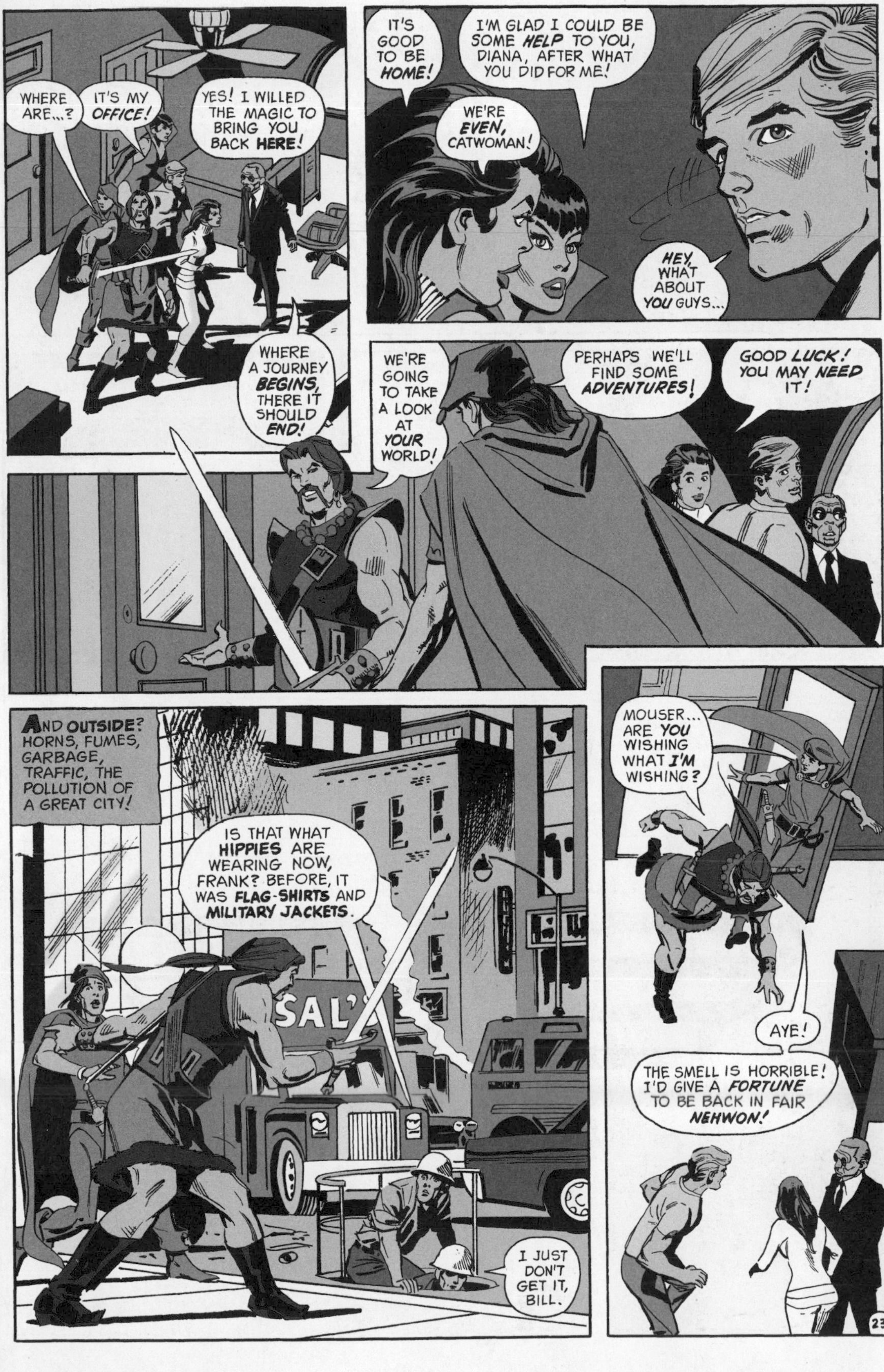
WHERE ARE...?
IT'S MY OFFICE!
YES! I WILLED THE MAGIC TO BRING YOU BACK HERE!
WHERE A JOURNEY BEGINS, THERE IT SHOULD END!
IT'S GOOD TO BE HOME!
I'M GLAD I COULD BE SOME HELP TO YOU, DIANA, AFTER WHAT YOU DID FOR ME!
WE'RE EVEN, CATWOMAN!
HEY, WHAT ABOUT YOU GUYS...
WE'RE GOING TO TAKE A LOOK AT YOUR WORLD!
PERHAPS WE'LL FIND SOME ADVENTURES!
GOOD LUCK! YOU MAY NEED IT!
AND OUTSIDE? HORNS, FUMES, GARBAGE, TRAFFIC, THE POLLUTION OF A GREAT CITY!
IS THAT WHAT HIPPIES ARE WEARING NOW, FRANK? BEFORE, IT WAS FLAG-SHIRTS AND MILITARY JACKETS.
SAL'S
I JUST DON'T GET IT, BILL.
MOUSER... ARE YOU WISHING WHAT I'M WISHING?
AYE!
THE SMELL IS HORRIBLE! I'D GIVE A FORTUNE TO BE BACK IN FAIR NEHWON!
23

ALMOST IN ANSWER, THE TWO DISPLACED SWORDSMEN ARE ENCASED IN A MYSTIC GLIMMER FROM THE JEWEL THE MOUSER STILL HOLDS...

THEY'RE VANISHING...

GONE! ANOTHER RANDOM JUMP OF THE JEWELS MUST HAVE CARRIED THEM BACK TO THEIR OWN WORLD!

THIS APPEARING AND DISAPPEARING--! MAKES ME WONDER IF IT ALL REALLY HAPPENED!

OUR UNDERSTANDING IS SMALL... AND THE UNIVERSE LARGE!

COME...

...I SENSE ADVENTURE AHEAD -- A KIND THAT IS A BIT MORE DOWN TO THE EARTH WE KNOW!

24   THE END.

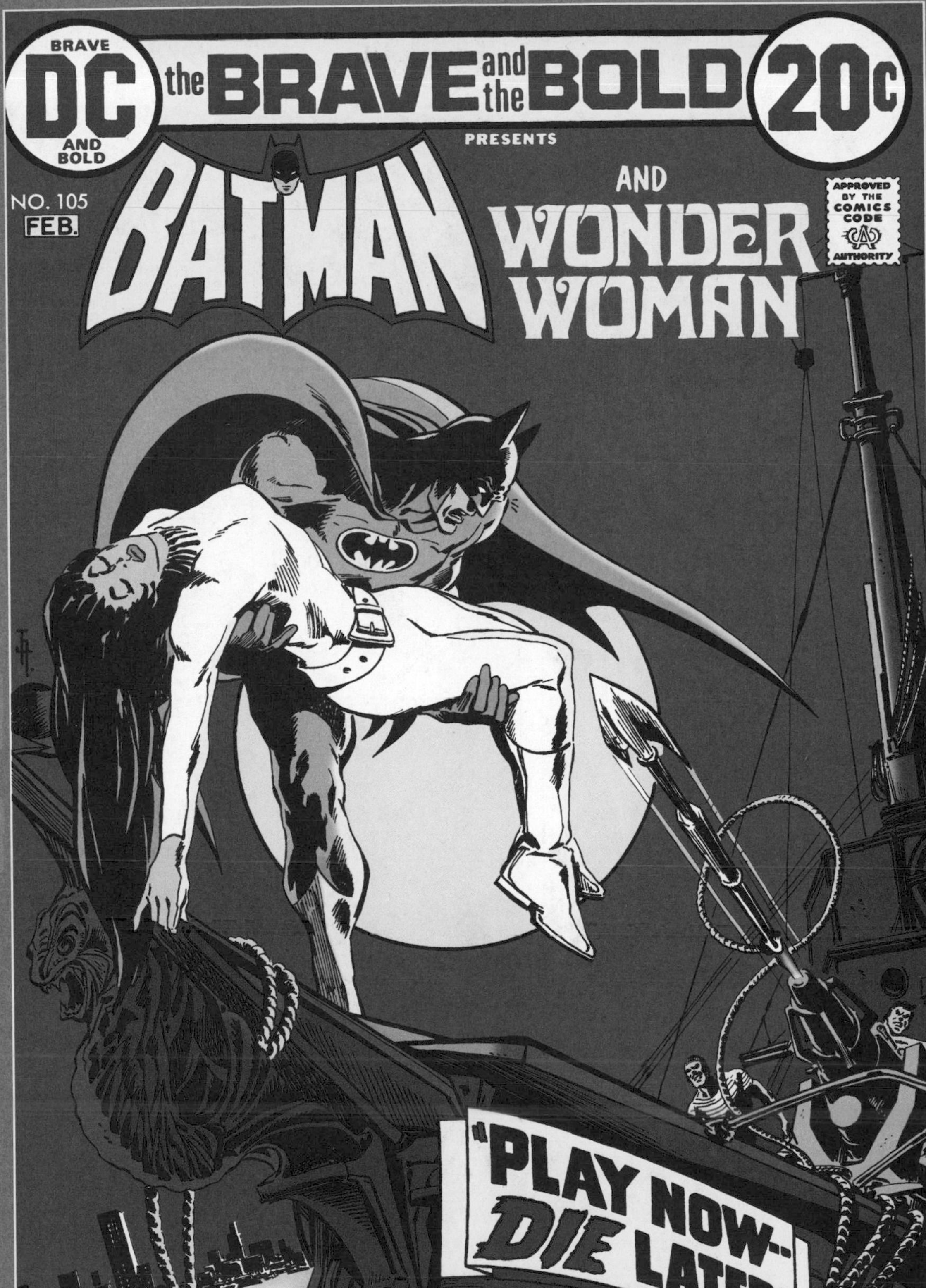
BRAVE DC AND BOLD
the BRAVE and the BOLD
20c
PRESENTS
BATMAN
AND
WONDER WOMAN
NO. 105
FEB.
APPROVED BY THE COMICS CODE AUTHORITY
"PLAY NOW-- DIE LATER"

The Brave and the Bold 105 Cover by Jim Aparo

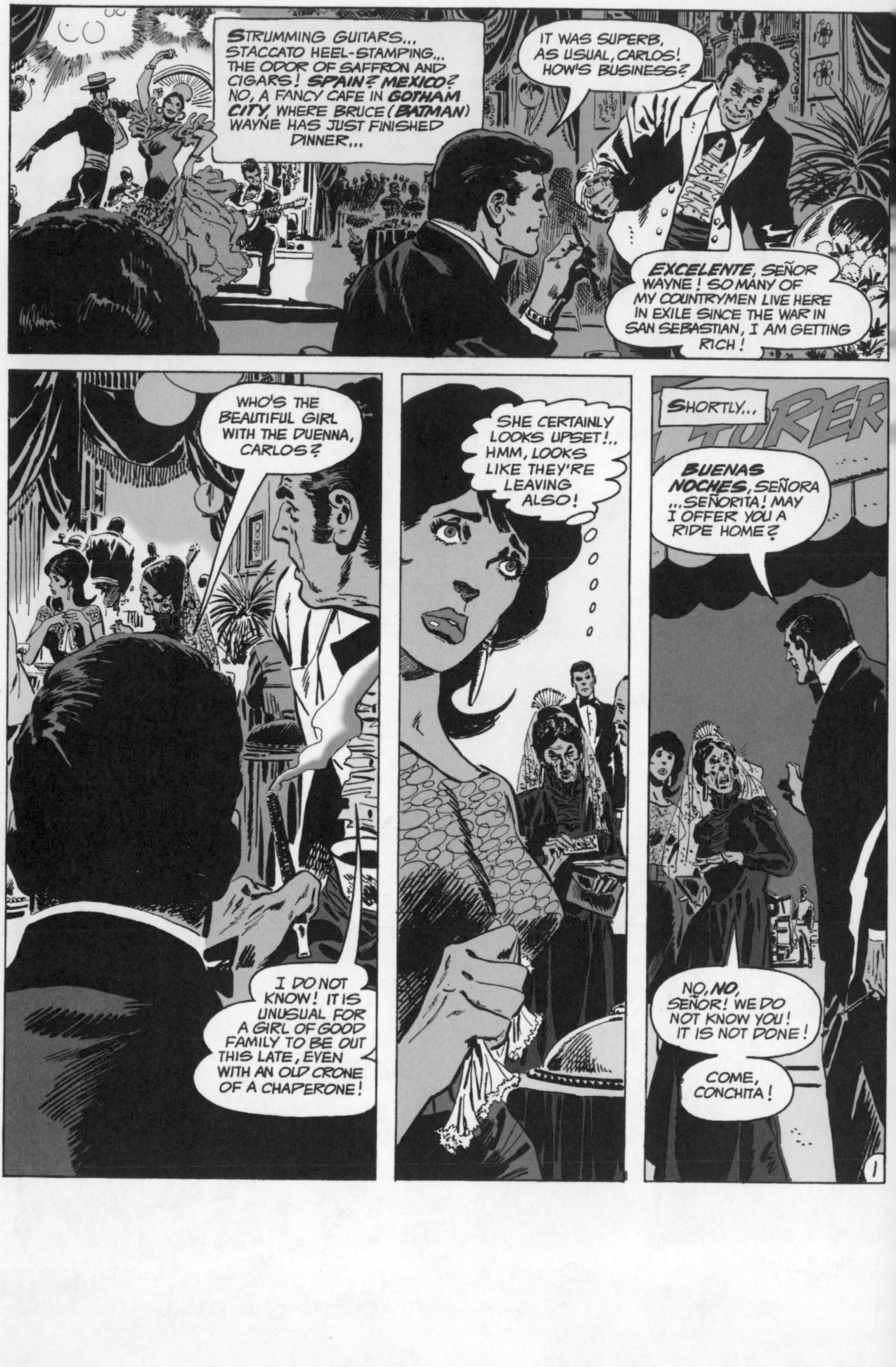
STRUMMING GUITARS... STACCATO HEEL-STAMPING... THE ODOR OF SAFFRON AND CIGARS! SPAIN? MEXICO? NO, A FANCY CAFE IN GOTHAM CITY, WHERE BRUCE (BATMAN) WAYNE HAS JUST FINISHED DINNER...
IT WAS SUPERB, AS USUAL, CARLOS! HOW'S BUSINESS?
EXCELENTE, SEÑOR WAYNE! SO MANY OF MY COUNTRYMEN LIVE HERE IN EXILE SINCE THE WAR IN SAN SEBASTIAN, I AM GETTING RICH!
WHO'S THE BEAUTIFUL GIRL WITH THE DUENNA, CARLOS?
I DO NOT KNOW! IT IS UNUSUAL FOR A GIRL OF GOOD FAMILY TO BE OUT THIS LATE, EVEN WITH AN OLD CRONE OF A CHAPERONE!
SHE CERTAINLY LOOKS UPSET!.. HMM, LOOKS LIKE THEY'RE LEAVING ALSO!
SHORTLY...
BUENAS NOCHES, SEÑORA ...SEÑORITA! MAY I OFFER YOU A RIDE HOME?
NO, NO, SEÑOR! WE DO NOT KNOW YOU! IT IS NOT DONE!
COME, CONCHITA!
1

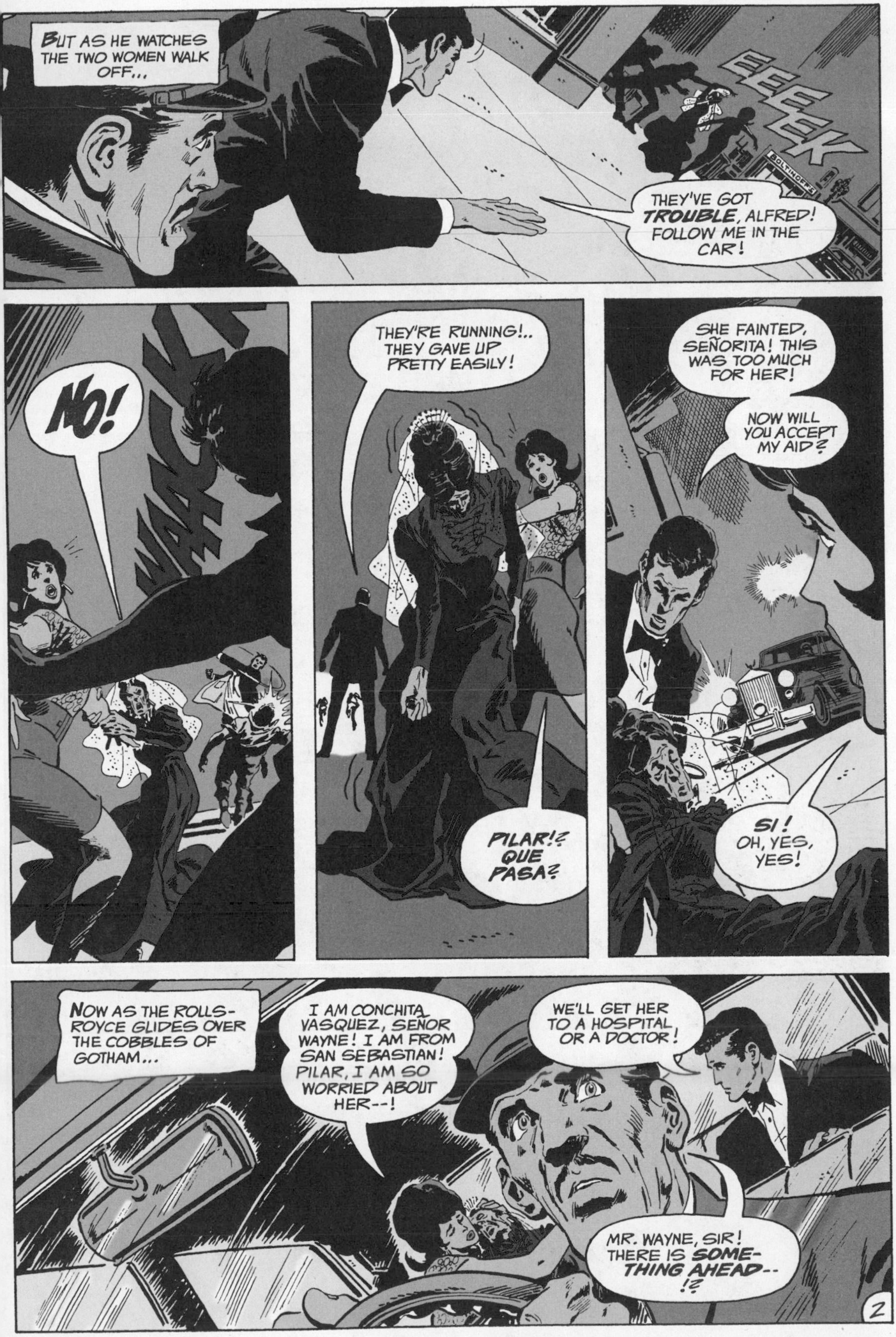
BUT AS HE WATCHES THE TWO WOMEN WALK OFF...
EEEEK
BOLTINOFF'S
THEY'VE GOT TROUBLE, ALFRED! FOLLOW ME IN THE CAR!
NO!
THEY'RE RUNNING!.. THEY GAVE UP PRETTY EASILY!
PILAR!? QUE PASA?
SHE FAINTED, SEÑORITA! THIS WAS TOO MUCH FOR HER!
NOW WILL YOU ACCEPT MY AID?
SI! OH, YES, YES!
NOW AS THE ROLLS-ROYCE GLIDES OVER THE COBBLES OF GOTHAM...
I AM CONCHITA VASQUEZ, SEÑOR WAYNE! I AM FROM SAN SEBASTIAN! PILAR, I AM SO WORRIED ABOUT HER--!
WE'LL GET HER TO A HOSPITAL OR A DOCTOR!
MR. WAYNE, SIR! THERE IS SOMETHING AHEAD--!?
2

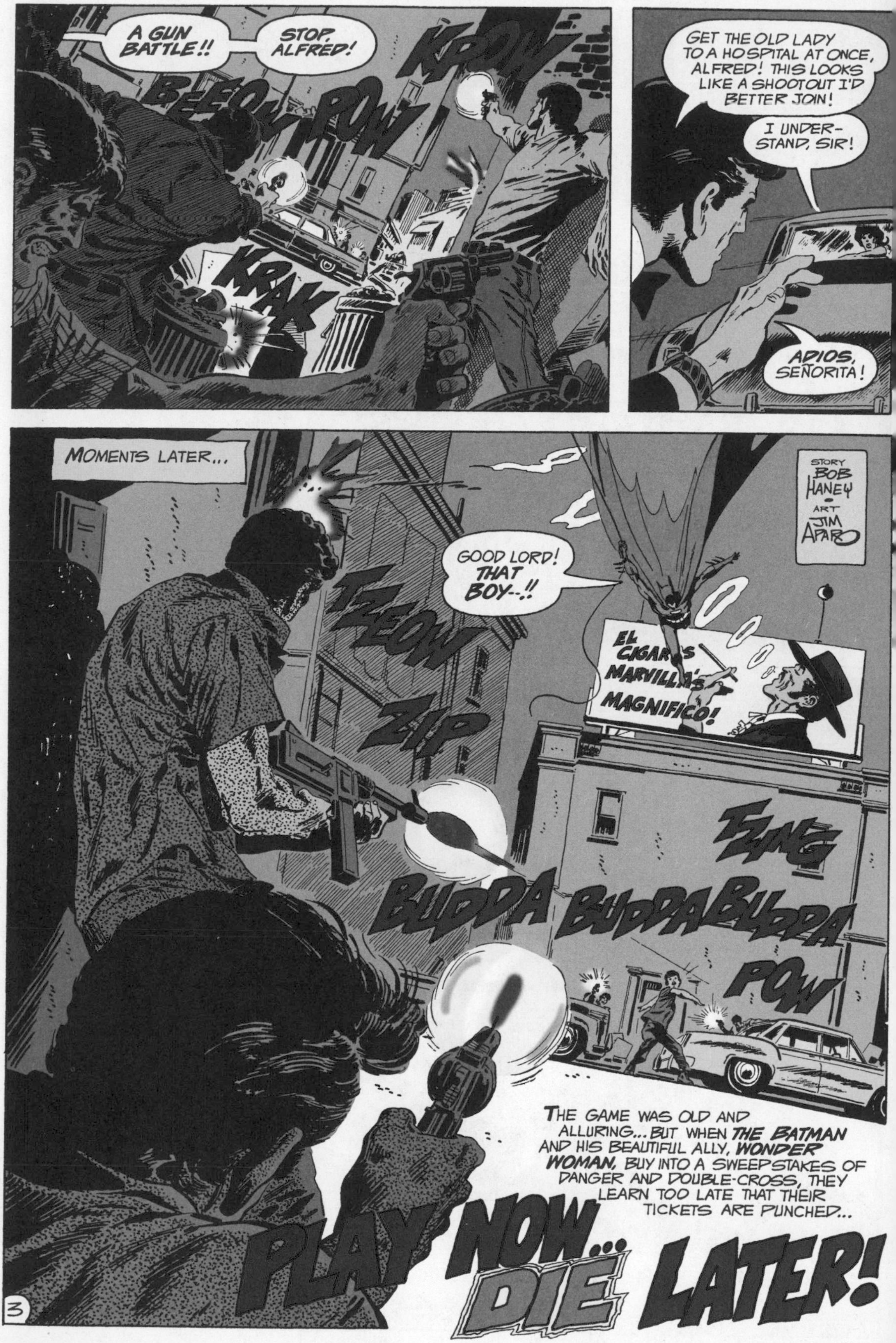
A GUN BATTLE!!
STOP, ALFRED!
KPOW
BEEOW
POW
KRAK
GET THE OLD LADY TO A HOSPITAL AT ONCE, ALFRED! THIS LOOKS LIKE A SHOOTOUT I'D BETTER JOIN!
I UNDERSTAND, SIR!
ADIOS, SEÑORITA!
MOMENTS LATER...
STORY BOB HANEY • ART JIM APARO
GOOD LORD! THAT BOY--!!
EL CIGARROS MARVILLAS MAGNIFICO!
TZEOW
ZIP
TZING
BUDDA BUDDABUDDA
POW
THE GAME WAS OLD AND ALLURING... BUT WHEN THE BATMAN AND HIS BEAUTIFUL ALLY, WONDER WOMAN, BUY INTO A SWEEPSTAKES OF DANGER AND DOUBLE-CROSS, THEY LEARN TOO LATE THAT THEIR TICKETS ARE PUNCHED...
PLAY NOW... DIE LATER!
3

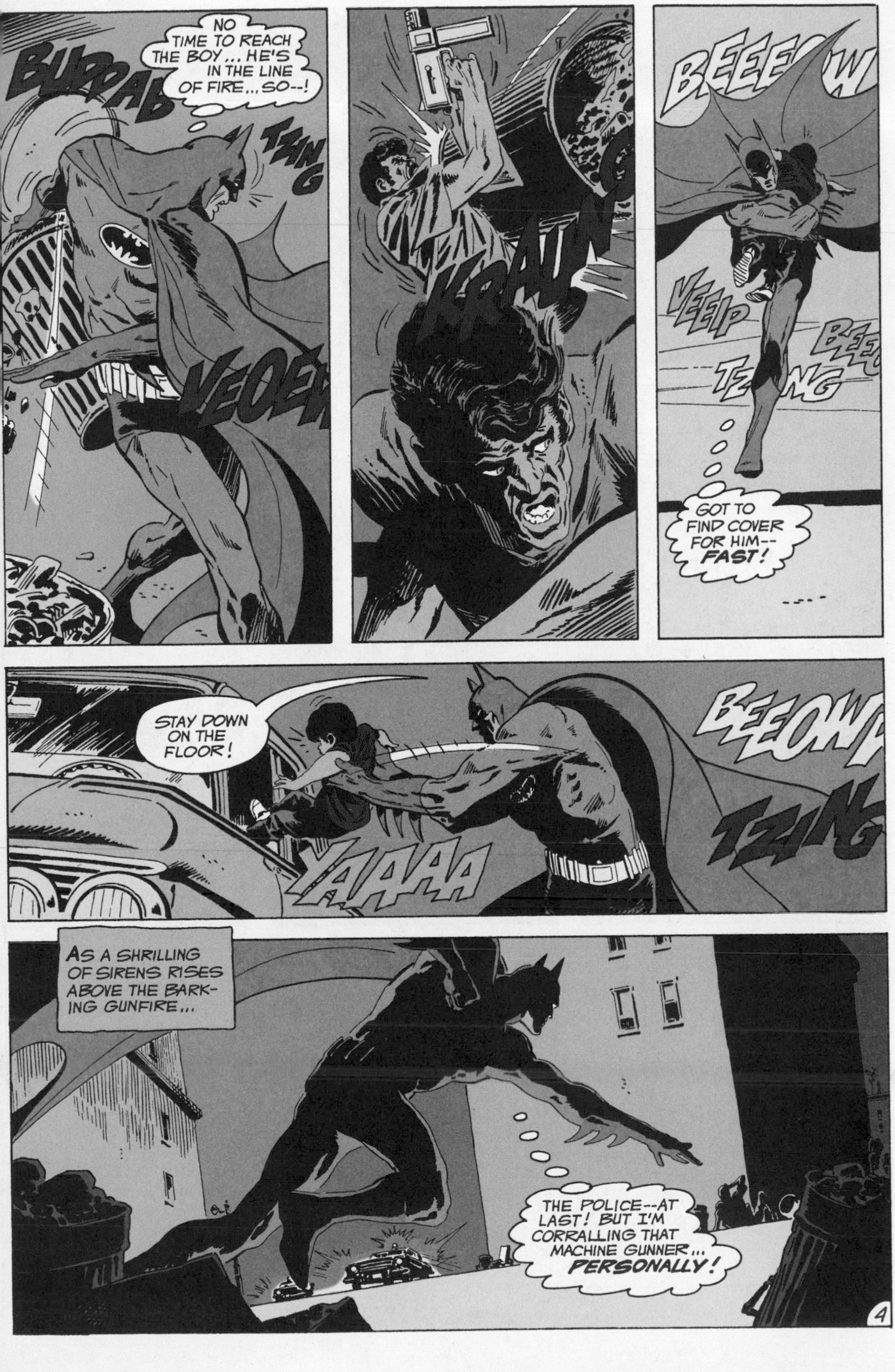
BUDDAB
NO TIME TO REACH THE BOY... HE'S IN THE LINE OF FIRE... SO--!
TZING
VEOEW
KRAUNG
BEEEOW
VEEIP
BEEO
TZING
GOT TO FIND COVER FOR HIM-- FAST!
STAY DOWN ON THE FLOOR!
BEEOW
TZING
YAAAA
AS A SHRILLING OF SIRENS RISES ABOVE THE BARKING GUNFIRE...
THE POLICE--AT LAST! BUT I'M CORRALLING THAT MACHINE GUNNER... PERSONALLY!
4

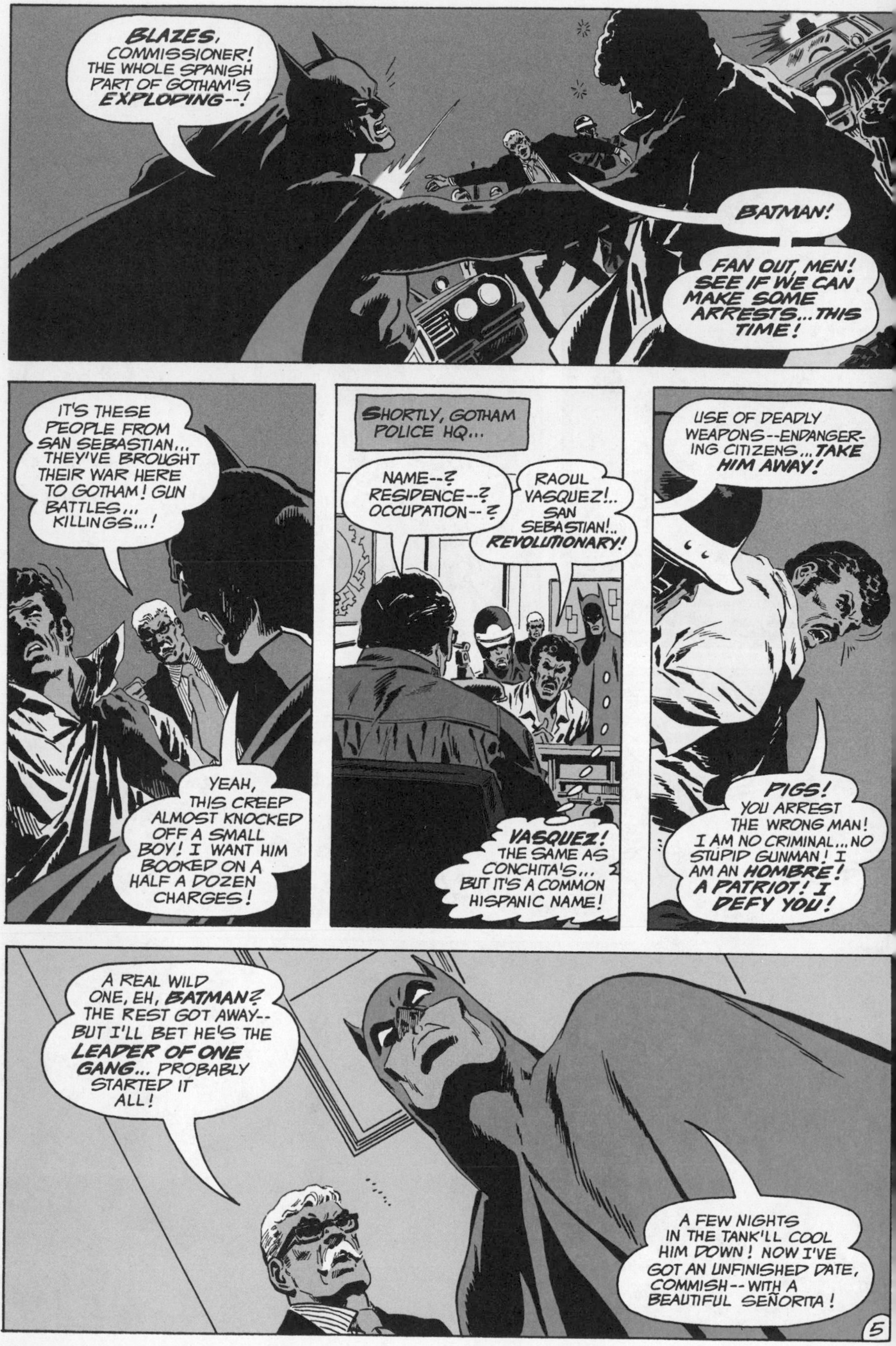
BLAZES, COMMISSIONER! THE WHOLE SPANISH PART OF GOTHAM'S EXPLODING--!
BATMAN!
FAN OUT, MEN! SEE IF WE CAN MAKE SOME ARRESTS...THIS TIME!
IT'S THESE PEOPLE FROM SAN SEBASTIAN... THEY'VE BROUGHT THEIR WAR HERE TO GOTHAM! GUN BATTLES... KILLINGS...!
YEAH, THIS CREEP ALMOST KNOCKED OFF A SMALL BOY! I WANT HIM BOOKED ON A HALF A DOZEN CHARGES!
SHORTLY, GOTHAM POLICE HQ...
NAME--? RESIDENCE--? OCCUPATION--?
RAOUL VASQUEZ!.. SAN SEBASTIAN!.. REVOLUTIONARY!
VASQUEZ! THE SAME AS CONCHITA'S... BUT IT'S A COMMON HISPANIC NAME!
USE OF DEADLY WEAPONS--ENDANGERING CITIZENS...TAKE HIM AWAY!
PIGS! YOU ARREST THE WRONG MAN! I AM NO CRIMINAL...NO STUPID GUNMAN! I AM AN HOMBRE! A PATRIOT! I DEFY YOU!
A REAL WILD ONE, EH, BATMAN? THE REST GOT AWAY-- BUT I'LL BET HE'S THE LEADER OF ONE GANG... PROBABLY STARTED IT ALL!
A FEW NIGHTS IN THE TANK'LL COOL HIM DOWN! NOW I'VE GOT AN UNFINISHED DATE, COMMISH--WITH A BEAUTIFUL SEÑORITA!
5

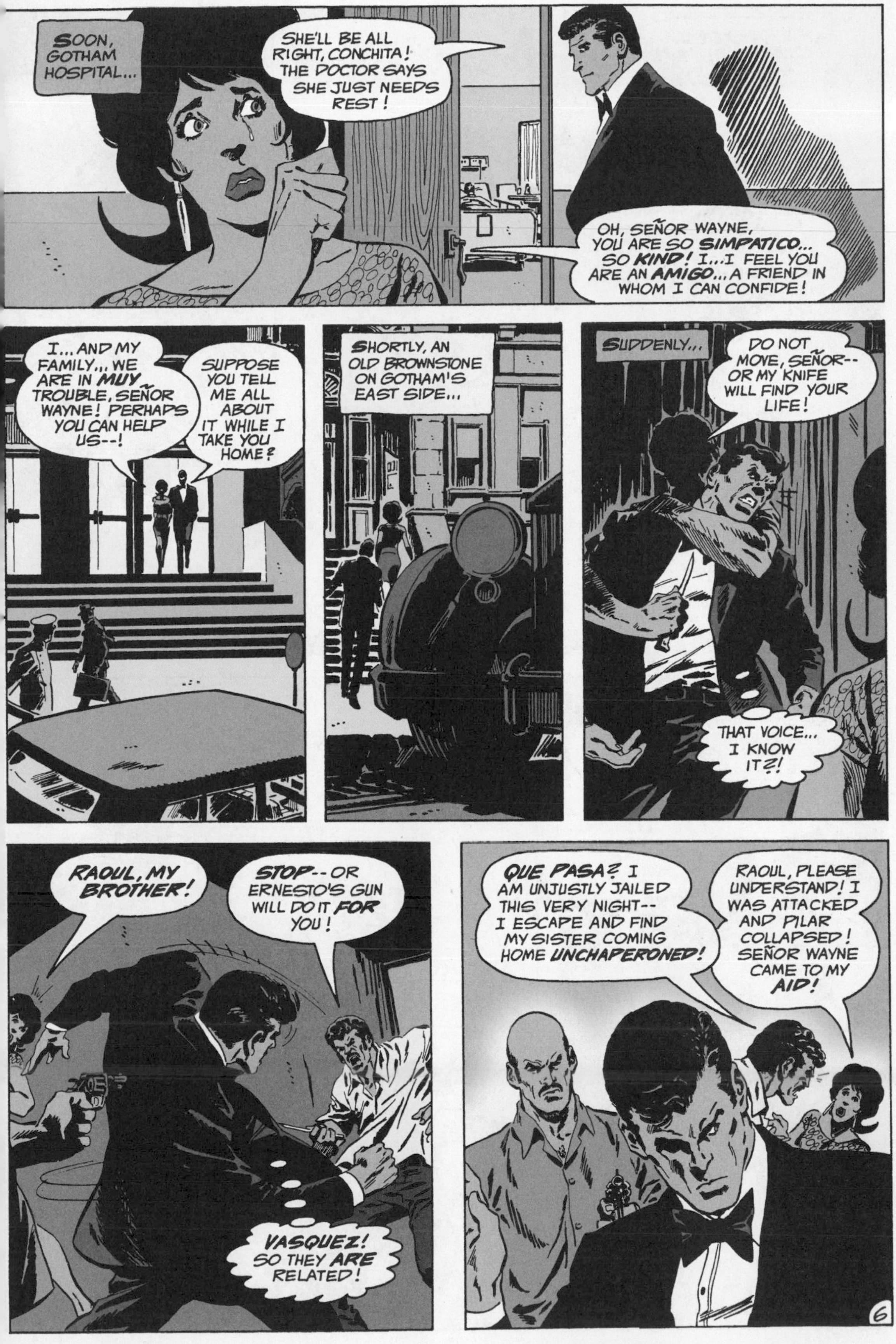
SOON, GOTHAM HOSPITAL...
SHE'LL BE ALL RIGHT, CONCHITA! THE DOCTOR SAYS SHE JUST NEEDS REST!
OH, SEÑOR WAYNE, YOU ARE SO SIMPATICO... SO KIND! I...I FEEL YOU ARE AN AMIGO...A FRIEND IN WHOM I CAN CONFIDE!
I...AND MY FAMILY...WE ARE IN MUY TROUBLE, SEÑOR WAYNE! PERHAPS YOU CAN HELP US--!
SUPPOSE YOU TELL ME ALL ABOUT IT WHILE I TAKE YOU HOME?
SHORTLY, AN OLD BROWNSTONE ON GOTHAM'S EAST SIDE...
SUDDENLY...
DO NOT MOVE, SEÑOR-- OR MY KNIFE WILL FIND YOUR LIFE!
THAT VOICE... I KNOW IT?!
RAOUL, MY BROTHER!
STOP--OR ERNESTO'S GUN WILL DO IT FOR YOU!
VASQUEZ! SO THEY ARE RELATED!
QUE PASA? I AM UNJUSTLY JAILED THIS VERY NIGHT-- I ESCAPE AND FIND MY SISTER COMING HOME UNCHAPERONED!
RAOUL, PLEASE UNDERSTAND! I WAS ATTACKED AND PILAR COLLAPSED! SEÑOR WAYNE CAME TO MY AID!
6

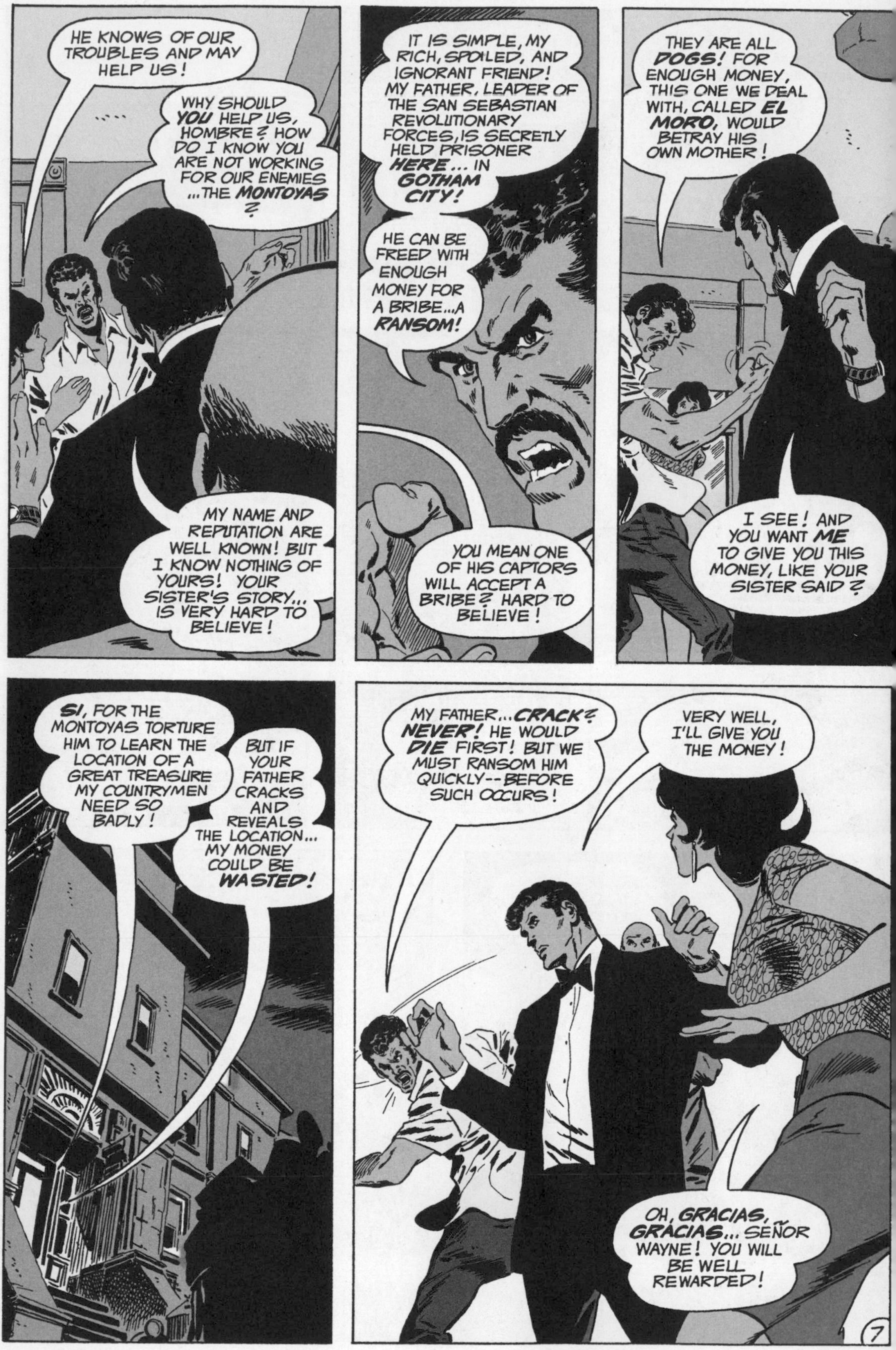
HE KNOWS OF OUR TROUBLES AND MAY HELP US!
WHY SHOULD YOU HELP US, HOMBRE? HOW DO I KNOW YOU ARE NOT WORKING FOR OUR ENEMIES ...THE MONTOYAS?
MY NAME AND REPUTATION ARE WELL KNOWN! BUT I KNOW NOTHING OF YOURS! YOUR SISTER'S STORY... IS VERY HARD TO BELIEVE!
IT IS SIMPLE, MY RICH, SPOILED, AND IGNORANT FRIEND! MY FATHER, LEADER OF THE SAN SEBASTIAN REVOLUTIONARY FORCES, IS SECRETLY HELD PRISONER HERE... IN GOTHAM CITY!
HE CAN BE FREED WITH ENOUGH MONEY FOR A BRIBE...A RANSOM!
YOU MEAN ONE OF HIS CAPTORS WILL ACCEPT A BRIBE? HARD TO BELIEVE!
THEY ARE ALL DOGS! FOR ENOUGH MONEY, THIS ONE WE DEAL WITH, CALLED EL MORO, WOULD BETRAY HIS OWN MOTHER!
I SEE! AND YOU WANT ME TO GIVE YOU THIS MONEY, LIKE YOUR SISTER SAID?
SI, FOR THE MONTOYAS TORTURE HIM TO LEARN THE LOCATION OF A GREAT TREASURE MY COUNTRYMEN NEED SO BADLY!
BUT IF YOUR FATHER CRACKS AND REVEALS THE LOCATION... MY MONEY COULD BE WASTED!
MY FATHER... CRACK? NEVER! HE WOULD DIE FIRST! BUT WE MUST RANSOM HIM QUICKLY--BEFORE SUCH OCCURS!
VERY WELL, I'LL GIVE YOU THE MONEY!
OH, GRACIAS, GRACIAS... SEÑOR WAYNE! YOU WILL BE WELL REWARDED!
7

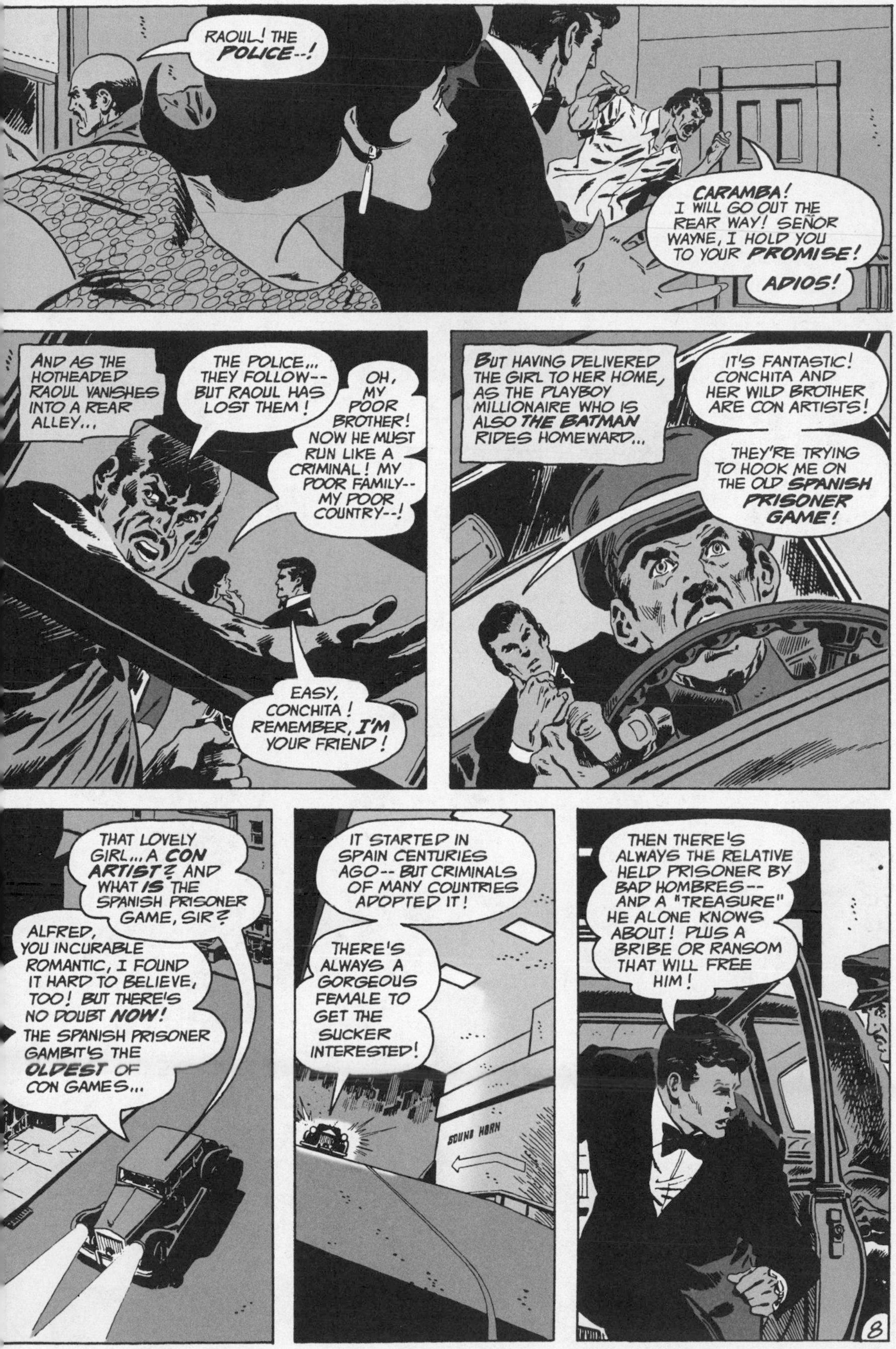
RAOUL! THE POLICE--!
CARAMBA! I WILL GO OUT THE REAR WAY! SEÑOR WAYNE, I HOLD YOU TO YOUR PROMISE!
ADIOS!
AND AS THE HOTHEADED RAOUL VANISHES INTO A REAR ALLEY...
THE POLICE... THEY FOLLOW-- BUT RAOUL HAS LOST THEM!
OH, MY POOR BROTHER! NOW HE MUST RUN LIKE A CRIMINAL! MY POOR FAMILY-- MY POOR COUNTRY--!
EASY, CONCHITA! REMEMBER, I'M YOUR FRIEND!
BUT HAVING DELIVERED THE GIRL TO HER HOME, AS THE PLAYBOY MILLIONAIRE WHO IS ALSO THE BATMAN RIDES HOMEWARD...
IT'S FANTASTIC! CONCHITA AND HER WILD BROTHER ARE CON ARTISTS!
THEY'RE TRYING TO HOOK ME ON THE OLD SPANISH PRISONER GAME!
THAT LOVELY GIRL... A CON ARTIST? AND WHAT IS THE SPANISH PRISONER GAME, SIR?
ALFRED, YOU INCURABLE ROMANTIC, I FOUND IT HARD TO BELIEVE, TOO! BUT THERE'S NO DOUBT NOW! THE SPANISH PRISONER GAMBIT'S THE OLDEST OF CON GAMES...
IT STARTED IN SPAIN CENTURIES AGO-- BUT CRIMINALS OF MANY COUNTRIES ADOPTED IT!
THERE'S ALWAYS A GORGEOUS FEMALE TO GET THE SUCKER INTERESTED!
SOUND HORN
THEN THERE'S ALWAYS THE RELATIVE HELD PRISONER BY BAD HOMBRES-- AND A "TREASURE" HE ALONE KNOWS ABOUT! PLUS A BRIBE OR RANSOM THAT WILL FREE HIM!
8

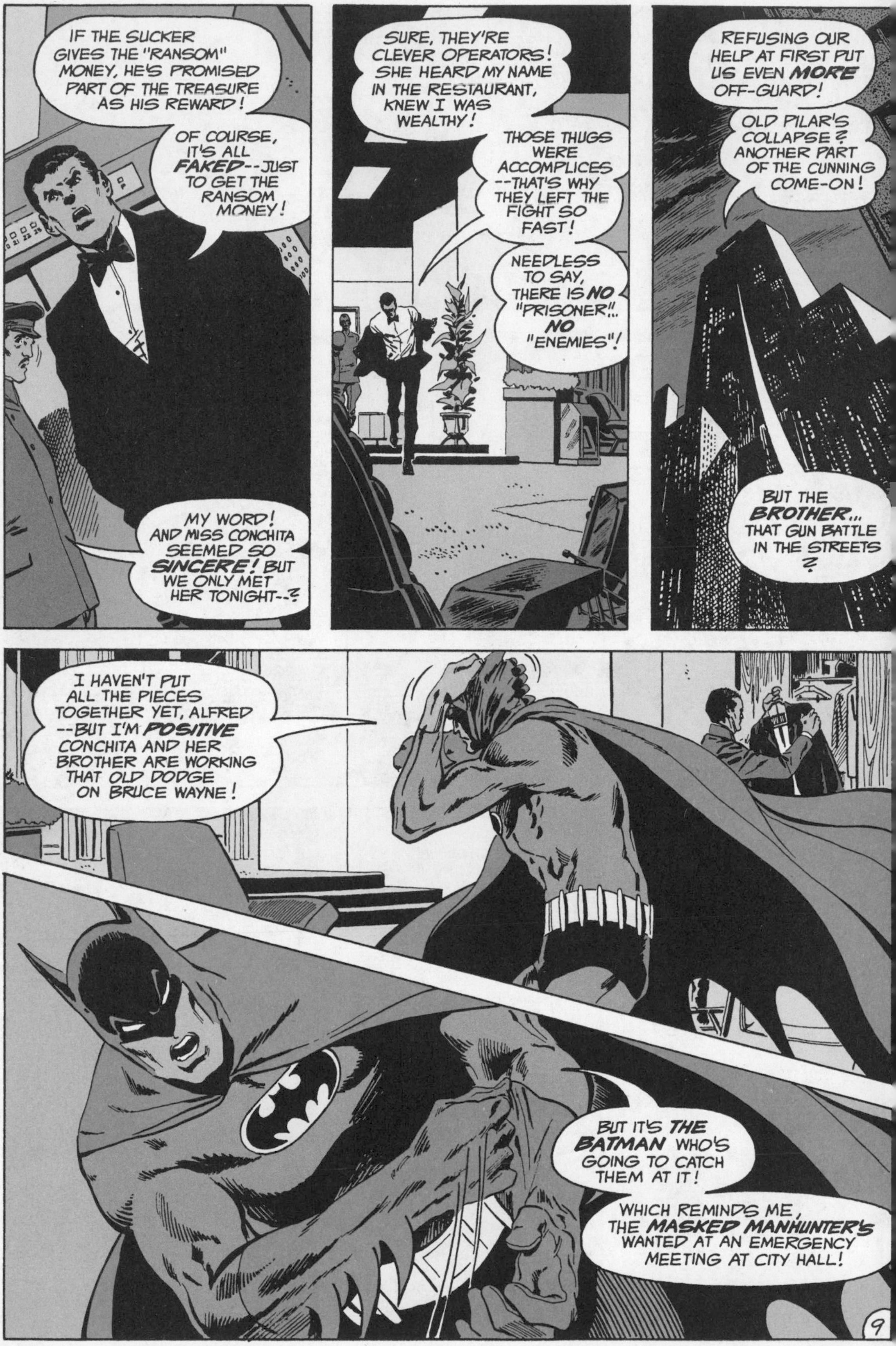
IF THE SUCKER GIVES THE "RANSOM" MONEY, HE'S PROMISED PART OF THE TREASURE AS HIS REWARD!
OF COURSE, IT'S ALL FAKED--JUST TO GET THE RANSOM MONEY!
MY WORD! AND MISS CONCHITA SEEMED SO SINCERE! BUT WE ONLY MET HER TONIGHT--?
SURE, THEY'RE CLEVER OPERATORS! SHE HEARD MY NAME IN THE RESTAURANT, KNEW I WAS WEALTHY!
THOSE THUGS WERE ACCOMPLICES --THAT'S WHY THEY LEFT THE FIGHT SO FAST!
NEEDLESS TO SAY, THERE IS NO "PRISONER"!.. NO "ENEMIES"!
REFUSING OUR HELP AT FIRST PUT US EVEN MORE OFF-GUARD!
OLD PILAR'S COLLAPSE? ANOTHER PART OF THE CUNNING COME-ON!
BUT THE BROTHER... THAT GUN BATTLE IN THE STREETS?
I HAVEN'T PUT ALL THE PIECES TOGETHER YET, ALFRED --BUT I'M POSITIVE CONCHITA AND HER BROTHER ARE WORKING THAT OLD DODGE ON BRUCE WAYNE!
BUT IT'S THE BATMAN WHO'S GOING TO CATCH THEM AT IT!
WHICH REMINDS ME, THE MASKED MANHUNTER'S WANTED AT AN EMERGENCY MEETING AT CITY HALL!
9

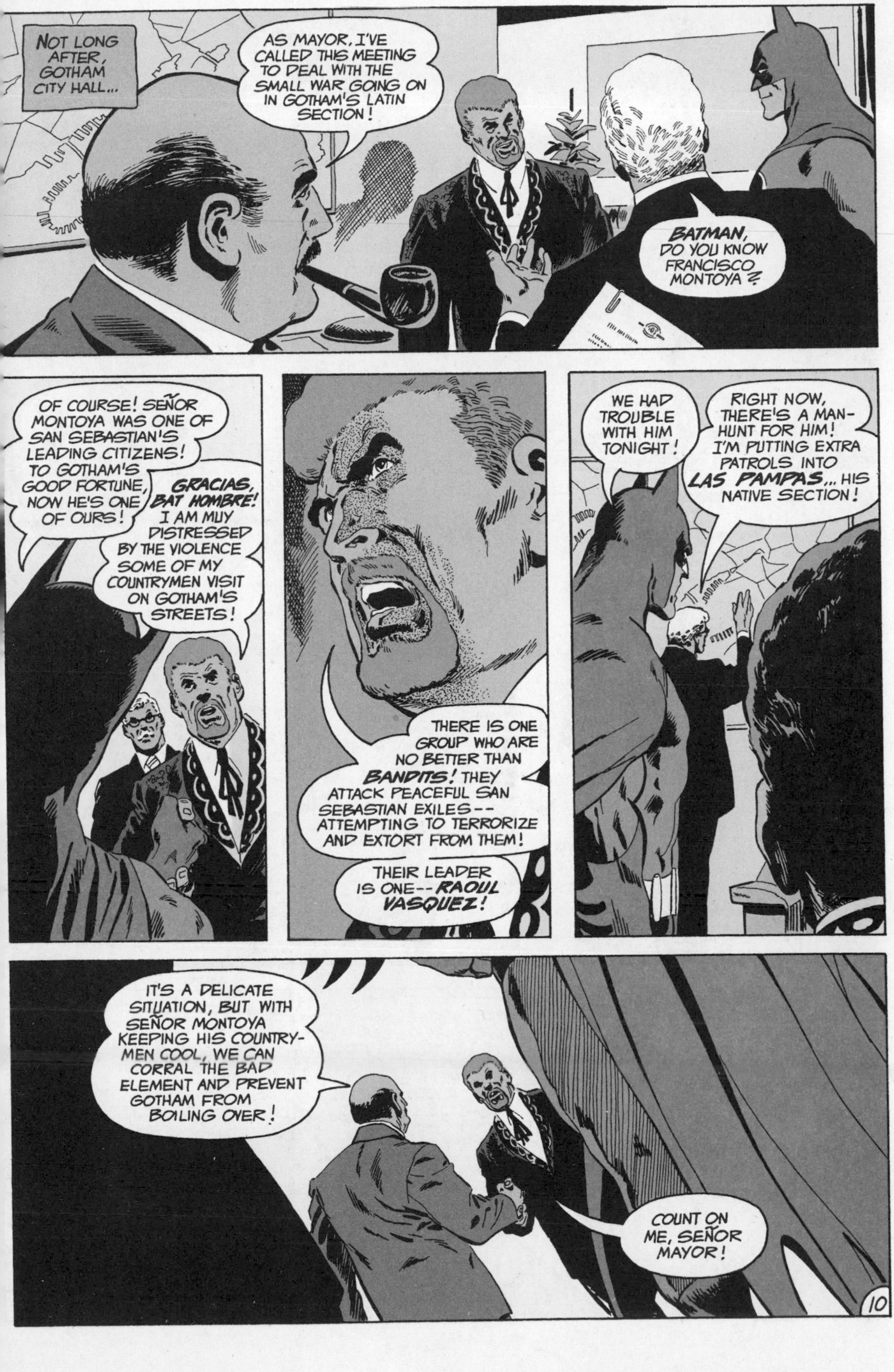
NOT LONG AFTER, GOTHAM CITY HALL...
AS MAYOR, I'VE CALLED THIS MEETING TO DEAL WITH THE SMALL WAR GOING ON IN GOTHAM'S LATIN SECTION!
BATMAN, DO YOU KNOW FRANCISCO MONTOYA?
OF COURSE! SEÑOR MONTOYA WAS ONE OF SAN SEBASTIAN'S LEADING CITIZENS! TO GOTHAM'S GOOD FORTUNE, NOW HE'S ONE OF OURS!
GRACIAS, BAT HOMBRE! I AM MUY DISTRESSED BY THE VIOLENCE SOME OF MY COUNTRYMEN VISIT ON GOTHAM'S STREETS!
THERE IS ONE GROUP WHO ARE NO BETTER THAN BANDITS! THEY ATTACK PEACEFUL SAN SEBASTIAN EXILES-- ATTEMPTING TO TERRORIZE AND EXTORT FROM THEM!
THEIR LEADER IS ONE-- RAOUL VASQUEZ!
WE HAD TROUBLE WITH HIM TONIGHT!
RIGHT NOW, THERE'S A MAN-HUNT FOR HIM! I'M PUTTING EXTRA PATROLS INTO LAS PAMPAS... HIS NATIVE SECTION!
IT'S A DELICATE SITUATION, BUT WITH SEÑOR MONTOYA KEEPING HIS COUNTRY-MEN COOL, WE CAN CORRAL THE BAD ELEMENT AND PREVENT GOTHAM FROM BOILING OVER!
COUNT ON ME, SEÑOR MAYOR!
10

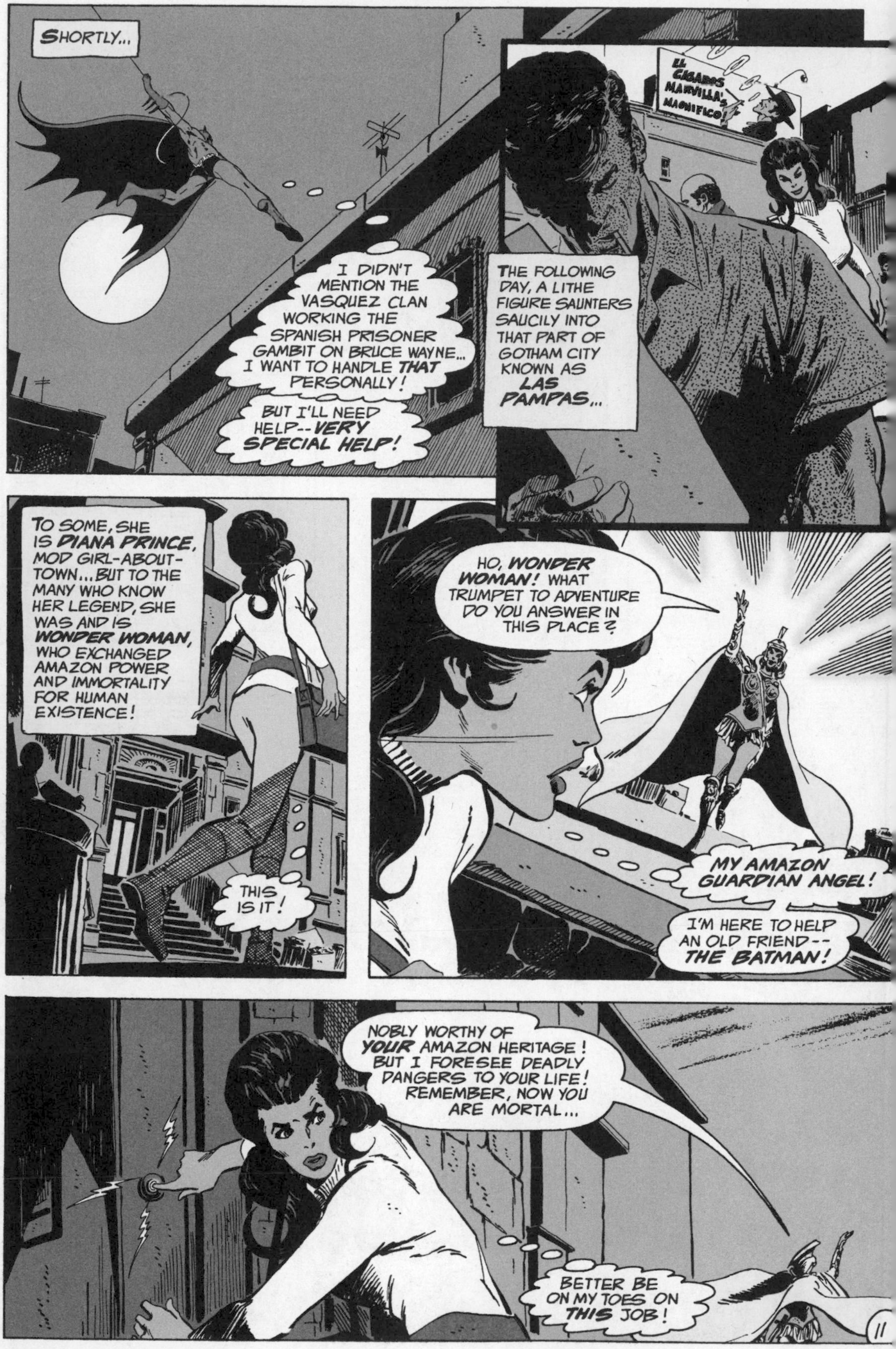
SHORTLY...
I DIDN'T MENTION THE VASQUEZ CLAN WORKING THE SPANISH PRISONER GAMBIT ON BRUCE WAYNE... I WANT TO HANDLE **THAT** PERSONALLY!
BUT I'LL NEED HELP--**VERY SPECIAL HELP!**
EL CIGAROS MARVILLA'S MAGNIFICO!
THE FOLLOWING DAY, A LITHE FIGURE SAUNTERS SAUCILY INTO THAT PART OF GOTHAM CITY KNOWN AS **LAS PAMPAS**...
TO SOME, SHE IS **DIANA PRINCE**, MOD GIRL-ABOUT-TOWN... BUT TO THE MANY WHO KNOW HER LEGEND, SHE WAS AND IS **WONDER WOMAN**, WHO EXCHANGED AMAZON POWER AND IMMORTALITY FOR HUMAN EXISTENCE!
THIS IS IT!
HO, **WONDER WOMAN!** WHAT TRUMPET TO ADVENTURE DO YOU ANSWER IN THIS PLACE?
MY AMAZON GUARDIAN ANGEL!
I'M HERE TO HELP AN OLD FRIEND-- **THE BATMAN!**
NOBLY WORTHY OF **YOUR** AMAZON HERITAGE! BUT I FORESEE DEADLY DANGERS TO YOUR LIFE! REMEMBER, NOW YOU ARE MORTAL...
BETTER BE ON MY TOES ON **THIS** JOB!
11

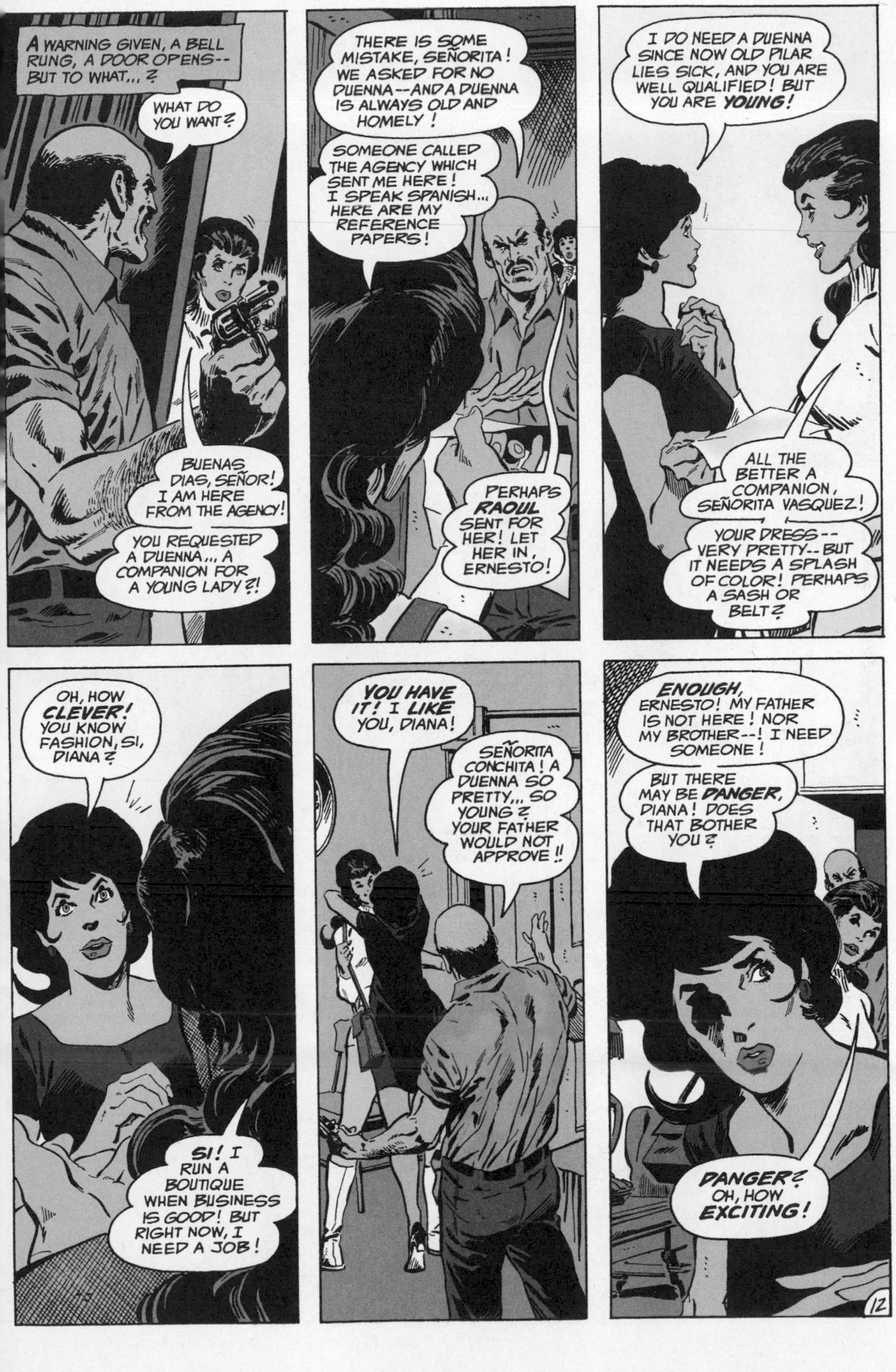
A WARNING GIVEN, A BELL RUNG, A DOOR OPENS-- BUT TO WHAT... ?
WHAT DO YOU WANT ?
BUENAS DIAS, SEÑOR! I AM HERE FROM THE AGENCY!
YOU REQUESTED A DUENNA... A COMPANION FOR A YOUNG LADY ?!
THERE IS SOME MISTAKE, SEÑORITA! WE ASKED FOR NO DUENNA--AND A DUENNA IS ALWAYS OLD AND HOMELY!
SOMEONE CALLED THE AGENCY WHICH SENT ME HERE! I SPEAK SPANISH... HERE ARE MY REFERENCE PAPERS!
PERHAPS RAOUL SENT FOR HER! LET HER IN, ERNESTO!
I DO NEED A DUENNA SINCE NOW OLD PILAR LIES SICK, AND YOU ARE WELL QUALIFIED! BUT YOU ARE YOUNG!
ALL THE BETTER A COMPANION, SEÑORITA VASQUEZ!
YOUR DRESS-- VERY PRETTY-- BUT IT NEEDS A SPLASH OF COLOR! PERHAPS A SASH OR BELT ?
OH, HOW CLEVER! YOU KNOW FASHION, SI, DIANA ?
SI! I RUN A BOUTIQUE WHEN BUSINESS IS GOOD! BUT RIGHT NOW, I NEED A JOB!
YOU HAVE IT! I LIKE YOU, DIANA!
SEÑORITA CONCHITA! A DUENNA SO PRETTY... SO YOUNG ? YOUR FATHER WOULD NOT APPROVE!!
ENOUGH, ERNESTO! MY FATHER IS NOT HERE! NOR MY BROTHER--! I NEED SOMEONE!
BUT THERE MAY BE DANGER, DIANA! DOES THAT BOTHER YOU ?
DANGER ? OH, HOW EXCITING!
12

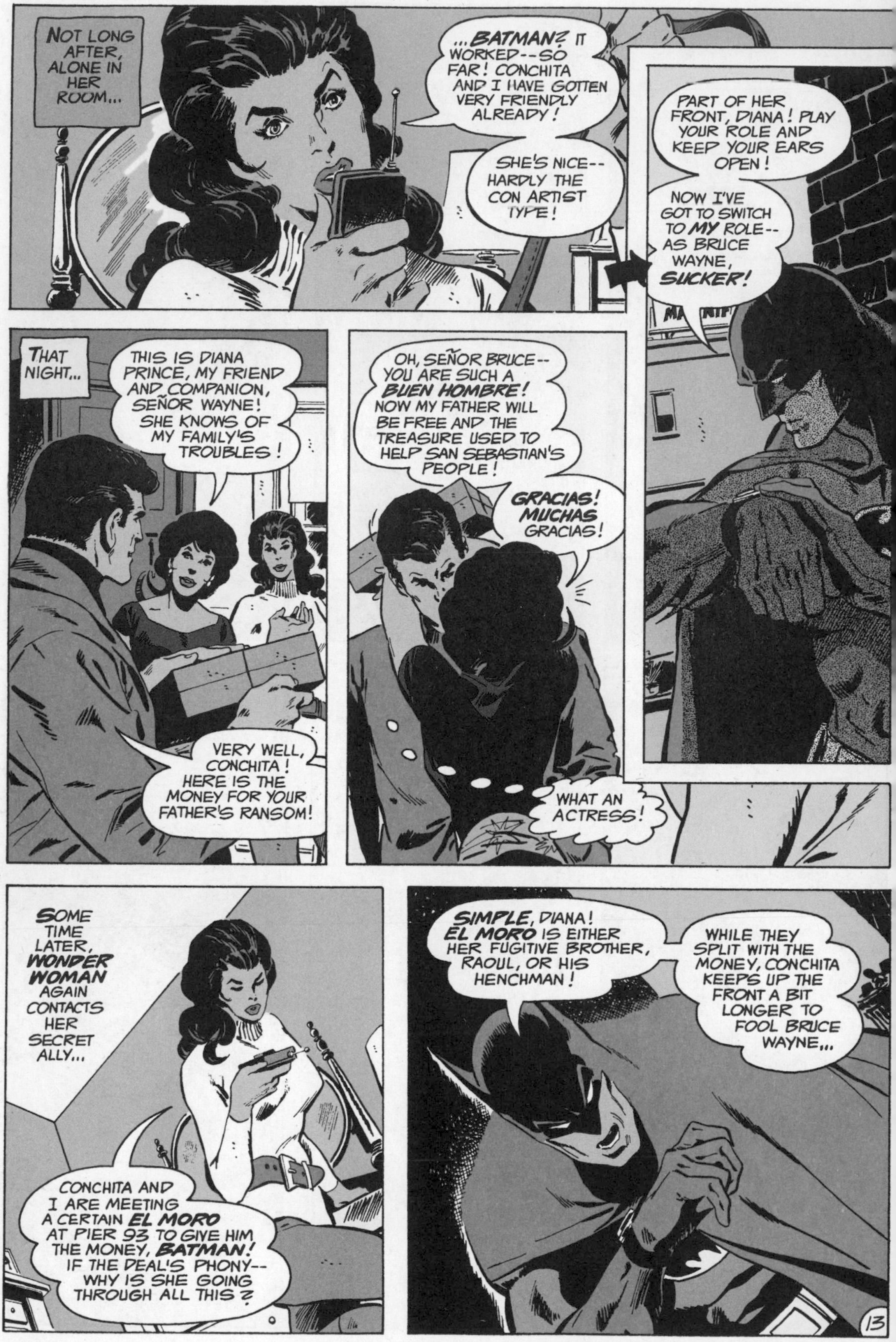

NOT LONG AFTER, ALONE IN HER ROOM...
...BATMAN? IT WORKED--SO FAR! CONCHITA AND I HAVE GOTTEN VERY FRIENDLY ALREADY!
SHE'S NICE--HARDLY THE CON ARTIST TYPE!
PART OF HER FRONT, DIANA! PLAY YOUR ROLE AND KEEP YOUR EARS OPEN!
NOW I'VE GOT TO SWITCH TO MY ROLE--AS BRUCE WAYNE, SUCKER!
THAT NIGHT...
THIS IS DIANA PRINCE, MY FRIEND AND COMPANION, SEÑOR WAYNE! SHE KNOWS OF MY FAMILY'S TROUBLES!
VERY WELL, CONCHITA! HERE IS THE MONEY FOR YOUR FATHER'S RANSOM!
OH, SEÑOR BRUCE--YOU ARE SUCH A BUEN HOMBRE! NOW MY FATHER WILL BE FREE AND THE TREASURE USED TO HELP SAN SEBASTIAN'S PEOPLE!
GRACIAS! MUCHAS GRACIAS!
WHAT AN ACTRESS!
SOME TIME LATER, WONDER WOMAN AGAIN CONTACTS HER SECRET ALLY...
CONCHITA AND I ARE MEETING A CERTAIN EL MORO AT PIER 93 TO GIVE HIM THE MONEY, BATMAN! IF THE DEAL'S PHONY--WHY IS SHE GOING THROUGH ALL THIS?
SIMPLE, DIANA! EL MORO IS EITHER HER FUGITIVE BROTHER, RAOUL, OR HIS HENCHMAN!
WHILE THEY SPLIT WITH THE MONEY, CONCHITA KEEPS UP THE FRONT A BIT LONGER TO FOOL BRUCE WAYNE...
13

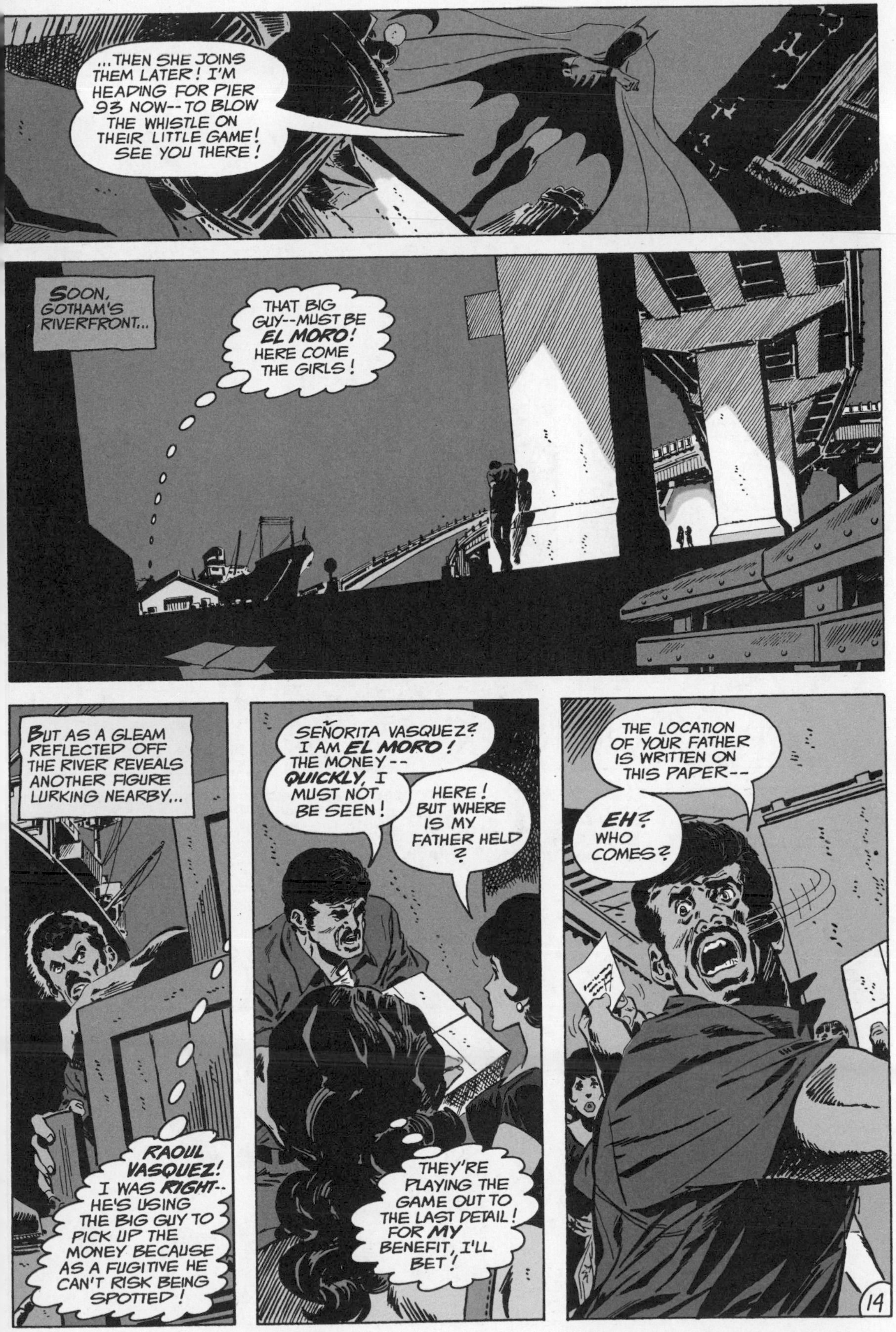
...THEN SHE JOINS THEM LATER! I'M HEADING FOR PIER 93 NOW--TO BLOW THE WHISTLE ON THEIR LITTLE GAME! SEE YOU THERE!
SOON, GOTHAM'S RIVERFRONT...
THAT BIG GUY--MUST BE EL MORO! HERE COME THE GIRLS!
BUT AS A GLEAM REFLECTED OFF THE RIVER REVEALS ANOTHER FIGURE LURKING NEARBY...
RAOUL VASQUEZ! I WAS RIGHT-- HE'S USING THE BIG GUY TO PICK UP THE MONEY BECAUSE AS A FUGITIVE HE CAN'T RISK BEING SPOTTED!
SEÑORITA VASQUEZ? I AM EL MORO! THE MONEY-- QUICKLY, I MUST NOT BE SEEN!
HERE! BUT WHERE IS MY FATHER HELD?
THEY'RE PLAYING THE GAME OUT TO THE LAST DETAIL! FOR MY BENEFIT, I'LL BET!
THE LOCATION OF YOUR FATHER IS WRITTEN ON THIS PAPER--
EH? WHO COMES?
14

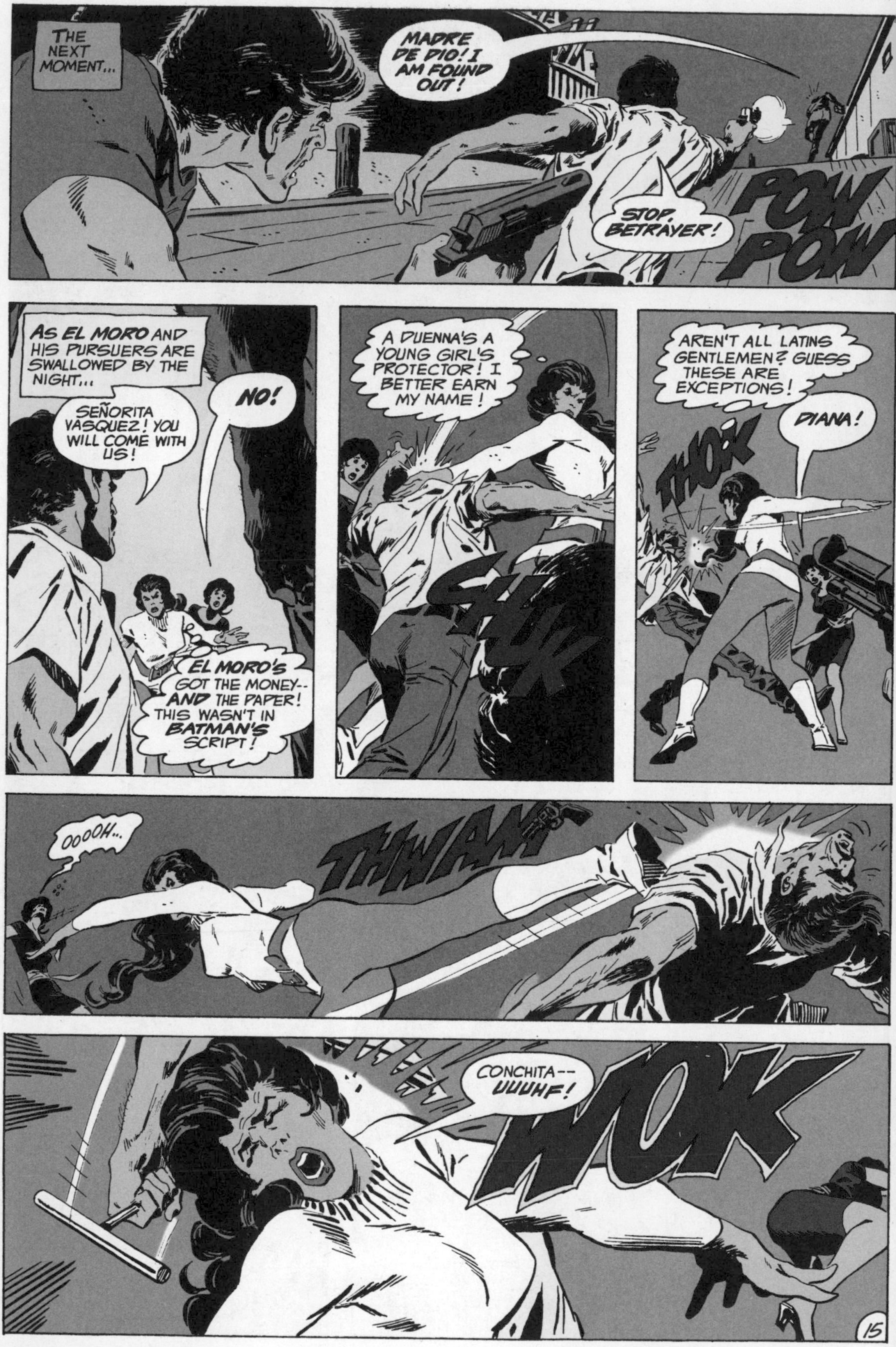
THE NEXT MOMENT...
MADRE DE DIO! I AM FOUND OUT!
STOP, BETRAYER!
POW POW
AS EL MORO AND HIS PURSUERS ARE SWALLOWED BY THE NIGHT...
SEÑORITA VASQUEZ! YOU WILL COME WITH US!
NO!
EL MORO'S GOT THE MONEY-- AND THE PAPER! THIS WASN'T IN BATMAN'S SCRIPT!
A DUENNA'S A YOUNG GIRL'S PROTECTOR! I BETTER EARN MY NAME!
SHUK
AREN'T ALL LATINS GENTLEMEN? GUESS THESE ARE EXCEPTIONS!
THOK
DIANA!
OOOOH...
THWAM
CONCHITA-- UUUHF!
WOK
15

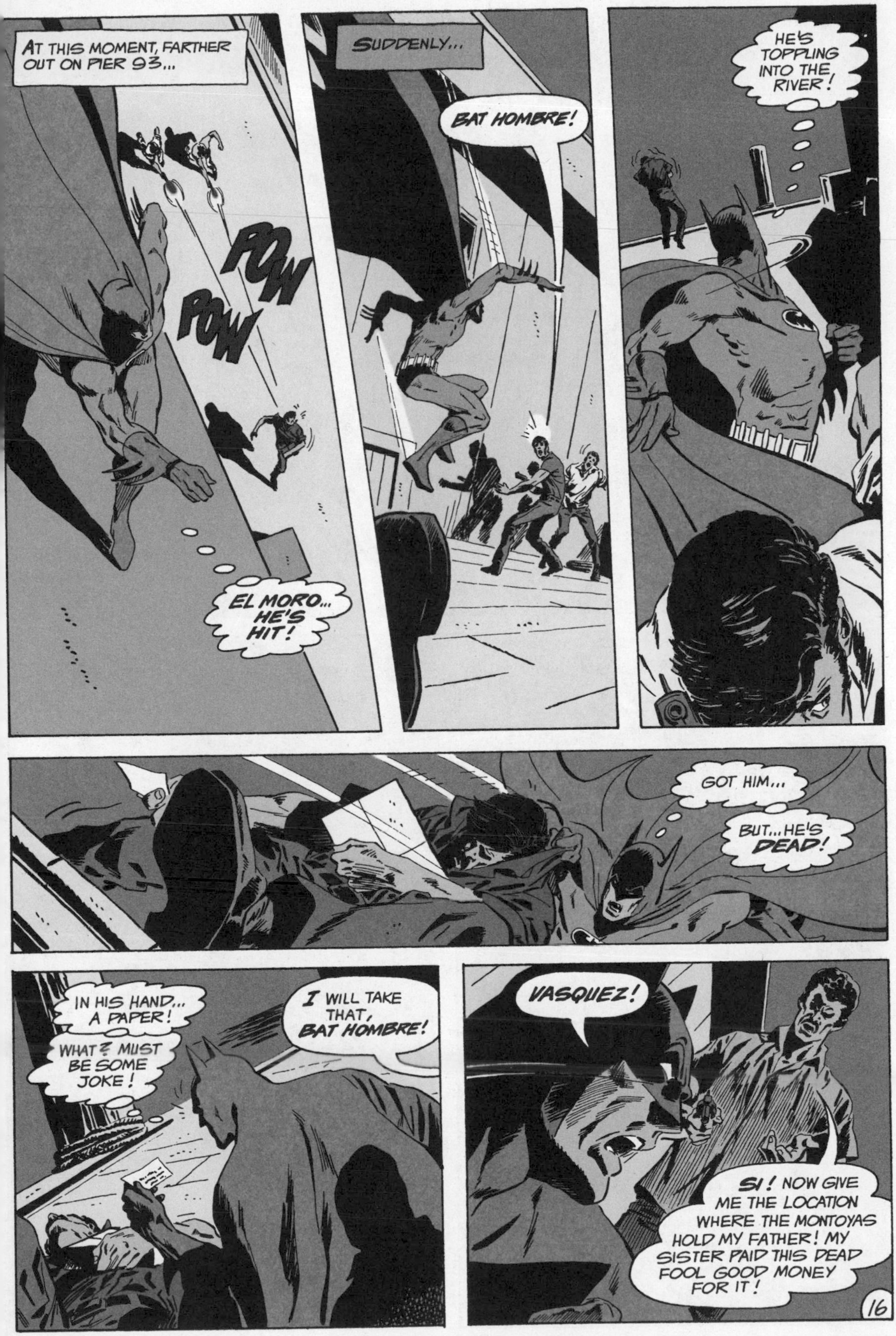
AT THIS MOMENT, FARTHER OUT ON PIER 93...
POW
POW
EL MORO... HE'S HIT!
SUDDENLY...
BAT HOMBRE!
HE'S TOPPLING INTO THE RIVER!
GOT HIM...
BUT... HE'S DEAD!
IN HIS HAND... A PAPER!
WHAT? MUST BE SOME JOKE!
I WILL TAKE THAT, BAT HOMBRE!
VASQUEZ!
SI! NOW GIVE ME THE LOCATION WHERE THE MONTOYAS HOLD MY FATHER! MY SISTER PAID THIS DEAD FOOL GOOD MONEY FOR IT!
16

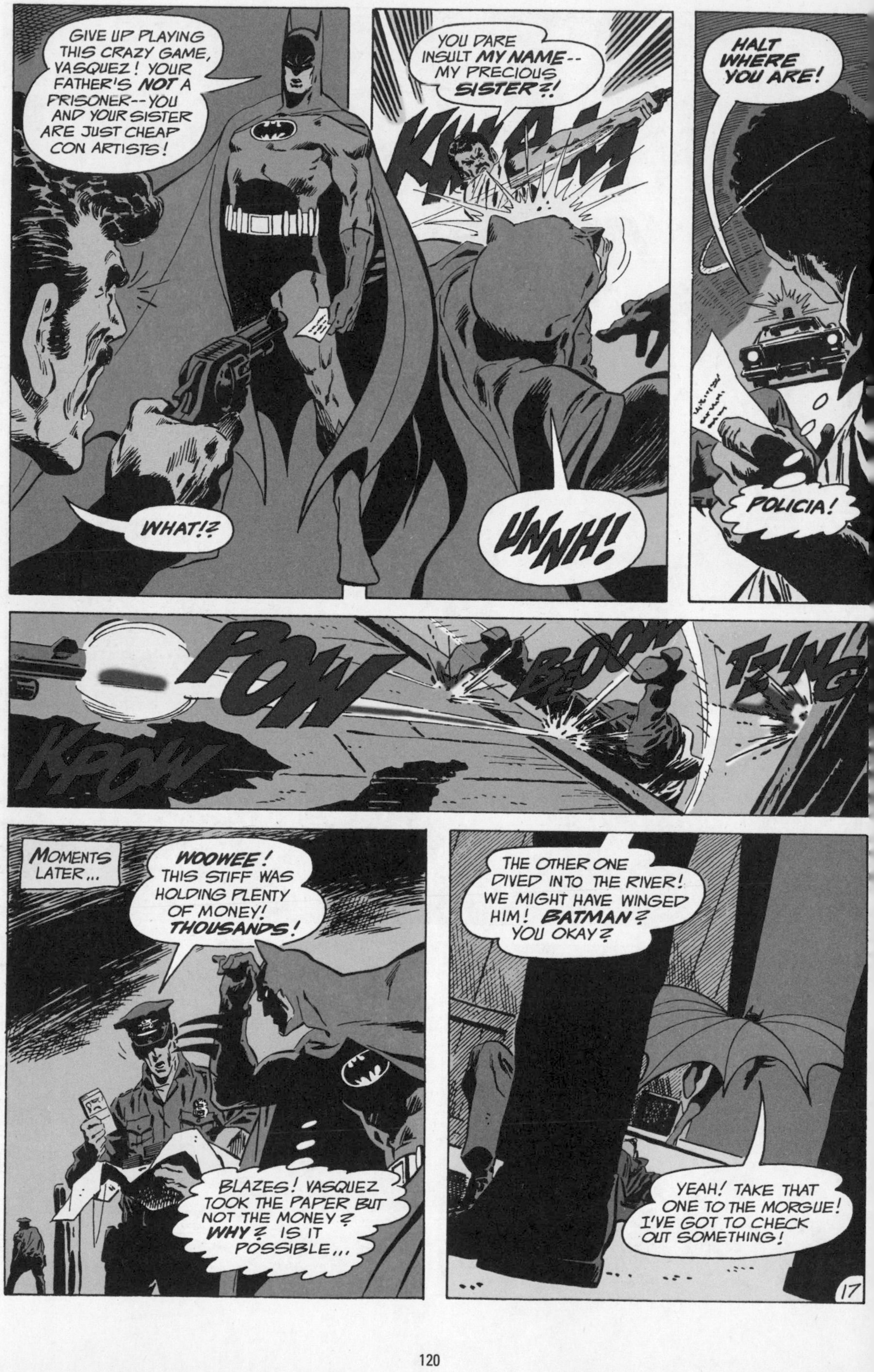
GIVE UP PLAYING THIS CRAZY GAME, VASQUEZ! YOUR FATHER'S NOT A PRISONER--YOU AND YOUR SISTER ARE JUST CHEAP CON ARTISTS!
WHAT!?
YOU DARE INSULT MY NAME-- MY PRECIOUS SISTER?!
KWAM
UNNH!
HALT WHERE YOU ARE!
POLICIA!
POW
KPOW
TZING
MOMENTS LATER...
WOOWEE! THIS STIFF WAS HOLDING PLENTY OF MONEY! THOUSANDS!
BLAZES! VASQUEZ TOOK THE PAPER BUT NOT THE MONEY? WHY? IS IT POSSIBLE...
THE OTHER ONE DIVED INTO THE RIVER! WE MIGHT HAVE WINGED HIM! BATMAN? YOU OKAY?
YEAH! TAKE THAT ONE TO THE MORGUE! I'VE GOT TO CHECK OUT SOMETHING!
17

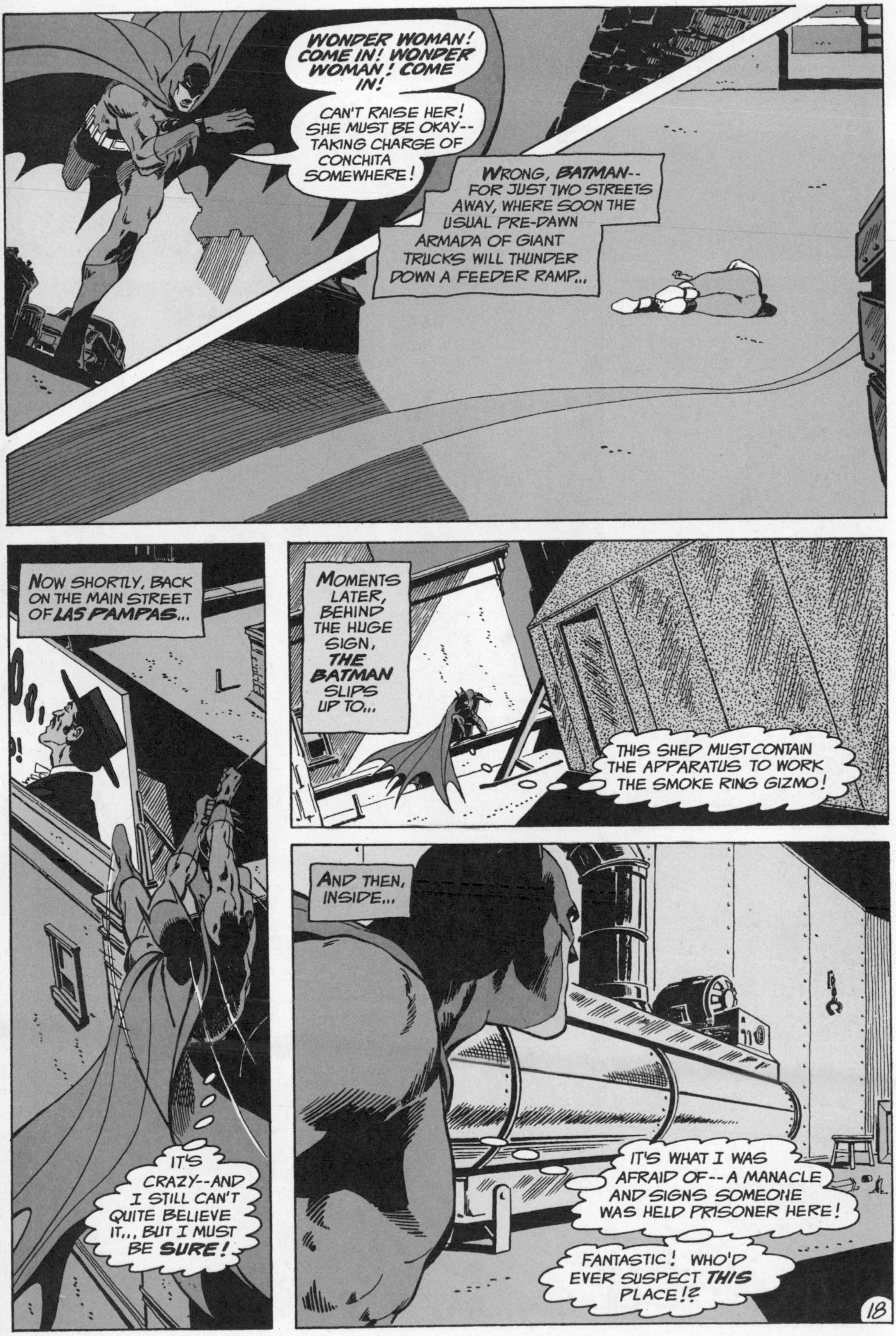
WONDER WOMAN! COME IN! WONDER WOMAN! COME IN!
CAN'T RAISE HER! SHE MUST BE OKAY-- TAKING CHARGE OF CONCHITA SOMEWHERE!
WRONG, BATMAN-- FOR JUST TWO STREETS AWAY, WHERE SOON THE USUAL PRE-DAWN ARMADA OF GIANT TRUCKS WILL THUNDER DOWN A FEEDER RAMP...
NOW SHORTLY, BACK ON THE MAIN STREET OF LAS PAMPAS...
IT'S CRAZY--AND I STILL CAN'T QUITE BELIEVE IT... BUT I MUST BE SURE!
MOMENTS LATER, BEHIND THE HUGE SIGN, THE BATMAN SLIPS UP TO...
THIS SHED MUST CONTAIN THE APPARATUS TO WORK THE SMOKE RING GIZMO!
AND THEN, INSIDE...
IT'S WHAT I WAS AFRAID OF-- A MANACLE AND SIGNS SOMEONE WAS HELD PRISONER HERE!
FANTASTIC! WHO'D EVER SUSPECT THIS PLACE!?
18

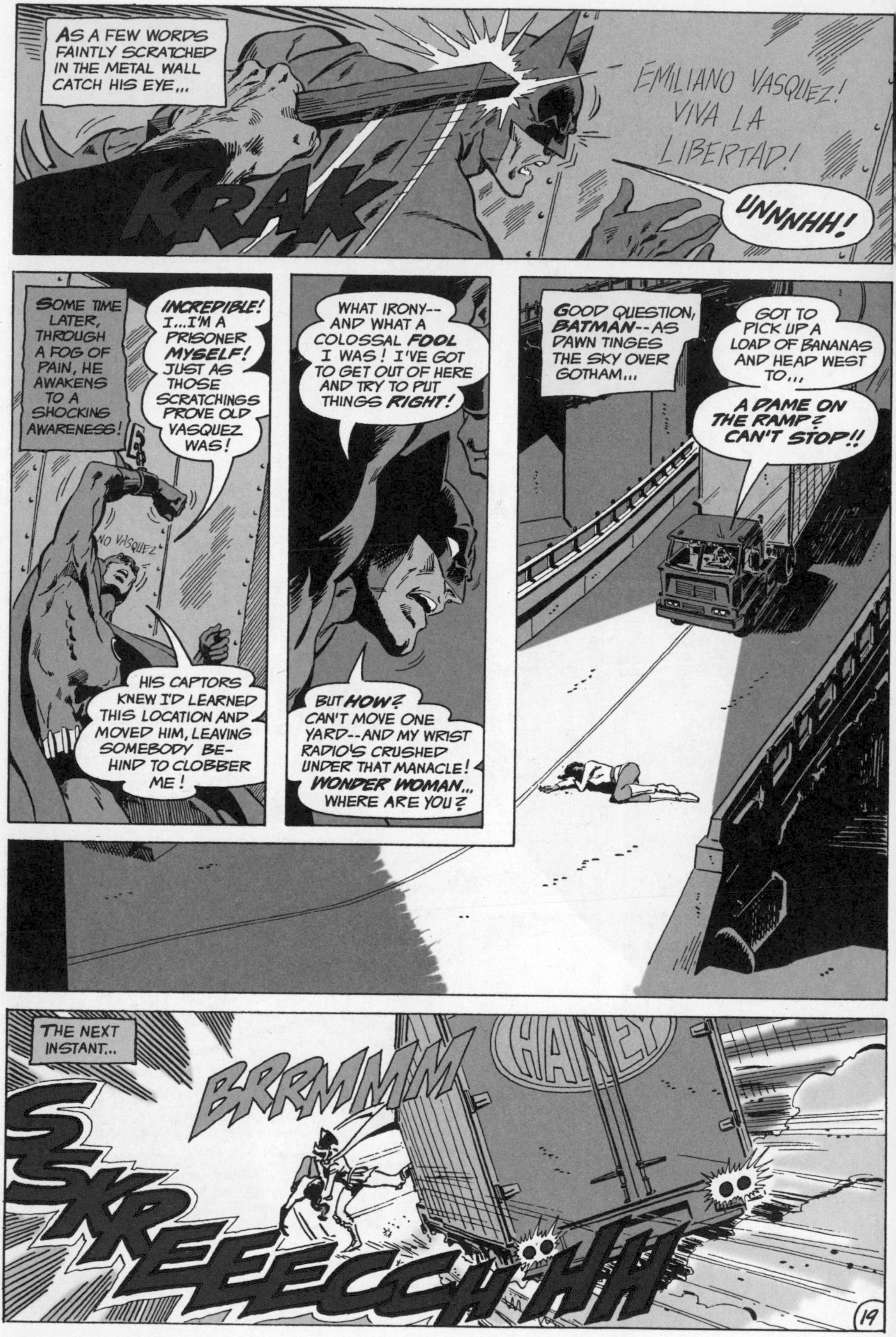
AS A FEW WORDS FAINTLY SCRATCHED IN THE METAL WALL CATCH HIS EYE...
EMILIANO VASQUEZ! VIVA LA LIBERTAD!
KRAK
UNNNHH!
SOME TIME LATER, THROUGH A FOG OF PAIN, HE AWAKENS TO A SHOCKING AWARENESS!
INCREDIBLE! I...I'M A PRISONER MYSELF! JUST AS THOSE SCRATCHINGS PROVE OLD VASQUEZ WAS!
NO VASQUEZ
HIS CAPTORS KNEW I'D LEARNED THIS LOCATION AND MOVED HIM, LEAVING SOMEBODY BE-HIND TO CLOBBER ME!
WHAT IRONY-- AND WHAT A COLOSSAL FOOL I WAS! I'VE GOT TO GET OUT OF HERE AND TRY TO PUT THINGS RIGHT!
BUT HOW? CAN'T MOVE ONE YARD--AND MY WRIST RADIO'S CRUSHED UNDER THAT MANACLE! WONDER WOMAN... WHERE ARE YOU?
GOOD QUESTION, BATMAN--AS DAWN TINGES THE SKY OVER GOTHAM...
GOT TO PICK UP A LOAD OF BANANAS AND HEAD WEST TO...
A DAME ON THE RAMP? CAN'T STOP!!
THE NEXT INSTANT...
BRRMMM
SSKREEEECCHHHH
19

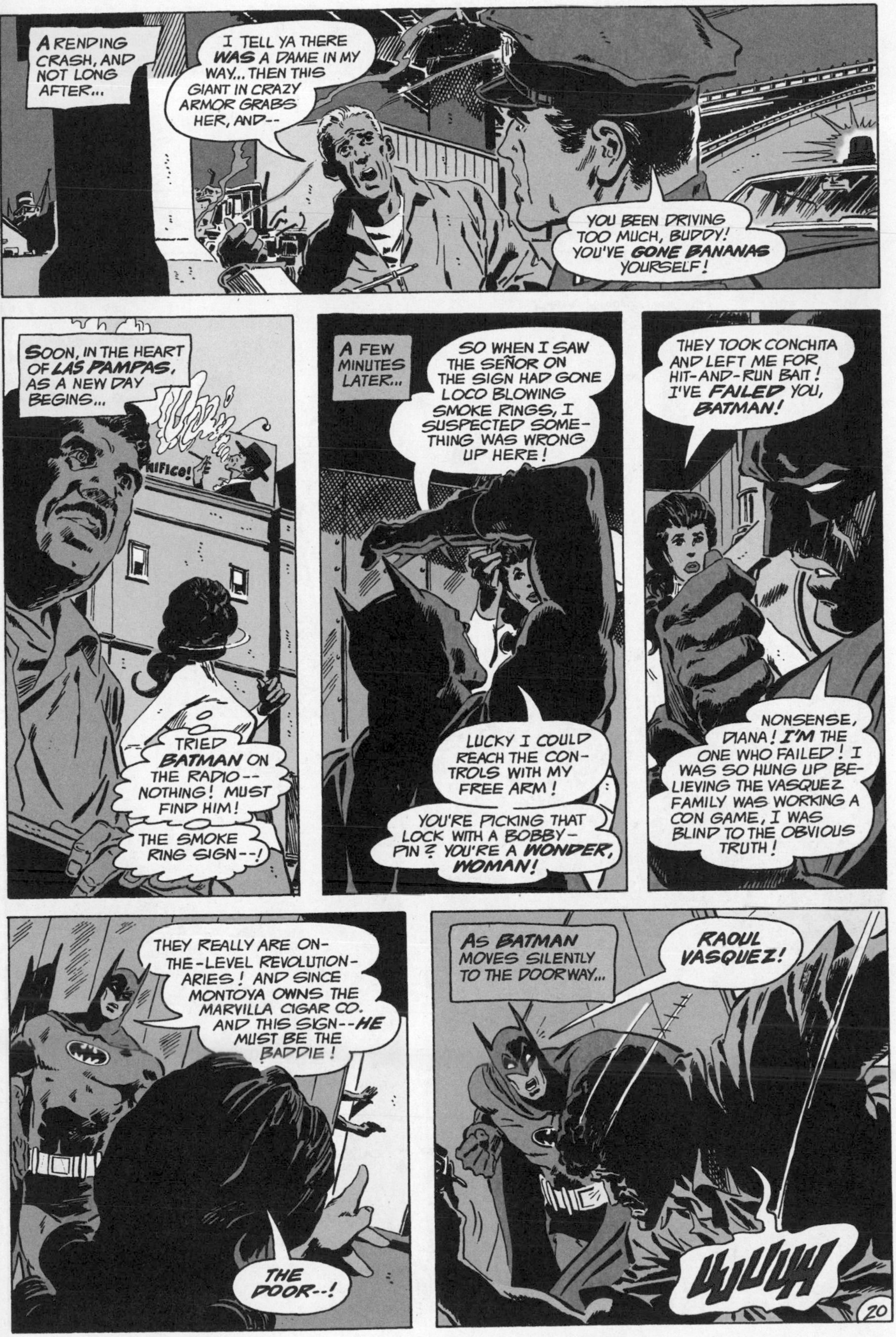

A RENDING CRASH, AND NOT LONG AFTER...
I TELL YA THERE WAS A DAME IN MY WAY... THEN THIS GIANT IN CRAZY ARMOR GRABS HER, AND--
YOU BEEN DRIVING TOO MUCH, BUDDY! YOU'VE GONE BANANAS YOURSELF!
SOON, IN THE HEART OF LAS PAMPAS, AS A NEW DAY BEGINS...
TRIED BATMAN ON THE RADIO-- NOTHING! MUST FIND HIM!
THE SMOKE RING SIGN--!
A FEW MINUTES LATER...
SO WHEN I SAW THE SEÑOR ON THE SIGN HAD GONE LOCO BLOWING SMOKE RINGS, I SUSPECTED SOMETHING WAS WRONG UP HERE!
LUCKY I COULD REACH THE CONTROLS WITH MY FREE ARM!
YOU'RE PICKING THAT LOCK WITH A BOBBY-PIN? YOU'RE A WONDER, WOMAN!
THEY TOOK CONCHITA AND LEFT ME FOR HIT-AND-RUN BAIT! I'VE FAILED YOU, BATMAN!
NONSENSE, DIANA! I'M THE ONE WHO FAILED! I WAS SO HUNG UP BELIEVING THE VASQUEZ FAMILY WAS WORKING A CON GAME, I WAS BLIND TO THE OBVIOUS TRUTH!
THEY REALLY ARE ON-THE-LEVEL REVOLUTIONARIES! AND SINCE MONTOYA OWNS THE MARVILLA CIGAR CO. AND THIS SIGN--HE MUST BE THE BADDIE!
THE DOOR--!
AS BATMAN MOVES SILENTLY TO THE DOORWAY...
RAOUL VASQUEZ!
UUUH
20

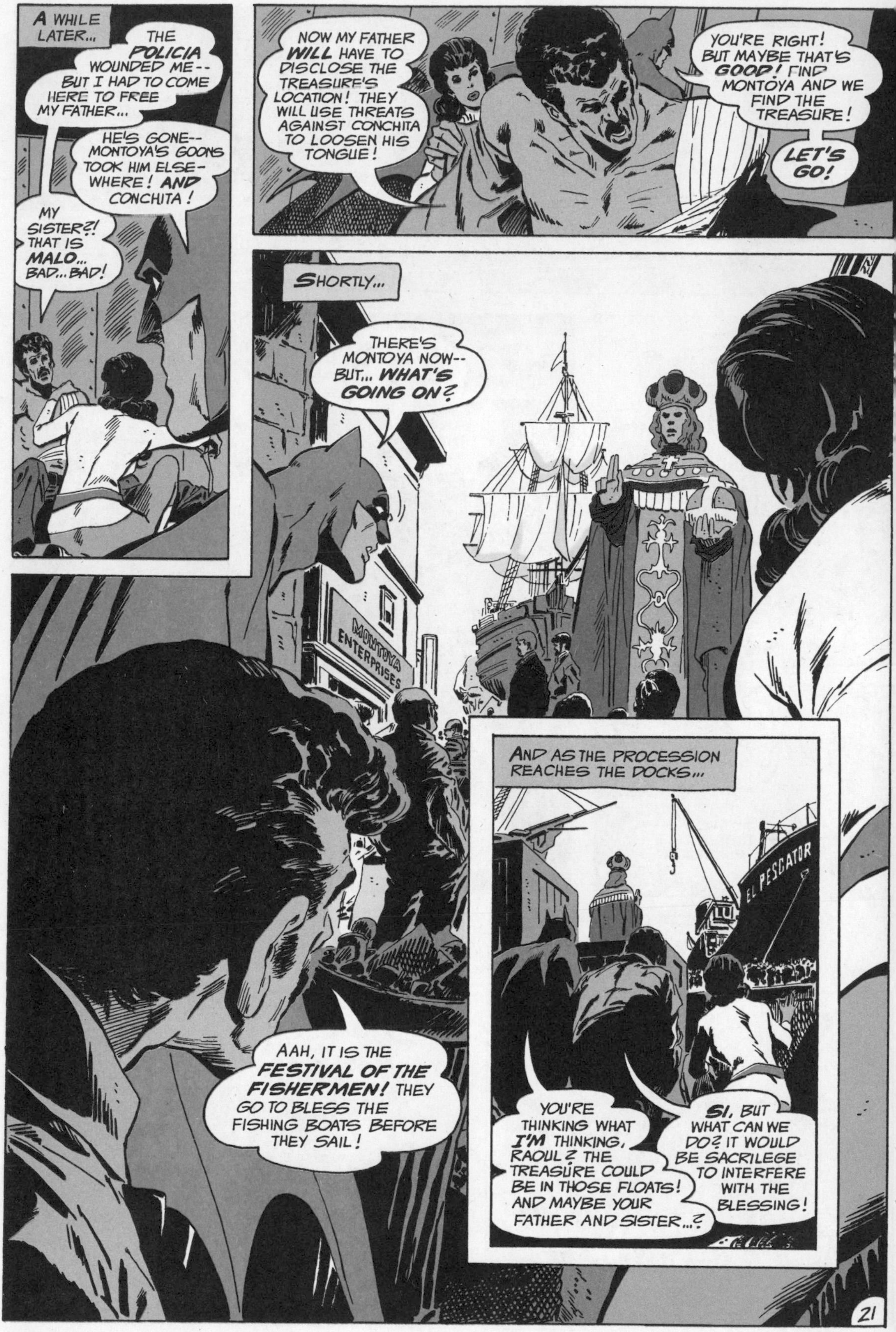
A WHILE LATER...
THE POLICIA WOUNDED ME-- BUT I HAD TO COME HERE TO FREE MY FATHER...
HE'S GONE-- MONTOYA'S GOONS TOOK HIM ELSEWHERE! AND CONCHITA!
MY SISTER?! THAT IS MALO... BAD...BAD!
NOW MY FATHER WILL HAVE TO DISCLOSE THE TREASURE'S LOCATION! THEY WILL USE THREATS AGAINST CONCHITA TO LOOSEN HIS TONGUE!
YOU'RE RIGHT! BUT MAYBE THAT'S GOOD! FIND MONTOYA AND WE FIND THE TREASURE!
LET'S GO!
SHORTLY...
THERE'S MONTOYA NOW-- BUT... WHAT'S GOING ON?
MONTOYA ENTERPRISES
AAH, IT IS THE FESTIVAL OF THE FISHERMEN! THEY GO TO BLESS THE FISHING BOATS BEFORE THEY SAIL!
AND AS THE PROCESSION REACHES THE DOCKS...
EL PESCATOR
YOU'RE THINKING WHAT I'M THINKING, RAOUL? THE TREASURE COULD BE IN THOSE FLOATS! AND MAYBE YOUR FATHER AND SISTER...?
SI, BUT WHAT CAN WE DO? IT WOULD BE SACRILEGE TO INTERFERE WITH THE BLESSING!
21

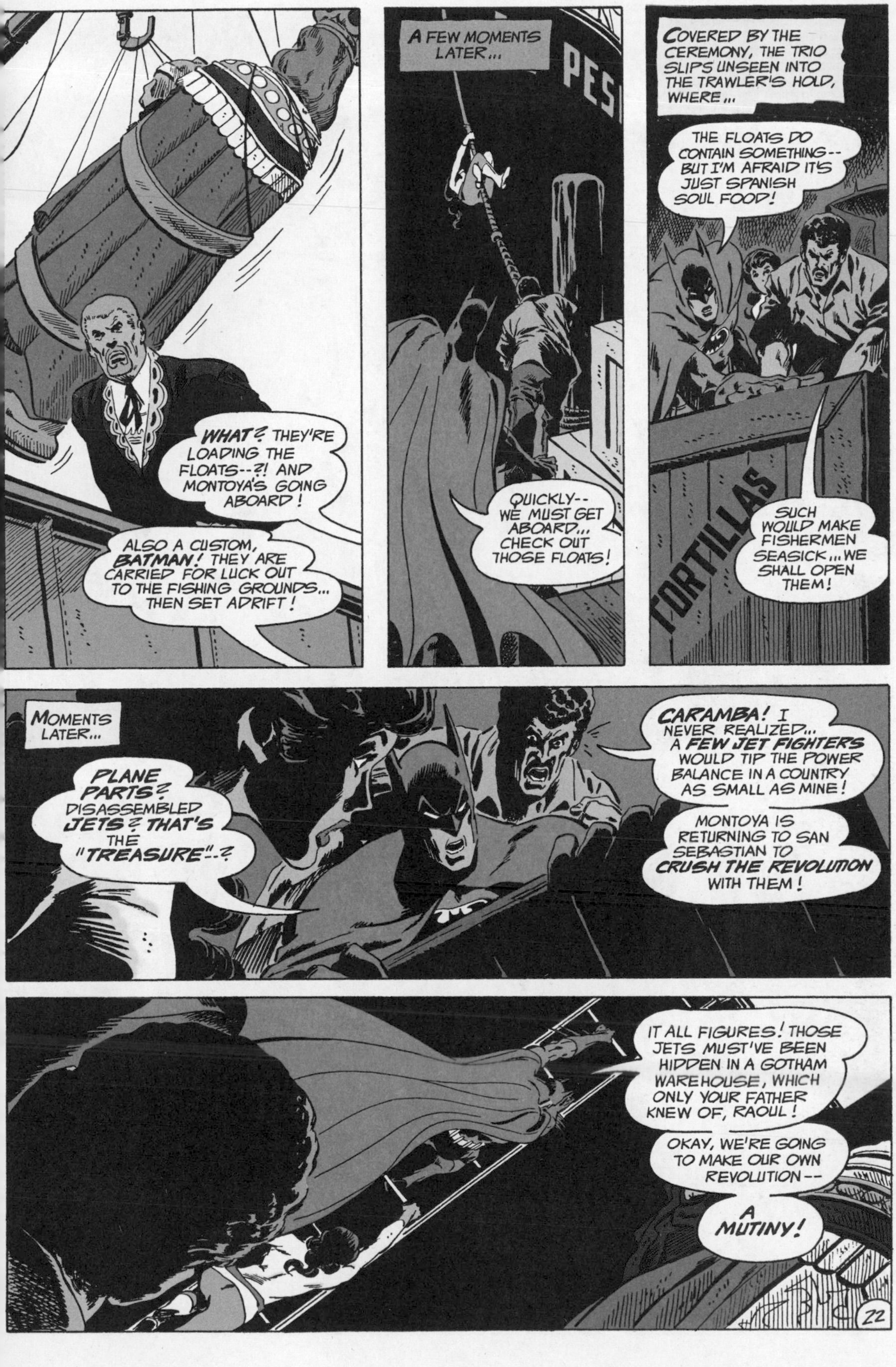
WHAT? THEY'RE LOADING THE FLOATS--?! AND MONTOYA'S GOING ABOARD!
ALSO A CUSTOM, BATMAN! THEY ARE CARRIED FOR LUCK OUT TO THE FISHING GROUNDS... THEN SET ADRIFT!
A FEW MOMENTS LATER...
PES
QUICKLY-- WE MUST GET ABOARD... CHECK OUT THOSE FLOATS!
COVERED BY THE CEREMONY, THE TRIO SLIPS UNSEEN INTO THE TRAWLER'S HOLD, WHERE...
THE FLOATS DO CONTAIN SOMETHING-- BUT I'M AFRAID IT'S JUST SPANISH SOUL FOOD!
TORTILLAS
SUCH WOULD MAKE FISHERMEN SEASICK... WE SHALL OPEN THEM!
MOMENTS LATER...
PLANE PARTS? DISASSEMBLED JETS? THAT'S THE "TREASURE"-?
CARAMBA! I NEVER REALIZED... A FEW JET FIGHTERS WOULD TIP THE POWER BALANCE IN A COUNTRY AS SMALL AS MINE!
MONTOYA IS RETURNING TO SAN SEBASTIAN TO CRUSH THE REVOLUTION WITH THEM!
IT ALL FIGURES! THOSE JETS MUST'VE BEEN HIDDEN IN A GOTHAM WAREHOUSE, WHICH ONLY YOUR FATHER KNEW OF, RAOUL!
OKAY, WE'RE GOING TO MAKE OUR OWN REVOLUTION --
A MUTINY!
22

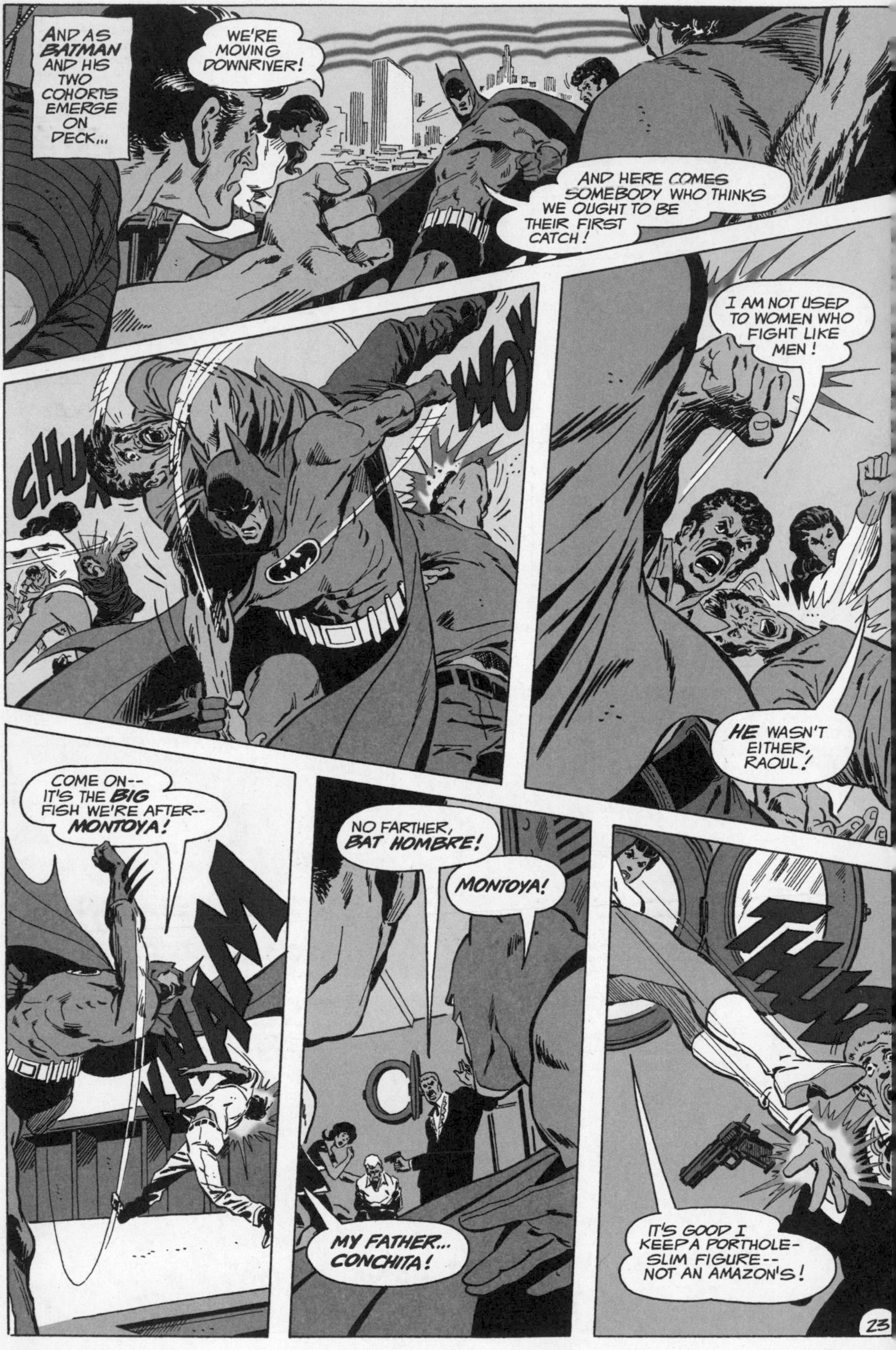
AND AS BATMAN AND HIS TWO COHORTS EMERGE ON DECK...
WE'RE MOVING DOWNRIVER!
AND HERE COMES SOMEBODY WHO THINKS WE OUGHT TO BE THEIR FIRST CATCH!
I AM NOT USED TO WOMEN WHO FIGHT LIKE MEN!
HE WASN'T EITHER, RAOUL!
COME ON-- IT'S THE BIG FISH WE'RE AFTER-- MONTOYA!
KHAM
NO FARTHER, BAT HOMBRE!
MONTOYA!
MY FATHER... CONCHITA!
IT'S GOOD I KEEP A PORTHOLE-SLIM FIGURE-- NOT AN AMAZON'S!
23

LATER...
THANKS TO YOU, SEÑOR BAT HOMBRE AND SEÑORITA DIANA, THE PLANES WILL GO TO THOSE WHO FIGHT FOR FREEDOM, AND SAN SEBASTIAN'S FUTURE WILL BE BRIGHT!
MAYBE IT MAKES UP FOR SUSPECTING YOUR FAMILY WAS PLAYING A CON GAME ON MY FRIEND, BRUCE WAYNE!
OF COURSE, BAT HOMBRE! BUT SINCE SEÑOR WAYNE CANNOT SHARE IN THE "TREASURE"-- AND I DID PROMISE HIM A REWARD...
...WHEN NEXT YOU SEE HIM, PLEASE GIVE HIM... THIS!
OLÉ!
THE END
24

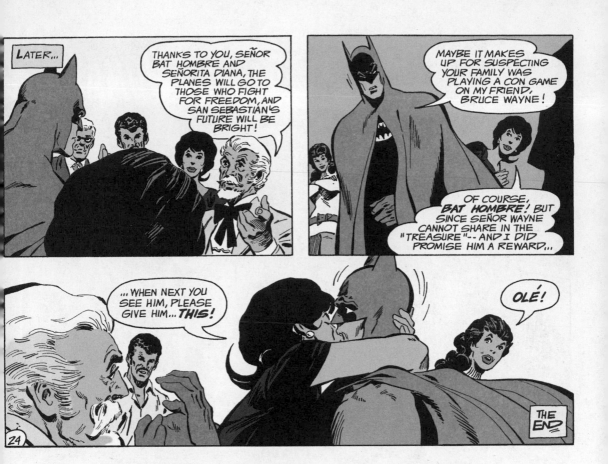

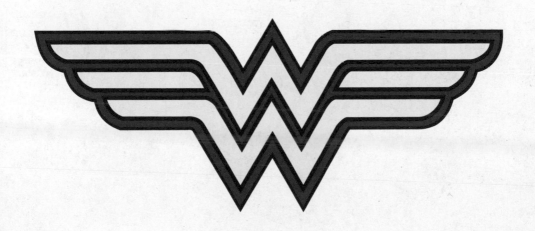

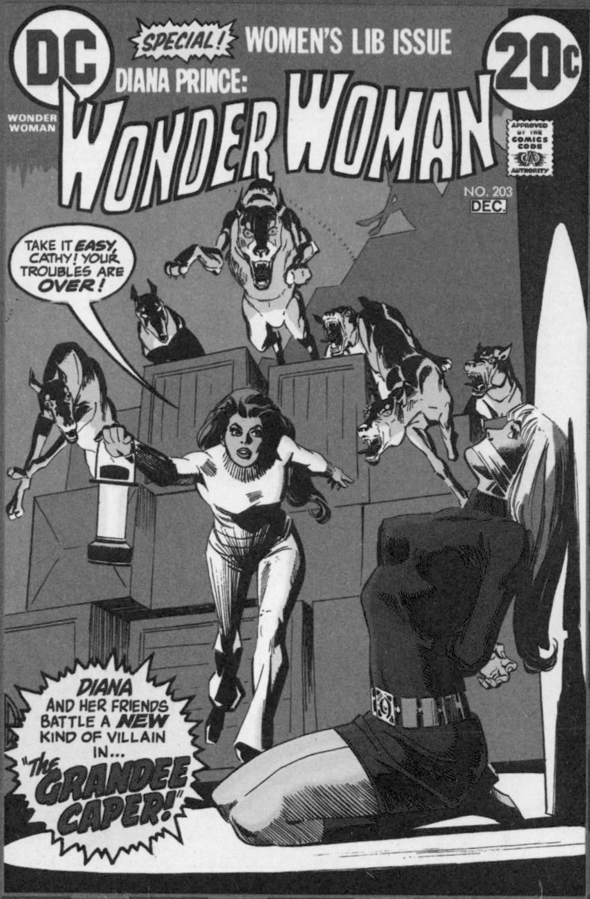
DC
SPECIAL! WOMEN'S LIB ISSUE
20¢
DIANA PRINCE:
WONDER WOMAN
WONDER WOMAN
NO. 203
DEC.
TAKE IT EASY, CATHY! YOUR TROUBLES ARE OVER!
DIANA AND HER FRIENDS BATTLE A NEW KIND OF VILLAIN IN... "The GRANDEE CAPER!"

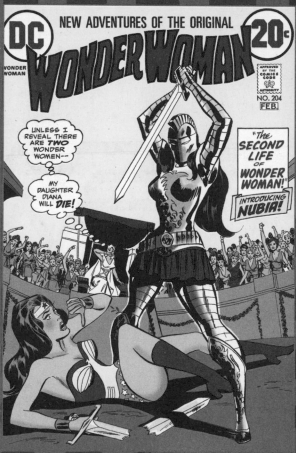

Wonder Woman 203
Cover by Dick Giordano

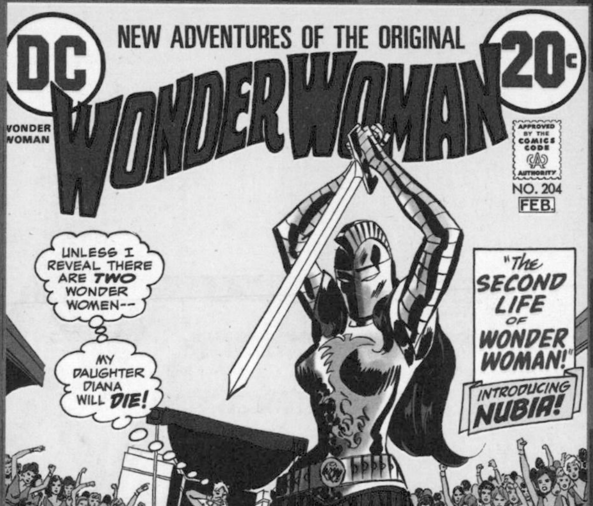
DC
NEW ADVENTURES OF THE ORIGINAL
20¢
WONDER WOMAN
WONDER WOMAN
NO. 204
FEB.
UNLESS I REVEAL THERE ARE TWO WONDER WOMEN--
MY DAUGHTER DIANA WILL DIE!
"The SECOND LIFE OF WONDER WOMAN!"
INTRODUCING NUBIA!

Wonder Woman 204
Cover by Don Heck / Dick Giordano

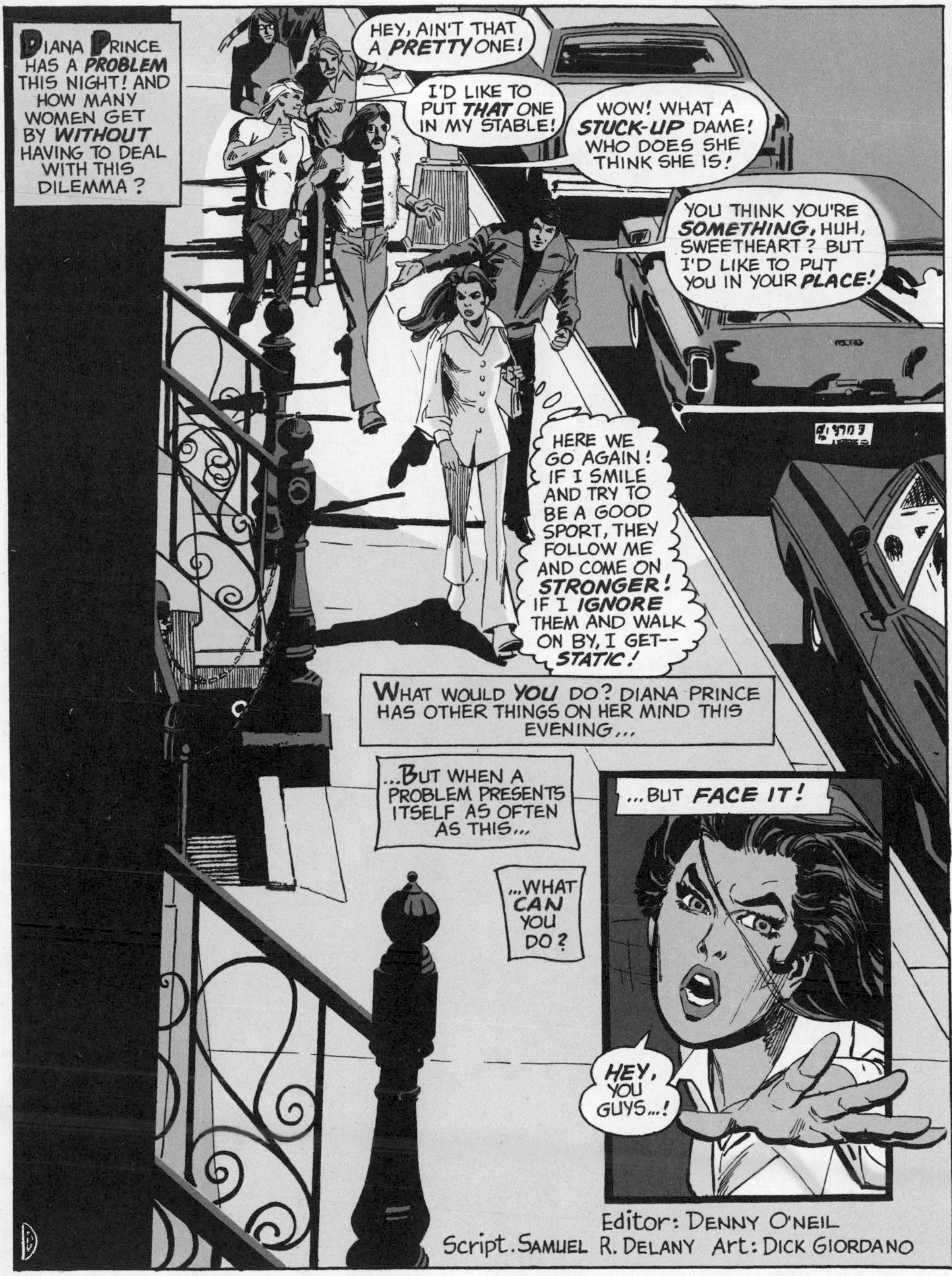
DIANA PRINCE HAS A PROBLEM THIS NIGHT! AND HOW MANY WOMEN GET BY WITHOUT HAVING TO DEAL WITH THIS DILEMMA?
HEY, AIN'T THAT A PRETTY ONE!
I'D LIKE TO PUT THAT ONE IN MY STABLE!
WOW! WHAT A STUCK-UP DAME! WHO DOES SHE THINK SHE IS!
YOU THINK YOU'RE SOMETHING, HUH, SWEETHEART? BUT I'D LIKE TO PUT YOU IN YOUR PLACE!
HERE WE GO AGAIN! IF I SMILE AND TRY TO BE A GOOD SPORT, THEY FOLLOW ME AND COME ON STRONGER! IF I IGNORE THEM AND WALK ON BY, I GET-- STATIC!
WHAT WOULD YOU DO? DIANA PRINCE HAS OTHER THINGS ON HER MIND THIS EVENING...
...BUT WHEN A PROBLEM PRESENTS ITSELF AS OFTEN AS THIS...
...WHAT CAN YOU DO?
...BUT FACE IT!
HEY, YOU GUYS...!
Editor: DENNY O'NEIL
Script. SAMUEL R. DELANY Art: DICK GIORDANO

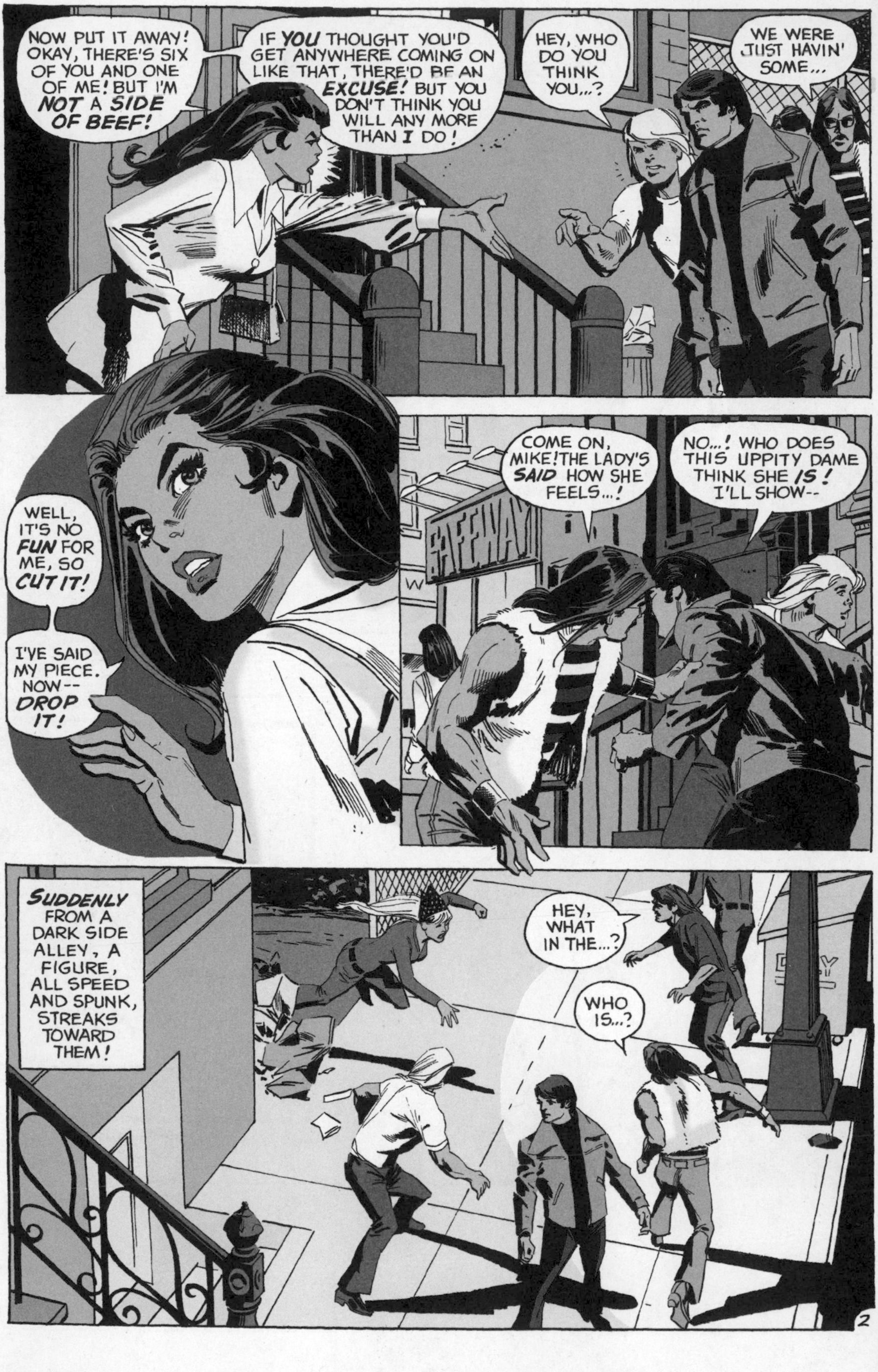
NOW PUT IT AWAY! OKAY, THERE'S SIX OF YOU AND ONE OF ME! BUT I'M NOT A SIDE OF BEEF!
IF YOU THOUGHT YOU'D GET ANYWHERE COMING ON LIKE THAT, THERE'D BE AN EXCUSE! BUT YOU DON'T THINK YOU WILL ANY MORE THAN I DO!
HEY, WHO DO YOU THINK YOU...?
WE WERE JUST HAVIN' SOME...
WELL, IT'S NO FUN FOR ME, SO CUT IT!
I'VE SAID MY PIECE. NOW-- DROP IT!
COME ON, MIKE! THE LADY'S SAID HOW SHE FEELS...!
NO...! WHO DOES THIS UPPITY DAME THINK SHE IS! I'LL SHOW--
SAFEWAY
SUDDENLY FROM A DARK SIDE ALLEY, A FIGURE, ALL SPEED AND SPUNK, STREAKS TOWARD THEM!
HEY, WHAT IN THE...?
WHO IS...?
2

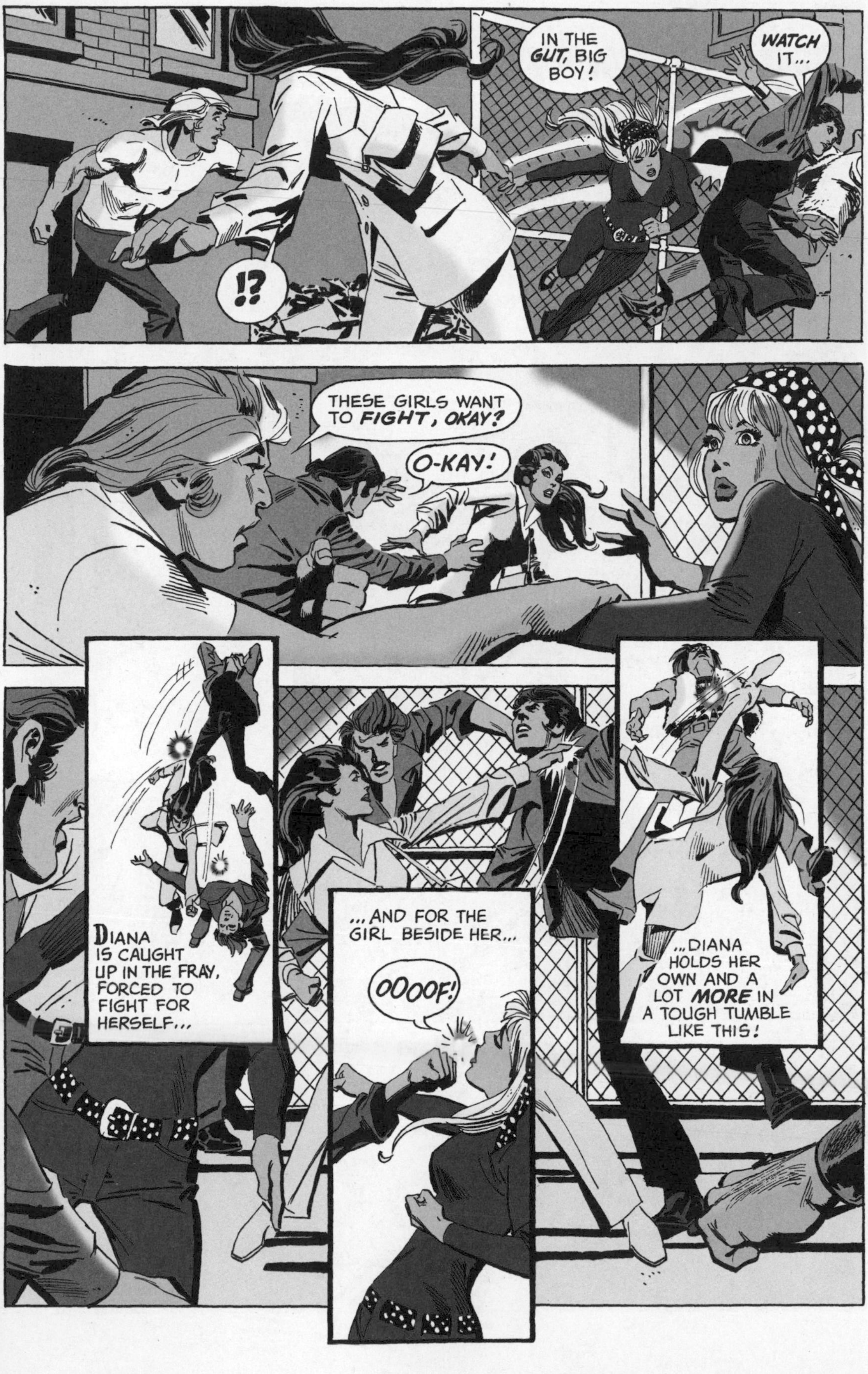
IN THE GUT, BIG BOY!
WATCH IT...
!?
THESE GIRLS WANT TO FIGHT, OKAY?
O-KAY!
DIANA IS CAUGHT UP IN THE FRAY, FORCED TO FIGHT FOR HERSELF...
...AND FOR THE GIRL BESIDE HER...
OOOOF!
...DIANA HOLDS HER OWN AND A LOT MORE IN A TOUGH TUMBLE LIKE THIS!

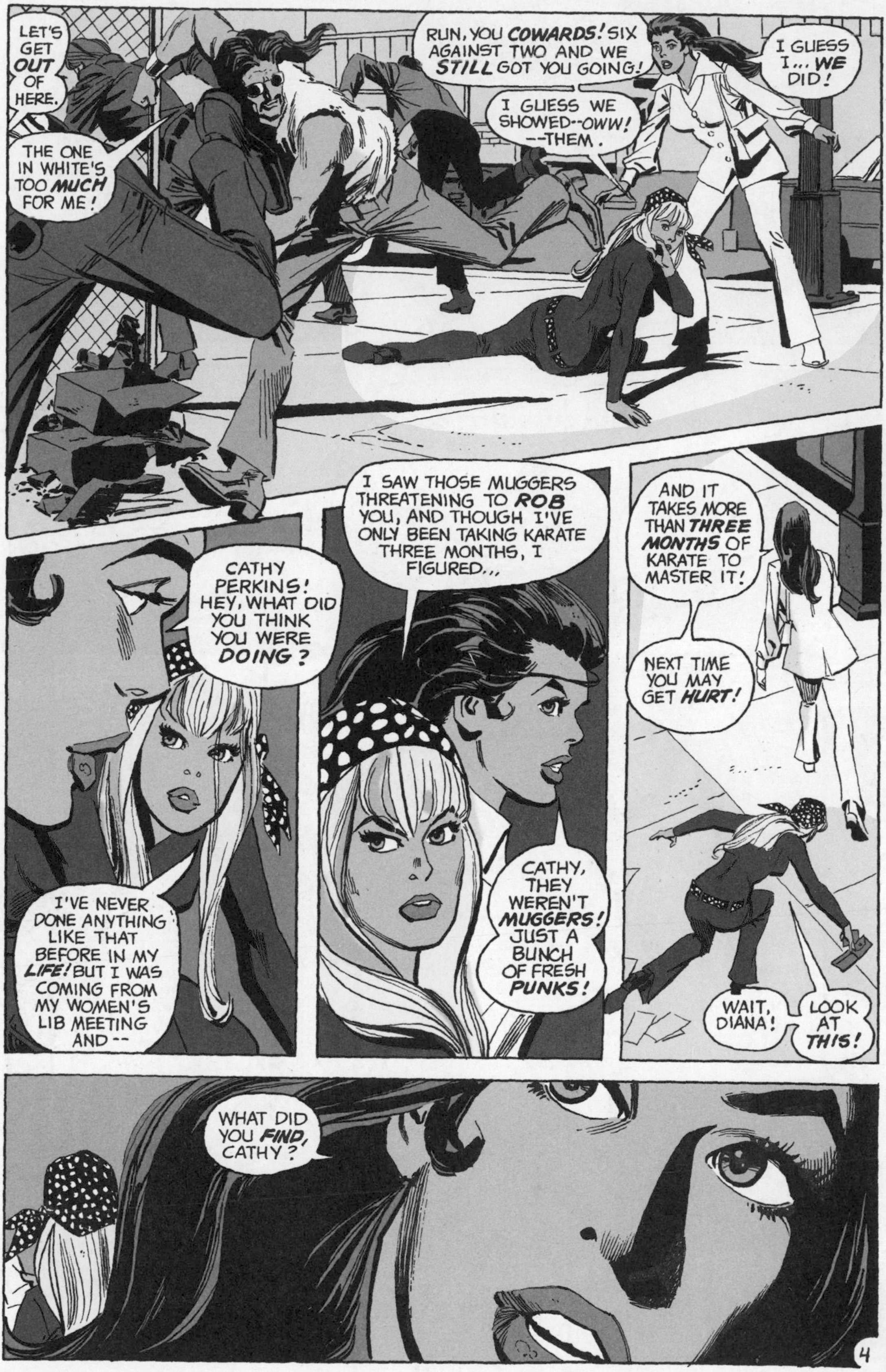
LET'S GET OUT OF HERE.
THE ONE IN WHITE'S TOO MUCH FOR ME!
RUN, YOU COWARDS! SIX AGAINST TWO AND WE STILL GOT YOU GOING!
I GUESS WE SHOWED--OWW! --THEM.
I GUESS I... WE DID!
CATHY PERKINS! HEY, WHAT DID YOU THINK YOU WERE DOING?
I'VE NEVER DONE ANYTHING LIKE THAT BEFORE IN MY LIFE! BUT I WAS COMING FROM MY WOMEN'S LIB MEETING AND --
I SAW THOSE MUGGERS THREATENING TO ROB YOU, AND THOUGH I'VE ONLY BEEN TAKING KARATE THREE MONTHS, I FIGURED...
CATHY, THEY WEREN'T MUGGERS! JUST A BUNCH OF FRESH PUNKS!
AND IT TAKES MORE THAN THREE MONTHS OF KARATE TO MASTER IT!
NEXT TIME YOU MAY GET HURT!
WAIT, DIANA!
LOOK AT THIS!
WHAT DID YOU FIND, CATHY?
4

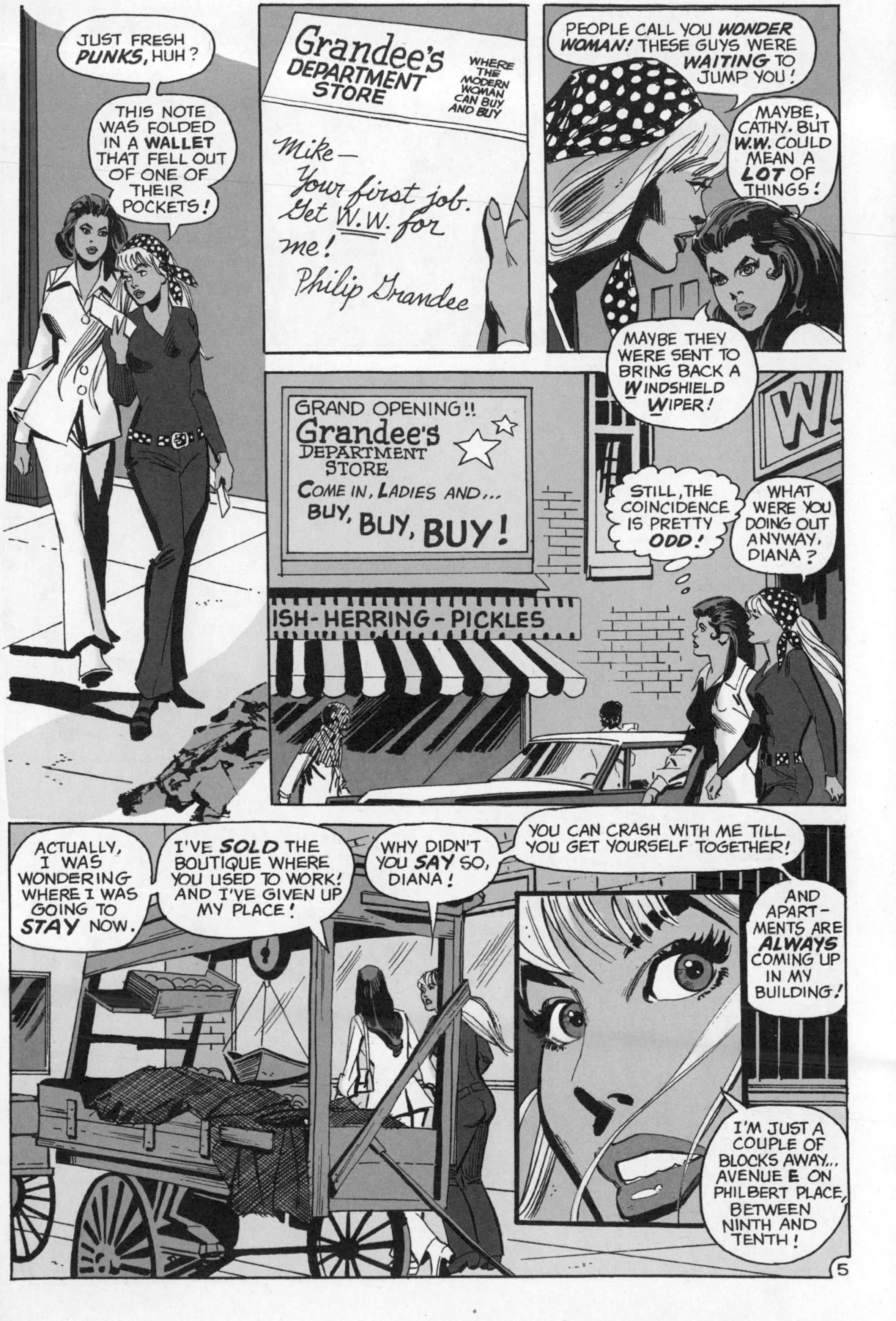

JUST FRESH PUNKS, HUH?
THIS NOTE WAS FOLDED IN A WALLET THAT FELL OUT OF ONE OF THEIR POCKETS!
Grandee's DEPARTMENT STORE
WHERE THE MODERN WOMAN CAN BUY AND BUY
Mike— Your first job. Get W.W. for me! Philip Grandee
PEOPLE CALL YOU WONDER WOMAN! THESE GUYS WERE WAITING TO JUMP YOU!
MAYBE, CATHY. BUT W.W. COULD MEAN A LOT OF THINGS!
MAYBE THEY WERE SENT TO BRING BACK A WINDSHIELD WIPER!
GRAND OPENING!! Grandee's DEPARTMENT STORE
COME IN, LADIES AND... BUY, BUY, BUY!
ISH-HERRING-PICKLES
STILL, THE COINCIDENCE IS PRETTY ODD!
WHAT WERE YOU DOING OUT ANYWAY, DIANA?
ACTUALLY, I WAS WONDERING WHERE I WAS GOING TO STAY NOW.
I'VE SOLD THE BOUTIQUE WHERE YOU USED TO WORK! AND I'VE GIVEN UP MY PLACE!
WHY DIDN'T YOU SAY SO, DIANA!
YOU CAN CRASH WITH ME TILL YOU GET YOURSELF TOGETHER!
AND APARTMENTS ARE ALWAYS COMING UP IN MY BUILDING!
I'M JUST A COUPLE OF BLOCKS AWAY... AVENUE E ON PHILBERT PLACE, BETWEEN NINTH AND TENTH!
5

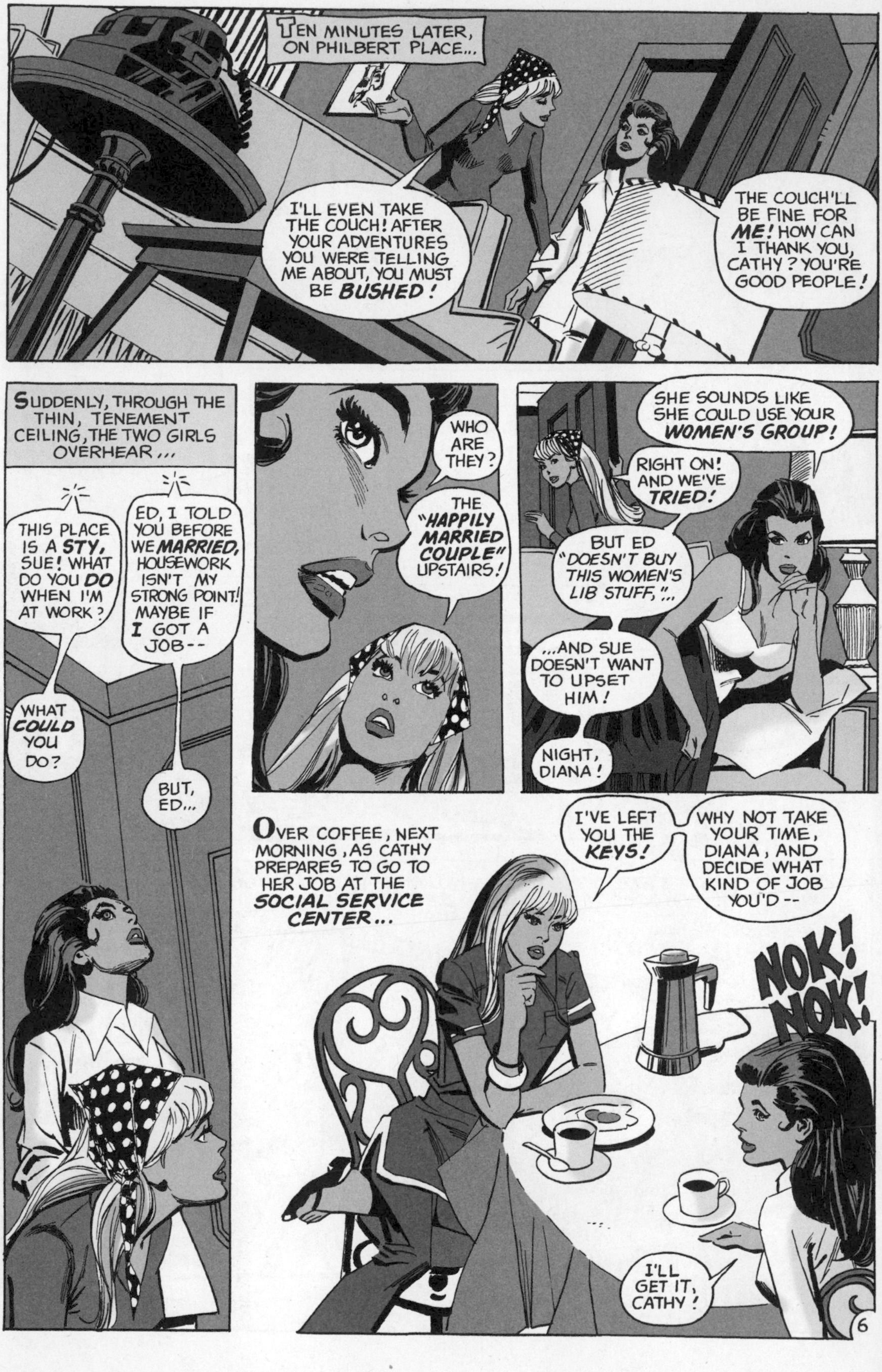

TEN MINUTES LATER, ON PHILBERT PLACE...
I'LL EVEN TAKE THE COUCH! AFTER YOUR ADVENTURES YOU WERE TELLING ME ABOUT, YOU MUST BE BUSHED!
THE COUCH'LL BE FINE FOR ME! HOW CAN I THANK YOU, CATHY? YOU'RE GOOD PEOPLE!
SUDDENLY, THROUGH THE THIN, TENEMENT CEILING, THE TWO GIRLS OVERHEAR...
THIS PLACE IS A STY, SUE! WHAT DO YOU DO WHEN I'M AT WORK?
ED, I TOLD YOU BEFORE WE MARRIED, HOUSEWORK ISN'T MY STRONG POINT! MAYBE IF I GOT A JOB--
WHAT COULD YOU DO?
BUT, ED...
WHO ARE THEY?
THE "HAPPILY MARRIED COUPLE" UPSTAIRS!
SHE SOUNDS LIKE SHE COULD USE YOUR WOMEN'S GROUP!
RIGHT ON! AND WE'VE TRIED!
BUT ED "DOESN'T BUY THIS WOMEN'S LIB STUFF,"...
...AND SUE DOESN'T WANT TO UPSET HIM!
NIGHT, DIANA!
OVER COFFEE, NEXT MORNING, AS CATHY PREPARES TO GO TO HER JOB AT THE SOCIAL SERVICE CENTER...
I'VE LEFT YOU THE KEYS!
WHY NOT TAKE YOUR TIME, DIANA, AND DECIDE WHAT KIND OF JOB YOU'D --
NOK! NOK!
I'LL GET IT, CATHY!
6

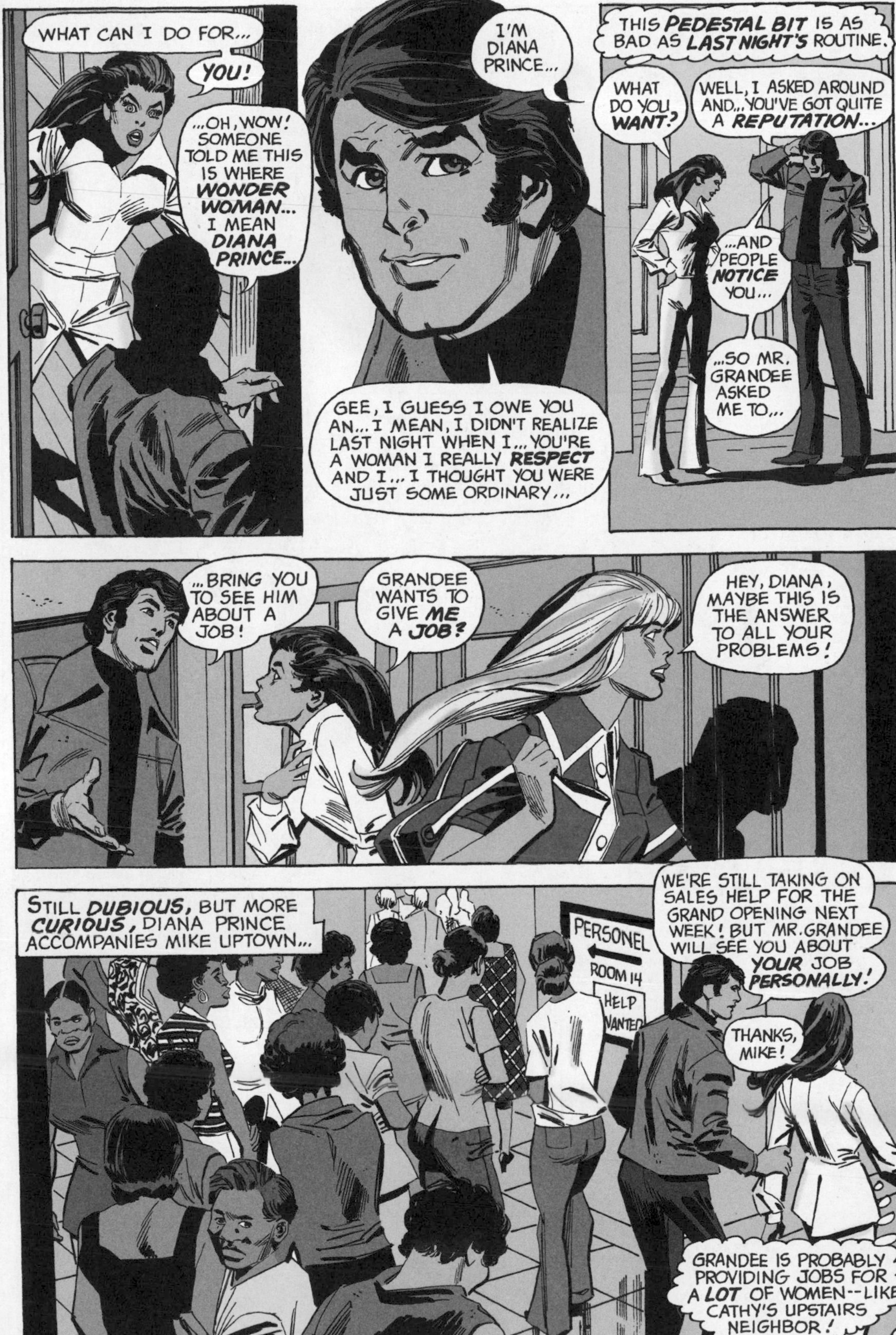
WHAT CAN I DO FOR...
YOU!
...OH, WOW! SOMEONE TOLD ME THIS IS WHERE WONDER WOMAN... I MEAN DIANA PRINCE...
I'M DIANA PRINCE...
GEE, I GUESS I OWE YOU AN... I MEAN, I DIDN'T REALIZE LAST NIGHT WHEN I... YOU'RE A WOMAN I REALLY RESPECT AND I... I THOUGHT YOU WERE JUST SOME ORDINARY...
THIS PEDESTAL BIT IS AS BAD AS LAST NIGHT'S ROUTINE.
WHAT DO YOU WANT?
WELL, I ASKED AROUND AND... YOU'VE GOT QUITE A REPUTATION...
...AND PEOPLE NOTICE YOU...
...SO MR. GRANDEE ASKED ME TO...
...BRING YOU TO SEE HIM ABOUT A JOB!
GRANDEE WANTS TO GIVE ME A JOB?
HEY, DIANA, MAYBE THIS IS THE ANSWER TO ALL YOUR PROBLEMS!
STILL DUBIOUS, BUT MORE CURIOUS, DIANA PRINCE ACCOMPANIES MIKE UPTOWN...
PERSONEL
ROOM 14
HELP WANTED
WE'RE STILL TAKING ON SALES HELP FOR THE GRAND OPENING NEXT WEEK! BUT MR. GRANDEE WILL SEE YOU ABOUT YOUR JOB PERSONALLY!
THANKS, MIKE!
GRANDEE IS PROBABLY PROVIDING JOBS FOR A LOT OF WOMEN--LIKE CATHY'S UPSTAIRS NEIGHBOR!
7

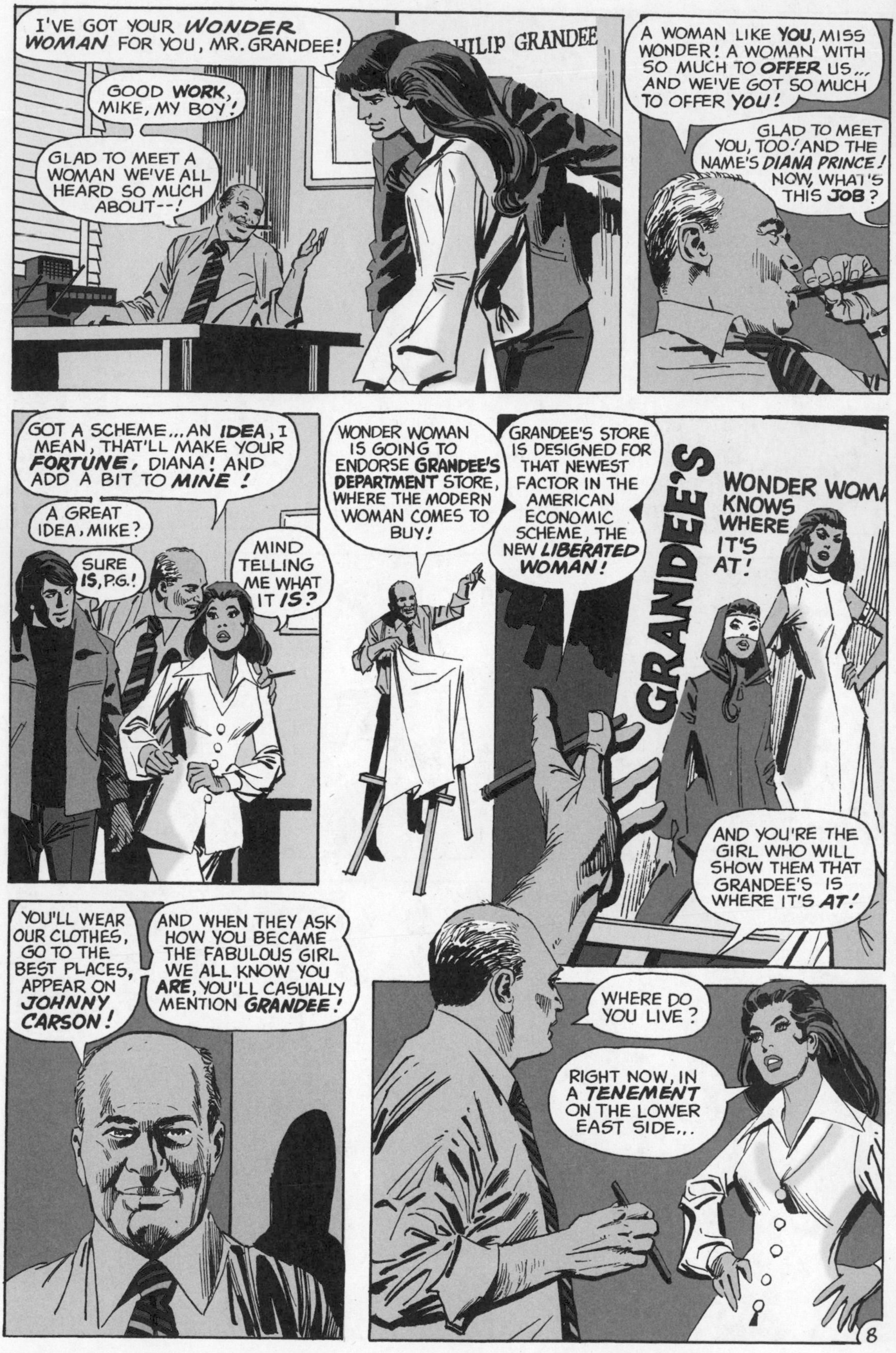

I'VE GOT YOUR WONDER WOMAN FOR YOU, MR. GRANDEE!
PHILIP GRANDEE
GOOD WORK, MIKE, MY BOY!
GLAD TO MEET A WOMAN WE'VE ALL HEARD SO MUCH ABOUT--!
A WOMAN LIKE YOU, MISS WONDER! A WOMAN WITH SO MUCH TO OFFER US... AND WE'VE GOT SO MUCH TO OFFER YOU!
GLAD TO MEET YOU, TOO! AND THE NAME'S DIANA PRINCE! NOW, WHAT'S THIS JOB?
GOT A SCHEME... AN IDEA, I MEAN, THAT'LL MAKE YOUR FORTUNE, DIANA! AND ADD A BIT TO MINE!
A GREAT IDEA, MIKE?
SURE IS, P.G.!
MIND TELLING ME WHAT IT IS?
WONDER WOMAN IS GOING TO ENDORSE GRANDEE'S DEPARTMENT STORE, WHERE THE MODERN WOMAN COMES TO BUY!
GRANDEE'S STORE IS DESIGNED FOR THAT NEWEST FACTOR IN THE AMERICAN ECONOMIC SCHEME, THE NEW LIBERATED WOMAN!
GRANDEE'S
WONDER WOMA
KNOWS WHERE IT'S AT!
AND YOU'RE THE GIRL WHO WILL SHOW THEM THAT GRANDEE'S IS WHERE IT'S AT!
YOU'LL WEAR OUR CLOTHES, GO TO THE BEST PLACES, APPEAR ON JOHNNY CARSON!
AND WHEN THEY ASK HOW YOU BECAME THE FABULOUS GIRL WE ALL KNOW YOU ARE, YOU'LL CASUALLY MENTION GRANDEE!
WHERE DO YOU LIVE?
RIGHT NOW, IN A TENEMENT ON THE LOWER EAST SIDE...
8

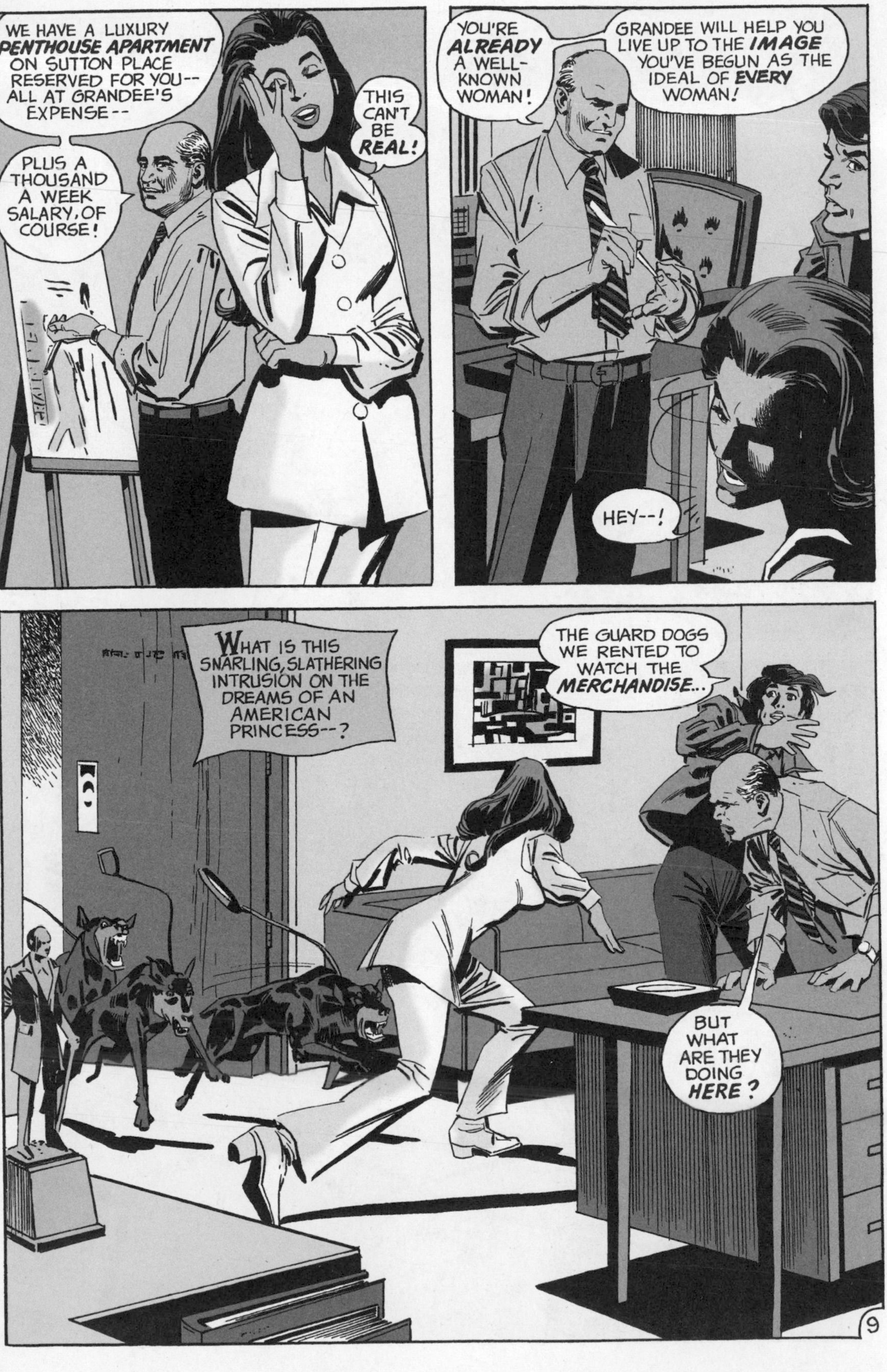
WE HAVE A LUXURY PENTHOUSE APARTMENT ON SUTTON PLACE RESERVED FOR YOU-- ALL AT GRANDEE'S EXPENSE--
PLUS A THOUSAND A WEEK SALARY, OF COURSE!
THIS CAN'T BE REAL!
YOU'RE ALREADY A WELL-KNOWN WOMAN!
GRANDEE WILL HELP YOU LIVE UP TO THE IMAGE YOU'VE BEGUN AS THE IDEAL OF EVERY WOMAN!
HEY--!
WHAT IS THIS SNARLING, SLATHERING INTRUSION ON THE DREAMS OF AN AMERICAN PRINCESS--?
THE GUARD DOGS WE RENTED TO WATCH THE MERCHANDISE...
BUT WHAT ARE THEY DOING HERE?
9

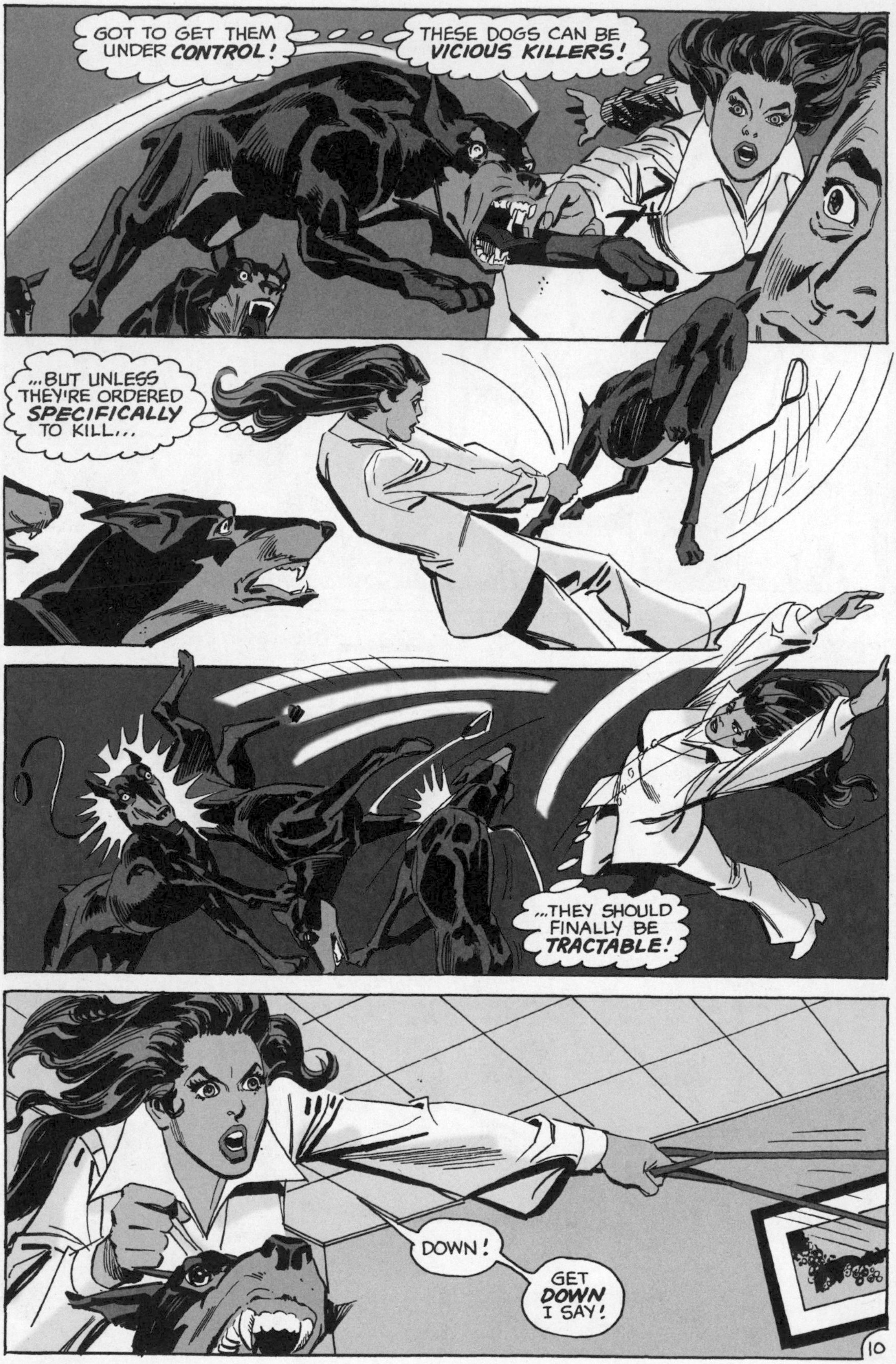
GOT TO GET THEM UNDER CONTROL!
THESE DOGS CAN BE VICIOUS KILLERS!
...BUT UNLESS THEY'RE ORDERED SPECIFICALLY TO KILL...
...THEY SHOULD FINALLY BE TRACTABLE!
DOWN!
GET DOWN I SAY!
10

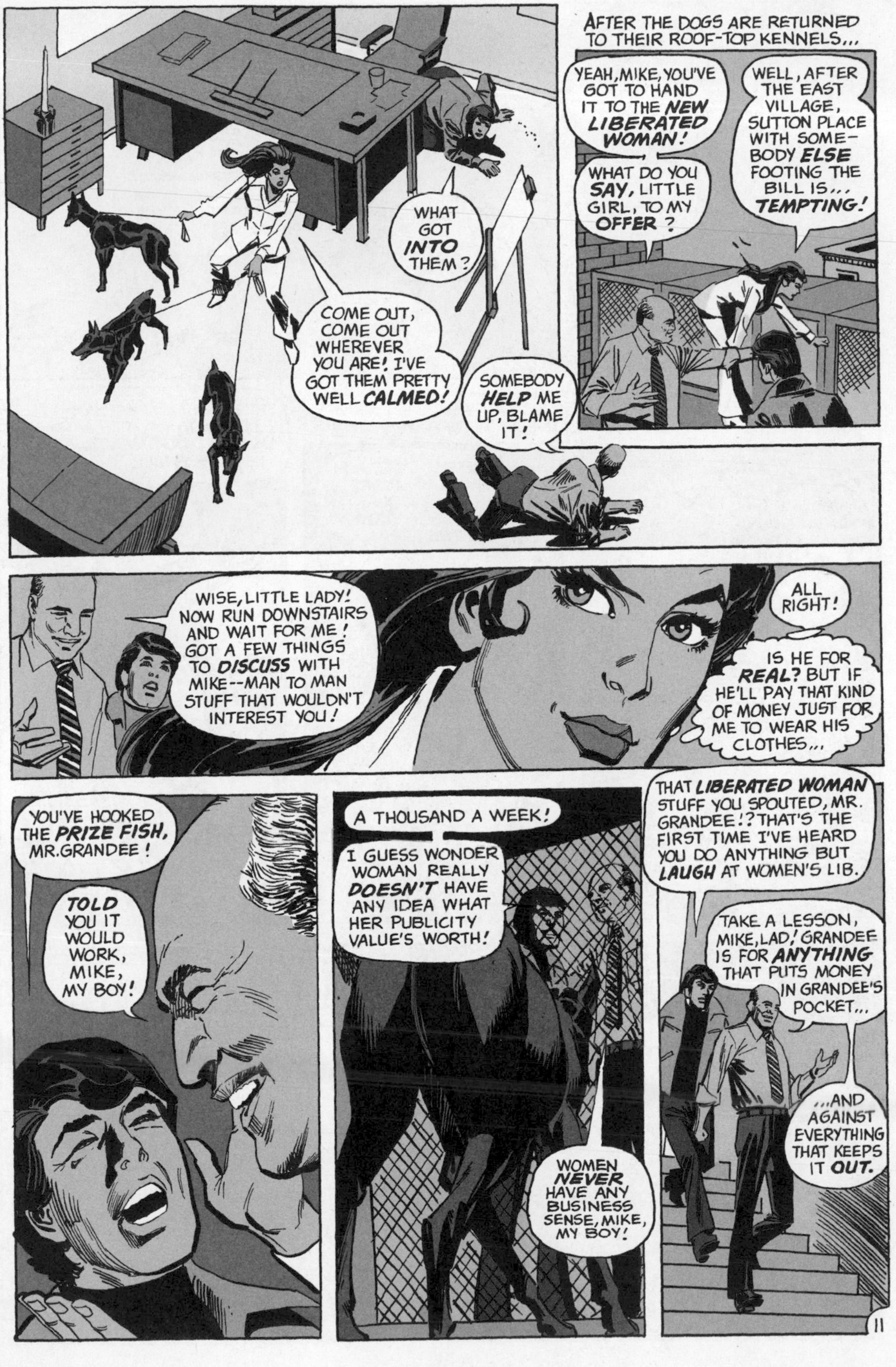
COME OUT, COME OUT WHEREVER YOU ARE! I'VE GOT THEM PRETTY WELL CALMED!
WHAT GOT INTO THEM?
SOMEBODY HELP ME UP, BLAME IT!
AFTER THE DOGS ARE RETURNED TO THEIR ROOF-TOP KENNELS...
YEAH, MIKE, YOU'VE GOT TO HAND IT TO THE NEW LIBERATED WOMAN!
WHAT DO YOU SAY, LITTLE GIRL, TO MY OFFER?
WELL, AFTER THE EAST VILLAGE, SUTTON PLACE WITH SOMEBODY ELSE FOOTING THE BILL IS... TEMPTING!
WISE, LITTLE LADY! NOW RUN DOWNSTAIRS AND WAIT FOR ME! GOT A FEW THINGS TO DISCUSS WITH MIKE--MAN TO MAN STUFF THAT WOULDN'T INTEREST YOU!
ALL RIGHT!
IS HE FOR REAL? BUT IF HE'LL PAY THAT KIND OF MONEY JUST FOR ME TO WEAR HIS CLOTHES...
YOU'VE HOOKED THE PRIZE FISH, MR. GRANDEE!
TOLD YOU IT WOULD WORK, MIKE, MY BOY!
A THOUSAND A WEEK!
I GUESS WONDER WOMAN REALLY DOESN'T HAVE ANY IDEA WHAT HER PUBLICITY VALUE'S WORTH!
WOMEN NEVER HAVE ANY BUSINESS SENSE, MIKE, MY BOY!
THAT LIBERATED WOMAN STUFF YOU SPOUTED, MR. GRANDEE!? THAT'S THE FIRST TIME I'VE HEARD YOU DO ANYTHING BUT LAUGH AT WOMEN'S LIB.
TAKE A LESSON, MIKE, LAD! GRANDEE IS FOR ANYTHING THAT PUTS MONEY IN GRANDEE'S POCKET...
...AND AGAINST EVERYTHING THAT KEEPS IT OUT.
11

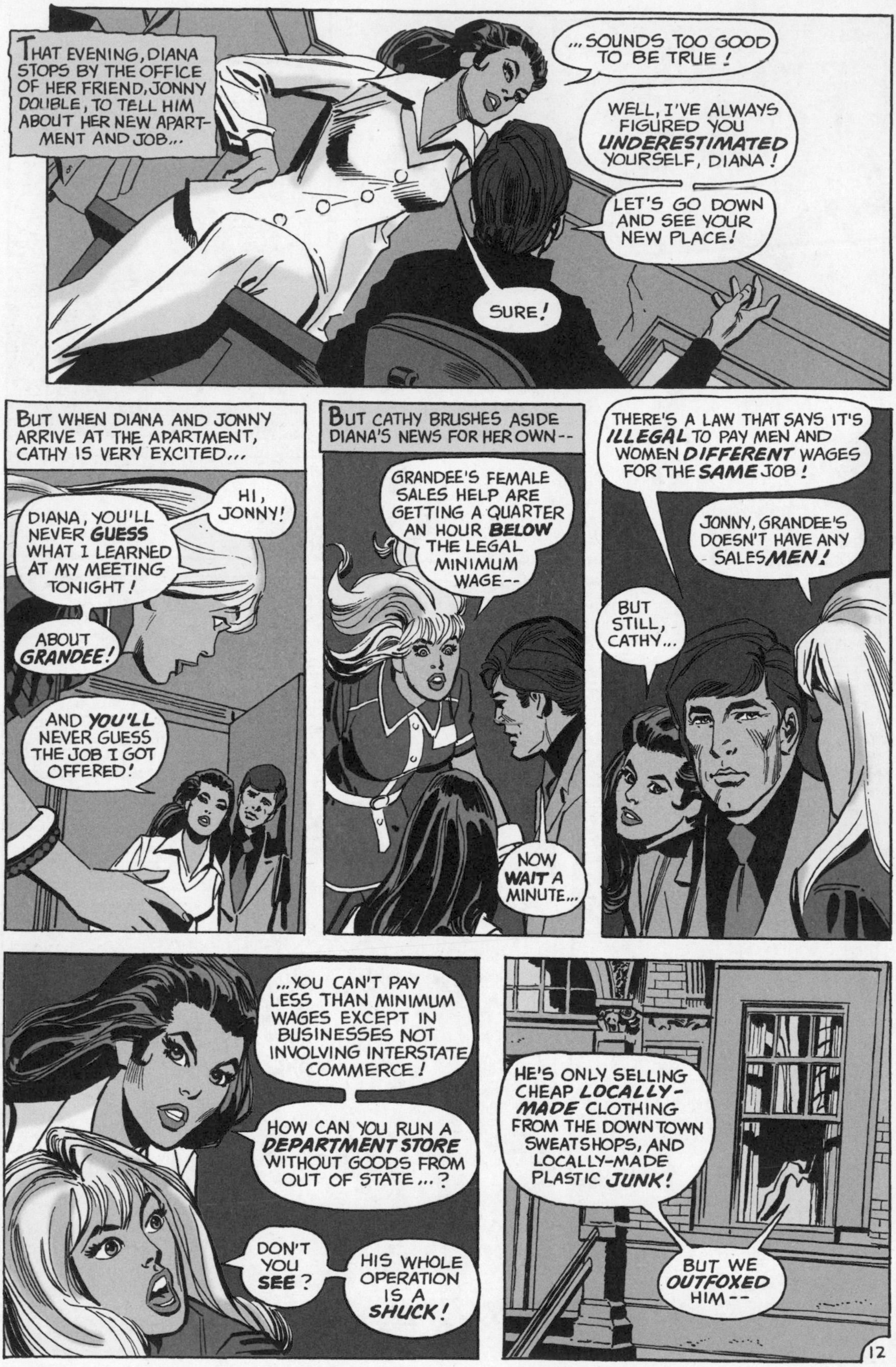
THAT EVENING, DIANA STOPS BY THE OFFICE OF HER FRIEND, JONNY DOUBLE, TO TELL HIM ABOUT HER NEW APARTMENT AND JOB...
...SOUNDS TOO GOOD TO BE TRUE!
WELL, I'VE ALWAYS FIGURED YOU UNDERESTIMATED YOURSELF, DIANA!
LET'S GO DOWN AND SEE YOUR NEW PLACE!
SURE!
BUT WHEN DIANA AND JONNY ARRIVE AT THE APARTMENT, CATHY IS VERY EXCITED...
HI, JONNY!
DIANA, YOU'LL NEVER GUESS WHAT I LEARNED AT MY MEETING TONIGHT!
ABOUT GRANDEE!
AND YOU'LL NEVER GUESS THE JOB I GOT OFFERED!
BUT CATHY BRUSHES ASIDE DIANA'S NEWS FOR HER OWN--
GRANDEE'S FEMALE SALES HELP ARE GETTING A QUARTER AN HOUR BELOW THE LEGAL MINIMUM WAGE--
NOW WAIT A MINUTE...
THERE'S A LAW THAT SAYS IT'S ILLEGAL TO PAY MEN AND WOMEN DIFFERENT WAGES FOR THE SAME JOB!
JONNY, GRANDEE'S DOESN'T HAVE ANY SALESMEN!
BUT STILL, CATHY...
...YOU CAN'T PAY LESS THAN MINIMUM WAGES EXCEPT IN BUSINESSES NOT INVOLVING INTERSTATE COMMERCE!
HOW CAN YOU RUN A DEPARTMENT STORE WITHOUT GOODS FROM OUT OF STATE...?
DON'T YOU SEE?
HIS WHOLE OPERATION IS A SHUCK!
HE'S ONLY SELLING CHEAP LOCALLY-MADE CLOTHING FROM THE DOWNTOWN SWEATSHOPS, AND LOCALLY-MADE PLASTIC JUNK!
BUT WE OUTFOXED HIM--
12

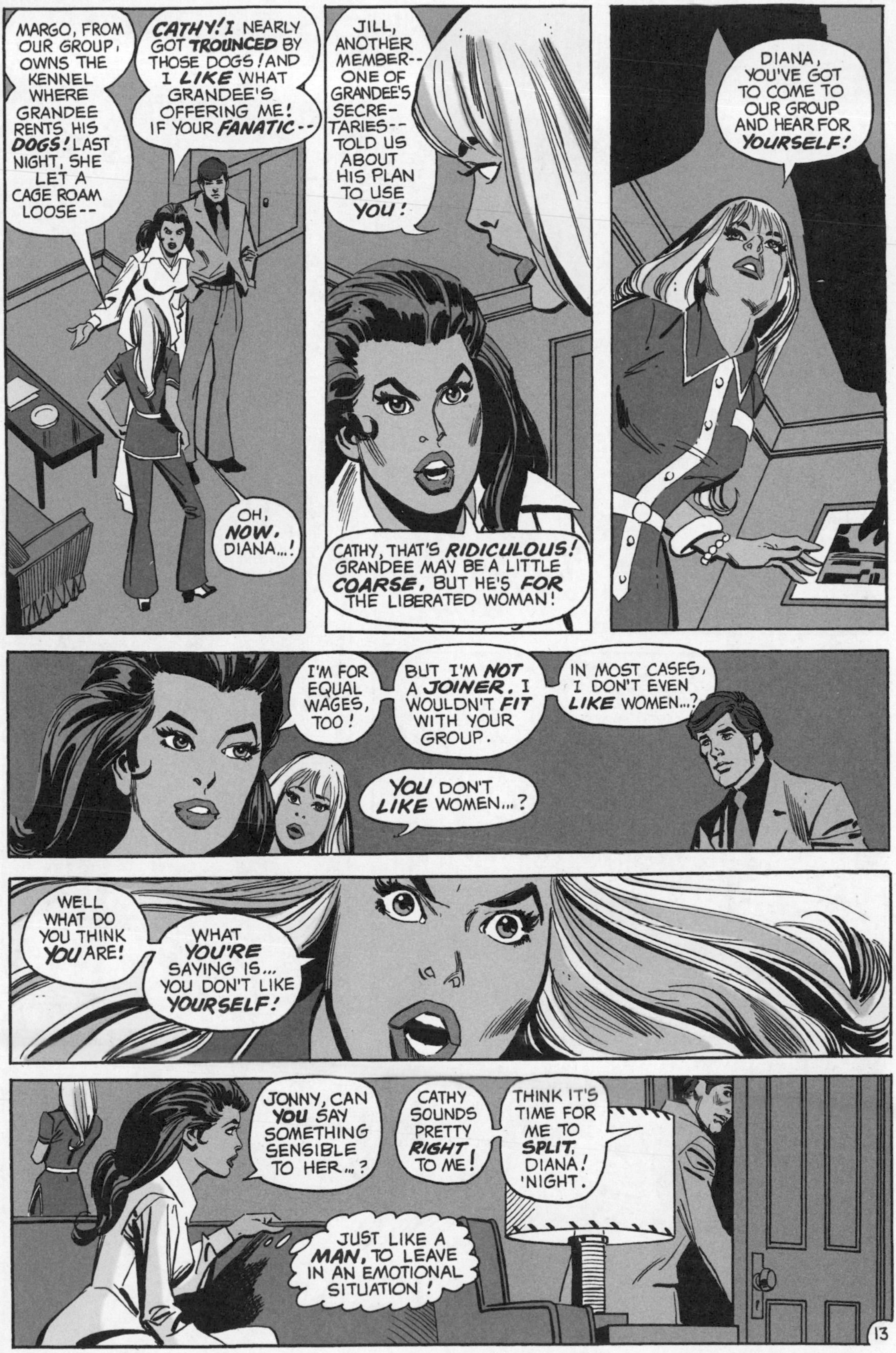
MARGO, FROM OUR GROUP, OWNS THE KENNEL WHERE GRANDEE RENTS HIS DOGS! LAST NIGHT, SHE LET A CAGE ROAM LOOSE--
CATHY! I NEARLY GOT TROUNCED BY THOSE DOGS! AND I LIKE WHAT GRANDEE'S OFFERING ME! IF YOUR FANATIC--
OH, NOW, DIANA...!
JILL, ANOTHER MEMBER--ONE OF GRANDEE'S SECRETARIES--TOLD US ABOUT HIS PLAN TO USE YOU!
CATHY, THAT'S RIDICULOUS! GRANDEE MAY BE A LITTLE COARSE, BUT HE'S FOR THE LIBERATED WOMAN!
DIANA, YOU'VE GOT TO COME TO OUR GROUP AND HEAR FOR YOURSELF!
I'M FOR EQUAL WAGES, TOO!
BUT I'M NOT A JOINER. I WOULDN'T FIT WITH YOUR GROUP.
IN MOST CASES, I DON'T EVEN LIKE WOMEN...?
YOU DON'T LIKE WOMEN...?
WELL WHAT DO YOU THINK YOU ARE!
WHAT YOU'RE SAYING IS... YOU DON'T LIKE YOURSELF!
JONNY, CAN YOU SAY SOMETHING SENSIBLE TO HER...?
CATHY SOUNDS PRETTY RIGHT, TO ME!
THINK IT'S TIME FOR ME TO SPLIT, DIANA! 'NIGHT.
JUST LIKE A MAN, TO LEAVE IN AN EMOTIONAL SITUATION!
13

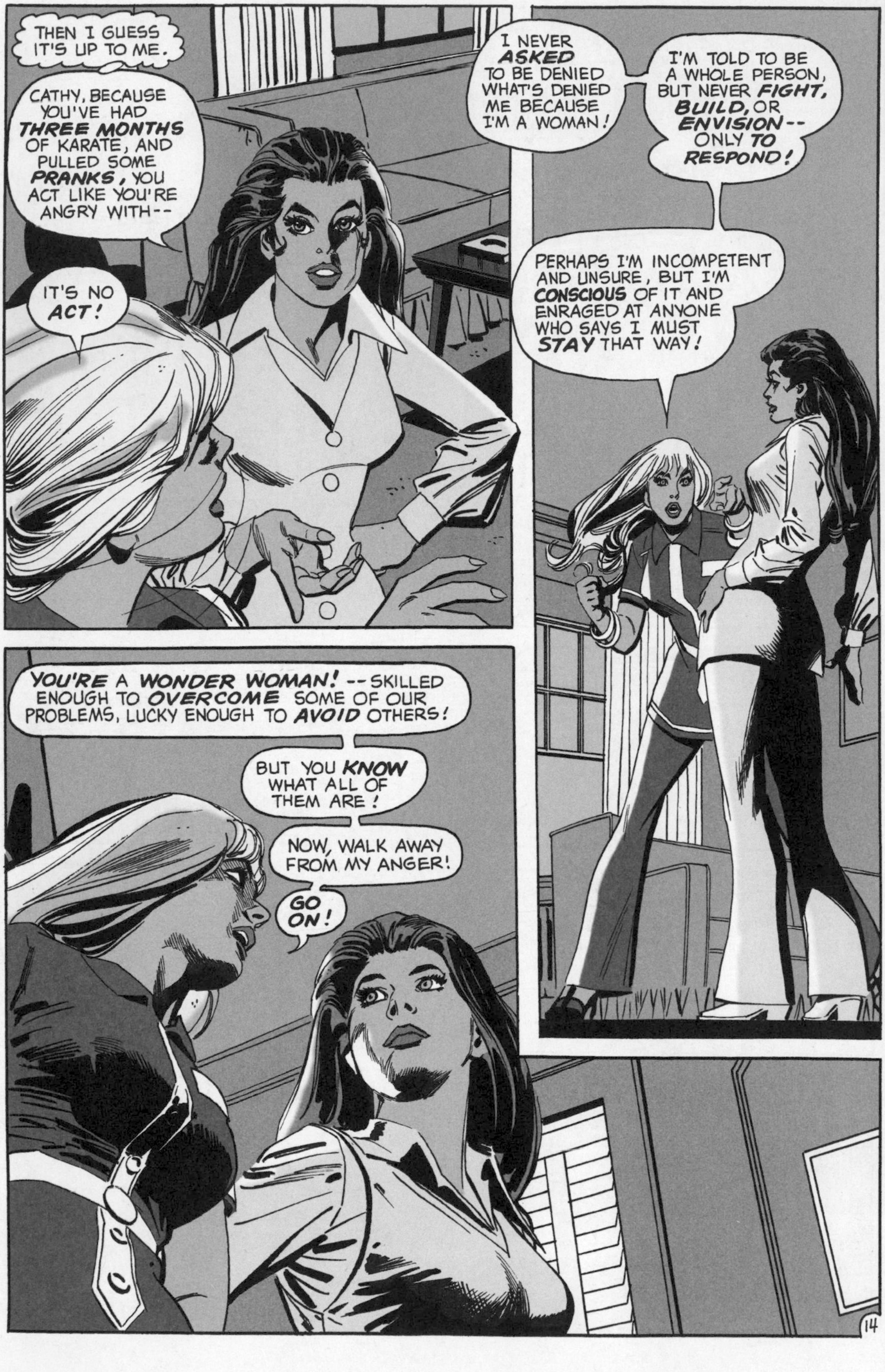
THEN I GUESS IT'S UP TO ME.
CATHY, BECAUSE YOU'VE HAD THREE MONTHS OF KARATE, AND PULLED SOME PRANKS, YOU ACT LIKE YOU'RE ANGRY WITH--
IT'S NO ACT!
I NEVER ASKED TO BE DENIED WHAT'S DENIED ME BECAUSE I'M A WOMAN!
I'M TOLD TO BE A WHOLE PERSON, BUT NEVER FIGHT, BUILD, OR ENVISION-- ONLY TO RESPOND!
PERHAPS I'M INCOMPETENT AND UNSURE, BUT I'M CONSCIOUS OF IT AND ENRAGED AT ANYONE WHO SAYS I MUST STAY THAT WAY!
YOU'RE A WONDER WOMAN! --SKILLED ENOUGH TO OVERCOME SOME OF OUR PROBLEMS, LUCKY ENOUGH TO AVOID OTHERS!
BUT YOU KNOW WHAT ALL OF THEM ARE!
NOW, WALK AWAY FROM MY ANGER!
GO ON!
14

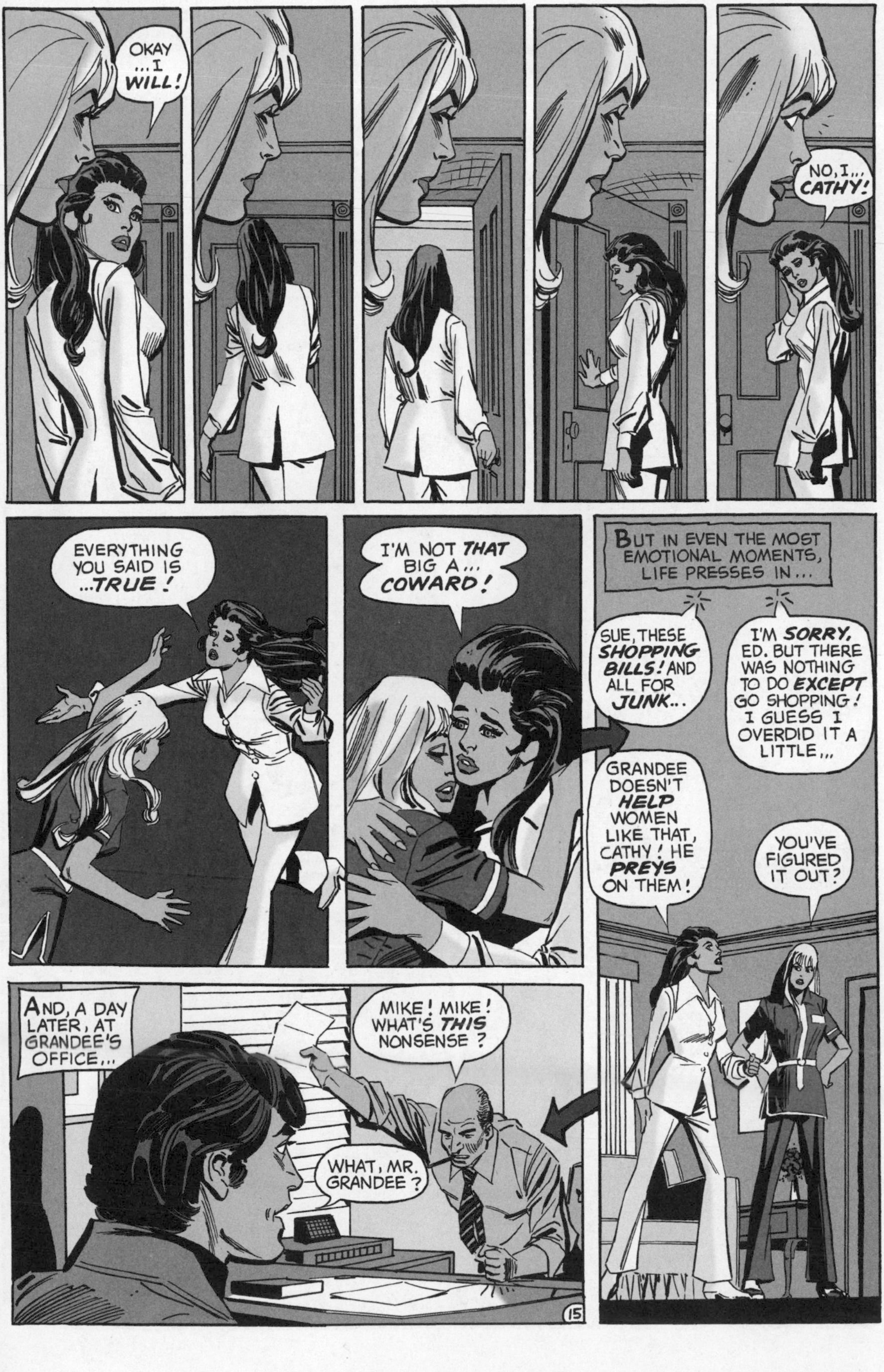
OKAY ...I WILL!
NO, I... CATHY!
EVERYTHING YOU SAID IS ...TRUE!
I'M NOT THAT BIG A... COWARD!
BUT IN EVEN THE MOST EMOTIONAL MOMENTS, LIFE PRESSES IN...
SUE, THESE SHOPPING BILLS! AND ALL FOR JUNK...
I'M SORRY, ED. BUT THERE WAS NOTHING TO DO EXCEPT GO SHOPPING! I GUESS I OVERDID IT A LITTLE...
GRANDEE DOESN'T HELP WOMEN LIKE THAT, CATHY! HE PREYS ON THEM!
YOU'VE FIGURED IT OUT?
AND, A DAY LATER, AT GRANDEE'S OFFICE...
MIKE! MIKE! WHAT'S THIS NONSENSE?
WHAT, MR. GRANDEE?
15

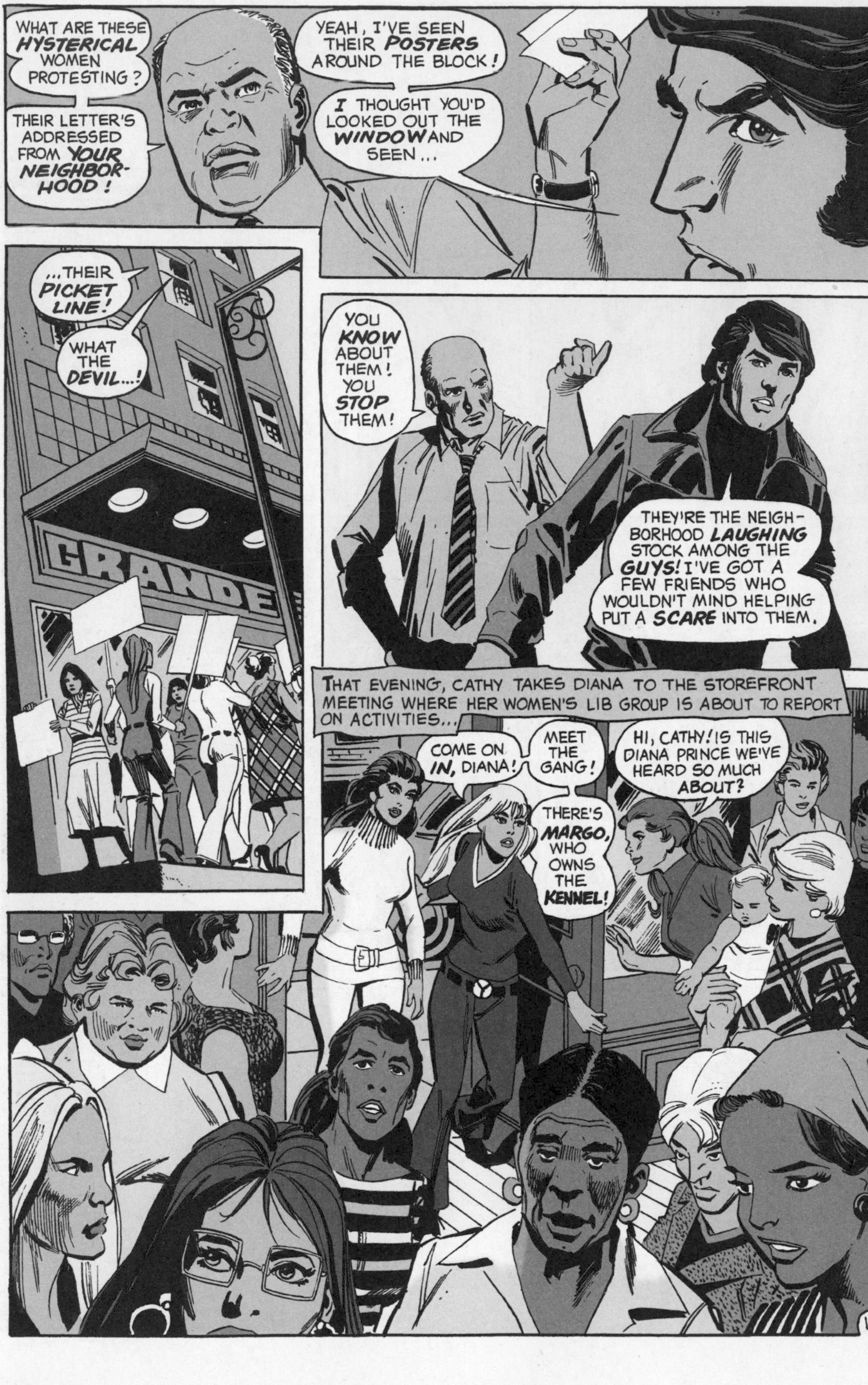
WHAT ARE THESE HYSTERICAL WOMEN PROTESTING?
THEIR LETTER'S ADDRESSED FROM YOUR NEIGHBOR-HOOD!
YEAH, I'VE SEEN THEIR POSTERS AROUND THE BLOCK!
I THOUGHT YOU'D LOOKED OUT THE WINDOW AND SEEN...
...THEIR PICKET LINE!
WHAT THE DEVIL...!
GRANDE
YOU KNOW ABOUT THEM! YOU STOP THEM!
THEY'RE THE NEIGH-BORHOOD LAUGHING STOCK AMONG THE GUYS! I'VE GOT A FEW FRIENDS WHO WOULDN'T MIND HELPING PUT A SCARE INTO THEM.
THAT EVENING, CATHY TAKES DIANA TO THE STOREFRONT MEETING WHERE HER WOMEN'S LIB GROUP IS ABOUT TO REPORT ON ACTIVITIES...
COME ON IN, DIANA!
MEET THE GANG!
THERE'S MARGO, WHO OWNS THE KENNEL!
HI, CATHY! IS THIS DIANA PRINCE WE'VE HEARD SO MUCH ABOUT?
16

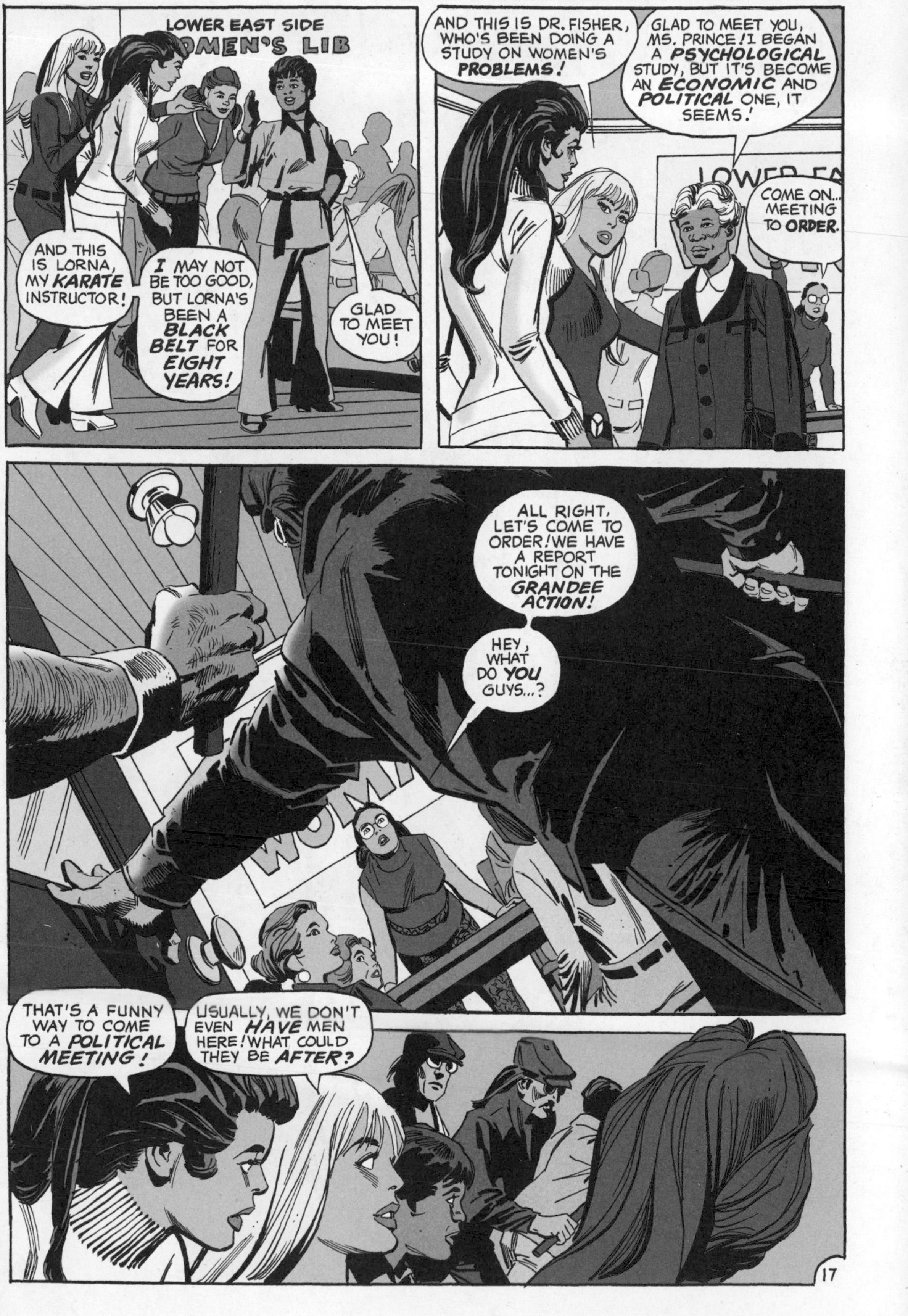
LOWER EAST SIDE
OMEN'S LIB
AND THIS IS LORNA, MY KARATE INSTRUCTOR!
I MAY NOT BE TOO GOOD, BUT LORNA'S BEEN A BLACK BELT FOR EIGHT YEARS!
GLAD TO MEET YOU!
AND THIS IS DR. FISHER, WHO'S BEEN DOING A STUDY ON WOMEN'S PROBLEMS!
GLAD TO MEET YOU, MS. PRINCE! I BEGAN A PSYCHOLOGICAL STUDY, BUT IT'S BECOME AN ECONOMIC AND POLITICAL ONE, IT SEEMS!
COME ON... MEETING TO ORDER.
ALL RIGHT, LET'S COME TO ORDER! WE HAVE A REPORT TONIGHT ON THE GRANDEE ACTION!
HEY, WHAT DO YOU GUYS...?
THAT'S A FUNNY WAY TO COME TO A POLITICAL MEETING!
USUALLY, WE DON'T EVEN HAVE MEN HERE! WHAT COULD THEY BE AFTER?
17

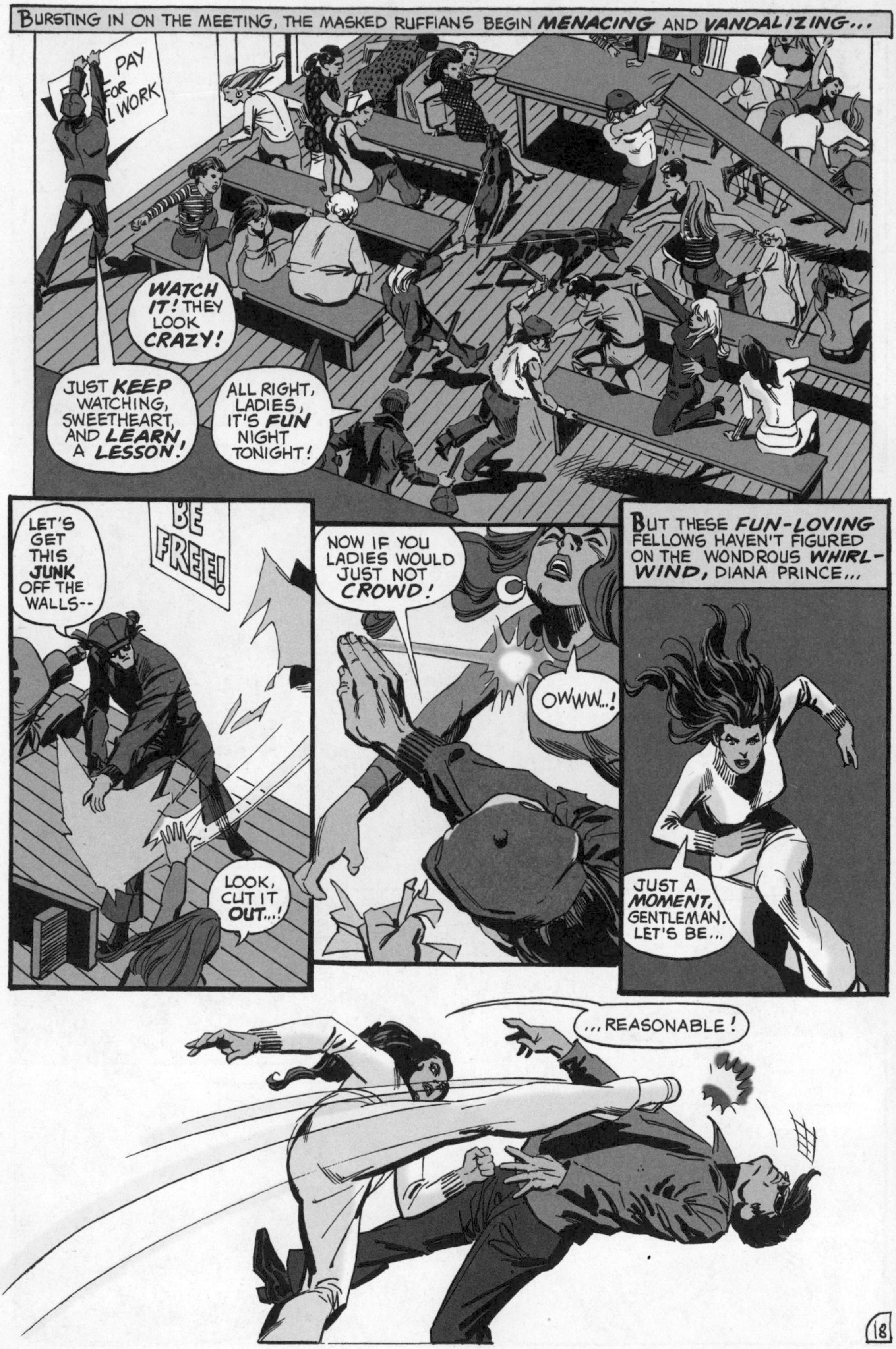
BURSTING IN ON THE MEETING, THE MASKED RUFFIANS BEGIN MENACING AND VANDALIZING...
WATCH IT! THEY LOOK CRAZY!
JUST KEEP WATCHING, SWEETHEART, AND LEARN A LESSON!
ALL RIGHT, LADIES, IT'S FUN NIGHT TONIGHT!
LET'S GET THIS JUNK OFF THE WALLS--
BE FREE!
LOOK, CUT IT OUT...!
NOW IF YOU LADIES WOULD JUST NOT CROWD!
OWWW...!
BUT THESE FUN-LOVING FELLOWS HAVEN'T FIGURED ON THE WONDROUS WHIRLWIND, DIANA PRINCE...
JUST A MOMENT, GENTLEMAN. LET'S BE...
...REASONABLE!
18

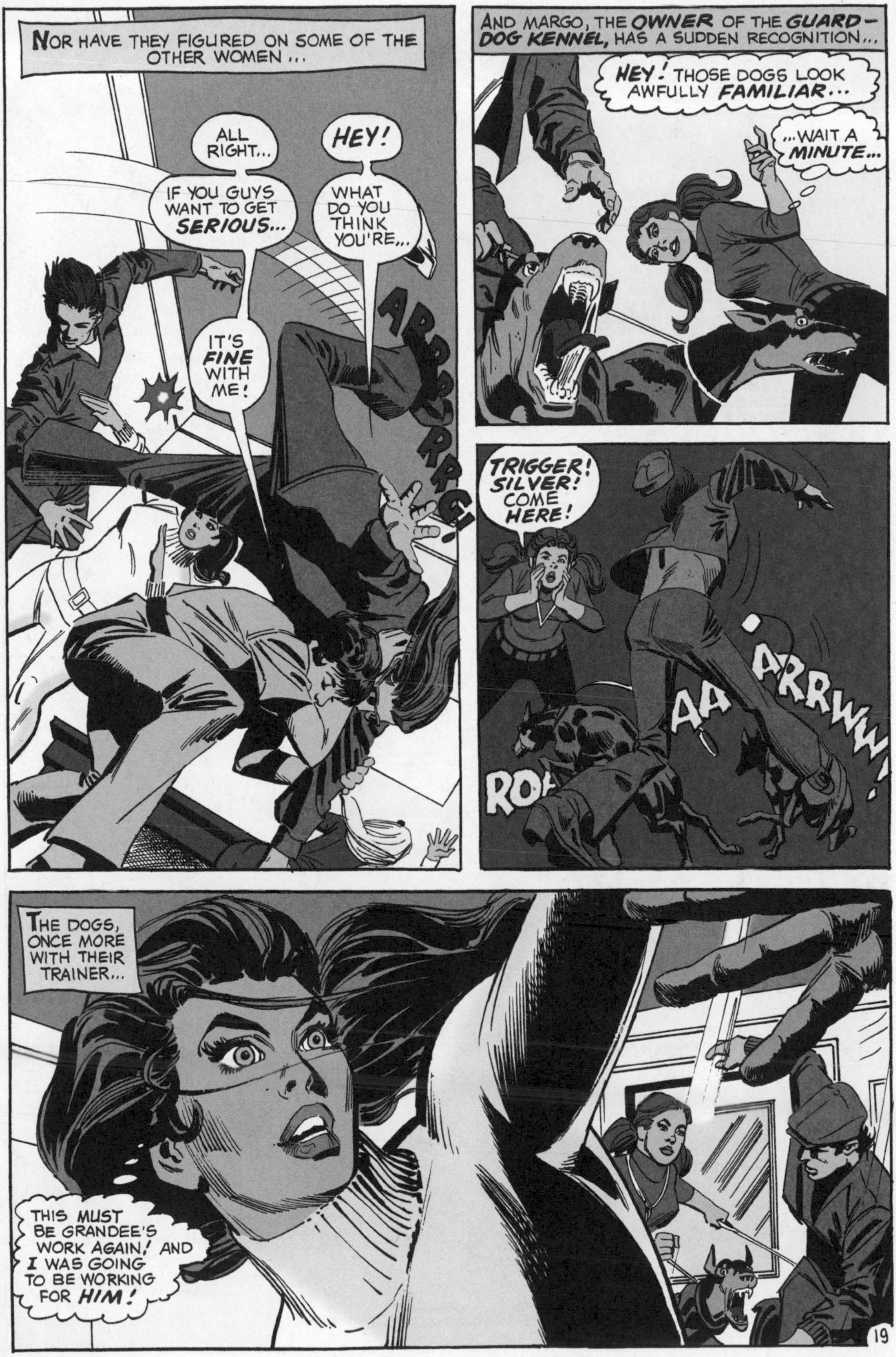
NOR HAVE THEY FIGURED ON SOME OF THE OTHER WOMEN...
ALL RIGHT...
IF YOU GUYS WANT TO GET SERIOUS...
IT'S FINE WITH ME!
HEY!
WHAT DO YOU THINK YOU'RE...
ARRRRRRG!
AND MARGO, THE OWNER OF THE GUARD-DOG KENNEL, HAS A SUDDEN RECOGNITION...
HEY! THOSE DOGS LOOK AWFULLY FAMILIAR...
...WAIT A MINUTE...
TRIGGER! SILVER! COME HERE!
AAARRRWW!
RO
THE DOGS, ONCE MORE WITH THEIR TRAINER...
THIS MUST BE GRANDEE'S WORK AGAIN! AND I WAS GOING TO BE WORKING FOR HIM!
19

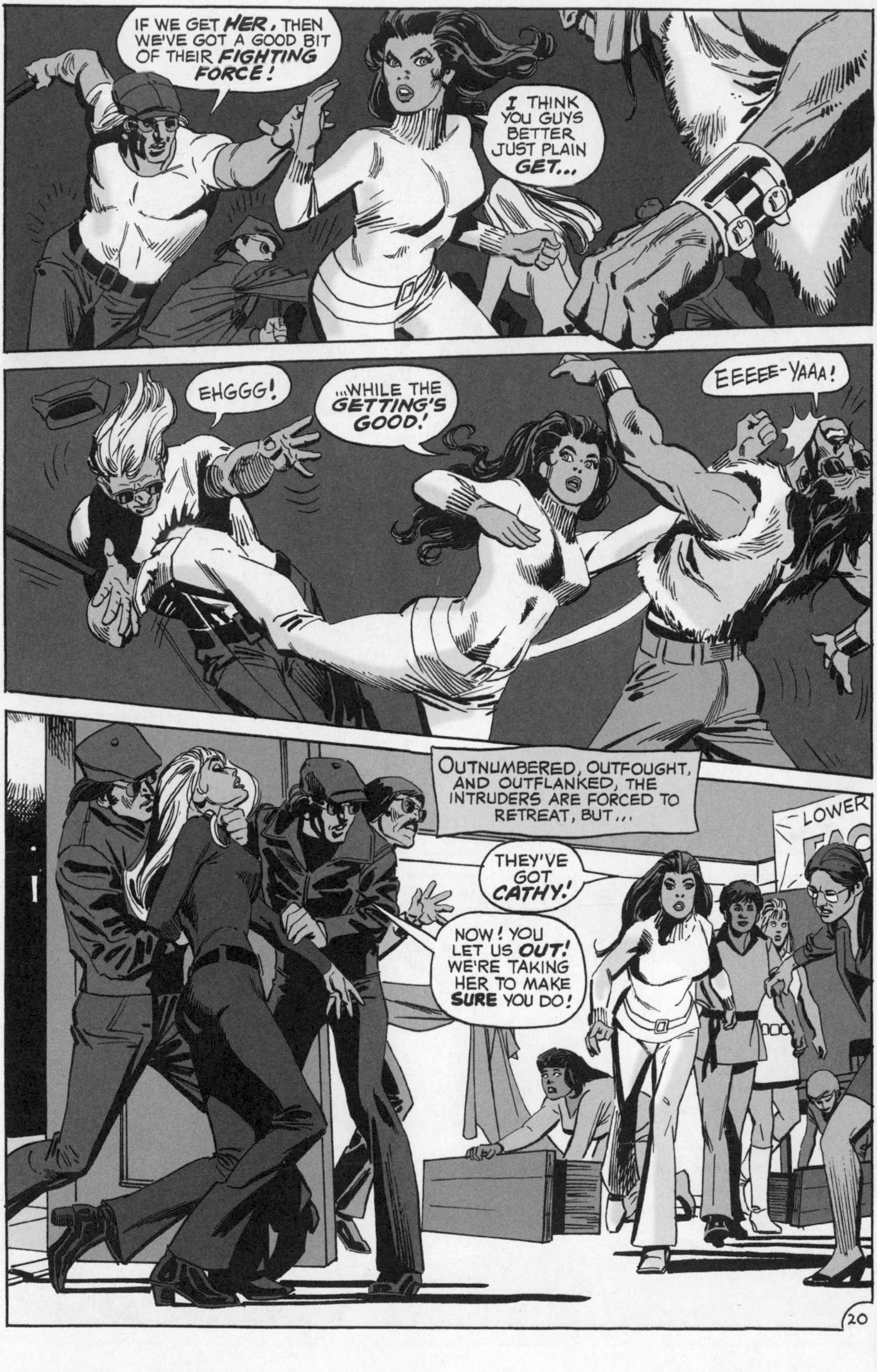
IF WE GET HER, THEN WE'VE GOT A GOOD BIT OF THEIR FIGHTING FORCE!
I THINK YOU GUYS BETTER JUST PLAIN GET...
EHGGG!
...WHILE THE GETTING'S GOOD!
EEEEE-YAAA!
OUTNUMBERED, OUTFOUGHT, AND OUTFLANKED, THE INTRUDERS ARE FORCED TO RETREAT, BUT...
LOWER
THEY'VE GOT CATHY!
NOW! YOU LET US OUT! WE'RE TAKING HER TO MAKE SURE YOU DO!
20

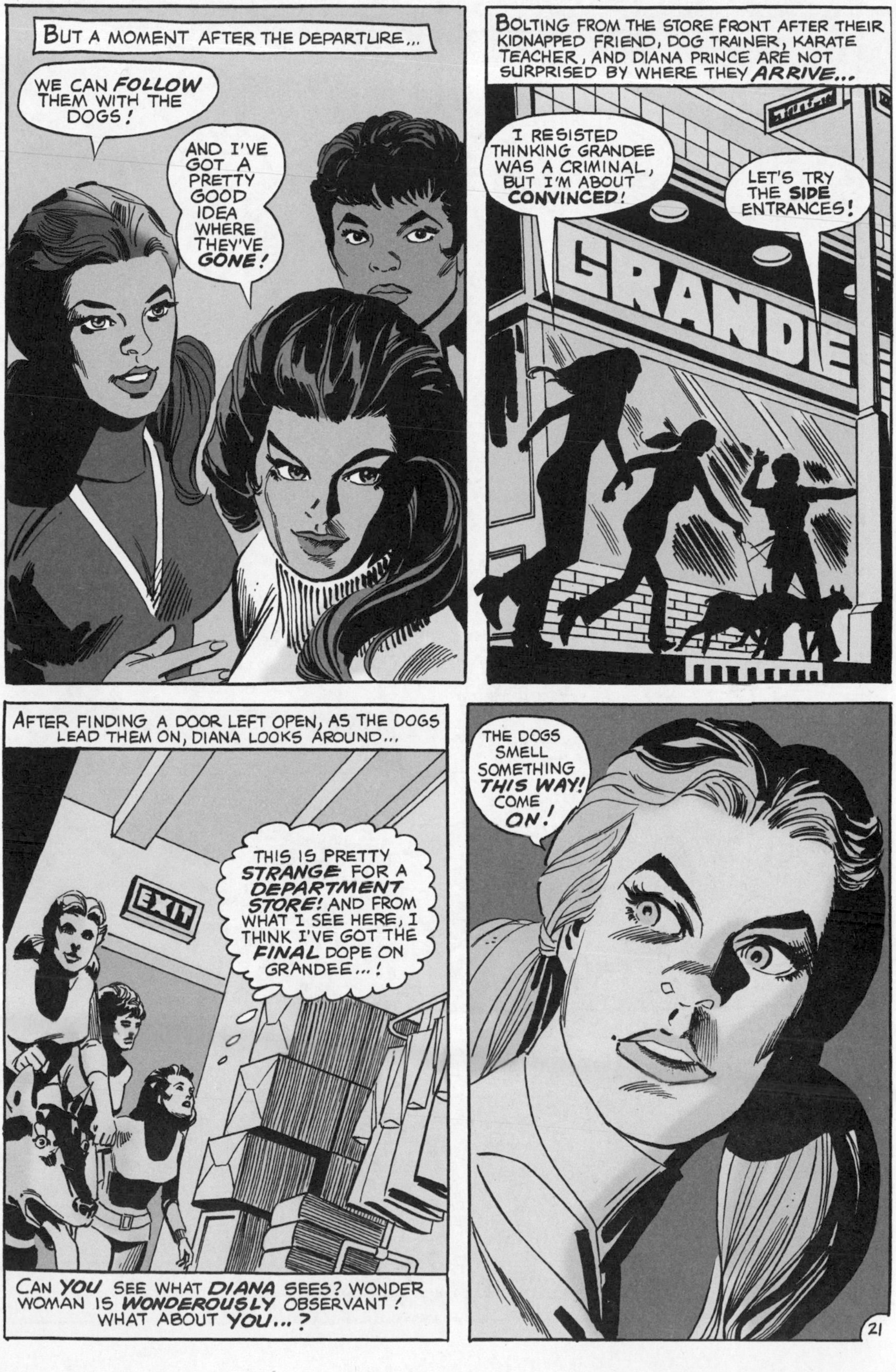
BUT A MOMENT AFTER THE DEPARTURE...
WE CAN FOLLOW THEM WITH THE DOGS!
AND I'VE GOT A PRETTY GOOD IDEA WHERE THEY'VE GONE!
BOLTING FROM THE STORE FRONT AFTER THEIR KIDNAPPED FRIEND, DOG TRAINER, KARATE TEACHER, AND DIANA PRINCE ARE NOT SURPRISED BY WHERE THEY ARRIVE...
I RESISTED THINKING GRANDEE WAS A CRIMINAL, BUT I'M ABOUT CONVINCED!
LET'S TRY THE SIDE ENTRANCES!
GRANDE
AFTER FINDING A DOOR LEFT OPEN, AS THE DOGS LEAD THEM ON, DIANA LOOKS AROUND...
EXIT
THIS IS PRETTY STRANGE FOR A DEPARTMENT STORE! AND FROM WHAT I SEE HERE, I THINK I'VE GOT THE FINAL DOPE ON GRANDEE...!
CAN YOU SEE WHAT DIANA SEES? WONDER WOMAN IS WONDEROUSLY OBSERVANT! WHAT ABOUT YOU...?
THE DOGS SMELL SOMETHING THIS WAY! COME ON!
21

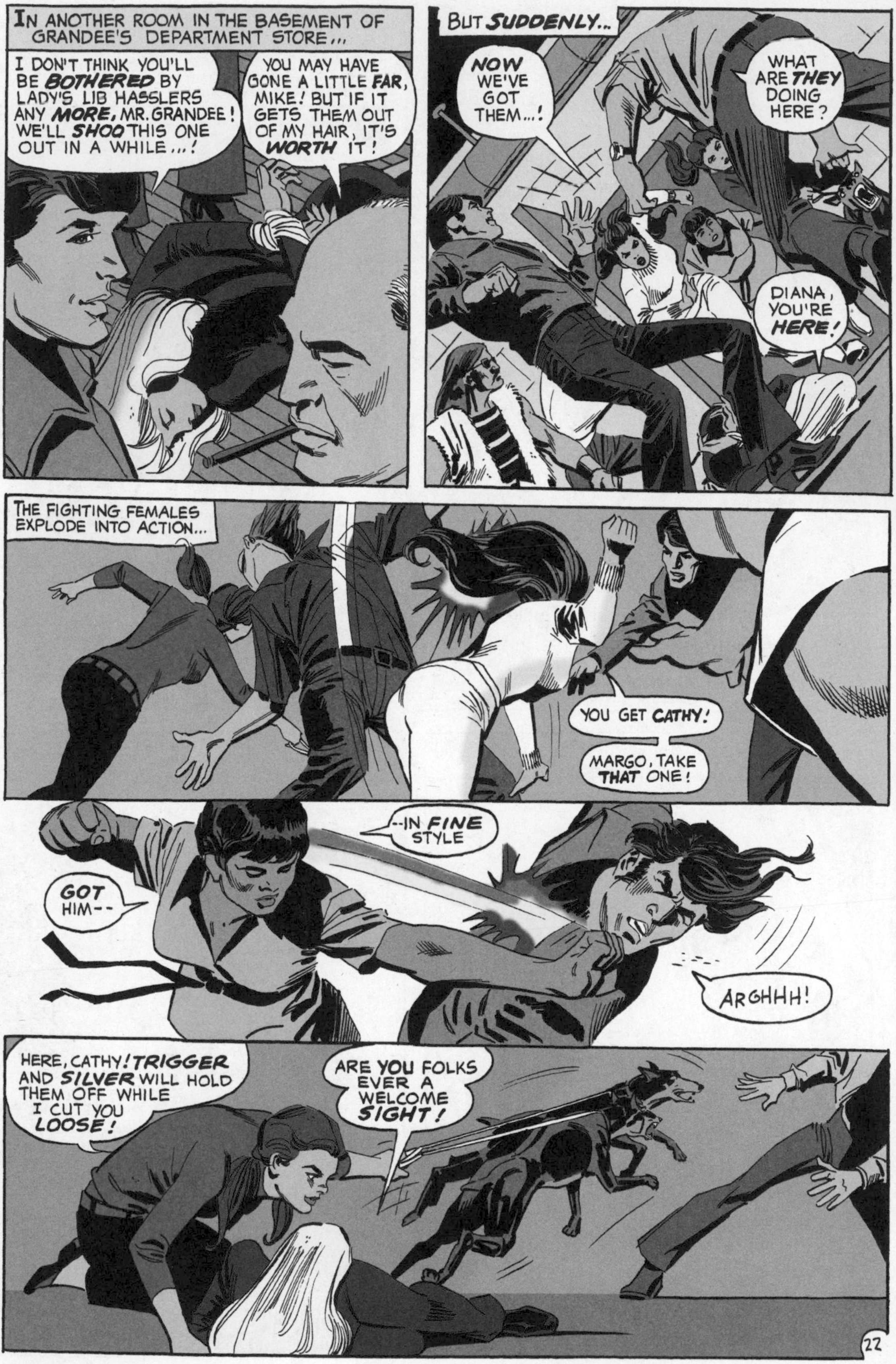
IN ANOTHER ROOM IN THE BASEMENT OF GRANDEE'S DEPARTMENT STORE...
I DON'T THINK YOU'LL BE BOTHERED BY LADY'S LIB HASSLERS ANY MORE, MR. GRANDEE! WE'LL SHOO THIS ONE OUT IN A WHILE...!
YOU MAY HAVE GONE A LITTLE FAR, MIKE! BUT IF IT GETS THEM OUT OF MY HAIR, IT'S WORTH IT!
BUT SUDDENLY...
NOW WE'VE GOT THEM...!
WHAT ARE THEY DOING HERE?
DIANA, YOU'RE HERE!
THE FIGHTING FEMALES EXPLODE INTO ACTION...
YOU GET CATHY!
MARGO, TAKE THAT ONE!
GOT HIM--
--IN FINE STYLE
ARGHHH!
HERE, CATHY! TRIGGER AND SILVER WILL HOLD THEM OFF WHILE I CUT YOU LOOSE!
ARE YOU FOLKS EVER A WELCOME SIGHT!
22

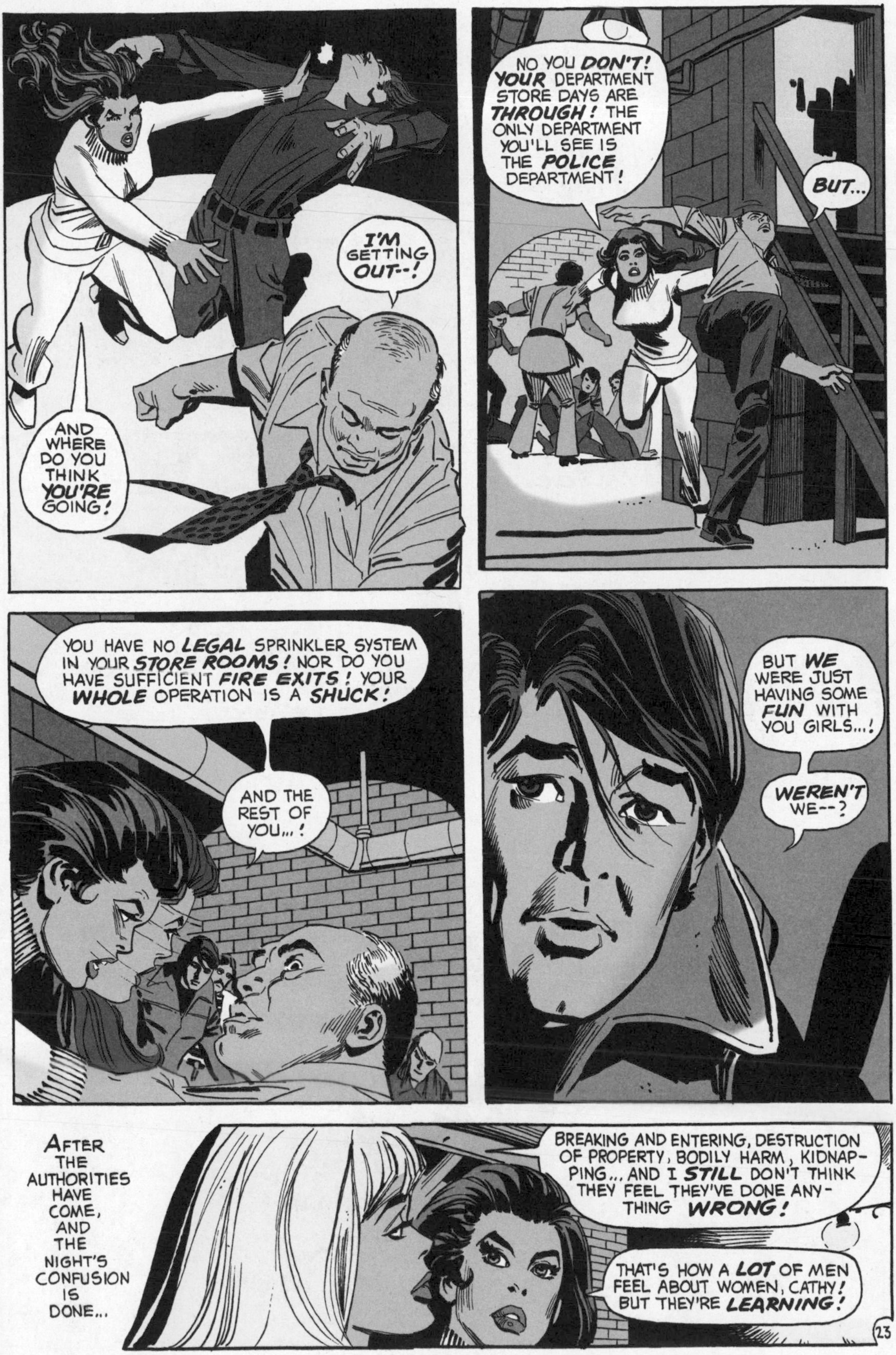
AND WHERE DO YOU THINK YOU'RE GOING!
I'M GETTING OUT--!
NO YOU DON'T! YOUR DEPARTMENT STORE DAYS ARE THROUGH! THE ONLY DEPARTMENT YOU'LL SEE IS THE POLICE DEPARTMENT!
BUT...
YOU HAVE NO LEGAL SPRINKLER SYSTEM IN YOUR STORE ROOMS! NOR DO YOU HAVE SUFFICIENT FIRE EXITS! YOUR WHOLE OPERATION IS A SHUCK!
AND THE REST OF YOU...!
BUT WE WERE JUST HAVING SOME FUN WITH YOU GIRLS...!
WEREN'T WE--?
AFTER THE AUTHORITIES HAVE COME, AND THE NIGHT'S CONFUSION IS DONE...
BREAKING AND ENTERING, DESTRUCTION OF PROPERTY, BODILY HARM, KIDNAP-PING... AND I STILL DON'T THINK THEY FEEL THEY'VE DONE ANY-THING WRONG!
THAT'S HOW A LOT OF MEN FEEL ABOUT WOMEN, CATHY! BUT THEY'RE LEARNING!
23

THE NEXT NIGHT, A VICTORIOUS ANNOUNCEMENT IS MADE AT THE MEETING...
GRANDEE'S DEPARTMENT STORE HAS BEEN *CLOSED* BY THE CITY! AND THE MAYOR IS SETTING UP A COMMITTEE TO REVIEW THE WAGE SITUATION OF WORKING WOMEN...
YOU IN THE *BACK*...?
NOW I FEEL I'VE *REALLY* ACCOMPLISHED SOMETHING FOR WOMEN'S IMAGE!
WE ACCUSE YOUR WOMEN'S LIBERATION GROUP OF PUTTING 250 WOMEN OUT OF WORK--WHO WOULD HAVE HAD JOBS AT GRANDEE'S DEPARTMENT STORE!
24
WHAT DO *YOU* SAY TO *THEM* NOW? AND WILL WE HAVE *TIME*? THEY LOOK LIKE THEY MEAN BUSINESS!
WHAT WILL DIANA DO NOW?

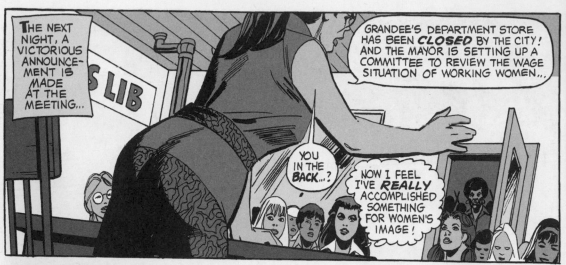

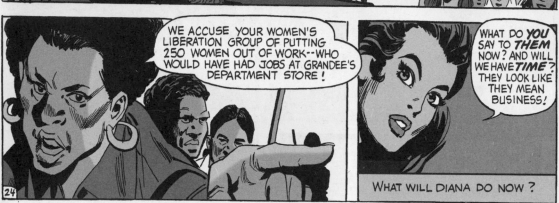

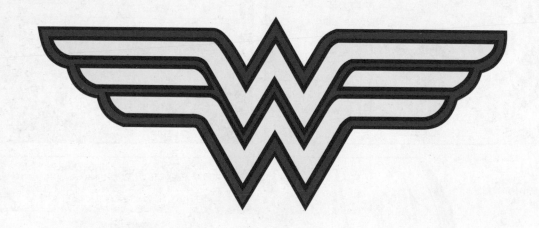

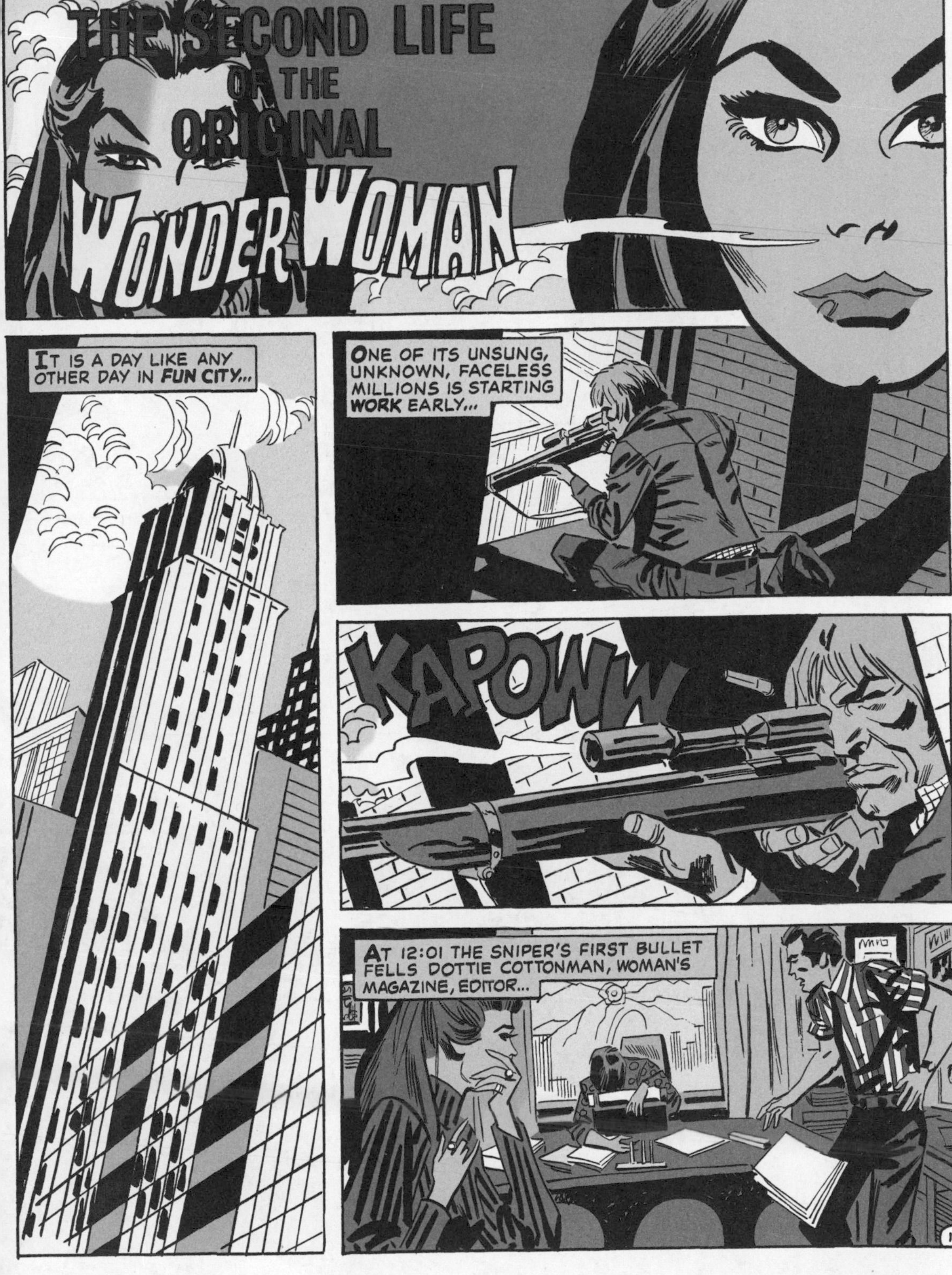
THE SECOND LIFE OF THE ORIGINAL WONDER WOMAN
IT IS A DAY LIKE ANY OTHER DAY IN FUN CITY...
ONE OF ITS UNSUNG, UNKNOWN, FACELESS MILLIONS IS STARTING WORK EARLY...
KAPOWW
AT 12:01 THE SNIPER'S FIRST BULLET FELLS DOTTIE COTTONMAN, WOMAN'S MAGAZINE, EDITOR...
1

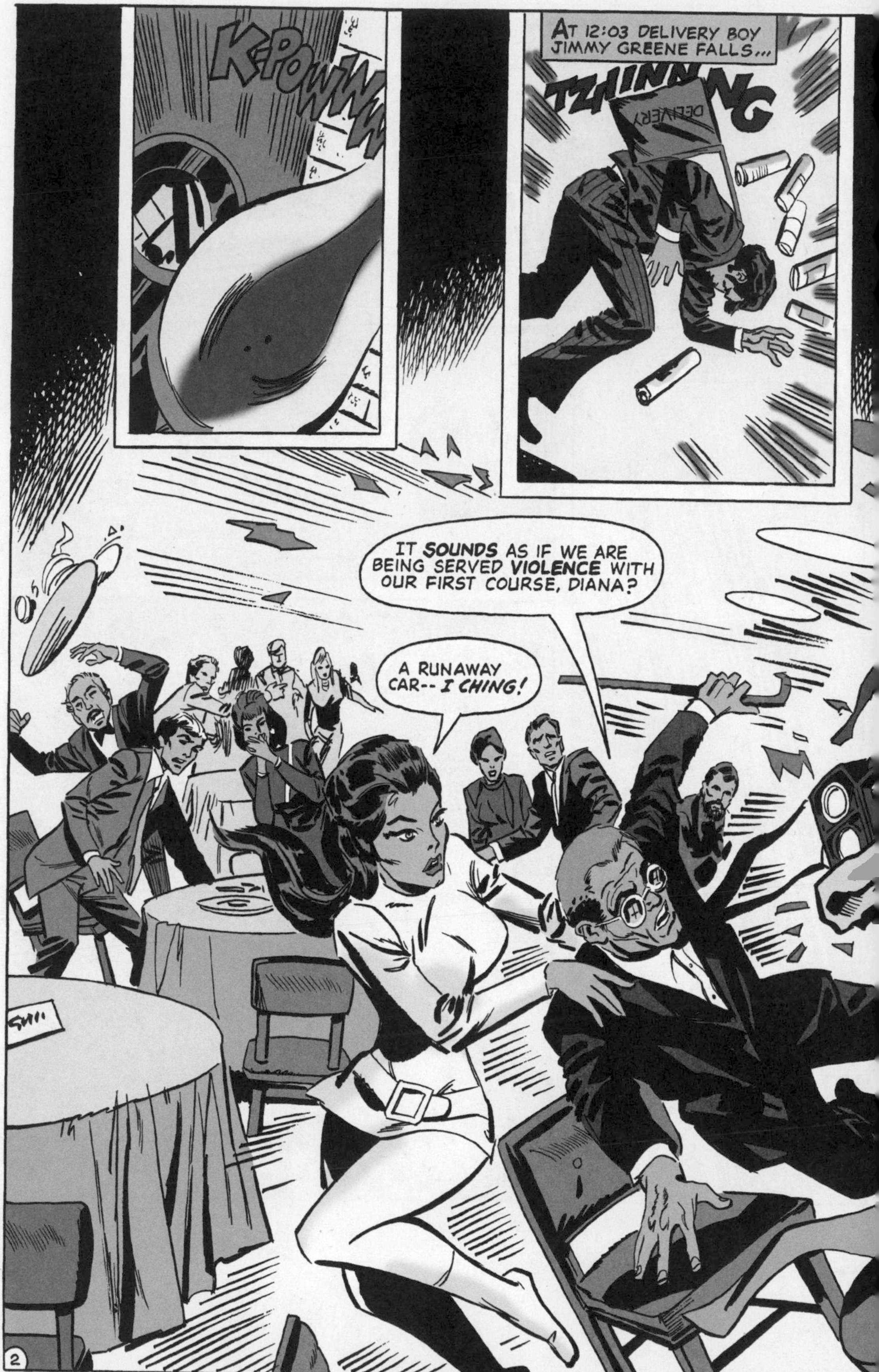
K-POWWW
AT 12:03 DELIVERY BOY JIMMY GREENE FALLS...
TZWINNNG
DELIVERY
IT SOUNDS AS IF WE ARE BEING SERVED VIOLENCE WITH OUR FIRST COURSE, DIANA?
A RUNAWAY CAR-- I CHING!
2

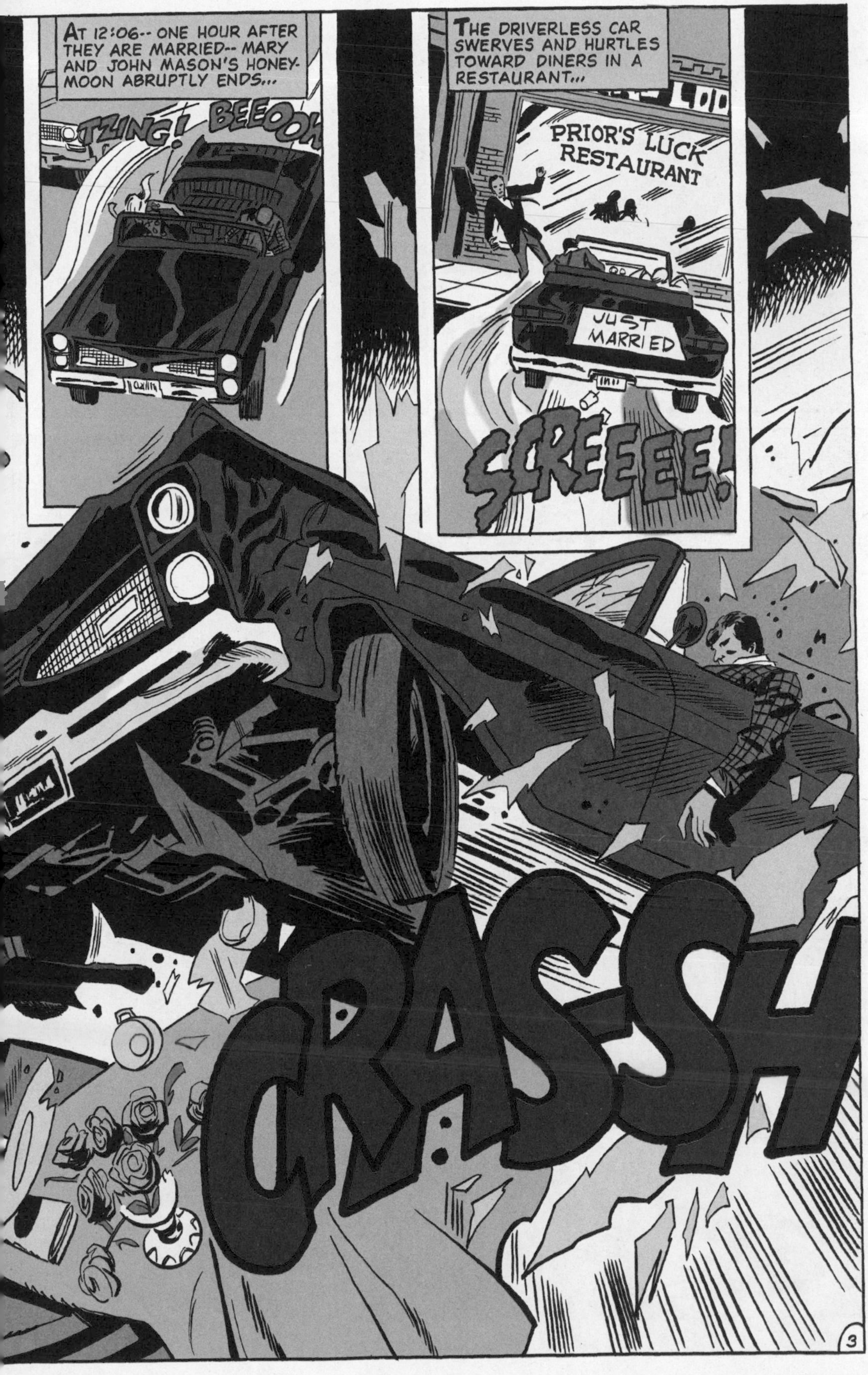
AT 12:06-- ONE HOUR AFTER THEY ARE MARRIED-- MARY AND JOHN MASON'S HONEY-MOON ABRUPTLY ENDS...
TZING! BEEOOOK
THE DRIVERLESS CAR SWERVES AND HURTLES TOWARD DINERS IN A RESTAURANT...
PRIOR'S LUCK RESTAURANT
JUST MARRIED
SCREEEEE!
CRASSH
3

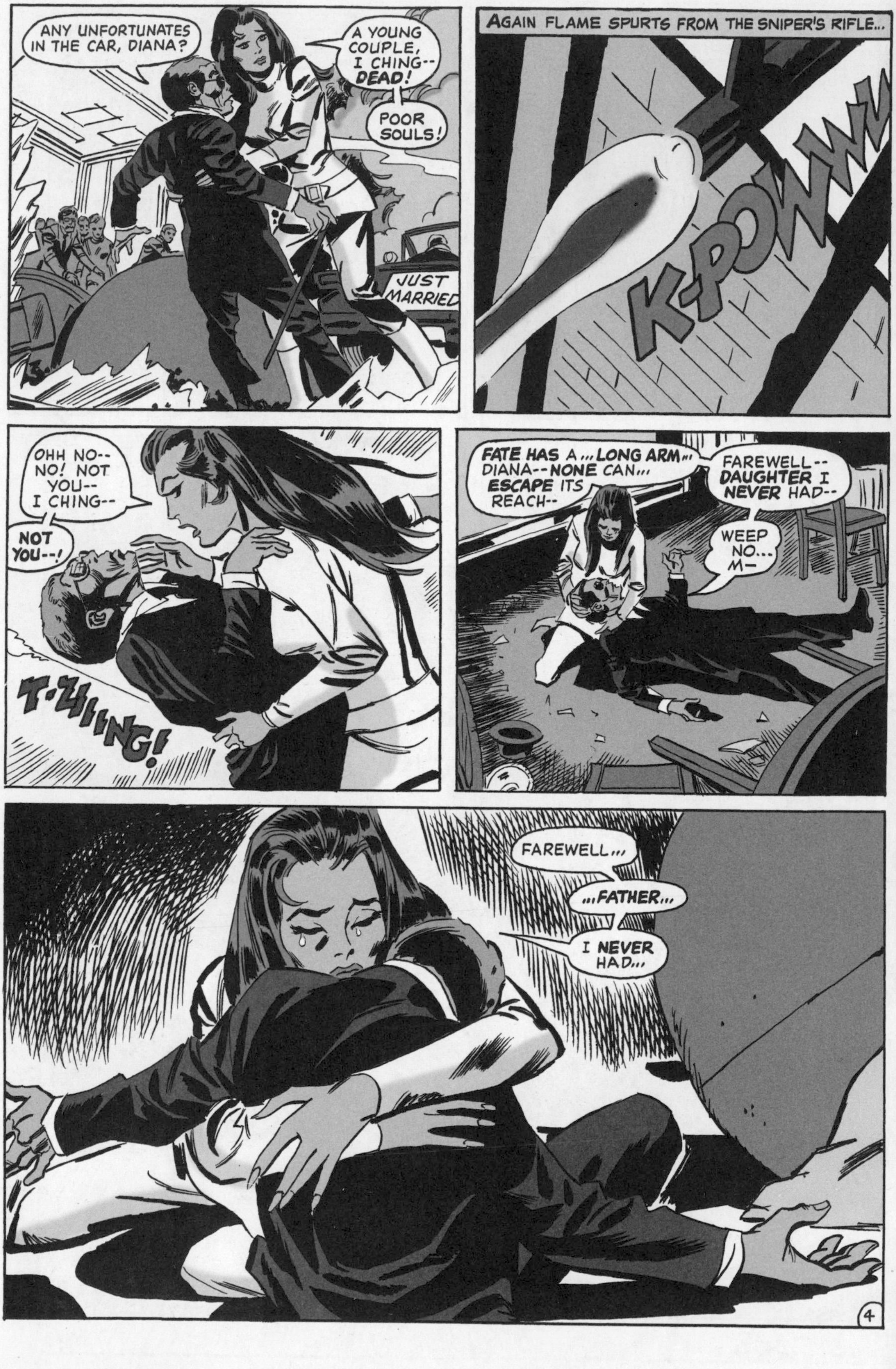
ANY UNFORTUNATES IN THE CAR, DIANA?
A YOUNG COUPLE, I CHING-- DEAD!
POOR SOULS!
JUST MARRIED
AGAIN FLAME SPURTS FROM THE SNIPER'S RIFLE...
K-POWWW
OHH NO-- NO! NOT YOU-- I CHING--
NOT YOU--!
T-ZIIING!
FATE HAS A... LONG ARM... DIANA--NONE CAN... ESCAPE ITS REACH--
FAREWELL-- DAUGHTER I NEVER HAD--
WEEP NO... M—
FAREWELL...
...FATHER...
I NEVER HAD...
4

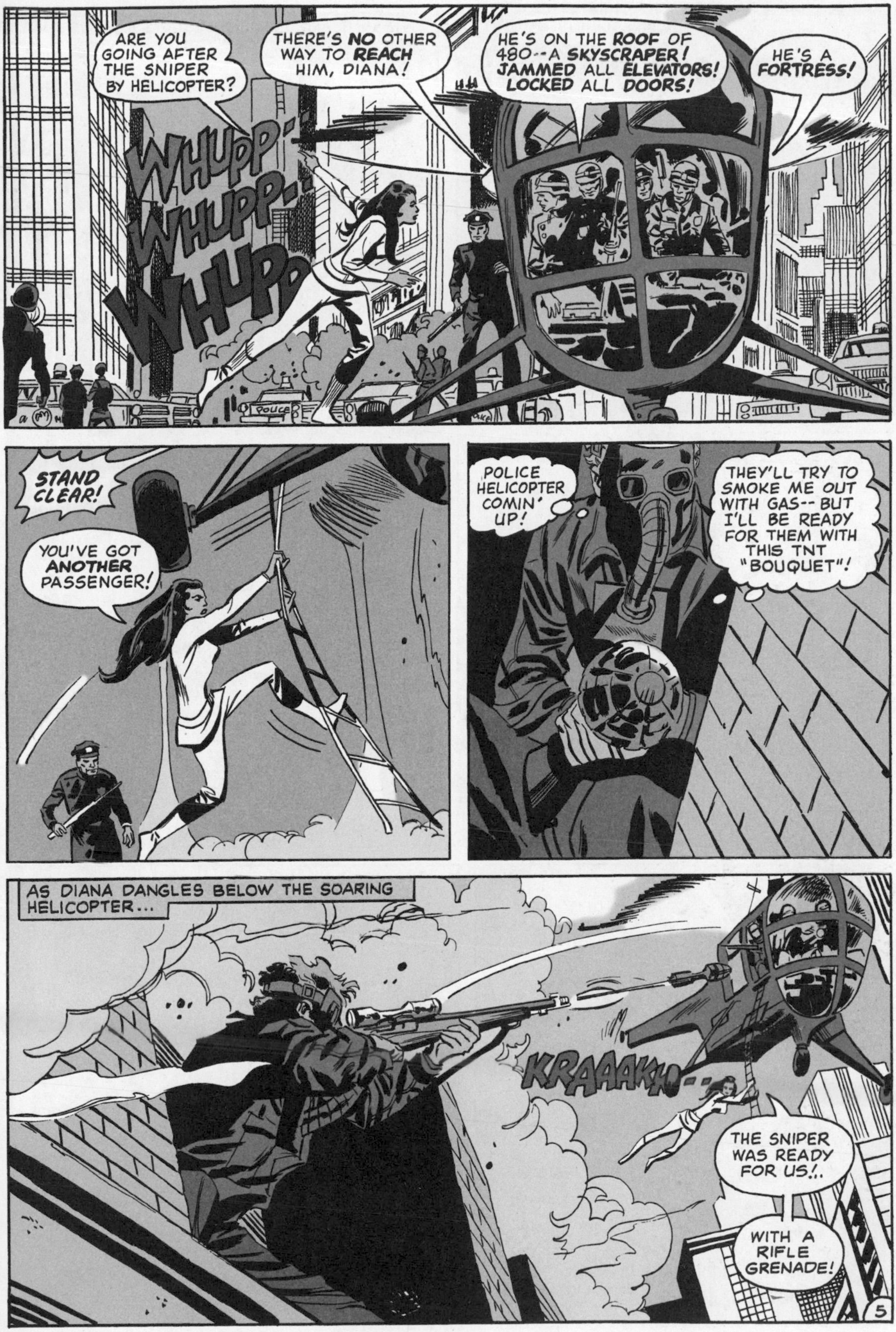
ARE YOU GOING AFTER THE SNIPER BY HELICOPTER?
THERE'S NO OTHER WAY TO REACH HIM, DIANA!
HE'S ON THE ROOF OF 480--A SKYSCRAPER! JAMMED ALL ELEVATORS! LOCKED ALL DOORS!
HE'S A FORTRESS!
WHUPP-WHUPP-WHUPP
STAND CLEAR!
YOU'VE GOT ANOTHER PASSENGER!
POLICE HELICOPTER COMIN' UP!
THEY'LL TRY TO SMOKE ME OUT WITH GAS-- BUT I'LL BE READY FOR THEM WITH THIS TNT "BOUQUET"!
AS DIANA DANGLES BELOW THE SOARING HELICOPTER...
KRAAAKK--
THE SNIPER WAS READY FOR US!..
WITH A RIFLE GRENADE!
5

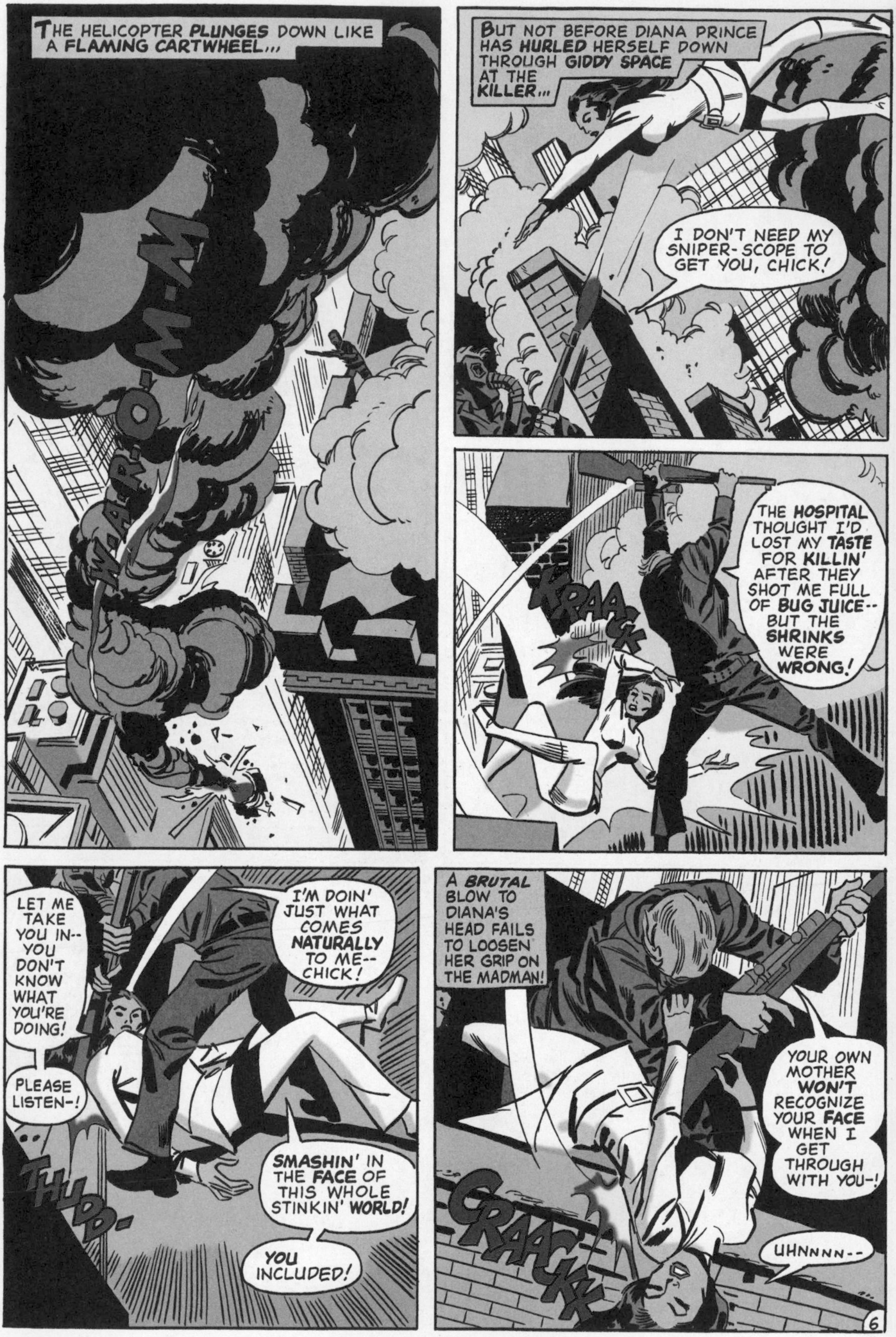
THE HELICOPTER PLUNGES DOWN LIKE A FLAMING CARTWHEEL...
WHA-R-O-O-M-M
BUT NOT BEFORE DIANA PRINCE HAS HURLED HERSELF DOWN THROUGH GIDDY SPACE AT THE KILLER...
I DON'T NEED MY SNIPER-SCOPE TO GET YOU, CHICK!
THE HOSPITAL THOUGHT I'D LOST MY TASTE FOR KILLIN' AFTER THEY SHOT ME FULL OF BUG JUICE-- BUT THE SHRINKS WERE WRONG!
KRAAACK
LET ME TAKE YOU IN-- YOU DON'T KNOW WHAT YOU'RE DOING!
PLEASE LISTEN-!
I'M DOIN' JUST WHAT COMES NATURALLY TO ME-- CHICK!
SMASHIN' IN THE FACE OF THIS WHOLE STINKIN' WORLD!
YOU INCLUDED!
THUDD-
A BRUTAL BLOW TO DIANA'S HEAD FAILS TO LOOSEN HER GRIP ON THE MADMAN!
YOUR OWN MOTHER WON'T RECOGNIZE YOUR FACE WHEN I GET THROUGH WITH YOU-!
CRAACKK
UHNNNNN--
6

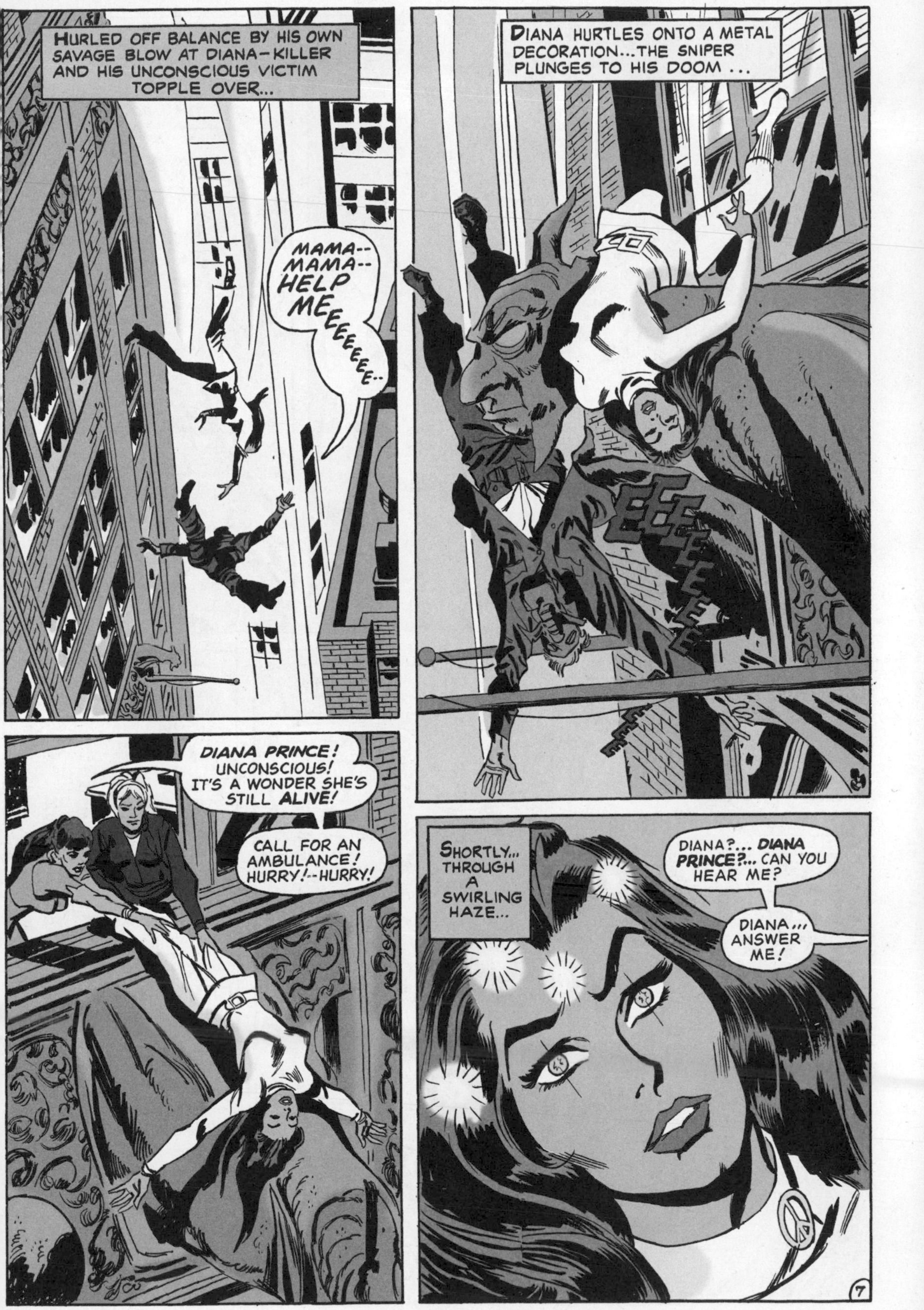
HURLED OFF BALANCE BY HIS OWN SAVAGE BLOW AT DIANA—KILLER AND HIS UNCONSCIOUS VICTIM TOPPLE OVER...
MAMA-- MAMA-- HELP MEEEEEEE..
DIANA HURTLES ONTO A METAL DECORATION...THE SNIPER PLUNGES TO HIS DOOM ...
EEEEEEEEE
DIANA PRINCE! UNCONSCIOUS! IT'S A WONDER SHE'S STILL ALIVE!
CALL FOR AN AMBULANCE! HURRY!--HURRY!
SHORTLY... THROUGH A SWIRLING HAZE...
DIANA?... DIANA PRINCE?... CAN YOU HEAR ME?
DIANA... ANSWER ME!
7

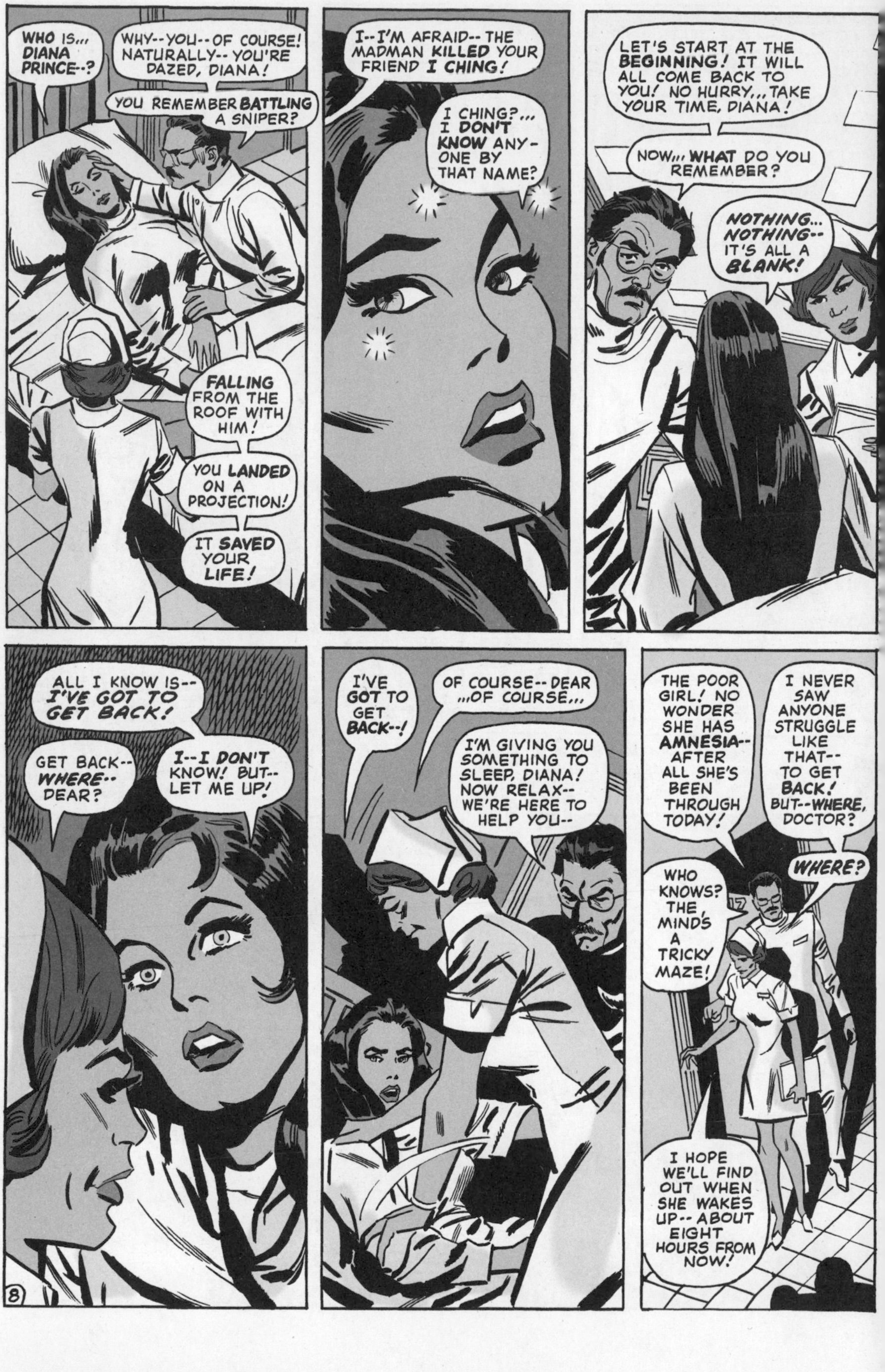
WHO IS... DIANA PRINCE--?
WHY--YOU--OF COURSE! NATURALLY--YOU'RE DAZED, DIANA!
YOU REMEMBER BATTLING A SNIPER?
FALLING FROM THE ROOF WITH HIM!
YOU LANDED ON A PROJECTION!
IT SAVED YOUR LIFE!
I--I'M AFRAID--THE MADMAN KILLED YOUR FRIEND I CHING!
I CHING?... I DON'T KNOW ANYONE BY THAT NAME?
LET'S START AT THE BEGINNING! IT WILL ALL COME BACK TO YOU! NO HURRY... TAKE YOUR TIME, DIANA!
NOW... WHAT DO YOU REMEMBER?
NOTHING... NOTHING--IT'S ALL A BLANK!
ALL I KNOW IS--I'VE GOT TO GET BACK!
GET BACK--WHERE--DEAR?
I--I DON'T KNOW! BUT--LET ME UP!
8
I'VE GOT TO GET BACK--!
OF COURSE--DEAR ...OF COURSE...
I'M GIVING YOU SOMETHING TO SLEEP, DIANA! NOW RELAX--WE'RE HERE TO HELP YOU--
THE POOR GIRL! NO WONDER SHE HAS AMNESIA--AFTER ALL SHE'S BEEN THROUGH TODAY!
I NEVER SAW ANYONE STRUGGLE LIKE THAT--TO GET BACK! BUT--WHERE, DOCTOR?
WHERE?
WHO KNOWS? THE MIND'S A TRICKY MAZE!
I HOPE WE'LL FIND OUT WHEN SHE WAKES UP--ABOUT EIGHT HOURS FROM NOW!

SHORTLY...

DOCTOR!-- DOCTOR!-- DIANA PRINCE IS GONE!

HER CLOTHES TOO!

SHE COULDN'T HAVE LEFT THROUGH THE DOOR-- I HAD MY EYE ON IT ALL THE TIME-- FROM THE HALL DESK!

THE WINDOW-- IT'S OPEN!

WHAT DROVE HER TO SHAKE OFF THE EFFECTS OF THE SEDATIVE? NO ORDINARY PERSON COULD!

SHE WAS DRIVEN BY A POWERFUL SUBCONSCIOUS DRIVE! THE SAME IRRESISTIBLE FORCE THAT PROPELS FISH AND BIRDS HALF-WAY ACROSS THE WORLD TO THEIR DESTINATION!

BUT-- WHAT IS DIANA'S?

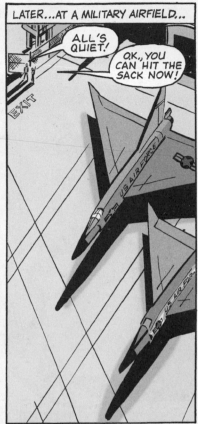

LATER...AT A MILITARY AIRFIELD...

ALL'S QUIET!

OK., YOU CAN HIT THE SACK NOW!

LOOK-! NO SHIP'S DUE TO TAKE OFF NOW! MUST BE A SABOTEUR! SOUND THE ALARM!

OFFICER OF THE GUARD!

AND IN THAT SUPERSONIC PLANE, DRIVEN BY AN OVERWHELMING FORCE, DIANA PRINCE ROCKETS THROUGH THE NIGHT SKIES TOWARDS A STARTLING RENDEZVOUS WITH FATE!

I'VE GOT TO GET BACK!-- I'VE GOT TO GET BACK!

9

THROUGH THE CLOUDY NIGHT... OVER DARK SEAS... DIANA HURTLES...

I--I DON'T KNOW **WHERE** I'M GOING--

BUT--I FEEL-- AS IF A HAND ON MINE-- IS **GUIDING** ME--

BACK-- BACK-- BACK!

OUT OF SIGHT IN THE SKIES BEHIND HER...

ROVER LEADER TO ROVER BASE! TARGET DOES NOT ANSWER CHALLENGE! HAVE TARGET ON RADAR GRID! --OVER!

ROVER BASE TO ROVER LEADER! TARGET MUST NOT FALL INTO HOSTILE HANDS! ATTACK! OVER!

FIRE!

VRUUMM VRUUMM VRUUMM...

LETHAL MISSILES SLASH THROUGH THE SKIES AT DIANA'S PLANE...

ROVER LEADER TO ROVER BASE! DIRECT HIT ON TARGET! OVER!

ROVER BASE TO ROVER LEADER! RETURN TO BASE! --OVER!

AT THAT MOMENT-- OUT OF SIGHT MILES AWAY-- DIANA PRINCE HURTLES SEAWARDS IN THE FLAMING PLANE--

WHREEEEE--

10

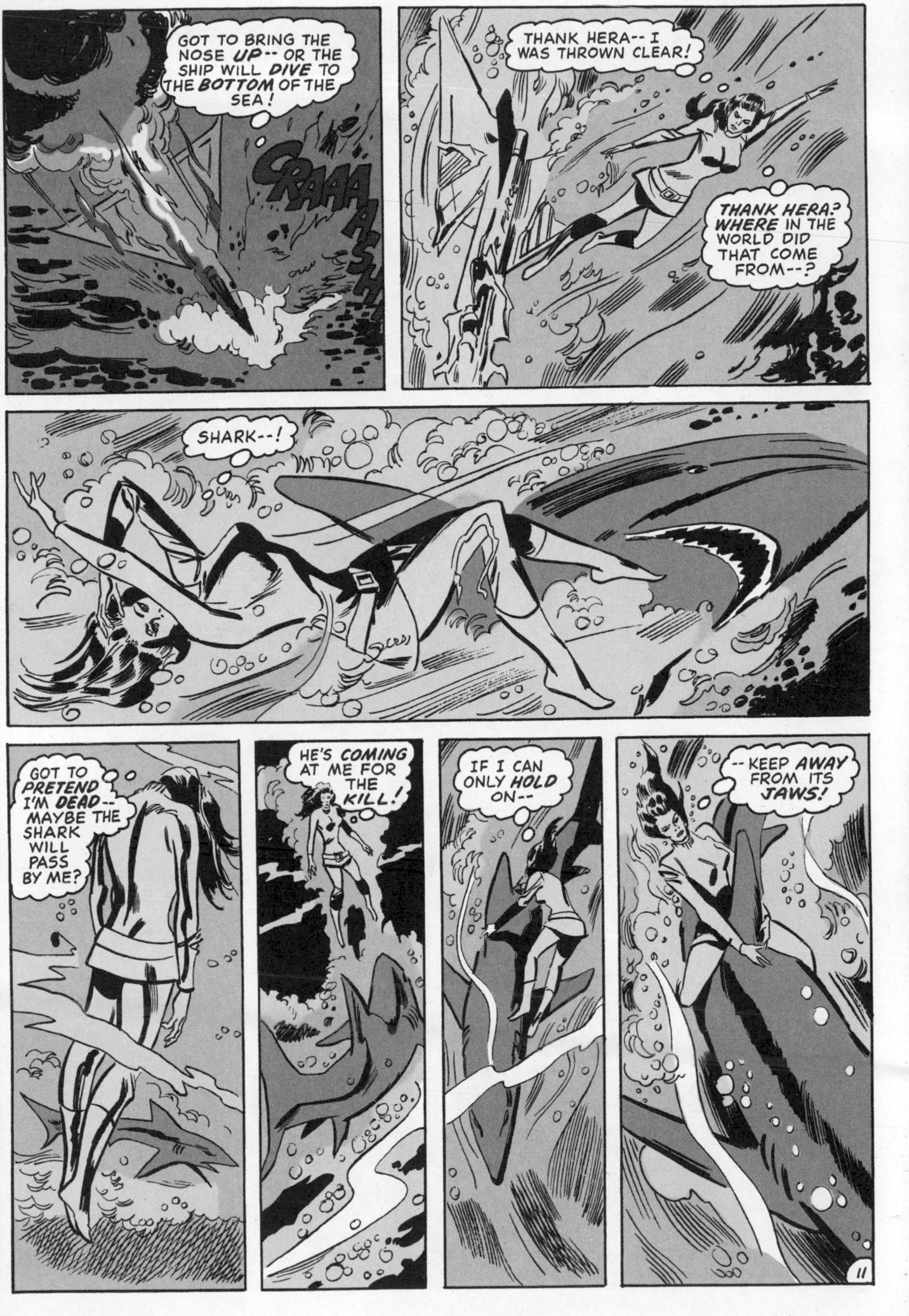
GOT TO BRING THE NOSE UP-- OR THE SHIP WILL DIVE TO THE BOTTOM OF THE SEA!
CRAAAASH!
THANK HERA-- I WAS THROWN CLEAR!
THANK HERA? WHERE IN THE WORLD DID THAT COME FROM--?
SHARK--!
GOT TO PRETEND I'M DEAD-- MAYBE THE SHARK WILL PASS BY ME?
HE'S COMING AT ME FOR THE KILL!
IF I CAN ONLY HOLD ON--
--KEEP AWAY FROM ITS JAWS!
11

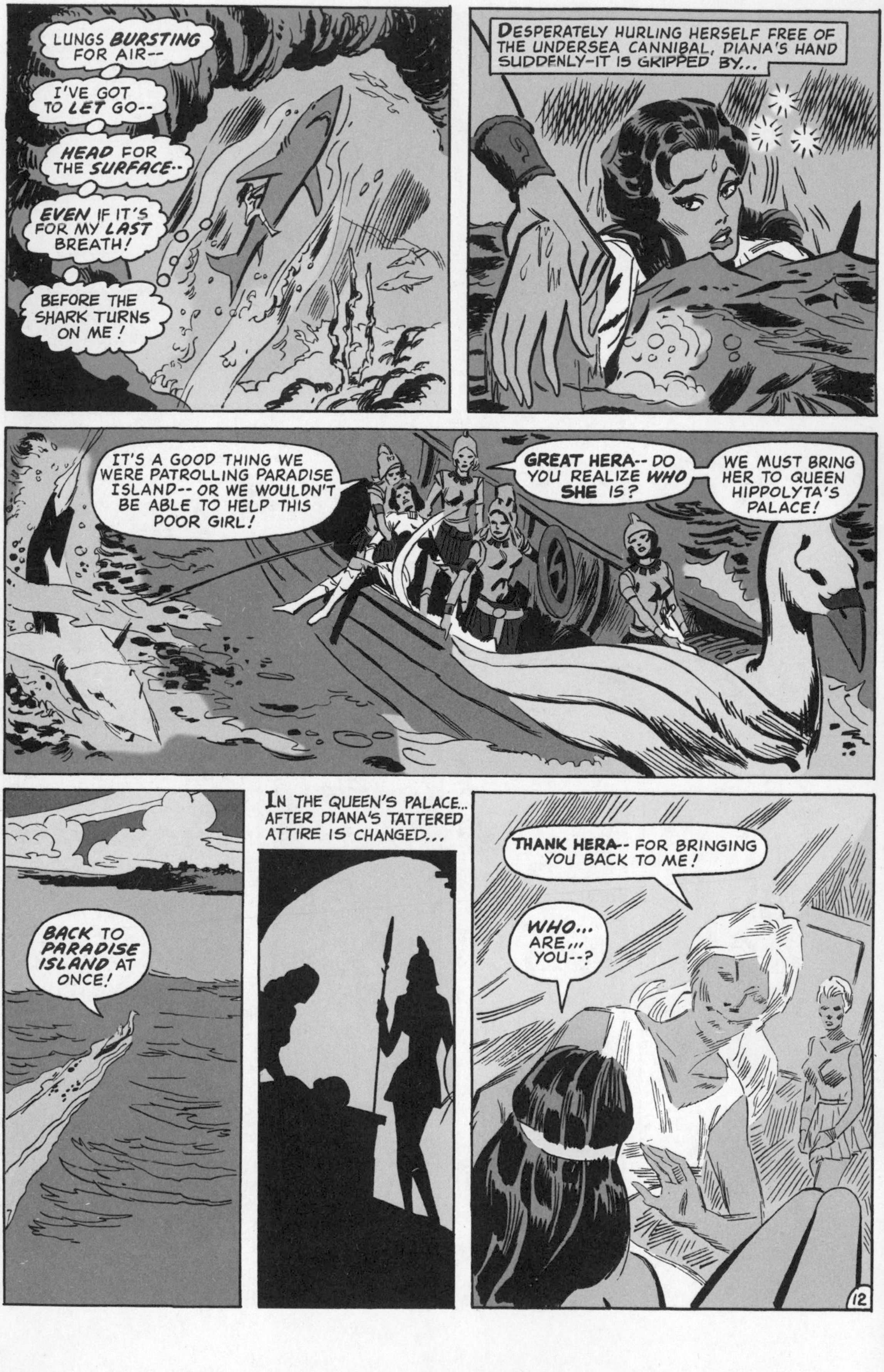
LUNGS BURSTING FOR AIR--
I'VE GOT TO LET GO--
HEAD FOR THE SURFACE--
EVEN IF IT'S FOR MY LAST BREATH!
BEFORE THE SHARK TURNS ON ME!
DESPERATELY HURLING HERSELF FREE OF THE UNDERSEA CANNIBAL, DIANA'S HAND SUDDENLY--IT IS GRIPPED BY...
IT'S A GOOD THING WE WERE PATROLLING PARADISE ISLAND-- OR WE WOULDN'T BE ABLE TO HELP THIS POOR GIRL!
GREAT HERA-- DO YOU REALIZE WHO SHE IS?
WE MUST BRING HER TO QUEEN HIPPOLYTA'S PALACE!
BACK TO PARADISE ISLAND AT ONCE!
IN THE QUEEN'S PALACE... AFTER DIANA'S TATTERED ATTIRE IS CHANGED...
THANK HERA-- FOR BRINGING YOU BACK TO ME!
WHO... ARE... YOU--?
12

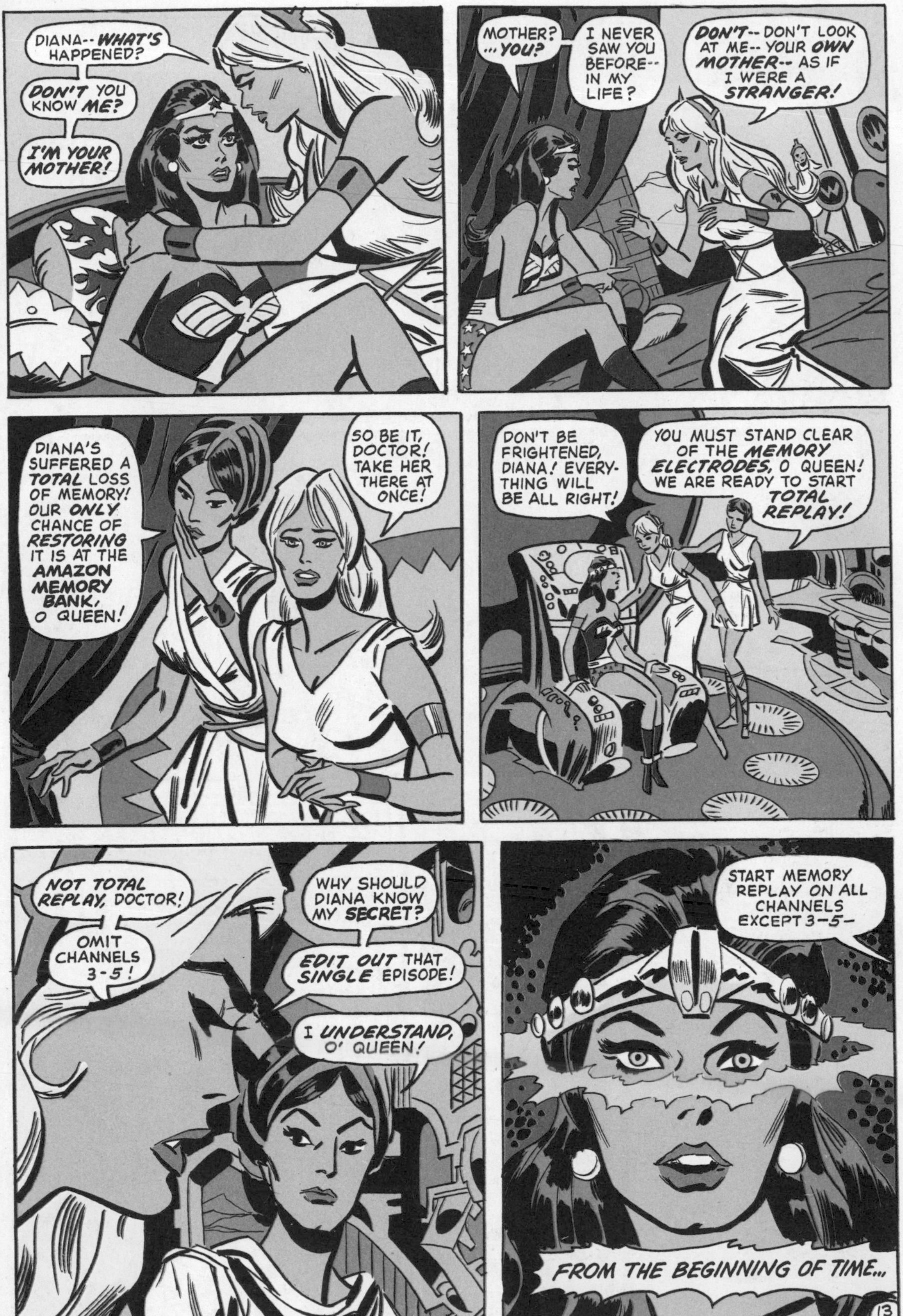
DIANA-- WHAT'S HAPPENED?
DON'T YOU KNOW ME?
I'M YOUR MOTHER!
MOTHER? ...YOU?
I NEVER SAW YOU BEFORE-- IN MY LIFE?
DON'T-- DON'T LOOK AT ME-- YOUR OWN MOTHER-- AS IF I WERE A STRANGER!
DIANA'S SUFFERED A TOTAL LOSS OF MEMORY! OUR ONLY CHANCE OF RESTORING IT IS AT THE AMAZON MEMORY BANK, O QUEEN!
SO BE IT, DOCTOR! TAKE HER THERE AT ONCE!
DON'T BE FRIGHTENED, DIANA! EVERYTHING WILL BE ALL RIGHT!
YOU MUST STAND CLEAR OF THE MEMORY ELECTRODES, O QUEEN! WE ARE READY TO START TOTAL REPLAY!
NOT TOTAL REPLAY, DOCTOR!
OMIT CHANNELS 3-5!
WHY SHOULD DIANA KNOW MY SECRET?
EDIT OUT THAT SINGLE EPISODE!
I UNDERSTAND, O' QUEEN!
START MEMORY REPLAY ON ALL CHANNELS EXCEPT 3-5-
FROM THE BEGINNING OF TIME...
13

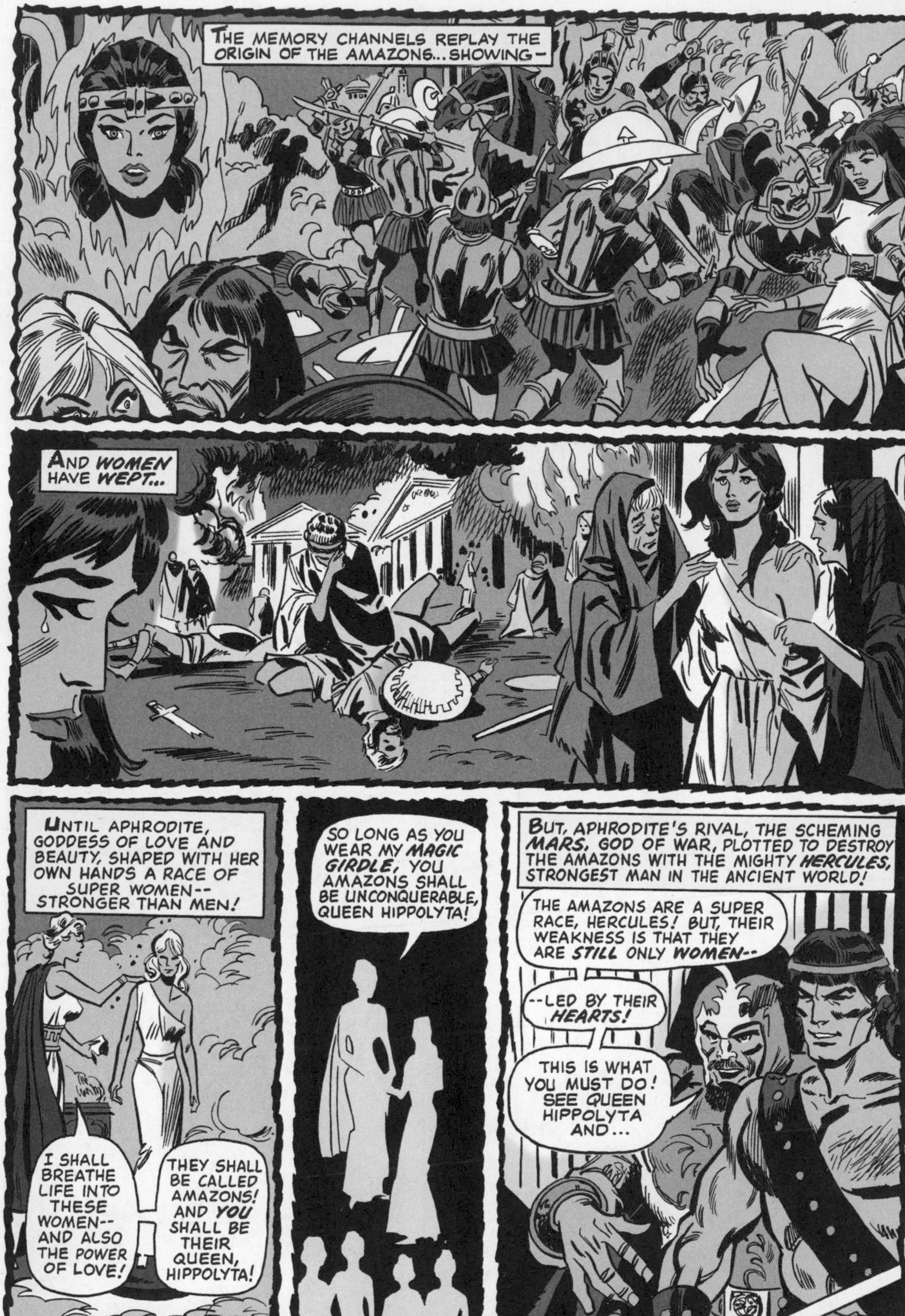
THE MEMORY CHANNELS REPLAY THE ORIGIN OF THE AMAZONS... SHOWING-
AND WOMEN HAVE WEPT...
UNTIL APHRODITE, GODDESS OF LOVE AND BEAUTY, SHAPED WITH HER OWN HANDS A RACE OF SUPER WOMEN-- STRONGER THAN MEN!
I SHALL BREATHE LIFE INTO THESE WOMEN-- AND ALSO THE POWER OF LOVE!
THEY SHALL BE CALLED AMAZONS! AND YOU SHALL BE THEIR QUEEN, HIPPOLYTA!
SO LONG AS YOU WEAR MY MAGIC GIRDLE, YOU AMAZONS SHALL BE UNCONQUERABLE, QUEEN HIPPOLYTA!
BUT, APHRODITE'S RIVAL, THE SCHEMING MARS, GOD OF WAR, PLOTTED TO DESTROY THE AMAZONS WITH THE MIGHTY HERCULES, STRONGEST MAN IN THE ANCIENT WORLD!
THE AMAZONS ARE A SUPER RACE, HERCULES! BUT, THEIR WEAKNESS IS THAT THEY ARE STILL ONLY WOMEN--
--LED BY THEIR HEARTS!
THIS IS WHAT YOU MUST DO! SEE QUEEN HIPPOLYTA AND...
14

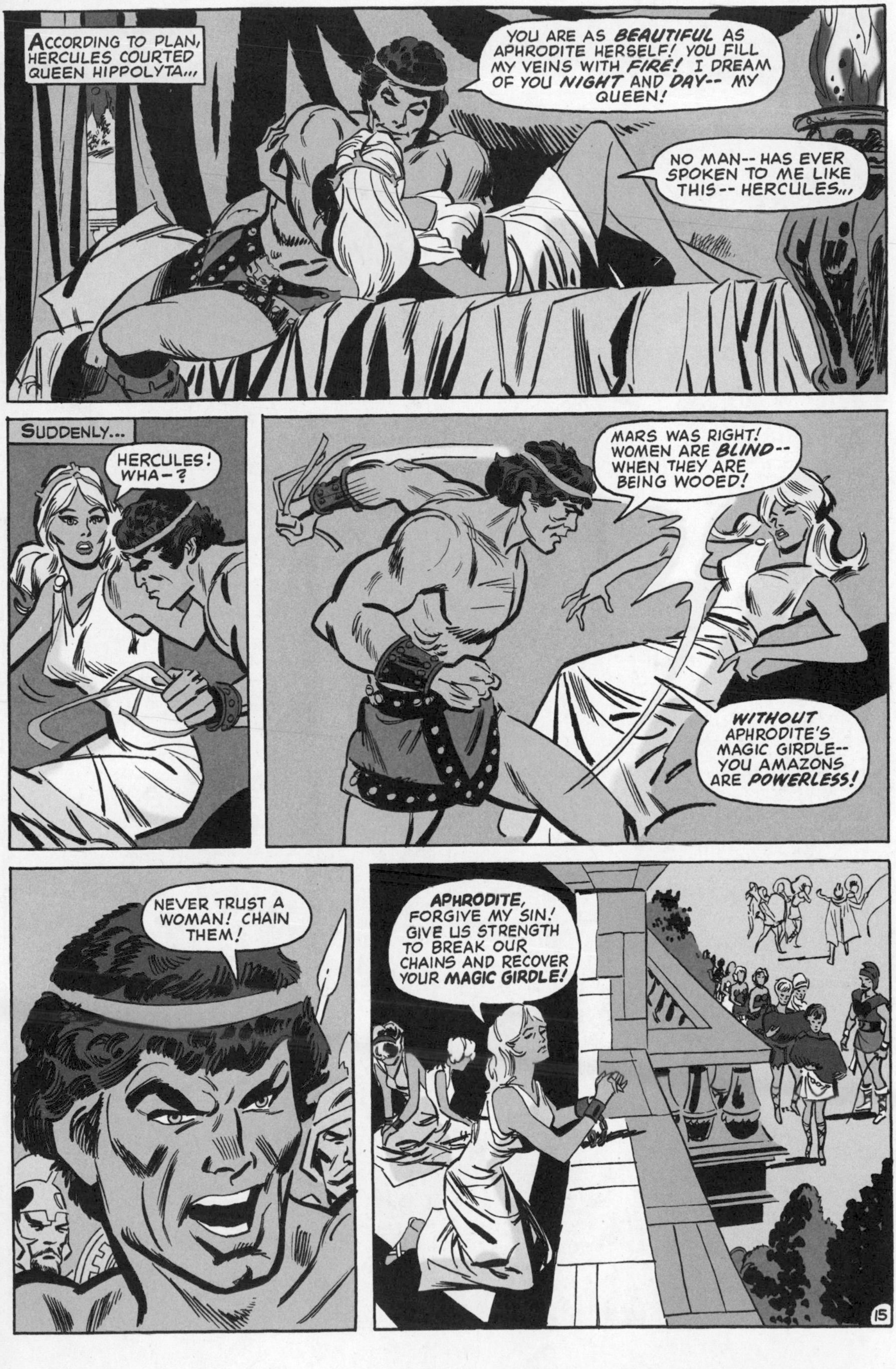
ACCORDING TO PLAN, HERCULES COURTED QUEEN HIPPOLYTA...
YOU ARE AS BEAUTIFUL AS APHRODITE HERSELF! YOU FILL MY VEINS WITH FIRE! I DREAM OF YOU NIGHT AND DAY-- MY QUEEN!
NO MAN-- HAS EVER SPOKEN TO ME LIKE THIS-- HERCULES...
SUDDENLY...
HERCULES! WHA-?
MARS WAS RIGHT! WOMEN ARE BLIND-- WHEN THEY ARE BEING WOOED!
WITHOUT APHRODITE'S MAGIC GIRDLE-- YOU AMAZONS ARE POWERLESS!
NEVER TRUST A WOMAN! CHAIN THEM!
APHRODITE, FORGIVE MY SIN! GIVE US STRENGTH TO BREAK OUR CHAINS AND RECOVER YOUR MAGIC GIRDLE!
15

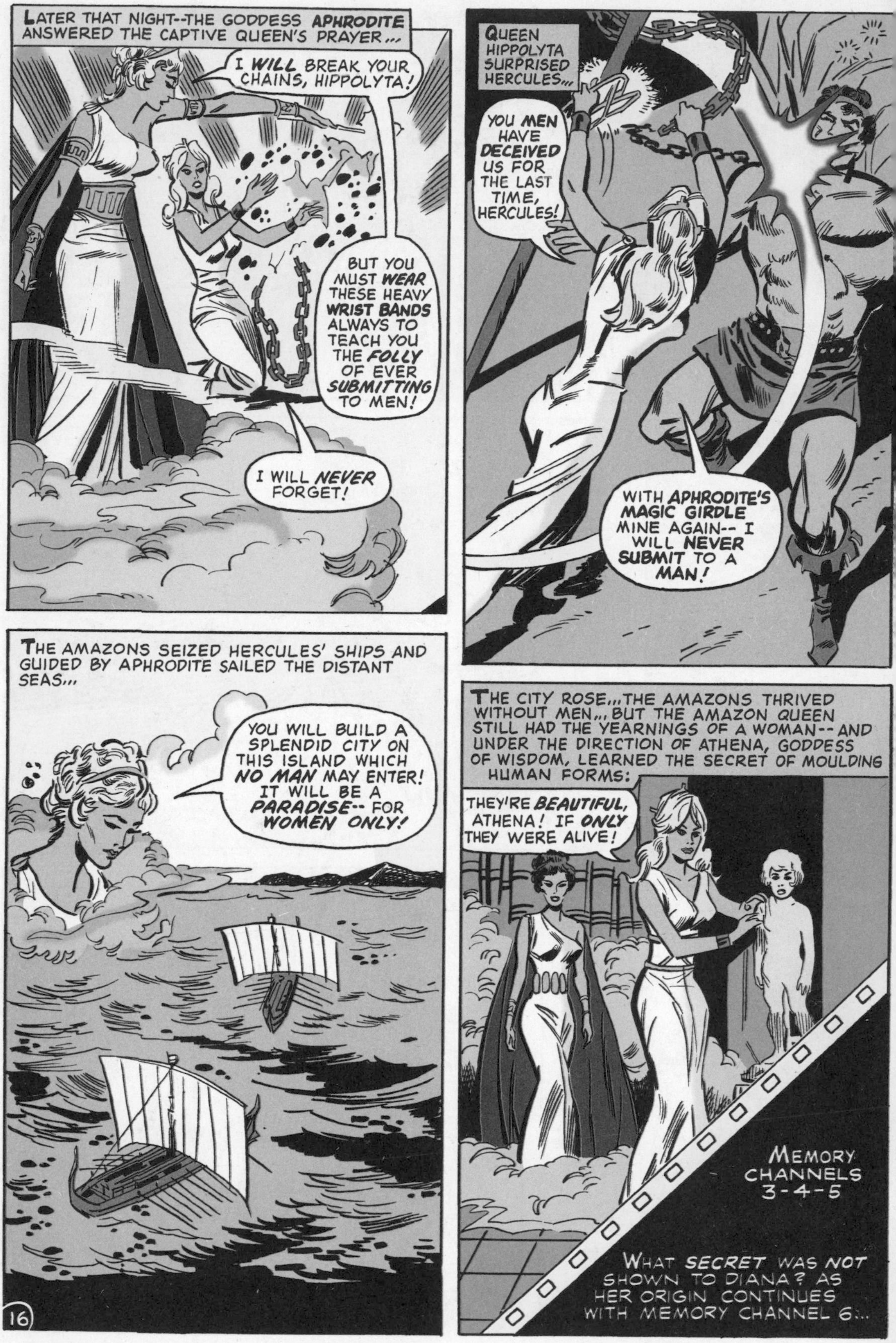
LATER THAT NIGHT--THE GODDESS APHRODITE ANSWERED THE CAPTIVE QUEEN'S PRAYER...
I WILL BREAK YOUR CHAINS, HIPPOLYTA!
BUT YOU MUST WEAR THESE HEAVY WRIST BANDS ALWAYS TO TEACH YOU THE FOLLY OF EVER SUBMITTING TO MEN!
I WILL NEVER FORGET!
QUEEN HIPPOLYTA SURPRISED HERCULES...
YOU MEN HAVE DECEIVED US FOR THE LAST TIME, HERCULES!
WITH APHRODITE'S MAGIC GIRDLE MINE AGAIN-- I WILL NEVER SUBMIT TO A MAN!
THE AMAZONS SEIZED HERCULES' SHIPS AND GUIDED BY APHRODITE SAILED THE DISTANT SEAS...
YOU WILL BUILD A SPLENDID CITY ON THIS ISLAND WHICH NO MAN MAY ENTER! IT WILL BE A PARADISE-- FOR WOMEN ONLY!
16
THE CITY ROSE... THE AMAZONS THRIVED WITHOUT MEN... BUT THE AMAZON QUEEN STILL HAD THE YEARNINGS OF A WOMAN-- AND UNDER THE DIRECTION OF ATHENA, GODDESS OF WISDOM, LEARNED THE SECRET OF MOULDING HUMAN FORMS:
THEY'RE BEAUTIFUL, ATHENA! IF ONLY THEY WERE ALIVE!
MEMORY CHANNELS 3-4-5
WHAT SECRET WAS NOT SHOWN TO DIANA? AS HER ORIGIN CONTINUES WITH MEMORY CHANNEL 6...

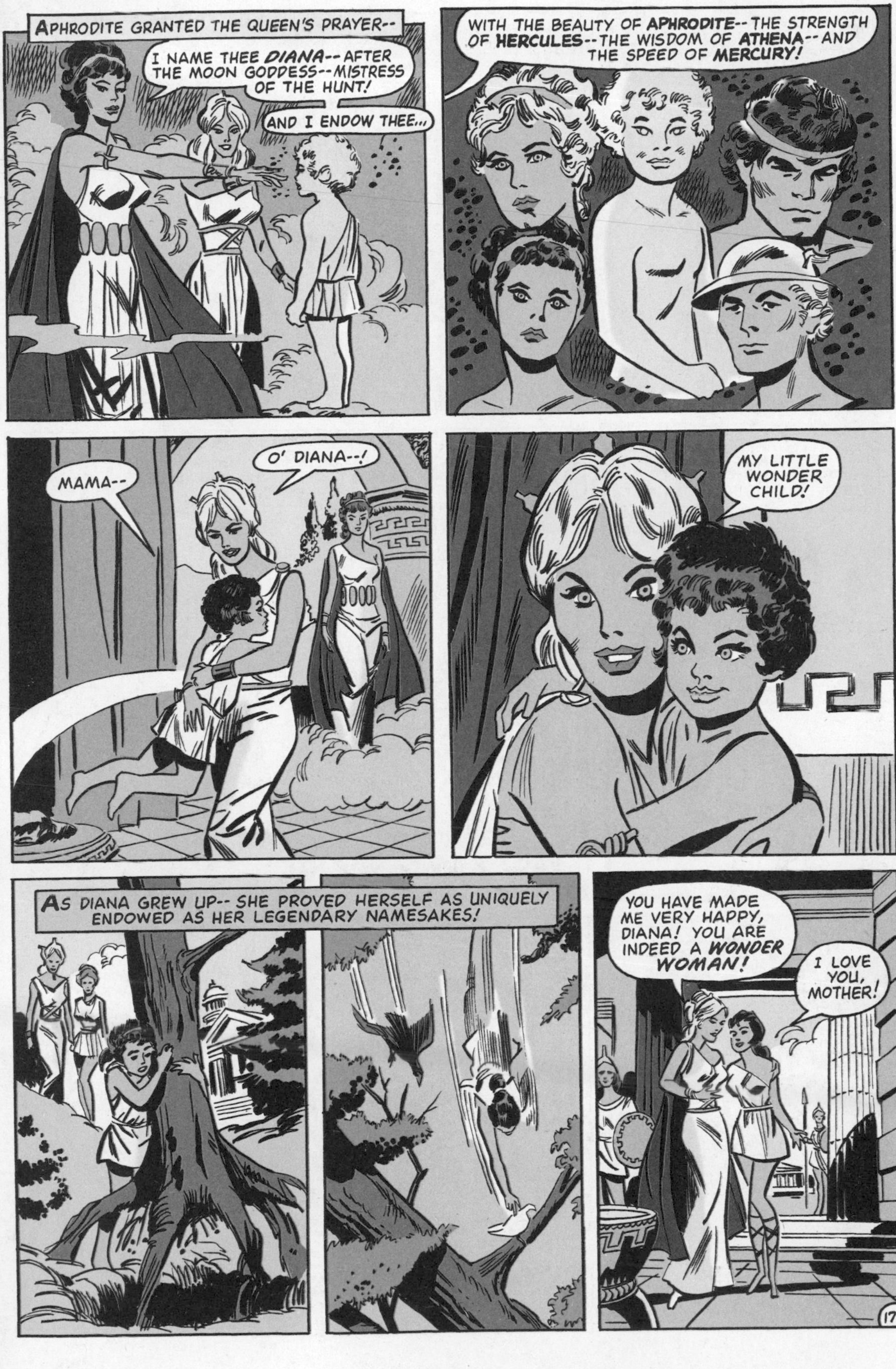
APHRODITE GRANTED THE QUEEN'S PRAYER--
I NAME THEE DIANA--AFTER THE MOON GODDESS--MISTRESS OF THE HUNT!
AND I ENDOW THEE...
WITH THE BEAUTY OF APHRODITE--THE STRENGTH OF HERCULES--THE WISDOM OF ATHENA--AND THE SPEED OF MERCURY!
MAMA--
O' DIANA--!
MY LITTLE WONDER CHILD!
AS DIANA GREW UP--SHE PROVED HERSELF AS UNIQUELY ENDOWED AS HER LEGENDARY NAMESAKES!
YOU HAVE MADE ME VERY HAPPY, DIANA! YOU ARE INDEED A WONDER WOMAN!
I LOVE YOU, MOTHER!
17

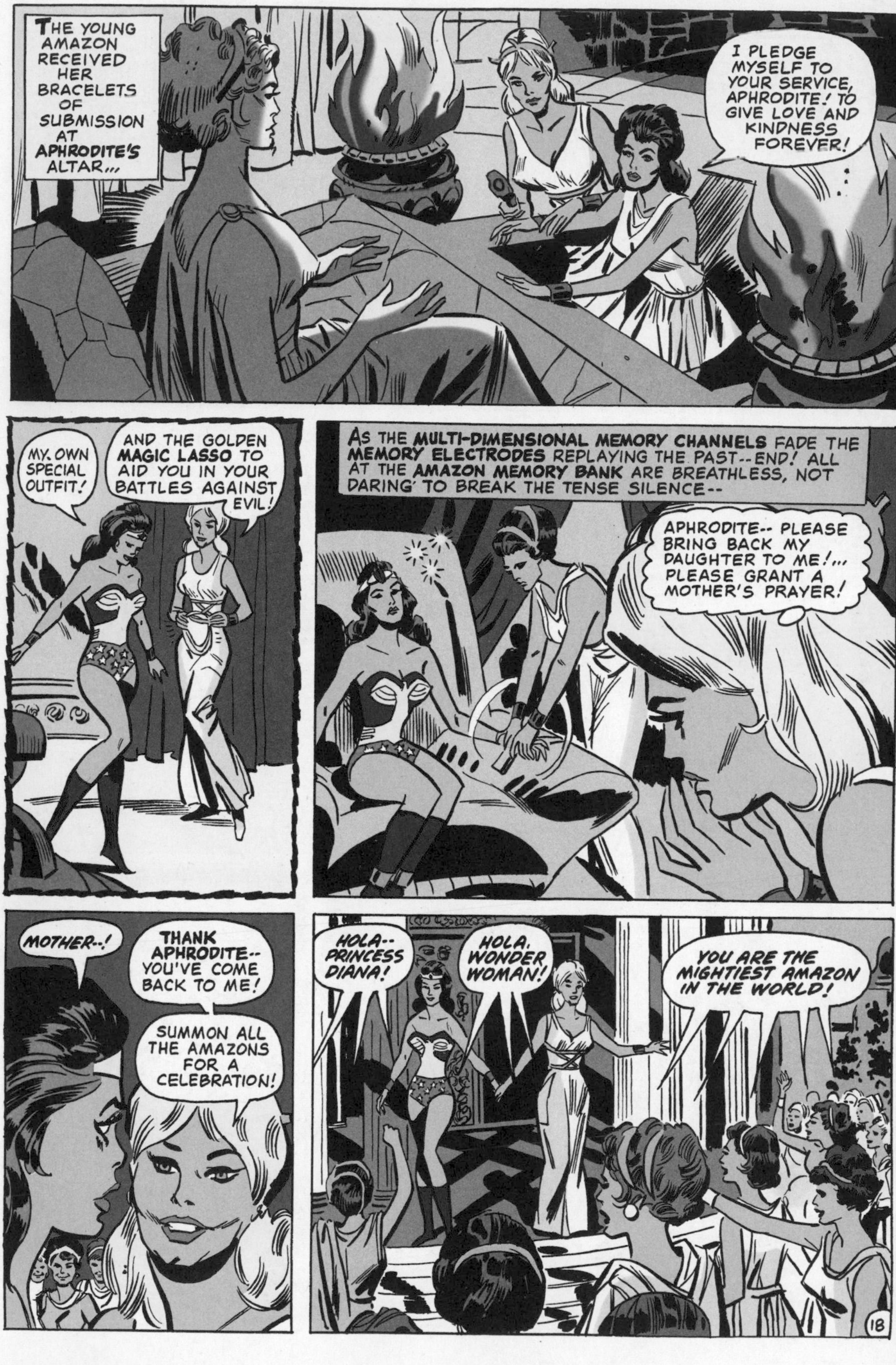
THE YOUNG AMAZON RECEIVED HER BRACELETS OF SUBMISSION AT APHRODITE'S ALTAR...
I PLEDGE MYSELF TO YOUR SERVICE, APHRODITE! TO GIVE LOVE AND KINDNESS FOREVER!
MY OWN SPECIAL OUTFIT!
AND THE GOLDEN MAGIC LASSO TO AID YOU IN YOUR BATTLES AGAINST EVIL!
AS THE MULTI-DIMENSIONAL MEMORY CHANNELS FADE THE MEMORY ELECTRODES REPLAYING THE PAST--END! ALL AT THE AMAZON MEMORY BANK ARE BREATHLESS, NOT DARING TO BREAK THE TENSE SILENCE--
APHRODITE-- PLEASE BRING BACK MY DAUGHTER TO ME!... PLEASE GRANT A MOTHER'S PRAYER!
MOTHER--!
THANK APHRODITE-- YOU'VE COME BACK TO ME!
SUMMON ALL THE AMAZONS FOR A CELEBRATION!
HOLA-- PRINCESS DIANA!
HOLA, WONDER WOMAN!
YOU ARE THE MIGHTIEST AMAZON IN THE WORLD!
18

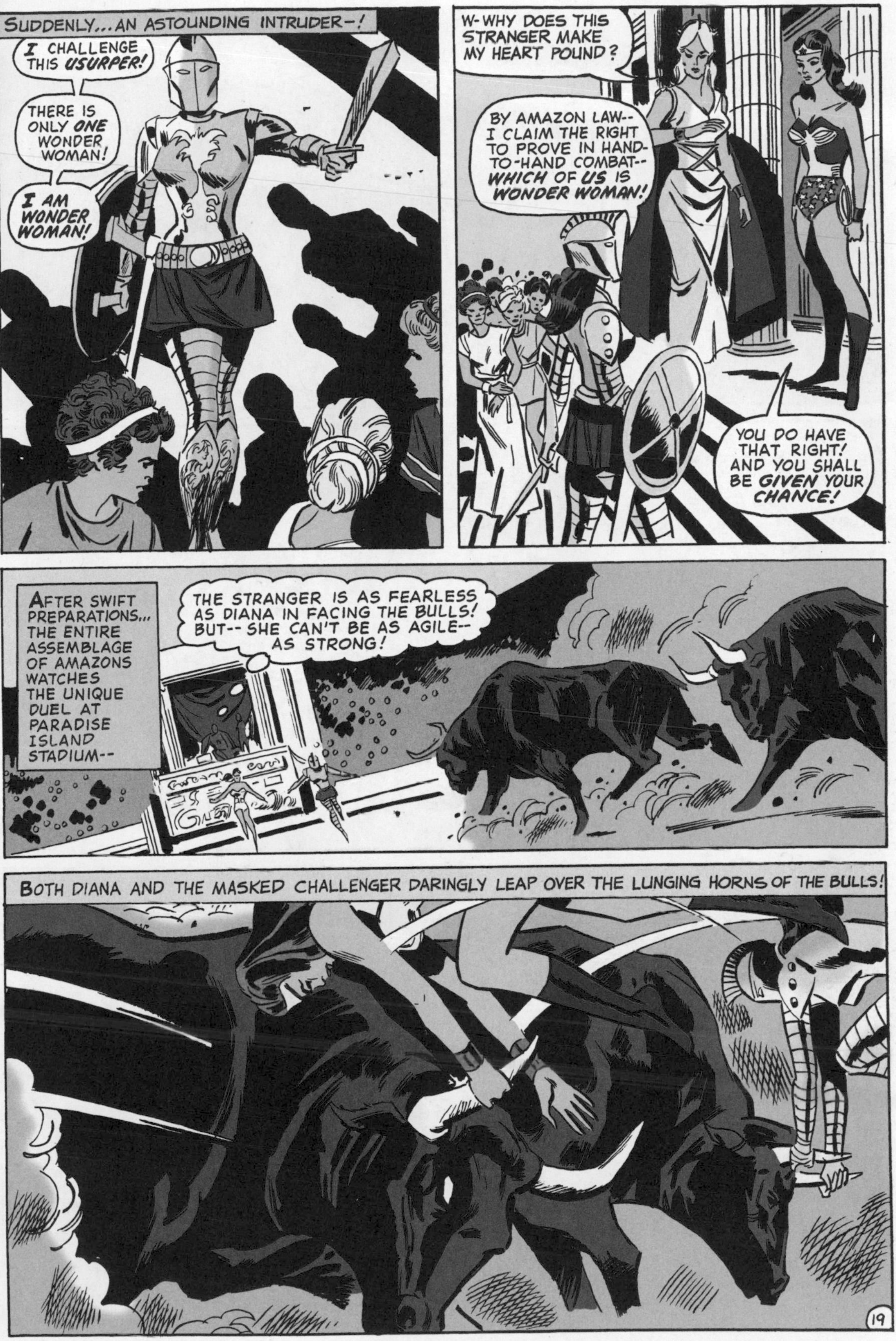
SUDDENLY... AN ASTOUNDING INTRUDER-!
I CHALLENGE THIS USURPER!
THERE IS ONLY ONE WONDER WOMAN!
I AM WONDER WOMAN!
W-WHY DOES THIS STRANGER MAKE MY HEART POUND?
BY AMAZON LAW-- I CLAIM THE RIGHT TO PROVE IN HAND-TO-HAND COMBAT-- WHICH OF US IS WONDER WOMAN!
YOU DO HAVE THAT RIGHT! AND YOU SHALL BE GIVEN YOUR CHANCE!
AFTER SWIFT PREPARATIONS... THE ENTIRE ASSEMBLAGE OF AMAZONS WATCHES THE UNIQUE DUEL AT PARADISE ISLAND STADIUM--
THE STRANGER IS AS FEARLESS AS DIANA IN FACING THE BULLS! BUT-- SHE CAN'T BE AS AGILE-- AS STRONG!
BOTH DIANA AND THE MASKED CHALLENGER DARINGLY LEAP OVER THE LUNGING HORNS OF THE BULLS!
19

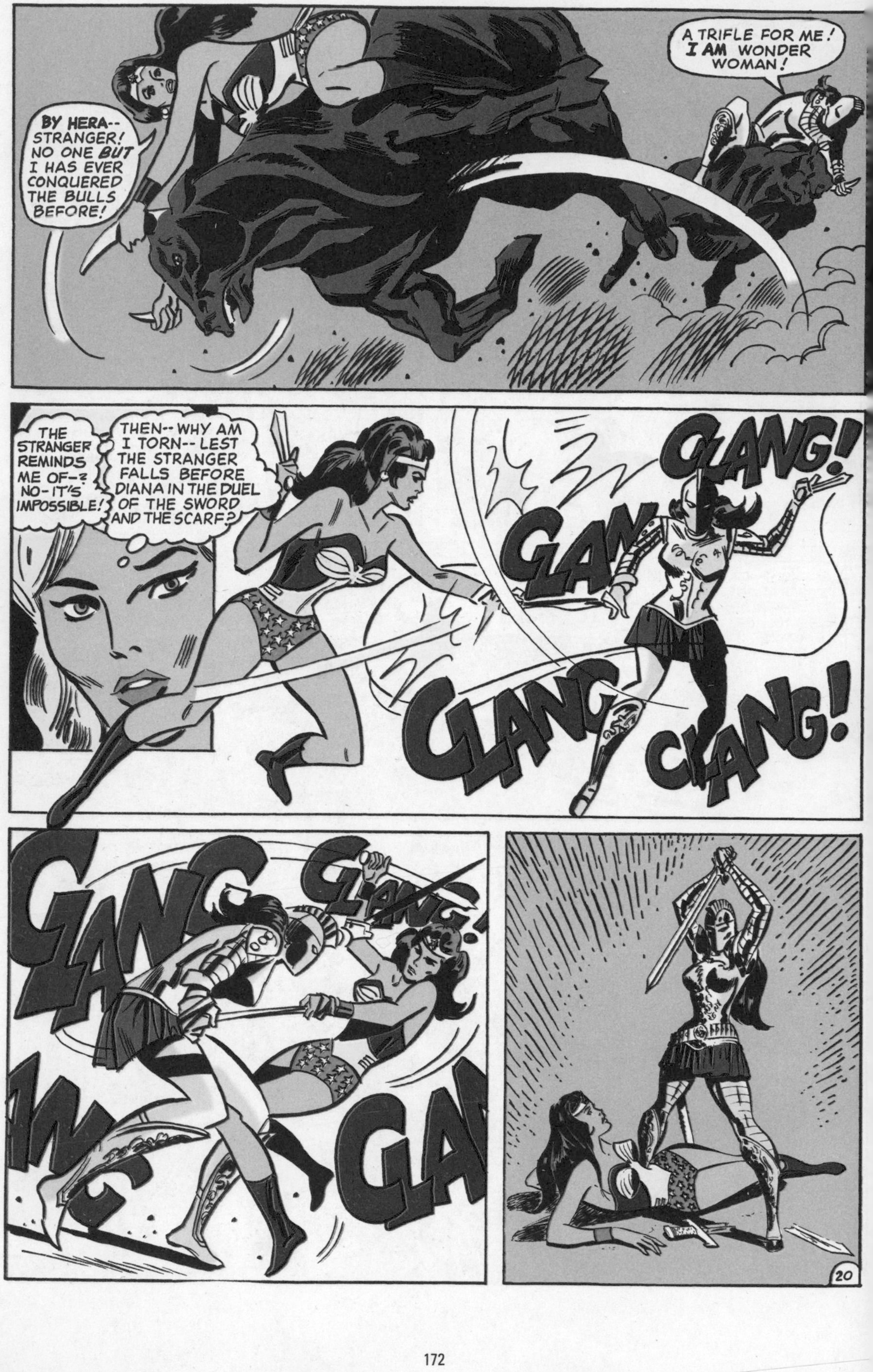
BY HERA-- STRANGER! NO ONE BUT I HAS EVER CONQUERED THE BULLS BEFORE!
A TRIFLE FOR ME! I AM WONDER WOMAN!
THE STRANGER REMINDS ME OF--? NO--IT'S IMPOSSIBLE!
THEN--WHY AM I TORN--LEST THE STRANGER FALLS BEFORE DIANA IN THE DUEL OF THE SWORD AND THE SCARF?
CLANG!
CLANG
CLANG
CLANG!
CLANG
CLANG
20

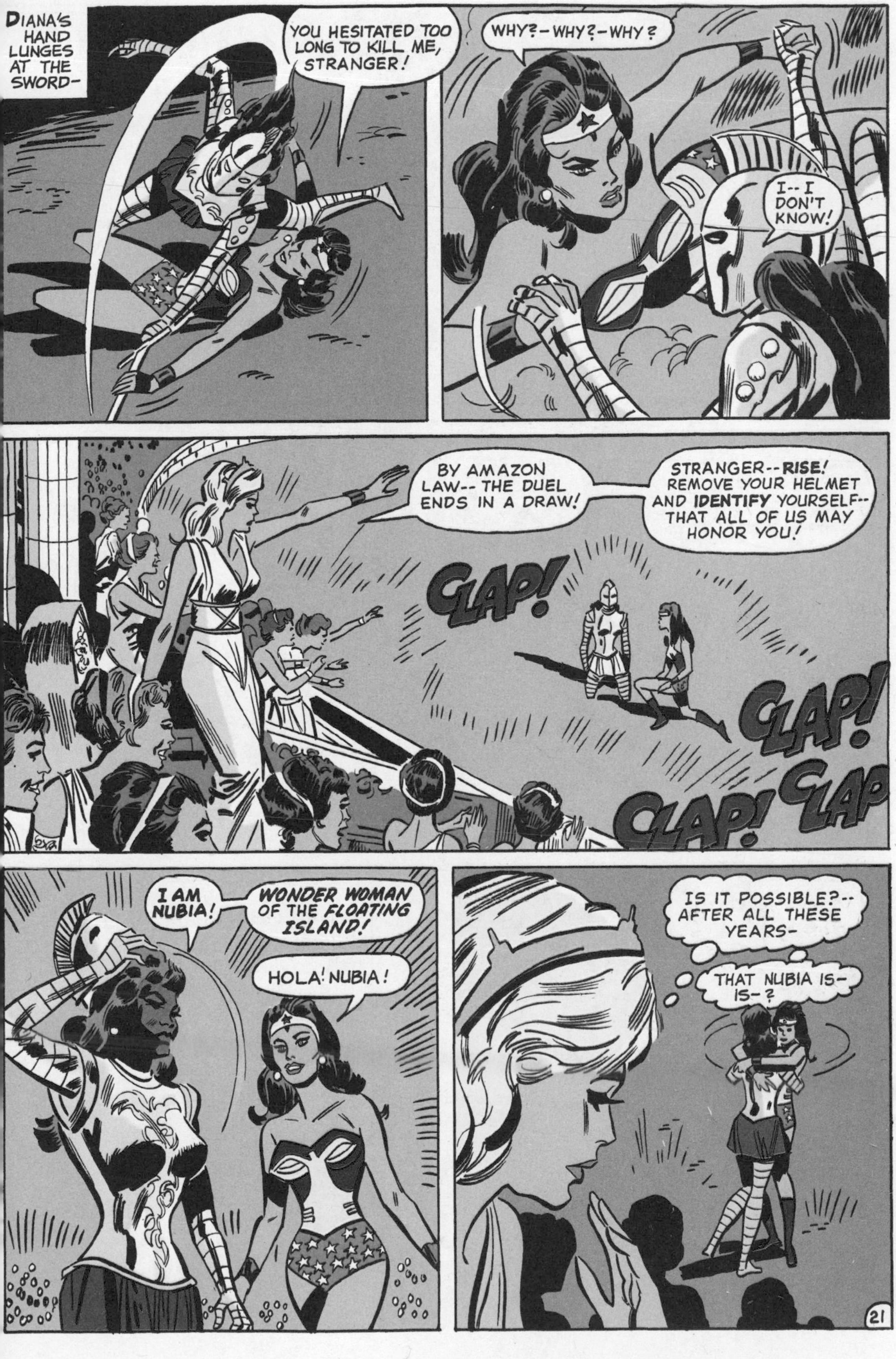
DIANA'S HAND LUNGES AT THE SWORD-
YOU HESITATED TOO LONG TO KILL ME, STRANGER!
WHY?-WHY?-WHY?
I-- I DON'T KNOW!
BY AMAZON LAW-- THE DUEL ENDS IN A DRAW!
STRANGER--RISE! REMOVE YOUR HELMET AND IDENTIFY YOURSELF-- THAT ALL OF US MAY HONOR YOU!
CLAP!
CLAP!
CLAP!
CLAP!
I AM NUBIA!
WONDER WOMAN OF THE FLOATING ISLAND!
HOLA! NUBIA!
IS IT POSSIBLE?-- AFTER ALL THESE YEARS-
THAT NUBIA IS- IS-?
21

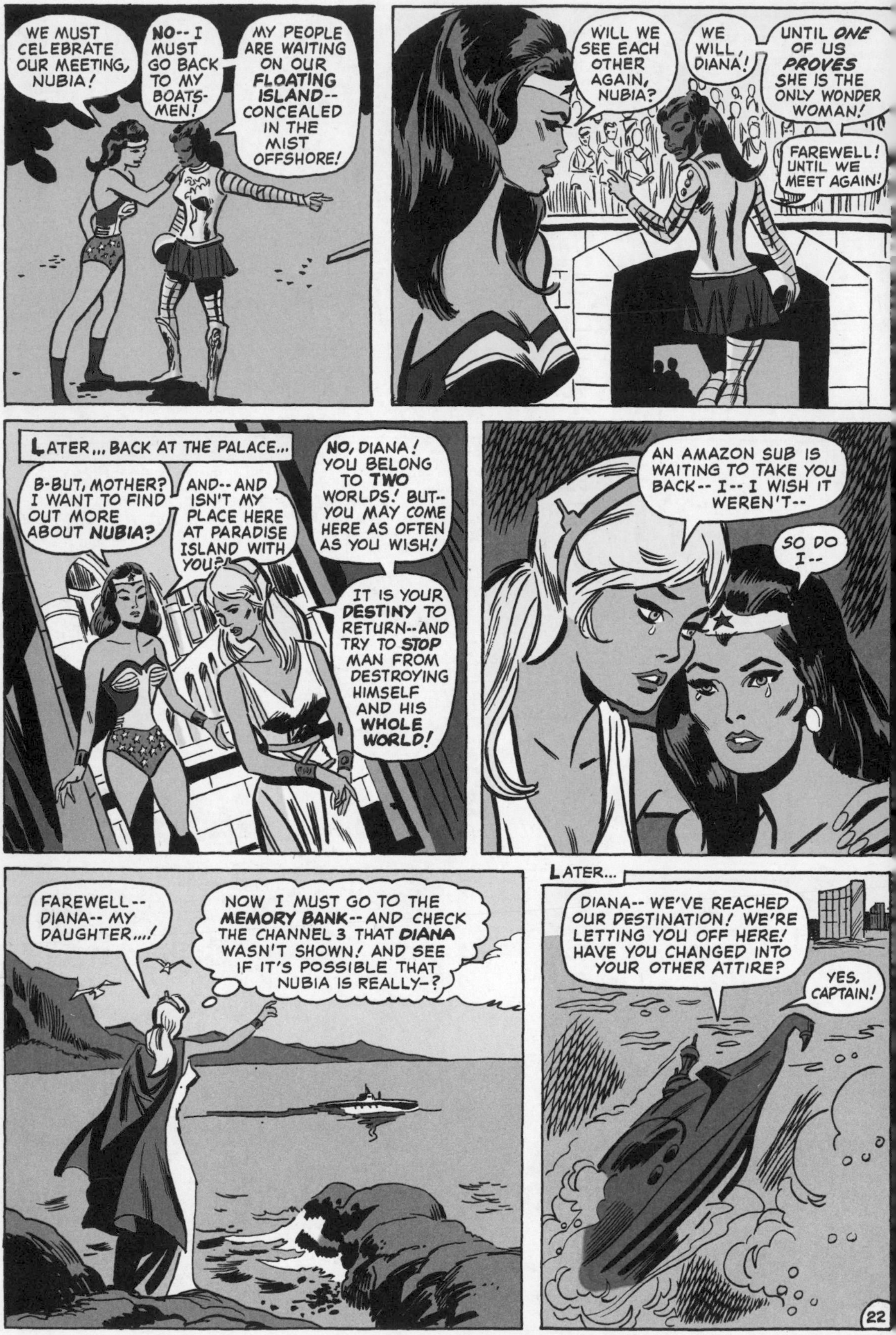
WE MUST CELEBRATE OUR MEETING, NUBIA!
NO-- I MUST GO BACK TO MY BOATS-MEN!
MY PEOPLE ARE WAITING ON OUR FLOATING ISLAND-- CONCEALED IN THE MIST OFFSHORE!
WILL WE SEE EACH OTHER AGAIN, NUBIA?
WE WILL, DIANA!
UNTIL ONE OF US PROVES SHE IS THE ONLY WONDER WOMAN!
FAREWELL! UNTIL WE MEET AGAIN!
LATER... BACK AT THE PALACE...
B-BUT, MOTHER? I WANT TO FIND OUT MORE ABOUT NUBIA?
AND-- AND ISN'T MY PLACE HERE AT PARADISE ISLAND WITH YOU?
NO, DIANA! YOU BELONG TO TWO WORLDS! BUT-- YOU MAY COME HERE AS OFTEN AS YOU WISH!
IT IS YOUR DESTINY TO RETURN--AND TRY TO STOP MAN FROM DESTROYING HIMSELF AND HIS WHOLE WORLD!
AN AMAZON SUB IS WAITING TO TAKE YOU BACK-- I-- I WISH IT WEREN'T--
SO DO I--
FAREWELL-- DIANA-- MY DAUGHTER...!
NOW I MUST GO TO THE MEMORY BANK--AND CHECK THE CHANNEL 3 THAT DIANA WASN'T SHOWN! AND SEE IF IT'S POSSIBLE THAT NUBIA IS REALLY-?
LATER...
DIANA-- WE'VE REACHED OUR DESTINATION! WE'RE LETTING YOU OFF HERE! HAVE YOU CHANGED INTO YOUR OTHER ATTIRE?
YES, CAPTAIN!
22

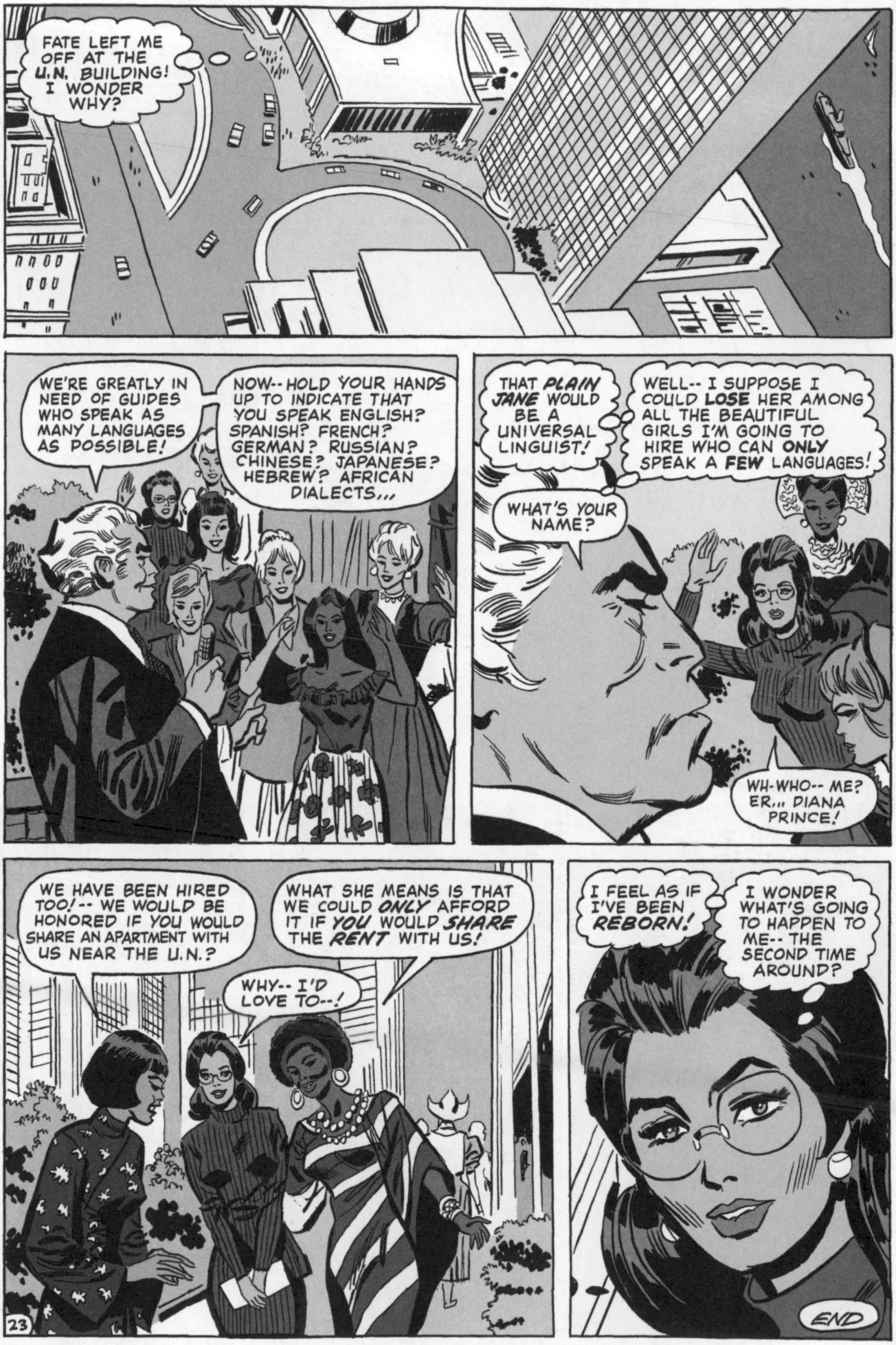
FATE LEFT ME OFF AT THE U.N. BUILDING! I WONDER WHY?
WE'RE GREATLY IN NEED OF GUIDES WHO SPEAK AS MANY LANGUAGES AS POSSIBLE!
NOW-- HOLD YOUR HANDS UP TO INDICATE THAT YOU SPEAK ENGLISH? SPANISH? FRENCH? GERMAN? RUSSIAN? CHINESE? JAPANESE? HEBREW? AFRICAN DIALECTS...
THAT PLAIN JANE WOULD BE A UNIVERSAL LINGUIST!
WELL-- I SUPPOSE I COULD LOSE HER AMONG ALL THE BEAUTIFUL GIRLS I'M GOING TO HIRE WHO CAN ONLY SPEAK A FEW LANGUAGES!
WHAT'S YOUR NAME?
WH-WHO-- ME? ER... DIANA PRINCE!
WE HAVE BEEN HIRED TOO! -- WE WOULD BE HONORED IF YOU WOULD SHARE AN APARTMENT WITH US NEAR THE U.N.?
WHAT SHE MEANS IS THAT WE COULD ONLY AFFORD IT IF YOU WOULD SHARE THE RENT WITH US!
WHY-- I'D LOVE TO--!
23
I FEEL AS IF I'VE BEEN REBORN!
I WONDER WHAT'S GOING TO HAPPEN TO ME-- THE SECOND TIME AROUND?
END